Architectural and Interior Models

Sanford Hohauser

Revised by Helen Demchyshyn

Architectural and Interior Models

Second Edition

VNR Van Nostrand Reinhold Company
New York

Copyright © 1982 by Van Nostrand Reinhold Company Inc.

Library of Congress Catalog Card Number 84-11933

ISBN 0-442-23668-9

Published by Van Nostrand Reinhold Company Inc.
115 Fifth Avenue
New York, New York 10003

Van Nostrand Reinhold Company Limited
Molly Millars Lane
Wokingham, Berkshire RG11 2PY, England

Van Nostrand Reinhold
480 La Trobe Street
Melbourne, Victoria 3000, Australia

Macmillan of Canada
Division of Canada Publishing Corporation
164 Commander Boulevard
Agincourt, Ontario M1S 3C7, Canada

16 15 14 13 12 11 10 9 8 7 6 5 4 3 2

Library of Congress Cataloging in Publication Data

Hohauser, Sanford, 1933-
  Architectural and interior models.

  Rev. ed. of: Architectural and interior models, design and
construction. 1970
  Includes index.
  1. Models and modelmaking. I. Demchyshyn, Helen.
II. Hohauser, Sanford, 1933-   . Architectural and
interior models, design and construction. III. Title.
TT154.H58 1984   720'.228   84-11933
ISBN 0-442-23668-9

  *All brand names, manufacturers, suppliers, and addresses
mentioned in this book are accurate as of publication date.*

  *Mention of products or equipment by trademark or by name
of manufacturer does not imply the authors' unqualified
endorsement.*

  *The authors have recommended specific tools and materials
for use with various techniques and procedures. These are, to
the best of their knowledge, efficient and safe if the modelbuilder is reasonably cautious. However, neither the authors
nor the publisher assumes liability for any personal injury,
wastage of material, breakage of tools, or imperfection of results that may be attributed to information found in this book.*

Contents

Part Two

Acknowledgments

As a tribute to the hundreds of individuals whose creative work make this edition possible, I would like to extend my thanks to the following for their generosity in providing photographic materials, information, and encouragement:

Allan Adams
Pam Adler Gallery
The Architects Collaborative
Asher Faure Gallery
Mark Boyle
Roger Brown
Chris Burden
Louis Checkman
Christo
Cooper Union School of Architecture
Charles Cowles Gallery
Daniel, Mann, Johnson & Mendenhall
Elisa D'Arrigo
Donna Dennis
Robert Duncan
The Eggers Group
Raymon Elozua
Andre Emmerich Gallery
Entertainment Effects Group
Rosa Esman Gallery
ESTO Photographics
Lauren Ewing
Ronald Feldman Fine Arts
Gallery Paule Anglim
Leslie Gill
Alexander Gorlin
The Grad Partnership
George Grant

James Grashow
Gresham, Smith and Partners
Red Grooms
Gwathmey Siegel Associates
Ira Joel Haber
Hellmuth Obata & Kassabaum
The Hillier Group
Jack Horner
Caroline Huber
Johnson/Burgee
Albert Kahn Associates
Kaplan/McLaughlin/Diaz
Ed Kerns
Phyllis Kind Gallery
Kohn Pederson Fox
Jeffrey Kusmick
The Ladd Company
Nathaniel Lieberman
Dr. Robert Mark
Marlborough Gallery
Rosemary Mauer
Michael C. McMillen
Lorna McNeur
Metz Train & Youngren
Moore Grover Harper
Gifford Myers
The NBBJ Group
Newark Museum
New Jersey Institute of Technology

OK Harris Gallery
Pace Gallery
Betty Parsons Gallery
I.M. Pei & Partners
Cesar Pelli & Associates
Princeton University Architectural Laboratory
RTKL Associates
Lucas Samaras
Schmidt, Garden & Erikson
Patrick Sherwood
Michael Seiler
Charles Simonds
SITE Inc.
Skidmore, Owings & Merrill
The Smith, Korach, Hayet, Haynie Partnership
Holly Solomon Gallery
Mark Stetson
Allan Stone Gallery
Hugh Stubbins and Associates
3/D International
Triumph Films
Ernest Trova
Urban Innovations Group
VVKR Incorporated
Donald Wall
Warner Bros.
Roger Welch

I would like to extend special thanks to:

Sanford Hohauser, whose expert knowledge and obvious enjoyment of every facet of modelmaking provided an excellent text from which to work; Wendy Lochner at Van Nostrand Reinhold, for the opportunity to pursue my interest in research; Donald Wall, for his advice and criticism and for contributing the foreword; Irene Demchyshyn, for her constant help throughout the project and for her expert editing of this edition; Oksana Demchyshyn, for her generous help in preparing the manuscript; and Pilar Almon, for her enthusiastic interest in the book and for her help in the final weeks of organizing the manuscript.

Foreword

This book is one of the better (if not the best) technical manuals on architectural modelmaking to date. The opinion is not mine alone: it is shared by various critics and reviewers, some of whom have employed this text as the standard against which all newcomers are compared. Hence, the book can be regarded as a model for texts on models—an exemplary parts manual, a treasure trove of details and methods for both the neophyte and the advanced professional.

It presents solutions to a sequence of propositional "ifs." If you want to keep cardboard from buckling, you can refer to the discussion of bracing in Chapter 6. If you are making a base for the first time, you will find in Chapter 12 accounts of all the major techniques developed for that purpose, including egg-crating, sandwiching, striating, molding, casting, and contours with or without spackle infill. If you want to make an intricate cornice detail, read about casting in Chapter 8. There is a dizzying kaleidoscope of additional salient data: steel milled window sections; curved paper structures; bronze casting; collaged papier mâché; pigmented wax emulsions; absorption rate of plaster; commercial and handcrafted window frames in styles from Colonial to Modernist; creating "weathering" effects with paints; using smoke blown on air currents for mists and theater atmospheres; specific f-stops for photography; animating traffic on conveyor belts; thermosetting plastic; making miniature picket fences, chain-link fences, split-rail fences, rustic fences; a microtaxonomy.

There are sections dealing with topological models; mechanical and structural models; site models; zoning models; conceptual/gestalt models; process models; analytic and synthetic models; interior and exterior models; dioramic models; models to be taken apart and put back together; models of verisimilitude and not-so-verisimilitude; anthropological/archaeological models; modern and post-modern models; traditional models; models of systemic logistics.

How then should one read this book? Certainly not just as a prosaic set of instructions, a how-to-do-it manual of tested and secure data. Such a reading would bypass the development of the text entirely—miss out, because in the world of artifice all technical data function philosophically, metaphysically, even poetically, as a critique of the human condition and of society. Diderot knew this when he undertook to illustrate the *Encyclopedia*. There, in plate after plate, he placed a technology-fraught mankind in the midst of a rural, bucolic, craft-laden mankind.

The revising author of *Architectural and Interior Models* demonstrates that she, too, knows of this by including illustrations of models that do *not* anticipate human-scale re-creation as habitable buildings in the near or distant future. Most of these models were not the achievements of professional architects but of sculptors, painters, photographers, film-makers, folk artists and story tellers, stage-set designers, and Sunday hobbyists and weekday children. This decision restores to architectural modeling its (lost) origins in personal human development in childhood and its (overlooked) origins in the historical development of theater. It appropriates architectural modeling for an expanded constituency among which *anyone*—whether a four-year-old armed with ice cream sticks for constructing a castle or a mathematician building a house for a geometry—can commit the act of architecture.

Meanwhile, the traditional concept of architectural modeling is maintained. Traditionally, the architectural model is conceived to be a simulation vehicle that provides an advanced view of what a building will look like when it is constructed. Leon Battista Alberti gave the following admonishment in his *De Re Aedificatoria*:

No man ought to begin a Building hastily, but should first take a good deal of time to consider and resolve in his Mind all the Qualities and Requisites of such a Work. And that he should judge carefully, Review and Examine with the advice of proper Judges, the Whole Structure in Itself, and the Proportions and Measures of Every Distinct Part, not only in

Draughts and Paintings, but in actual Models of wood or some other Substance, that when he has finished his Building, he may not Repent of his labor. . . . You ought to make such Models, and consider them yourself, and with others, so Diligently, and examine them over and over, so often, that there should not be a Single Part in the Whole Structure but what you are thoroughly acquainted with.

The architect hence turns to modeling for security of knowledge, for validation of intent, for consensual agreement, for purposes of refining details and ideas, for deeper speculation and contemplation, and to stave off embarrassment and guilt—and does so despite the fact that models are expensive to produce (in Alberti's day, cabinet makers were enlisted to produce large, intricate, precisely executed models, which served as legal contract documents and as definitive guides during actual building construction for sizing capitals, column shafts, stair widths, and so forth), are time-consuming, require specialized skills, are often extraordinarily susceptible to damage, and are bulky to store and cumbersome to transport. Nonetheless, models communicate with an immediacy not shared by any architectural drawings except fully-rendered perspectives (which are a form of modeling-in-the-flat).

Obviously models have established ideological destinies in circumstances in which a building's actual construction was economically, politically or societally prohibited, addressing itself to the cultural thought of that day.

The revising author of *Architectural and Interior Models* continues this tradition: she provides numerous illustrations of the conventional model, from schematic to highly rendered stages and in degrees of cost ranging from five-dollar analog models constructed from scraps of materials to models costing over a quarter of a million dollars; models constructed from steel, brass, oak, or plastics; models completely outfitted with interior lights; models in scales varying from the tiniest miniaturized replica to the full-scale detail; models expressing various professional concerns of the practitioner. Each age has a preferred manner of imbedding the signified (the future work) into the signifier (the model). The model, therefore, has its own intelligibility—one not always identical with the building as constructed.

Also included is a more recent class of models *different in kind* from the traditional sort. These models do not look, feel, smell, or sound like their traditional counterparts. They are profoundly new, implicating new audiences, new creators, new forms of delivery and receiving, new criticism, and new demands on the modelmaker. Such models may employ the human body (as geographical site), continuous tape recordings, colored

gel spotlights, full-size industrial electrical conduits (from subway stations), shotguns, air-conditioning fan blades, smoke machines, conveyor belts, live ferns and bushes, binoculars, toy trains and airplanes, old chemistry-set boxes, television monitors, burned and make-believe burned constructions . . . all of these added to the usual wood, ceramic, metal, cardboard, paper, plaster, and plastic . . . veritably and irrevocably a vast explosion in subject matter created by those who are far exceeding the architectural profession's ability to achieve signification in modeling.

The new architectural model has made its appearance in the work of such individuals as Dennis, Simonds, Grooms, Trova, Welch, Oppenheim, Samaras, Elozua, Insley, Burden, Christo, Aycock, Balint, Westerman, Christenberry, Graves, Acconci, Hejduk, Libeskind, Eisenman, Keinholz, and the Poiriers. These people's models reflect a multitude of concerns: they stand for memory, speculation, analysis, continuum, and discharge.

Above all, an architectural model of the new type seeks to be accepted for itself; its content does not reside in its forecasting of a future building but in its own integral existence. While the traditional model endeavors to maintain illusion as much as possible, the modern architectural model operates in the world of allusion. Whereas the traditional model prefers simulations, the modern architectural model prefers literalism. Whereas in the traditional model, vision and comprehension are directed outwards, *away* from the model, away from the room containing the model, away from what is being perceived, *out* to the building's intended site and geography, the vision and comprehension of the modern architectural model is centered *in* the model. Vision is not allowed to escape the here and now of the perceiver. No attempt is made to direct the viewer's thought anywhere other than into consciousness of the model's own genealogical-existential self. The modern model is, therefore, place-specific, with a real-time identity and a real-material identity.

Fifteen or twenty years ago, the architectural model was rarely encountered in museums, galleries, or magazines (except in professional journals or in the real estate section of the Sunday newspaper). Instead, they were to be seen in bankers' and land developers' offices and, of course, in architectural drafting studios. Today, the layperson can hardly turn around without encountering the modern architectural model in newspapers, monthly magazines, art periodicals, commercial galleries, and museums. From Maine to California, miniaturized environments appear and reappear, in guise after guise. And, as the traditional model declares its nature by its name (*Chase Manhattan Bank; Assembly Hall for the*

University of Illinois), the modern model declares its nature similarly: *Monument at 3 A.M.; Tree House for Poisoned Soil; Ghost Town; Waiting Room for the Midnight Special (A Thought Collision Factory for Ghost Ships); Klansville; Champagne House With Net; (House) Object with a Memory; Empty Gallery with Light in Basement; The Blue-Eyed Blond Facade; The Castle of Preserverance—A Moral Model; Jail Break; Gate of Souls; The Seven Gates of Eden; House Eleven Odd; The Devil's Bridge in a Chemistry Set; Red School House for Thomas Paine; Plan for a Circular Utopia; Ritual Furnace; The Last Temple; Passage Space Spiral; Illusion Facade with Parthenon; Pyramid for Little People.*

The difference is between models of concepts and models of notions; models of prose and models of poetry; models of science/technology and models of philosophy. In discussing the differences he saw between scientific and philosophical ideas, Jean-Paul Sartre gave expression to the precise difference that also exists between traditional and modern modeling in *Life Situations:*

I try to be rigorous with notions. The way I differentiate between concepts and notions is this: a concept is a way of defining things from the outside, and it is atemporal. A notion, as I see it, is a way of defining things from the inside, and it includes not only the time of the object about which we have the notion, but also its own time of knowledge. In other words, it is a thought that carries time within itself . . . therefore you have two temporal elements, how thought—my thought, in this case—takes hold of it and develops it; and where it comes from and how it develops. All of this is included in the idea of notion. The distinction I make between concepts and notions is similar to the distinction I make between knowledge and understanding.

When Sanford Hohauser wrote the first edition of this book, the modern architectural model was not an available option; only the traditional model existed. Models were miniaturized representations of projects-to-be-built (or projects-already-built in the case of archaeological models). Sometimes, as with Mies van der Rohe and especially with Saarinen, huge or full-scale models would be constructed out of wood and canvas to evoke the projected building. Occasionally, too, an esoteric model would appear, such as the one that included a photograph of Corbusier's hand inserting a modular component into the model's structural frame. But these were rare perturbations. Standard models prevailed through the sixties: block-study massing models or highly detailed realistic models; topological

contouring on a wooden base; layered cardboard constructions. The model was photographed either against a black background or against a real-life background of clouds scudding across the sky.

This does not mean that subtlety in modelmaking could not be found. Numerous examples identified by Hohauser continue to exhibit delectable nuances. For example, SOM's Yale Rare Book Library model has an engrossing foray into two-dimensional linear illusion that belies its three-dimensional context; Saarinen's detail of the TWA Terminal captures a poetic tone; Hugh Hardy's theater interior shows dust that conceptually fills the viewer's nostrils; Mies's Seagram Office Building, a snared urbanism, is an aesthetic proclamation of verisimilitude and *precision.*

The fact that modern architecture had been interpreted by all too many to mean predominately undecorated surfaces, overall homogeneity, gestalt outlining, rectilinear framing without a resulting tranformation—in short, as a simplified idea controlling an entire range of thematic expressiveness—allowed the modelmaking task to be undertaken without undue difficulty. Three or four well-crafted models could stand for ninety percent of state-of-the-art modelmaking in America. More examples were needed to illustrate the greater visual and constructional quality of architecture that relied on structure for aesthetic visual content. Hence, Hohauser included (and the revising author retains) a broad range of model typology/technics, documenting buildings with post and beam construction, poured concrete, steel cable suspension systems, and so forth.

Classification and subclassification developed from office practice procedures. There were study models, more refined models, highly representational models, take-apart models, zoning envelope models, and detail models. Then there were engineering models intended to verify loading factors, lighting conditions, and so on. But there were no models that directly addressed the relationship of model to thought, to symbolic logic, to semiotics. Idea was never related to idea, for this would have required the building to be subservient to the model.

The revising author, Helen Demchyshyn, is a witness to the development of the modern architectural model alongside the traditional model—a development that began with a retrograde movement. What Demchyshyn saw in the early stage of the modern model was modeling pushed back one stage, to a time just before Alberti, to Brunelleschi who, in addition to creating realistic wood models of the great dome of Florence, also produced stage set models for the Church of Saints Annunzia depicting the descent of the Holy Ghost in the town square and other sacred representations. Models of this type were often very large, measuring up to twenty feet in length, and came complete with gears and machinery, moving figures, tableaux, and scripts. They were intended to capture the psychological response to the architectural settings of real life—that is, architecture as used and as residue. This is categorically different from models based on the anticipated use of architecture—of architecture as trajectory, as prognostication, as traditional from the time of Alberti.

It was this other modeling tradition that Demchyshyn saw, in darkened gallery rooms where silhouettes of archetypal towns cast their eerie shadows on the walls, while tape recorders broadcast a shoot-out with radio memory of the Lone Ranger; where sidewalk/street slabs made of stone with a single cutout window were tilted against one another to replicate the view of a person about to commit suicide.

The narrative response which used to be carried by theatrical architectural models in Brunelleschi's time was displaced by the rise of perspective illusion in painting, wherein narrative subsequently took place. This left narrative in modeling to be found in sideshow maquettes—often in travelling circus shows—from which it was resurrected only in the late twentieth century, in a form intrinsic to narrative sculpture. This late resurrection could be traced to the rise of nonobjective painting which followed upon the decline of figurative painting, which itself left a vacuum for narrative imagery that was filled exclusively by literature in the interim; and to the resumption of neorealist painting where *used* architecture was depicted as an absence of users. The same vacancy of narrative in painting thus prevailed, as it had prevailed since Hopper. Consequently, the construct of this book: two traditions; two times; a seamlessness.

DONALD WALL

Part One

1:Planning the Model

Many models inadequately fulfill their function because the builder did not take the time to analyze the precise purpose of the model. The following questions must be asked before starting construction:

Use. What will this model be used for? Will it be a general massing form, semidetailed, or superdetailed? Will it be photographed? Will it be displayed? How long should the model last?

Detail. What is the minimum detail that must be shown? If time and money permit, how far should this minimum be exceeded to fulfill its uses?

Budget. How much time and expense should be allotted for the model? If the budget were to be raised, could the model be put to greater use?

Techniques. What construction techniques could do the job economically? What materials and tools would be needed? Could they be purchased in time?

CHOOSING A CONSTRUCTION TECHNIQUE

A knowledge of the variety of models commonly used to depict architectural designs will help you decide which type of model best suits your purposes and budget. Model types range from the simplest massing study to the most detailed presentation model. (Each type is discussed in fuller detail in Part 2 of the book.)

Massing models, described in chapter 15, are frequently used in the beginning stages of design to study the shape or zoning envelope of a building. These are basic, not literal, forms used to explore such things as volume, setbacks at the top floors, a single structure versus a cluster of several buildings, and so on. Because many different solutions are being considered, the models must be executed quickly and should be suitable for modifications, such as cutting away or additions. These should also be inexpensive since they will probably be discarded later. *Solid block models* are best used here,

especially since internal detail is not yet being shown (figure 1-1). These can be made of roughly cut clay or wood, or made as Strathmore or chipboard boxes built to approximate dimensions. These models can be revised as more detail is required. Textures and patterns can be worked into or drawn on them, and elements such as moldings, overhangs, or balconies can be added on. As the design becomes more refined, block models can be rebuilt to exact dimensions, with major details built into the models.

Hollow models (see chapter 16) should be used if the model must show interior details or window fenestration. These can be made of cardboard, wood, or acrylic, with clear plastic or cut-out windows. Floor slabs, which will also serve as internal bracing, may have to be included in these models. A final *presentation model* may be highly detailed, showing color, texture, and major elements accurately. It may even include all interior furnishings or have internal lighting (figure 1-2).

When choosing the kind of detail to show on the model, be sure to follow it through consistently. For example, if you are showing 2″ mullions, do not leave out 3′ high and 8″ thick parapet walls. It is best to determine the minimum size of detail before proceeding. The amount of detail shown on the model may determine its price to a far greater extent than does its size or the materials used.

PLANNING CONSIDERATIONS

Make and review approximate time and cost estimates when making even a minimum model. Assemble all construction details and reference materials. A list of photographs to be taken should also be secured because of its bearing on the technique eventually chosen. For example, if interior shots are needed, the model may have to be constructed in such a way that it can be disassembled easily to reveal the inside (see figures 6-16 and 18-4). Or if a model is to be photographed

1-1.
Blade Runner, Tyrell Pyramid
Warner Bros., Inc. (A Ladd Company Release)
Special photographic effects: Entertainment Effects Group
Scale: approximately 1:1000. Dimensions: 2½' H × 9' W

The "Pyramid" building was one of many special effects miniatures used in the film, *Blade Runner.* Shown here is a mock-up of the building; this was used to study shape and scale, as well as to plan the viewing angles from which the final model was to be shot. The mock-up was made out of double-thick cardboard, on which drawings of the exterior details were applied. (*Photograph by Mark Stetson*)

exclusively in black and white, attention to the shades of gray that appear in the photograph may be more important than achieving a realistic depiction of the building's actual colors. Decisions about painting will also affect the assembly schedule. Because, once they have been assembled, abutting parts cannot be painted different colors easily or neatly, much of the painting has to be done beforehand.

Before you begin a model, assemble the plans and drawings from which you will work. Keep in mind that designers are notorious for making constant changes. Modelmakers who work in an architectural or interior design firm expect these changes and will accommodate the designers. In fact, many offices have in-house model studios because models are frequently used to test various design solutions. An outside professional modelmaker, on the other hand, will either refuse to make changes because the model was exactly specified in the contract, or will add the cost of changes to the price

1-2.
Shown here is the final model of the Tyrell Pyramid from *Blade Runner* (see figure 1-1), under construction. The walls were made of ⅛″ acrylic sheets supported on wood frames and backpainted, with the paint partially scratched away later, allowing the internal light to pass through. The richly textured surface is a second layer, made of cast plastic and acid-etched brass panels, applied onto the acrylic sheets. The model was filmed with computerized motion-control cameras in a smoke room, which gave the miniature set a greater illusion of depth. The studio's special lighting and atmospheric conditions, combined with the model's richly detailed design, produced a spectacular opening sequence in the film. (*Photograph by Mark Stetson*)

of the model. In either case, while revisions may be necessary, they add to the work-time and materials expenses. For this reason, as much information as possible should be assembled before beginning a model; and it is important, therefore, for designers to understand the modelmaking process and schedule and to communicate any changes in the design as soon as they come up.

A quick sketch with dimensions shown may be all that is necessary for a rough study model. For a more detailed or complicated model, a set of plans, elevations, and sections should be assembled. It is easiest to work from drawings that are at the same scale as the model is to be. Check all prints to make sure that they have not been distorted by the printing process, atmospheric changes, or aging. Also check for accuracy the measurements given on the drawings. Because models have their own construction details, such as the thickness of the material being used or the internal bracing needed for the model, redraw important parts of the building according to these details.

If the building being modeled is intended for a specific site, visit the site, if possible, to collect information that may be useful for the model (see figure 11-1). Note the shape and color of adjacent buildings or rooms, size and type of flora, color of roads and sidewalks, ground texture, amount of pedestrian or vehicular traffic, and, in the case of a renovation or space-planning model, details of existing conditions. A camera is indispensable for recording most of this information. You may also want to take photographs that can be used on the model, or background shots; these can be superimposed on model pictures to form an effective photocomposite.

SCALE SELECTION

By the time you have reviewed the planning considerations discussed above, you may have developed some definite feelings about the scale that will best satisfy your needs. You must consider the degree of realism you want to convey in the model and photographs as well as the amount and kind of detail to be shown. Minimum and maximum scale ranges can then be formulated (table 1-1).

Large-scale models allow you to show more detail, can be used to study smaller intersections and parts of the design, and are (sometimes) more impressive.

Table 1-1. Scales Used in Model Building

Scale	Proportion
	1:2000
1″ = 100′	1:1200
	1:1000
1″ = 60′	1:720
1″ = 50′	1:600
	1:500
1″ = 40′	1:480
1/32″ = 1′	1:384
1″ = 30′	1:360
1″ = 20′	1:240
1/16″ = 1′	1:192
OOO or N model-train gauge	1:152
3/32″ = 1′	1:128
1″ = 10′ (TT model-train gauge)	1:120
	1:100
1/8″ = 1′	1:96
HO model-train gauge	1:87
OO model-train gauge	1:76
3/16″ = 1′ (S model-train gauge)	1:64
1/4″ = 1′ (O model-train gauge)	1:48
3/8″ = 1′	1:32
1/2″ = 1′	1:24
3/4″ = 1′	1:16
1″ = 1′	1:12
	1:10

Smaller-scale models take less time to construct, if details are simplified or omitted, and are easier to protect and ship.

Check the scale at which ready-made parts (simulated building materials, structural shapes, etc.) can be obtained. If these can be appropriately used in the model, you may save a great deal of time by simply incorporating them into the model rather than constructing them yourself.

The following are the scales usually used for various types of models:

Town-planning models can be built at 1:2000 to 1:1000 scale if only a block model is required. If some indication of fenestration, balconies, parapets, or other building parts is required, 1:500 (about 1″ = 40′) is a better scale.

Building models used for massing studies can also be made at 1:500. For modeling very small buildings, you may want to increase the scale to 1:200 (about 1/16″ = 1′). Detailed models of large buildings may be done at 1/32″ = 1′ or 1/16″ = 1′. At these scales, complete fenestration and columns can be shown satisfactorily. If superdetailing, such as small mullions, grillework, or stairs, for example, is required, your scale may have to be as large as 1/8″ = 1′ for large buildings and up to 1/4″ = 1′ for small buildings.

Factory and *office layout models* are best at 1/4″ = 1′ if available castings are used. If you intend to construct the pieces yourself and little detail is required, 1/8″ = 1′ may prove acceptable.

Landscape models can be scaled as small as 1:500 if only a rough layout of trees and bushes is needed, to as large as 1/16″ = 1′ (about 1:200) for a fairly accurate rendition of plant size, shape, and texture.

Interior design models or *stage set models* may range from 1/4″ = 1′ scale for rough models to 1/2″ = 1′ and 1″ = 1′ for models that must show greater detail.

PLANNING CONSTRUCTION TECHNIQUES

More mistakes in craftsmanship are due to the lack of planning than to lack of skill. You must plan the technique used for each object before starting the work. One way is to compare it to similar already-modeled objects. Ask yourself what the simplest ways to make what you need are.

After two or three techniques have come to mind, analyze them to see if they will give satisfactory results. Do these techniques require trips to different, hard-to-locate suppliers? Do they require additional tools? Do they require greater skills than you possess? These kinds of questions can probably eliminate all but the most practical system.

This type of decision-making process was used by one designer who was working on a model of a display that included three washer-shaped pieces of decorative trim with outside diameters of 2″. These objects were to be about $\frac{1}{32}$″ thick and have a cross-sectional shape similar to that of a bowl with a large hole cut in the bottom. Forming the curved concave surface posed the greatest problem. The designer brought drawings of the objects to a modelmaker, whose first response was to consult a nearby supplier of parts for handbag manufacturing in order to buy brass or copper collars of the approximate dimensions needed. This is a typical first thought, full of intended cleverness but impractical for two reasons: it might take too much time and legwork to secure such parts, and the acquired parts probably will not duplicate the outside and inside diameters and the curved contours exactly.

The second idea was to obtain polystyrene sheet material of the necessary thickness and, by pivoting an X-Acto blade around the center point, to scrape out the concavity. The outside diameters could be cut on an electric jigsaw, the center holes drilled, and then the objects sanded. This technique, requiring a time-consuming shopping trip and the difficult process of carving with the blade, seemed too complicated on further consideration, even if feasible.

The third thought was to form a shallow cone from 3-ply Bristolboard. The point could then be cut off, leaving a washer-shaped object that could be reinforced and made thicker with additional layers. This technique had been useful in previous work with curved objects.

On comparing the three techniques, it seemed obvious that the third was the most reasonable for modeling accuracy and time expenditure. When it was suggested to the designer, however, he appeared unimpressed and favored the second idea instead. It seems he had experienced past difficulty with paper construction warping (probably due to improper bracing or waterproofing). After reflection, however—and no little coercion on the modelmaker's part—he accepted the paper technique. It required only a few minutes of construction, and the efforts resulted in an accurate and, so far, durable model.

This illustration demonstrates three psychological factors involved in selecting techniques: the handbag idea represents a desire to be ingenious; the polystyrene carving is an attempt to devise a new, perhaps magical technique; and the reluctance to accept the simple paper construction illustrates a distrust of a previously used technique that did not work because of a lack of knowledge and improper handling.

As your modelmaking experience increases, impractical ideas and prejudices will decrease, and you will recognize basic truths about techniques:

1. First try to locate suppliers or stores where you can buy the object already fabricated.

2. If a technique has been used by others successfully, it can, in all probability, be perfected and adapted by you with adequate tools and instruction.

3. If you intend the use of a particular technique that has never been heard of before, you must undertake a thorough investigation and experimentation well before a deadline date.

4. An assembly of tools and up-to-date references will save you time and money.

5. Obtaining new materials almost always takes more time than anticipated.

6. An unsuccessful technique should be analyzed to discover what went wrong.

Faced with the problem of construction, you should select the techniques with which you have had prior experience and for which you have the requisite tools on hand. Some of the construction methods and materials discussed in this book often will not be suitable. However, to increase your modelmaking skills, you should know alternate methods and should experiment with new ones. Before starting the model, try to ascertain whether or not less widely used systems could save time and expense and/or greatly increase the quality of your model.

It is also important to determine the intended longevity of the model. Its construction can be simplified if it is only going to be photographed, or if it is going to be shown for a short time and then stored away for possible (but not probable) future use. On the other hand, a 10% to 20% increase in model cost can sometimes ensure that a model will last for decades.

2:The Workspace

Most work areas are a compromise in space, but care must be taken that economizing does not result in cramped or dangerous working conditions or in a workspace that exposes the rest of your home or office to fire hazards, noise, dust, smells, and distractions. Setting up a separate room will eliminate most of these problems, especially if the modelmaking activities involve even small power tools and spray-painting operations. In fact, because of the relatively large floor area needed for each modelbuilder and because of health and insurance considerations, large design firms often prefer to locate model shops in totally separate quarters.

SMALL SHOPS

Even if you plan to build simple models, if two or more models will be under construction at the same time, it would probably be wise of you to have a separate shop. A minimal two-person, 100'-square shop is shown in figure 2-1. Its freestanding model table affords access to all sides of the models being constructed. The workbenches should be sufficiently large to hold mounted power tools (circular saws, jigsaws, and so forth). The tables can also be used to set up the model for photography. A portable spray-painting booth may be made from a 2'-square (or larger) corrugated cardboard carton, set up when needed on a workbench and stored the rest of the time under the model table (make sure the shop is well ventilated when you are painting). Since shop equipment must be supplemented periodically, future needs must be carefully estimated to keep a shop from becoming crowded and inefficient.

LARGER SHOPS

If you intend to make many solid wood block models, machined Plexiglas models, or wood model bases, you will need heavy power tools permanently mounted on stands. Such tools require sufficient workspace around

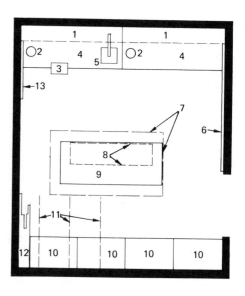

2-1.
A two-person workshop with a minimum of power tools: (1) 12" deep shelf at 5'6", 6', 7', and 8' levels—keep plastic small parts cabinets on the lowest shelf and infrequently used materials and tools on the top shelves; (2) table lamp; (3) vise; (4) 24" × 60" workbench with a single full-length 3" deep drawer and two 18" wide, 12" high drawers—one bench is for rough, messy work, the other is for drafting and for paper and board cutting; (5) portable electric jigsaw—store it in workbench drawers with other portable power tools; (6) tackboard or Homosote board on which to pin up drawings and photographs; (7) border of maximum-size model that can be comfortably fabricated in this shop (3' × 5'6"); (8) ceiling light; (9) 24" × 60" model table with low shelf—store clay, plaster, and other heavy supplies on the shelf; (10) steel small-drawer cabinets 38" high and 12" to 18" deep; drawers measure 3'6" high × 18" deep × 24" wide; 3'6" × 16" × 9"; or 5" × 24" × 11"; store tools, paint, and materials in drawers; finished models can be stored in a vertical position on top of the cabinets; (11) rack made of 1" diameter pipe (1'6" oc) connected by elbow joints to vertical pipes that are screwed to the ceiling; the bottom of the rack should be 6'6" above the floor; store sheet material, dowels, stripwood, and rolled plans on racks; (12) board storage; and (13) perforated Masonite board for storing hand tools.

them (table 2-1), to ensure safety and to accommodate the large sizes of materials that are sold in lumberyards.

Before planning the room, you must decide what types of operations will be performed on each machine.

Table 2-1. Recommended Location of Various Bench-Mounted Power Tools

Tool	Workspace Required	Location in Room
Drill press	Front, sides	Wall, corner
Jigsaw	Front, sides	Wall, corner
Band saw	Front, sides	Wall
Table circular saw	Front, rear, sides	Center
Radial arm saw	Front, sides	Wall
Disc sander	Front	Center, wall
Belt sander	Sides	Center, wall
Grinder	Front	Center, wall, corner
Lathe	Front	Wall, corner
Jointer	Front, rear	Center, wall
Shaper	Front, sides	Wall

2-2.
Untitled
Allan Adams
Scale: 1:1
Material: wood

All the tools in this 1:1 scale wooden replica of the artist's workshop depict the tools necessary for its construction. Everything has been cut and carved out of wood, including the table saw, with its blade and miter gauge, drill press, standing lamp and extensions cords, hand tools, spray cans, and apron. Naturally, the planks and sawdust are also made of wood. (*Photograph by Colin C. McRae, courtesy of Gallery Paule Anglim*)

Cutting baseboards out of 4′ × 8′ plywood sheet will probably be the most space-consuming operation, but regular work on the jigsaw, band saw, radial arm saw, drill press, sander, and jointer will also require considerable space. A shop containing five heavy power tools and the same amount of workbench and storage space will require 150 to 200 square feet.

To conserve space, you can take the following steps:

1. Mount the tool stands on casters and move them to the center of the shop when they are required to hold large materials.

2. Substitute a Lazy Susan revolving table (called a tool turret) for individual tool stands. The turret can be made from sheet metal and mounted on a 2″- to 4″-diameter pipe pedestal that is attached to a workbench. Two or three tools can be kept on this table, which requires the wall space of only one conventional tool.

3. Buy multipurpose tools, such as radial arm saws, that perform several operations and reduce the number of individual tools required.

2-3.
Entertainment Effects Group modelmaking studio. Large table surface areas are needed for laying out objects such as the many rows of edged brass facade silhouettes for urban landscape scenes shown here as well as for tools and supplies. Ample amounts of open floor space are also needed for constructing larger-scale buildings, such as the one seen in the background. Even though the overall lighting in the workshop is even and bright, movable lamps could be used for close-up work.

If you intend to spray paint with lacquers, your insurance company will probably require that the painting be done in a separate room and that paints be stored in steel cabinets. Certain insurance policies will not allow the storage of lacquers on the premises under any circumstances. Incidentally, keeping painting activities away from the dust of other working areas facilitates good finishes. Larger shops may require areas for hot casting, photo taking, and model storage, as well as clothing lockers, water supply, and a slop sink.

WORKBENCHES

There are several types of furniture that may be efficiently used as workbenches: old drafting tables, commercially made woodshop benches, and flush doors set on sawhorses. Benches should be about 36″ high. They should contain one or more drawers (for tool and flat material storage) and perhaps a lower open storage shelf. Tops of benches should be covered with a sheet of material that can be replaced when it becomes badly mutilated. Use ⅛″ Masonite or plywood held in place by countersunk screws on a rough workbench and an inexpensive illustration board stapled or tacked on a workbench where delicate work can be performed. If the bench is located against a wall, the table should have a low rear barrier to prevent small parts from falling off. Bench tops should overhang in front to facilitate fastening vises and clamps.

Commercial benches are made in several styles. The machine and layout bench without a built-in vise or drawers has a low, open storage shelf. The elementary workbench has a built-in wood vise, drawers, and a storage shelf. The woodshop bench has a built-in wood vise, drawers, and holes in its top for tool storage.

Flush wood doors, 1″ or 2″ thick, may be used to make workbenches of almost any length. Sawhorse legs for these can be made by using five pieces of 2″ × 4″ lumber with prefabricated Dalton brackets and completed with a cross-member made out of 2″ lumber; or they can be bought from companies that sell prefabricated wood or steel bipods.

STORAGE

Even if you contemplate making only an occasional model in a drafting room, keeping an organized stock of model materials and tools will save time and money. Various papers and boards, as well as a cutting surface, can be stored in plan file drawers. Tapes, glue, and tools, such as mat knives or rulers, can be stored on shelves or in file cabinets.

When a modelmaking workshop is being set up, adequate storage space must be provided to keep it uncluttered and efficient and to preserve tools. An almost universal tendency is to underestimate the number of tools and material samples that will be collected and to be unprepared for storage expansion. Storage space must be provided for many basic types of materials:

1. Large (30″ × 40″ to 4′ × 8′) sheets of board and plywood are best stored flat in shallow plan drawers. Vertical storing may result in warping unless the boards are kept exactly vertical. Overhead pipe racks are also a possibility. A sheet of Mylar plastic will keep the boards dust-free.

2. Heavy bulk material—plaster and clay, for example—should be stored near floor level in drawers or cabinets.

3. Portable power tools and light but bulky materials can be stored on wall shelves or in cabinets (save small corrugated cardboard cartons or shipping boxes to keep tools and materials protected from dust). If shelves are used, they should be adjustable, with wall-mounted, slotted metal strips into which shelf brackets can be fitted.

4. Hand tools should be kept on pegs or wire brackets on wall-hung, perforated Masonite sheets. Each tool should have a permanent location on the board, shown by a painted outline. To prevent blade damage, cutting tools should never be piled into drawers.

5. For blocks of wood and other materials, 38″-high small-drawer steel cabinets, with 4½″-high, 24″-deep, and 10½″-wide drawers, are suitable. The largest blocks can be stored on open shelves. Steel cabinets are available at office supply stores.

6. Sheets of balsa and Plexiglas may be stored in the long, low drawers of workbenches or in a plain storage cabinet.

7. Stripwood, structural shapes, dowels, and wire are stored inside 1″- to 2″-diameter cardboard tubes near the balsa and Plexiglas sheets.

8. Small material and assemblies—trees, cars, people, furniture, electrical equipment, camera supplies, and so forth—should be stored by category in individual drawers or bins. A system of storage should be organized as early as possible, and room should be made to store boxes or small compartment chests as they begin to pile up. A 38″-high shallow-drawer steel cabinet with 3½″ × 16″ × 9″ drawers is a good system. Valuable equipment can be safeguarded with a locking bar. One method for storing small materials is to build 2″ × 2″ compartments (or compartments of whatever dimensions are required) out of ⅜″-thick cardboard. Glue the card-

board in an egg-crate pattern on cardboard bases that have been set into the drawers of steel cabinets. The advantage of making your own compartments is that these waste less space than does fitting various-size plastic chests and bins into drawers.

9. Small bottles and tubes of paint and glue can also be stored in narrow-drawer steel cabinets.

10. Small tools—those that cannot be pegged onto Masonite racks practically—may also be kept in steel cabinets.

11. Very small tools and fasteners (nails, screws, drills, knife blades, and so forth) should be kept in the plastic drawers of small metal or plastic cabinets, which can be found in hobby or hardware stores. The cabinets contain from four to about twenty drawers. They can be stored on a low shelf or on top of large steel cabinets. Extremely small things can be kept in divided plastic boxes; these come with compartments as small as $1'' \times 1''$ and can also be stored in steel cabinets. Another system is to use small food jars hung with mounting clips from a pegboard. No matter which system you use, you should buy enough small drawers and boxes so that practically every size screw, nail, washer, and so on, can be allotted to a separate compartment. Drills, knife blades, burrs, and other small sharp tools should be kept in some sort of protective rack or stand.

12. Catalogs of tool and material suppliers as well as articles on tools and modelbuilding can be kept in one or more filing cabinet drawers.

ELECTRICITY AND LIGHT

All power tools made for the hobbyist and home craftsperson run on 110-volt, 60-cycle alternating current. It is a good policy to provide two outlets for each workbench. Some shops have continuous plug-in strips located a foot above the top of the workbench and these have outlets every 18″. If there are a number of power tools, two or more electrical circuits should be available to separate the energy supply for the shop's lighting from the supply for its tools. Thus, if a tool causes an overload and blows a fuse, the lights will remain on. Make sure to note the rated amperage of tools and provide the proper fusing for them.

Use three-prong plugs with power tools. If receptacles in the shop will take only two-prong plugs, buy an adapter equipped with a pigtail. To ensure that the tool is safely grounded, screw the pigtail to the receptacle's coverplate. Since overloading can occur much more easily with shop tools than with home appliances, do not use adapters that allow more than one tool or lamp on an outlet. Also use heavy-duty extension cords. The longer the cord, the heavier gauge its wire must be. If photographs are to be taken in the shop, make sure that the circuits have sufficient capacity for floodlights—a minimum of 1,000 to 1,500 watts.

A lighting level equal to that maintained in drafting areas is desirable. This may be provided by a combination of ceiling fixtures (for overall lighting) and individual adjustable drafting lamps located at each workbench and power-tool stand. Many bench-mounted power tools have already-mounted accessory lamps. Movable lamps can be directed at the work from different angles to reveal defects. Table-fixture lights must be angled in such a way that your body does not block light from the work.

VENTILATION, WATER, AND HUMIDITY

Take care to ventilate shop and paint areas properly. Forced ventilation will probably be needed for rapid clearance of the fumes produced by some paints. Ideally, air should be evacuated from the area where the workers stand, across the workbench, and directly out of the building.

Running water is not necessary in small shops. A sufficient supply of water for occasional plaster casting and tempera painting can be kept in plastic bottles. Larger shops should be equipped with a slop sink.

Humidity and temperature levels must be reasonably stable. Extreme variations in temperature can cause warping of models made from a combination of several materials and can also make it difficult to assemble parts made to exact size because they may have expanded or contracted. Excess humidity can cause wood and paper constructions to buckle, and paint in a humid place may take much longer to dry between coats. Air conditioners, humidifiers, and, where necessary, dehumidifiers help maintain an even shop environment.

SOUND AND DUST CONTROL

Some cutting operations will create acoustical disturbances, no matter what sound control measures have been taken. However, to deaden shop noises appreciably, mount acoustic tile on the ceiling and use perforated Masonite (from which tools may be hung) on the walls. Placing power tools on rubber casters also cuts vibration noise.

Dust caused by sanding and cutting is a persistent problem. Some power sanders are equipped with built-in vacuum cleaners that allow little dust to escape. However, any shop will benefit from having a small electric vacuum cleaner that could also provide suction for vacuum sheet forming of plastic.

Dust is especially troublesome during painting, since the slightest amount in the air can ruin a model's finish. A separate paint room or paint booth can solve this problem.

SHOP SAFETY

It is wise to review basic shop safety rules periodically. Following them and being alert to the dangers inherent in working with tools can prevent many accidents:

1. Keep your shop uncluttered. Put away tools and materials as soon as you have finished with them.

2. Use sharp tools. Dull ones that require excessive pressure to make cuts may be dangerous to use.

3. Do not store wet rags with paint.

4. Concentrate on the cutting surfaces of the hand tool in use and on the direction in which it is moving. Make sure you are not in the line of its path or the path it may take if it is somehow deflected.

5. Have on hand a well-supplied first aid kit.
When using power tools:

6. Be sure you are thoroughly acquainted with the proper use and care of power tools.

7. Do not wear loose clothing; remove ties, scarves, necklaces, and so forth, and roll up sleeves.

8. Wear goggles whenever working with a machine that throws out sparks, chips, or sawdust.

9. Make sure you have a firm grip on any portable power tool you are using, and make sure your material is held firmly in place while you are working. Concentrate on the direction in which you are moving the tool.

10. Be careful not to let cutting blades bind. If they do, the material or tool will be kicked back or out of control. Secure material down with clamps when drilling. When cutting small pieces on a table saw, keep fingers at least 3″ away from blade by using push sticks to guide the material.

11. Analyze blind cuts; make sure your hand is not in the way of the cutting blades.

12. Use blade guards.

13. Cover all motor belts.

14. Do not allow tools to overheat.

15. Do not overload your electrical supply.

Since prolonged inhalation of the fumes of certain paints, solvents, and cements is dangerous, adequate shop and paint-room ventilation should be provided. Use applicators and wear polyethylene throwaway gloves to avoid skin contact with certain elements. Always read and respect the warnings that are printed on the labels of products.

A dust mask should be worn during hand sanding, power sanding, and power cutting of various materials because of the huge amount of dust that is produced. Safety respirators with replaceable filters can screen out most nontoxic paint fumes. Other, more expensive devices, obtainable from spray equipment manufacturers, will render less harmful any type of fumes that may be encountered.

FIRE SAFETY. Common sense (and your insurance company) requires that fire extinguishers be located in the work areas. Small CO_2 or CO_2 powdered dry chemical (sodium bicarbonate) extinguishers are effective in fighting all types of fires (including those in electrical equipment). Test them yearly by reading the gauges or indicators (if available) or by weighing the CO_2 cartridge. A weight loss of ¼ ounce or more suggests that a recharge is necessary.

Foam extinguishers are of marginal use since they do not work on all types of electrical fires. Soda acid extinguishers will not work on electrical fires or on inflammable liquids. Vaporizing liquid (Carbona, and so on) extinguishers and small aerosol units can themselves cause noxious fumes.

3:The Minimal Toolbox

For making a rough clay model, you may only need one tool: a modeling knife. On the other hand, making a finished acrylic model requires many tools, including a table saw and power sander. The following numbered toolboxes (corresponding to eight different categories of modelmaking techniques) will help you inventory and purchase the tools you will need most for each type of project. Table 3-1 lists all the tools and specifies the toolboxes in which they should be included (hand tools are described in detail in chapter 4 and power tools in chapter 5).

Table 3-1. Minimal Tool Boxes for Various Modeling Techniques

Tools	Toolbox Numbers
MARKING TOOLS	
Pencils (HB, 3H, and 6H)	1–8
Drafting set (including inking pen and compass)	2, 3, 5, 8
MEASURING TOOLS	
Architect's (or engineer's) scale	1–3, 5–8
18″ metal ruler	2–8
Zigzag ruler (6′ long with slide-out extensions)	4
Straightedge (18″, 3′, and 5′ lengths)	2–8
Divider	1–3, 5–8
Beam compass	2–5, 8
1″ micrometer	3, 5–8
Caliper or caliper rule	3, 5, 6, 8
Combination square	1–8
Sliding T-bevel	8
Marking gauge	8
Contour marker	3, 5, 8
Magnifier	3, 6, 8
Burnisher (for overlays)	2, 3, 5, 8
VISES	
Bench vise	2–8
Woodworking vise	4, 5, 8
Mechanic's vise	8
Instrument vise	8
Hand vise	3
CLAMPS	
Improvise clamps (several)	1, 2, 5–8
Magnetic holders (2 or more)	3, 7, 8

Tools	Toolbox Numbers
CLAMPS (*continued*)	
Multipurpose spring clamps (2 or more)	3, 4, 5, 8
C-clamps (4 or more)	1–8
Clamps for large flat surfaces	1–5, 8
Workbench-mounted hold-down clamps (2 or more)	3, 8
Common wood hand screws	4
Tourniquet clamps	3, 8
PLIERS	
Round-nose pliers	2–8
Flat-nose pliers	2, 3, 5–8
Combination pliers	1, 3, 6–8
Diagonal-cutters or side-cutters	2, 3, 5, 6, 8
End-cutting nippers	7
Bernard side-cutters	8
Tweezers	1–8
Forceps	6, 7
WIRE BENDERS	
Bending jig	3, 7, 8
Wire-bending die	2, 3, 5–8
Sheet metal bending tool (homemade)	7
SCREWDRIVERS	
Standard blade (2 or more sizes)	2–8
Phillips head screwdriver	2–4
Jeweler's screwdriver set	3, 7, 8
HAMMERS	
10 oz. bell-face curved claw	1–3, 5–8
16 oz. bell-face curved claw	4
10 oz. soft-face	3, 5, 8
KNIVES AND ACCESSORIES	
Plywood or Masonite cutting surface	1–8
Mat-cutter and beveler	3, 8
Balsa stripper	2, 3, 5, 8
Razor blades (single-edge) or throwaway razor blade knives	1–3, 5–8
X-Acto knives (a lightweight and a heavyweight handle, with a selection of blades)	2, 3, 5, 6, 8
Mat knife	1–5, 7, 8
Paper cutter	2, 3, 8
CIRCLE CUTTERS	
Beam compass and circle cutter	2, 3, 8
Artist's cutting blade	2, 3

Tools	Toolbox Numbers	Tools	Toolbox Numbers
SCRIBERS		**CARVING TOOLS**	
Improvised scribers	1–3, 5, 6, 8	X-Acto, small-size blades	
Awl	3, 5, 7, 8	(5 or more)	2, 3, 6, 7
Multiple-line scriber	1–3, 5, 6, 8	X-Acto, heavier set	
SCISSORS		(5 or more)	2, 3, 5, 8
2½″ and 6″	2–3, 6–8	Spokeshave, standard	4–6
Snips (combination)	2, 3, 5–8	Spokeshave, miniature	3–6
DRILLS		Hand scraper	4
Wheel brace	1–8	**PUNCHES**	
Pin vise or pin tong	1–3, 5–8	Dot punch	2–8
TWIST DRILLS		90° punch	4, 7, 8
10 to 15 selected sizes	1–7		
Complete set	8	**PLASTER-WORKING TOOLS**	
Screw bits (several sizes)	4, 8	Wood surface	3, 5, 6
Large hole drill	4, 5, 8	Mixing bowl	3, 5, 6
Countersink bits	4, 8	Mixing spoon	3, 5, 6
FILES		Metal scrapers (2 or 3)	3, 5, 6
Jeweler's files (5 or more)	2, 3, 5–8	Steel rasps (perforated or	
Full-size files (several)	3–5, 8	unperforated, 2 or 3)	3, 5, 6
Abrasive paper (a selection		Miscellaneous running outriggers	
of 10 coarsenesses)	1–8	and slipper-board assemblies	3, 5, 6
Sanding block (homemade		Brushes (to apply separators	
or bought)	1–8	and to dust sanded surfaces)	3, 5, 6
CEMENTING TOOLS		**CASTING TOOLS**	
Hypodermic glue gun	2–6, 8	Melting ladle (stainless steel	
Porcelain enamel solvent		or iron)	6, 8
trays (several)	3, 8	Glass, slate, or marble surface	3, 6–7
Mixing cups	3–5, 7, 8	Electric heater or Bunsen burner	6, 8
Annealing oven	8	**PAINTING EQUIPMENT**	
CLAY-WORKING TOOLS		Paint brushes (selection)	1–6, 8
Joint knife	1	Air gun or airbrush, air	
Putty knife	1	compressor or compressed air	
Wire-end modeling tools (3 or 4)	1, 6	tank, hose paint cups	3–6, 8
Boxwood modeling tools (3 or 4)	1, 6	Masking tape or other masking material	2–6, 8
Polyethylene film or wax paper	1, 6	Rags	2–6, 8
		Spray booth with turntable	2–6, 8
SAWS		Flock applicator	2–6, 8
Razor saw or dovetail saw		**PLASTIC-FORMING TOOLS**	
(with blade having 50 or more		Infrared lamps or electric	
teeth per inch)	2, 3, 5–8	heating elements (2 or more;	
Multiple-tool saw, saw knife,		lamps may also be used to	
back saw, or dovetail saw (with		speed the drying of paint	
blade having 32 teeth per inch)	1–3, 5–8	resin and some cements)	3, 8
Keyhole saw, all-purpose saw,		Thermometer	3, 8
or general-purpose saw	4	Electric oven	3, 8
Jeweler's saw or fine		Homemade or toy pressure	
coping saw	1–3, 5, 6, 8	chamber for vacuum forming	3, 8
Fret saw	4	**SOLDERING TOOLS**	
Hacksaw	4, 7	50-watt soldering iron or gun	2, 3, 5–8
Jab saw	4	Pencil iron or torch	2, 3, 5–8
Ripsaw	4	Table protector	2, 3, 5–8
Crosscut saw	4	**POWER TOOLS FOR:**	
Miter box, small	2, 3, 5, 8	Portable saber sawing	4
Miter box, large	4, 5, 8	Circular sawing	2–5
PLANES		Band sawing	5, 8
Modelmaker's plane	3, 5, 8	Light-duty jigsawing	2, 3, 5, 7, 8
Block plane	2–5	Accurate heavy drilling	3–5, 8
Smoothing plane	5, 8	Portable orbital or	
Fore plane	4	reciprocating sanding	4
Cabinetmaker's rabbet plane	4	Bench-mounted belt sanding	4, 5, 8
Chisel (heavy-duty)	4	Bench-mounted disc sanding	3–5, 8
		Grinding	3–5, 8

Tools	Toolbox Numbers
POWER TOOLS FOR:	
Dadoing and molding	4, 8
High-speed turning of small drills, cutters, emery wheels, cutoff discs, cloth-backed abrasive discs, polishing wheels, etc. (toolboxes 3 and 5 will need a rheostat and shaping table)	2, 3, 5–8
Light lathe turning	2, 3, 5, 8
Heavy lathe turning	8
TOOL CARE EQUIPMENT	
Grinder	3–5, 8
Honing stone	1–8
Strop	2–8
Oil	1–8

Key:

Toolbox 1: clay massing models
Toolbox 2: rough hollow models
Toolbox 3: detailed hollow models
Toolbox 4: baseboards, carrying boxes
Toolbox 5: precise solid block models
Toolbox 6: cast parts
Toolbox 7: metal forming and soldering
Toolbox 8: highly detailed acrylic models

Toolbox 1 provides the tools needed to construct *rough clay* or *plasticine massing models*, which can be mounted on unfinished pieces of composition board or heavy cardboard.

Toolbox 2 contains the tools necessary for the construction of *rough hollow models* made of cardboard or wood, supported on light wood carcasses. Thin sheets of plastic may also be used for this type of model. The model can be mounted on unfinished pieces of composition board or heavy cardboard.

Toolbox 3 lists the tools used to construct *detached hollow models* made of cardboard and wood, as well as of plaster and vacuum-formed sheet plastic.

Toolbox 4 shows the tools needed to construct heavy wood and plywood *bases* and *carrying boxes*.

Toolbox 5 has the tools for *precise solid block models* made of hardwood or plastic.

Toolbox 6 indicates the tools needed to *cast assemblies* from rubber, plastic, and plaster molds.

Toolbox 7 lists the tools for *metal forming* and *soldering*.

Toolbox 8 provides tools for producing *highly detailed models* built from acrylic plastic.

POWER TOOL REQUIREMENTS

Toolbox 1 does not require power tools.

Toolbox 2 requirements include some power tools (rented or bought) if many rough, hollow models are to be made. Because some tools can be used for a variety of functions (as indicated in table 5-1), the best starting tools would be either a small portable hand motor tool with stand and a light bench-mounted jigsaw or a Dremel combination tool.

Toolbox 3 probably requires buying or renting several tools if many elaborate built-up models are to be made. There are quite a few possible combinations of tools that will encompass all the required operations. The least expensive set is probably a Dremel combination tool, a ¼″ portable drill with drill press stand and horizontal bench stand, and a grinding tool rest. To these tools, add a good assortment of blades, cutters, and sanders.

Toolbox 4 definitely requires the rental or purchase of power tools unless you do not mind hard work and less-than-perfect results. There are many possible tool combinations available. The least expensive of these is probably a ¼″ portable drill (with accessory drill press stand, horizontal bench stand, orbital sander attachment, and rubber disc), a bench-mounted table saw with dado blade, and a bench-mounted belt sander. Add to these tools various blades, sanding discs, and molding heads.

Toolbox 5 also requires some power-tool rental or purchase unless balsa is substituted for harder woods and the extra work involved in finishing is taken into account. Again, there are a great number of possible tool combinations, the least expensive of which is a small portable hand motor tool with rheostat and shaping table, a bench-mounted band saw, and a ¼″ portable drill with drill press stand, horizontal stand, and rubber disc. Add to these an assortment of blades, cutters, and sanders.

Toolbox 6 requires a small portable hand motor tool with miscellaneous cutters and sanders.

Toolbox 7 does not require power tools unless you will be doing a lot of metal cutting. Then, either a small portable hand power tool and a light bench-mounted jigsaw, or a Dremel combination tool will probably suffice.

Toolbox 8 requires a shop full of tools. This is one of the reasons the types of models made with these tools are usually done in a professional modelmaking shop. A makeshift tool collection could produce moderately well-machined acrylic or similar types of models. Even with this array of equipment, however, you would be much less well-equipped than are professional modelbuilders who invest in thousands of dollars worth of power tools.

Before starting your first model, make a survey of your home or office toolbox. Employees or associates should also take an inventory of their stock. Add to

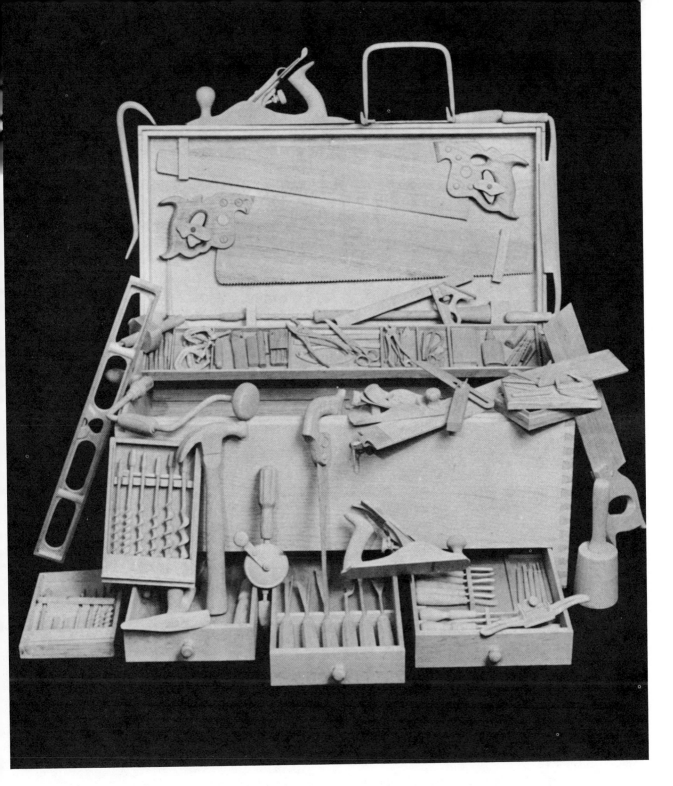

these tools only as the need arises, but keep in mind that completing the first of each type of model will probably mean having the complete minimal toolbox it requires. As you make more types of models, your supply of additional types and sizes of tools will grow.

3-1.
Tool Box, 1977
Allan Adams
Dimensions: 18″ × 42″ × 42″
Material: sugar pine

This toolbox, showing a complete set of hand tools, is made entirely out of sugar pine. Although power tools are recommended for building this type of detailed solid model, the craftsmanship in this sculpture shows the precision and detail that can be achieved with hand tools. (*Collection of Modesto Lanzone*)

4:Hand Tools and Their Use

The greatest investment made in modelbuilding—after paying the rent—will be in tools. While you can economize on rent by working in unused drafting space, for example, it is best to purchase tools of quality and adequacy, regardless of the cost. Cheap tools will be more expensive in the long run because of the need for frequent replacement, sharpening, and adjustment. Inadequate tools can prove a liability on even the first model undertaken. Wasted time and spoiled materials involving just one part of a model can add up to the price of an expensive tool.

High-quality tools are, surprisingly enough, more essential to the beginner than they are to the expert, since the easily discouraged neophyte does not have the skill to compensate for malfunctioning tools. Models have been successfully built using only a straightedge, a razor blade, sandpaper, and a pencil. However, if models are to be constructed periodically, it is reasonable to purchase tools whose time savings, effected on even the first model, will equal as much as one-third of the tool's price.

In the case of power tools, there is always the possiblity of renting. Rental fees can be kept low through careful scheduling of work. Most rental contracts now also allow a deduction of the rent from the price of any tool subsequently purchased. However, most available rentable tools are intended for the home craftsperson and the construction worker and tend to be too heavy and over-powered. Their use is therefore unfeasible except for the construction of baseboards, cases, and block models.

Listed in Appendix 1 are the names of suppliers or manufacturers of many well-made tools that have proved themselves to be of special use to the modelmaker and are competitively priced. One or more tools of each type may be purchased in any large hardware store. Check large local discount houses for bargains. Obtain catalogs of large mail-order companies before making an extensive purchase of tools.

TOOL CARE

Tools should be kept in good condition, free from rust that can so easily build up. If the shop is humid, all metal tools must be wiped with a light machine oil or paste wax. Convenient antirust oils in spray cans are also available. Jars of silica gel or magnesium chloride may be used to dry out the air inside cabinets and drawers. If rust does form, it can be removed with fine steel wool or abrasive paper. If these are found to be too abrasive, use a prepared rust remover. From time to time, all moving parts should be oiled.

After a tool is used, it should be cleaned and replaced on the tool pegboard. Heavy accumulations of grease and dirt may be removed by dipping the tool in cleaning fluids or solvents. Hard-to-remove gum deposits found on saw blades or router and shaper cutters can be removed with solvents, called gum and pitch removers, which are best applied with a toothbrush.

TOOL SHARPENING

It is extremely important to keep tools sharp. Dull tools make for sloppy models and wasted time and materials, and they create safety hazards. It is probably more expedient to have dull saw teeth reshaped and ground professionally, but it is also possible to grind and whet knives, planes, chisels, and scrapers yourself. In general, you will need a grinder, a honing stone, a slip stone, and a strop to do this work.

Grinding wheels are for grinding. Use a motor-driven circular Carborundum or emery grinding wheel equipped with a tool rest. You can buy a special motor or stand to convert portable electric drills into grinders. A conversion kit may include a stand, a wheel guard, a grinding wheel, and a drill-sharpening attachment. Horizontal shafts that can be turned by the motors of other power tools are also available. Multiuse power tools and radial arm saws can be fitted with grinding wheels, and belt sanders may also be used to sharpen tools.

In an improvised grinder, the wheel should not be turned too quickly. If you exceed the manufacturer's recommended speed, the wheel may burst. Always wear goggles when grinding, even if the tool rest is equipped with an eye shield. Purchase or make jigs to hold tool blades at the correct angle against the wheel (see figure 4-8F). When the wheel becomes worn, it can be dressed with a Carborundum stick. The grinder may also be converted into a sander, further defraying its cost.

Honing stones, used for tool sharpening, are best made artificially of Carborundum or Aloxite. Stones must be kept wet with oil or their pores will clog with metal particles. Carborundum stones may be used dry, with water, or with oil, which works the best. Most hones have a coarse and a fine side. To prevent stones from becoming gummy, store them in a piece of cloth moistened with oil. If gum does form, place the stone on nails in the bottom of a shallow pan. Slowly heat the pan until the oil runs free, but be careful not to allow it to evaporate. Wipe the stone dry while it is still hot. If the stone is worn, its surface may be re-smoothed by rubbing it with a piece of metal covered with a creamy mixture of water and aluminum oxide powder, whose grit is somewhat coarser than that of the stone.

Slip stones are used to sharpen gouges. Aluminum oxide stones (sometimes called tool room sticks) come in three grades and with square, triangular, half-round, or round cross-sections.

Strops are used to bring honed tools to razor sharpness. They can be formed with a strip of leather glued to a hard wood block.

MEASURING AND LAYOUT TOOLS

Architect's or *engineer's scales* may be used to lay out dimensions precisely on modeling materials.

Zigzag rules (figure 4-1A) or *metal tape rules* are for large layout work on baseboards, tables, and cases. They come in several models, with maximum extended lengths of from 2' to 8'. *Metal rules* are for measuring and for use as knife guides in cutting sheet material. Sizes run from 6" to 24". For making longer cuts, or when cutting thick material, use heavier metal *straight-edges*. These come in lengths of up to 60".

Dividers and *compasses* are for circle drawing or for transferring dimensions from the drawing to the model material. Use old drafting tools or, for large work, purchase a wing divider.

Beam compasses are for drafting large circles. Use an old drafting tool or buy trammel heads and mount them on a wood beam.

Micrometers (figure 4-1B) come in a wide range of accuracy and cost. In general, they are calibrated down to $\frac{1}{1000}''$ or $\frac{1}{10000}''$ and have a 1" capacity (0 to 1", 1" to 2", and so forth). For work that is not too exacting, an inexpensive tool will suffice, but for the fine machining of Plexiglas, for example, you will need a better-grade micrometer.

Vernier calipers (figure 4-1C) are used for inside and outside measurements and for the transfer of dimensions from one object to another. Some models have an outside measuring capacity of $3\frac{1}{4}''$ and an inside one of between $\frac{3}{16}''$ and $\frac{3}{4}''$, and are graduated in increments of $\frac{1}{32}''$. Others have an outside measuring tool that is calibrated down to $\frac{1}{1000}''$.

Combination squares (figure 4-1D) are multipurpose tools that combine the functions of an inside and outside try square, 45° miter square, level, depth gauge, marking gauge, scribe, and straightedge. They are 9" or 12" long, with calibrations down to $\frac{1}{32}''$.

Sliding T-bevels (figure 4-1E) lay out and test bevels of any angle. They are useful in a baseboard construction.

Marking gauges (figure 4-1F) make lines parallel to an edge of a sheet of material. The sliding head resting against the material's edge is fastened by a thumbscrew. These tools are useful in making baseboards and other pieces of heavy carpentry.

Contour markers (figure 4-1G) transfer complex contours from drawing to material or from material to material. Lay them against the curve to be copied and push the sliding slats into positions; then snap the lock to capture the curve. This tool also makes a very useful variable template.

Magnifiers are a great aid for work with small parts. These are available with stands or handles, and some have built-in battery-operated lights.

  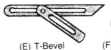 

(A) Zigzag Rule   (B) Micrometer   (C) Vernier Caliper   (D) Combination Square   (E) T-Bevel   (F) Boxwood Marking Gauge   (G) Contour Marker

4-1.
Measuring and layout tools

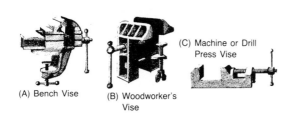

(A) Bench Vise   (B) Woodworker's Vise   (C) Machine or Drill Press Vise

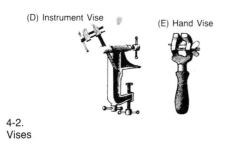

(D) Instrument Vise   (E) Hand Vise

4-2.
Vises

GRIPPING TOOLS

Vises

Odd-shaped objects may be held in a vise if they are first precast into a block of low-melting-point metal. After the object has been worked on, the metal, whose melting point is lower than the flash or melting point of the object, can easily be melted off.

Bench, workshop, or *utility vises* (figure 4-2A) are the most useful all-round vises, even though they are basically intended for metal and their unprotected jaws might scar wood. The jaws have either serrated faces for firm gripping or smooth faces for use with finished work. Sharp pointed jaws, facilitating metal bending, are also available. More expensive vises have interchangeable jaws. Always use jaws softer than your work material. Bench vises have stationary bases, swivel bases, or swiveling bases and swiveling rear jaws. The latter vise aids in holding tapered work. Vises can be either clamped on the workbench—providing greater flexibility of use but less rigidity—or screwed into place. The machinist's vise is a heavier version of the bench vise.

Woodworker's vises (figure 4-2B) have long jaws faced with replaceable wood facings. Some have metal "dogs" on their outer jaws; these can be raised and used for clamping long work against a bench stop. Some also have quick-acting jaws that slide open and closed without the usual handle turning.

Machine or *drill press vises* (figure 4-2C) are used to precisely position small work that is being machined.

They are meant to be bolted to a drill press table. These vises come in several models: stationary, with a swivel base, with a tilting (up-and-down) base, with a swiveling and tilting base (called an angle vise), or with a sideways sliding and swiveling base.

Instrument vises (figure 4-2D) hold small work in position and *hand vises* (figure 4-2E) are used to hand-grip small work.

Clamps

Clamps must be properly positioned before you can start work. Test clamp positions to make sure that the pieces being held are not pulled out of line. Pieces of cardboard or wood placed between the clamp and the work should be used to prevent surface marring of soft materials.

Improvised clamps include paper clips, bulldog letter clips, binder clips, clothespins, and rubber bands. Drops of sealing wax can also be used to clamp small, oddly shaped joints together.

Tweezers and *forceps* are also useful in working with small parts.

Magnetic holders keep metal parts together while they are being soldered or hold parts of nonmagnetic material in position on a metal work surface. Some magnets will hold parts in a perfect 90° (or any other) angle intersection.

Multipurpose spring clamps (figure 4-3A) have pivoting jaws allowing surfaces to be gripped at practically any angle.

Carriage makers or *C-clamps* (figure 4-3B, C, and D) are the most important clamps encountered in model work. Small clamps are made of nylon, malleable iron, or magnesium. Nylon clamps have ⅜″ to ¾″ jaw sizes. Malleable iron ones have ¾″, 1″, and 2″ throat depths. Magnesium clamps with throat depths of 1″ and 1½″ have 1″ and 1½″ jaw sizes. Large clamps made of malleable iron come with a 2″ × 3″ to 4″ × 8″ opening.

Clamps for large flat surfaces (figure 4-3E) can be made out of scrap wood or a pile of heavy books. For curved surfaces, use small sandbags.

Workbench-mounted hold-down clamps are permanent clamps that secure work to a table. The clamp slides into a bolt projecting from the bench. When not in use, the clamp can be removed and the bolt dropped into a counterbored hole, leaving the bench surface clear.

Tourniquet clamps (figure 4-3F) can be tightly wound with string and used on moderate-size jobs. Place wood blocks between the object and the cord to prevent damage to the surface of the work.

Common wood hand screws (figure 4-3G) are heavy clamping tools for making glued baseboards. *Bar clamps* (figure 4-3H) are used to butt glue planks into wide boards. *Cleat* and *wedge clamps* (figure 4-3I and J) or

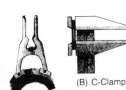

(A) Multipurpose
Spring Clamp

(B) C-Clamp

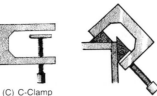

(C) C-Clamp

(D) C-Clamp and
Corner-Clamping
Blocks

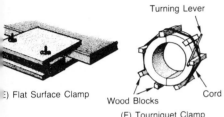

E) Flat Surface Clamp

Turning Lever

Wood Blocks   Cord

(F) Tourniquet Clamp

(G) Common Wood
Hand Screw

crimp clamps (figure 4-3K), made in a variety of sizes, can be used as substitutes for bar clamps; these facilitate gluing baseboards or model assemblies.

Pliers and Cutters

Pliers and cutters should be made of hammer-forged, tempered steel. They must be tested for closely fitting jaws. Some have built-in wire cutters, which come in three basic styles: first, squared sections on each jaw that cut with a shearing action (this type of cutter has a tendency to loosen up); second, side cutters consisting of short chisellike blades on each jaw (these are more reliable than the squared style); and third, button cutters with wire-size notches on each jaw (the notches shift past one another as the pliers close and cut the wire).

Round nose pliers (figure 4-4A) are for making curved bends and for holding wire and strips. *Combination nose pliers* (figure 4-4B) have one nose rounded and the other flat. *Chain nose* (figure 4-4C) and *flat nose*

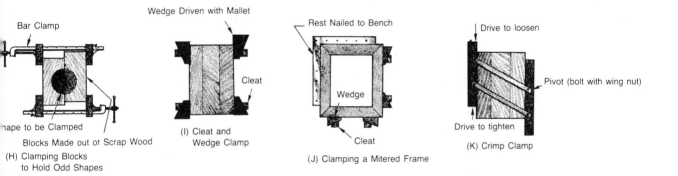

Bar Clamp

Shape to be Clamped

Blocks Made out of Scrap Wood

(H) Clamping Blocks
to Hold Odd Shapes

Wedge Driven with Mallet

Cleat

(I) Cleat and
Wedge Clamp

Rest Nailed to Bench

Wedge

Cleat

(J) Clamping a Mitered Frame

Drive to loosen

Pivot (bolt with wing nut)

Drive to tighten

(K) Crimp Clamp

4-3.
Clamps

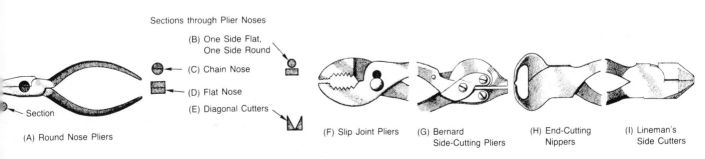

Sections through Plier Noses

(B) One Side Flat,
One Side Round

(C) Chain Nose

(D) Flat Nose

(E) Diagonal Cutters

Section

(A) Round Nose Pliers

(F) Slip Joint Pliers

(G) Bernard
Side-Cutting Pliers

(H) End-Cutting
Nippers

(I) Lineman's
Side Cutters

4-4.
Pliers and cutters

(figure 4-4D) *pliers* make sharp bends in wire and strips. They are for holding small parts and are used as small wrenches. These pliers come in long nose and needle nose lengths.

Diagonal-cutting pliers (figure 4-4E) or *sharp nippers* are used to cut small wire, nails, or screws. They have the ability to cut close to the surface from which the nail projects.

Slip joint or *combination pliers* (figure 4-4F) have a slip joint that allows the jaws to be opened extra-wide. These pliers are used for gripping rods and small pipes and for bending wire and sheet metal. Because of possible marring, they should not be used on nuts and bolts.

Bernard side-cutting pliers (figure 4-4G) have compound leverage, giving great holding and cutting power. Jaws are parallel, allowing this tool to be used as a wrench.

End-cutting nippers (figure 4-4H) have long handles. Compound leverage makes these tools more powerful than diagonal-cutting pliers. They may also be used to pull nails.

Lineman's side cutter pliers (figure 4-4I) or *side cutters* are used for cutting and splicing all types of wire except piano wire and tempered steel wire.

The pliers most useful for modelmakers can be obtained in sets that include round nose, flat nose, diagonal-cutting, end-cutting, snipe nose, and combination pliers.

Wrenches

Adjustable wrenches (figure 4-5A) are for turning nuts and bolts. They come in various sizes, ranging in maximum jaw capacity from ½″ to 1¾″.

Open-end wrenches (figure 4-5B) are also used to turn nuts and bolts, but the wrench must exactly fit the object being turned or it will damage it. Open-end wrenches come with openings at various angles to their handles to facilitate turning hard-to-reach nuts.

Box wrenches (figure 4-5C) are for use on nuts and bolts unreachable with an open-end wrench.

Six-sided socket wrenches are for use with small nuts and bolts and are fitted to a screwdriverlike handle.

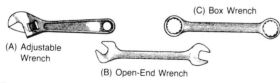

(A) Adjustable Wrench

(B) Open-End Wrench

(C) Box Wrench

4-5.
Wrenches

SCREWDRIVERS

The tip of a screwdriver must be square. If use has rounded it, restore it to its original shape on a grinding wheel. Long handles transmit more power to the screw. Short drivers (stubbies) are used to reach otherwise inaccessible screws. Use insulated drivers when working on electrical hookups.

Standard blades are for normal work and *cabinet blades* (figure 4-6A) are for use on deeply set screws.

Phillips screwdrivers have blades that fit into the cross-shaped slots of Phillips screws. Because of their greater driver-to-screw-bearing surface, Phillips screws seldom cause driver slip. They are used extensively where screws are visible and where driver slippage could mar a finished surface.

Spiral ratchet screwdrivers (figure 4-6B) have blades that turn when the handle is pushed down. Some come with interchangeable bits that permit drilling or countersinking holes.

Jeweler's screwdrivers have small interchangeable blades that can be locked into a handle.

Screwdriver bits are used with standard bit braces to create the necessary amount of driving thrust for large screws.

Screw-holding screwdrivers are useful for starting screws in hard-to-reach places. They are made for standard and Phillips screws.

Nut drivers have a hexagonal blade opening that fits standard nuts.

Allen wrenches (figure 4-6C) have hexagonal heads that fit Allen cap screws.

Set screw wrenches are metal bars that fit into the head groove of set screws.

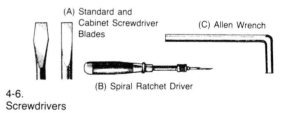

(A) Standard and Cabinet Screwdriver Blades

(C) Allen Wrench

(B) Spiral Ratchet Driver

4-6.
Screwdrivers

HAMMERS

Hammers come with hickory, tubular steel, solid steel (the strongest), and fiberglass handles. Striking faces may be plain (flat), bell (slightly convex), ball-peen (very convex), checkered, or soft (plastic faced). A plain face is easiest to use, but a bell face can drive a nail flush without leaving marks on the wood. A ball-peen head is for spreading rivets. A checkered face is for rough, ast work such as crating. A soft face is used with wood-andled chisels.

Hammers are graded by the weight of the head, 10 ounces being the size most often found in the household toolbox. A hammer that is too light will bend nails, as will the imperfectly made heads of cheap hammers. Hammerheads should be of drop-forged steel, with a hardened striking surface.

Claws come in two styles: curved, which is best for nail pulling; and ripping (straight), usable for nail pulling or for prying nailed joints apart. When pulling nails, place a block of wood between the hammer's head and the work to prevent damage to the latter.

When hammering, hold the nail near its point until a few light blows from the hammer have started embedding it. Then hold the hammer near the handle's end for best leverage. The head should be brought down squarely on the nail. If the nail bends, retract it and start over with a new one.

CUTTING TOOLS

Knives and Cutters

All cutting should be done on a sheet of Masonite or heavy cardboard attached to the workbench. When the cutting surface has become badly marred, replace it. Use a metal straightedge to guide the blade in straight cuts. Put a strip of masking tape along the underside of the metal to prevent it from sliding under the pressure of the knife. Straightedges of varying lengths will facilitate long or short cuts without unnecessary maneuvering. An 18″ metal rule will suffice for most long cuts, and the ruler part of a combination square is good for short work. The square may be used as a guide for cutting perfect 45° or 90° angles.

When cutting all but the thinnest materials, make several light runs over the cut line rather than attempting to sever the material at once. A sharp single cut can result in beveled cuts, deviation from the intended line, and possible stab wounds.

Mat cutters and *bevelers* come in the form of a 30″ straightedge. These can be used to guide the knife when you are making perpendicular or beveled cuts.

Balsa strippers have a knife-holding guide that can be used to cut perfect strips (1/16″ to 1/2″ wide) from a 1/32″- to 3/16″-thick balsa sheet. These tools permit cutting odd-size strips that are unobtainable ready-made.

Common *single-edge razor blades* are the handiest cutting tools. The thin, sharp blade allows the cutting of thin, fragile material without damage. Some people find it difficult to get the proper leverage with blades, and some fear them. With practice, however, a razor blade can be made to perform most of the cutting required on paper, cardboard, and balsa models and will cause fewer accidents.

X-Acto knives come in a complete line of knife handles and interchangeable blades. They can be used for fine or heavy cutting, carving, chiseling, routing, punching, and sawing.

Mat knives are very handy for cutting the heavy cardboard used for laminated contours, cardboard baseboards, and templates.

Paper cutters are useful for rapidly cutting out a large number of objects. Their built-in squaring edges allow cutting of perfect 90° corners.

Scissors can be used to cut paper and fabric, and are available in 2″ to 10″ lengths.

Swivel knives, *circle cutters*, and *compass cutters* can be used for making small radial cuts. *Large circle cutters* can be fabricated easily in the shop. At the end of a strip of wood, cut a groove perpendicular to the length of the strip. Clamp a mat knife into the groove. Drive a long sharply pointed nail through the other end of the wood strip parallel to the knife, with the nail point on the same side as the blade of the knife. The distance between the nail and the blade determines the radius of the desired circle.

Scratch awls and *engineer's scribers* are used for marking lines on acrylic and metal.

Multiple-line scribers can be shop-fabricated to make an endless variety of line patterns.

Saws

Material being sawed should be held in a vise or, if too large or oddly shaped, placed on a sawhorse and held steady with the left hand or knee. Start saw cut by cutting a kerf: position the blade with the thumb and then draw the saw over the material in the direction opposite to the cutting stroke if cutting wood, or in the direction of the cutting stroke if cutting metal. Once the kerf is deep enough to support the blade, start the actual cut. Keep checking the position of the saw to be sure the material is being cut squarely. Test by using a try square or develop a practiced eye.

Sawing should be accomplished with long, easy strokes, and pressure should be applied only when the blade is moving in the cutting direction. Let the blade lift slightly on the return stroke. If the blade starts to wander from its intended path, twist the saw slightly to move it back into line. If a cut turns out crooked despite the use of reasonable skill in following the guideline, it may be due to a dull blade, not enough tension on the blade, or lack of alignment of the saw's frame.

The coarseness of a saw blade is measured by the

number of tooth points per inch. The more and finer the teeth, the cleaner the cut. Saw teeth are bent alternately to the left and to the right of the plane of the blade. This is called set, and the extent of its divergence from the plane of the blade determines the width of the cut. Set comes in various patterns. A *wavy set*, on finer metal-cutting blades, has one unbent tooth, then three that are bent in one direction (the first bent tooth is slightly bent, the next has maximum set, the third is slightly bent), then another unbent tooth, then three teeth bent in the other direction: this pattern then repeats. A *raker set* has an unbent tooth flanked on both sides by single teeth bent in opposite directions. This pattern is found on wood- and coarser metal-cutting blades.

Spiral saw blades (used on piercing, coping, and fret saws) can be used to cut plaster, plastic, and other materials that clog regular saw teeth. *Backsaws* (figure 4-7A) are used to make fine, straight, not-too-long wood cuts. Their crosscutlike blades have 18 to 32 teeth per inch.

Dovetail saws are small backsaws used for very fine cutting and miter cutting. Their blades have 32 to 60 teeth per inch.

Keyhole saws (figure 4-7B) cut square or curved holes in the centers of panels. They can be used after being inserted into holes drilled through the material. Their blades, containing 10 to 18 teeth per inch, cut well with or against the grain. *Compass saws* are large versions of the keyhole saw.

Junior saws (figure 4-7C) are small versions of the coping saw. They have 32 teeth per inch on their replaceable blades.

Coping saws (figure 4-7D) have blades with 14 teeth per inch. They are used for cutting intricate curves in thin (up to about 1"-thick) wood and plastic. Since the blade may be turned in the frame, the depth of cut is unlimited. The teeth should point toward the handle so that the saw cuts on its back stroke. Spiral blades cut in any direction without having to be turned in the frame.

Piercing or *jeweler's saws* are like coping saws but have less clearance between their blades and the rear of the frame. Their blades have 32 to 80 teeth per inch.

Fret saws are also like coping saws but have more clearance between the blade and the rear of the frame. Their blades have 16 to 32 teeth per inch.

Razor saws (figure 4-7E) are among the finest-cut saws obtainable, having about 40 teeth per inch on their replaceable blades. They are used for making delicate cuts in cardboard, wood, and metal and may be used in small miter boxes. They cannot, however, make curved cuts.

Ripsaws (figure 4-7F) have 5 to 7 teeth per inch and a small amount of set (figure 4-7K). They are used to cut with the wood's grain. The saw should be held at a 60° angle between the blade and the work. When ripping a long board, insert a screwdriver into the cut to prevent the board from binding the saw blade.

All-purpose saws (figure 4-7G) can be used to cut holes in the centers of panels and to cut curves.

Pad saws use hacksaw, keyhole saw, or pad saw blades that have 10 to 32 teeth per inch; when equipped with a hacksaw blade, they may be used for cutting metal.

Saw knives (figure 4-7H) are available in sets that include five replaceable blades and a handle.

Jab saws (figure 4-7I) have hacksaw blades that may be extended out from the handle and flexed to lie flat against a surface. This facilitates making flush cuts.

Crosscut saws have 8 to 12 teeth per inch and a great amount of set (figure 4-7J). Their blades are between 16" and 26" long. The saw should be held at a 45° angle between blade and work. If the crosscut blade is polished, the reflection of the board will be mirrored in it and this will help to make perfect 90° cuts. If you hold the saw exactly perpendicular to the edge, the reflection of the wood's edge will appear continuous with the actual edge. Make a perfect 45° miter cut by placing the blade in such a position that the reflection of the board's edge is perpendicular to the front (the edge that the saw will first enter) of the wood.

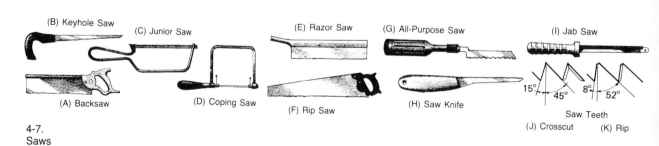

4-7.
Saws

Miter boxes are boxlike devices in which stripwood to be crosscut is placed. The saw fits into slots in the box; these position it to make exact 90° or 45° (miter) cuts. Miter boxes come in various sizes. Small wood ones are used with razor or dovetail saws. Larger boxes are sometimes made of metal, and some can be adjusted to make cuts of all angles. These boxes are used with backsaws.

Saws with thin blades, such as coping saws and hacksaws, break easily. If the blade twists and then breaks, the frame is not holding it with enough tension. If it breaks without twisting first or breaks near an end, it is being held with too much tension. A blade may also break because it is too coarse for the stock being sawed, because it was twisted during sawing, or because it was pushed with too much pressure.

Since saws are very prone to rust, apply a light oil as a preventive measure. If rust does form, emery cloth will remove it. When a crosscut saw, ripsaw, or backsaw becomes dull, leave the sharpening, blade reshaping, and the restoration of the saw's set to a professional.

Planes

After wood has been cut, it must be planed down to its approximate dimensions before being sanded to a smooth finish. The proper adjustment of a plane is necessary for accurate performance. The blade must project evenly just below the bottom of the plane. Shavings are deflected by the cap iron (the plate that rests on top of the blade).

The cap iron should be secured slightly back from the cutting edge of the blade, so that shavings are not caught between it and the blade. The throat of the plane (the slot through which the shavings feed) can be adjusted: wide for deep cuts in soft wood, and narrow for cuts in hard or cross-grained woods. From time to time, clear shavings from the throat of the plane with a wooden stick.

To make a cut of consistent thickness, press down slightly on the front of the plane at the start of a planing stroke. At the end of the stroke (as you approach the end of the wood), press down on the rear of the plane. If the cut is even, the shaving will be of uniform thickness. Always hold the plane perpendicular to the work. Never tilt it from this position when removing a high spot. Planing must be done with the grain, not against it. A long plane will cut a flat surface; a short one will ride curves in the wood. Thus, a shorter plane should be used only on level wood or for curved surfaces.

To avoid splitting the corners of a board when planing its end, you must either plane from both edges to the center or plane from one edge to the other—first clamping a scrap board to the work so the plane will finish its stroke on the scrap. When planing the thin edge of a board, clamp a scrap board along the edge to give the plane sufficient surface on which to rest. If planing produces a rough or torn finish, reverse the direction. Wide boards should be planed by a series of diagonal cuts.

Fasten planing work in a vise or, if planing the top of a plank, use a bench stop to keep the wood in position on the worktable.

Plane irons must be kept sharp. Remove dullness by whetting the edge on an oilstone. When nicks develop or the bevel is no longer the correct shape because of repeated whetting, you will either have to regrind the blade in the shop or send it to a knife grinder.

To whet a plane, clamp an oilstone in a vise and move the blade's cutting edge back and forth at a 30° to 35° angle to the stone. Be careful to move the blade without rocking it. When the cutting edge is sharp, rub the blade on its flat side until the burr caused by the first rubbing is removed. Be careful not to taper the flat side of the blade because, if you do, it will not refit against the cap iron. After whetting, strop the cutting edge on a piece of leather or on a smooth wood block.

Use a circular grinding wheel to grind the plane. Place the blade as shown in figure 4-8F. The bevel must be cut at a 25° to 30° angle to the flat side of the blade; it must be straight and at a perfect 90° angle to the thin edges of the blade. Hold the blade on a tool rest and move it from side to side across the wheel's edge. If the 90° angle is lost, it should be restored by rubbing the blade on a perfectly flat, medium-fine oilstone. Use a try square to test the 90° side angles.

Razor planes use double-edged razor blades and can be used on balsa and other soft materials.

Modelmaker's or *violin planes* (figure 4-8A) have a curved bottom and a conforming curved blade. They are used for planing flat, concave, or convex (down to a 12″ radius) surfaces. These planes are 3″ to 4″ long.

Block planes (figure 4-8B) are for smoothing the end grain of large boards, shaping small boards, making chamfers, and so on. The blade fits into the plane with its bevel side up.

Jack planes (11½″ to 15″ long), *fore planes* (18″ long) (figure 4-8C), and *jointer planes* (22″ to 24″ long) are basically the same tool in different lengths. The longer planes eliminate peaks, and the shorter planes smooth level work. Blades are set with their bevel side down. The cap iron should be placed about 1/16″ behind the blade's cutting edge for cutting with the grain and as near the edge as possible for cutting across the grain or on curly wood.

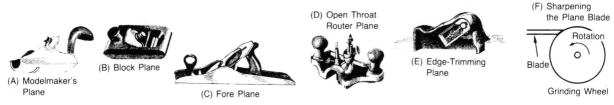

4-8.
Planes

Smoothing planes are small (5½" to 10" long) versions of the jack plane and are used for finishing. The blade is set into the plane with its bevel side up.

Low-angle planes have blades set at a low angle to give a smooth cut across grain. This type of plane is used on work too heavy for a block plane.

Open throat router planes (figure 4-8D) are used to make grooves, dadoes, and so on.

Rabbet planes have a frame only on one side. The blade extending to the side edge of the plane will cut extremely close to a vertical obstruction; thus, the plane may be used to smooth out the insides of boxes, to cut rabbets, and so forth. *Cabinetmaker's rabbet planes* are 4" to 5½" long. *Bull-nosed rabbet planes* can cut into corners because the blades are at the very front of the plane.

Edge-trimming block planes (figure 4-8E) are used to trim and square off the edges of boards of up to 1" thicknesses. They are a great aid in planing edges squarely. When used for beveling, a wood block (cut to the desired bevel) can be attached to the bottom of the plane in order to tilt it to the desired angle.

Chisels

Chisels are used to cut away surface material. Secure work so that it cannot move before you do any cutting with a chisel. Cuts are accomplished by a series of light passes—penetrating too deeply may split the work. Cut with the grain (figure 4-9A) or directly across it, holding the chisel at a slight angle toward the cut. The chisel's bevel should be face down for heavy cutting and face up for lighter shaving. Cut from a penciled guideline into the waste area, so that a slip will not carry you into good wood. Push the chisel with the palm of your right hand, guiding the top of the blade with the left. Make the initial outlining cuts with a parting tool.

To maintain razor-sharp edges, whet blades frequently. Secure an oilstone to the bench and rub the chisel's bevel on the stone's rough side, maintaining a 25° to 30° bevel edge. Then whet the bevel on the fine side of the stone, smoothing the rough bevel to a 30° to 35° angle. Remove any burr that may have formed

by rubbing the flat side of the chisel on the fine side of the oilstone. Finally, whet the edge on a piece of leather. It takes skill to rub the blade at a constant angle across the stone; a poor job will cause a rounded bevel.

When the edge becomes badly nicked or when the bevel has become rounded or distorted, the chisel will have to be reground, either in the shop or at a hardware store. You will need an emery or Carborundum wheel with an adjustable tool rest if you do the grinding yourself. Avoid overheating the blade (which will cause it to lose its temper and hardness) by keeping the wheel wet with a constant application of water or kerosene. If the wheel is not smooth or true, it can be dressed with a Carborundum stick. Move the chisel from side to side across the wheel, which should be turning toward it. After you complete the grinding, whet the chisel. Hollow-ground or V-point edges may be produced by grinding the chisel on the wheel's edge.

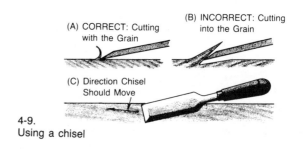

4-9.
Using a chisel

Chisels come in three handle constructions: *tang chisels*, designed for hand pushing or light mallet driving; *socket chisels*, which can be driven by a heavy mallet; and *everlasting chisels*, which are strong enough to be driven by a steel hammer. Chisels also come in various blade shapes. *Paring chisels* have thin blades for hand driving. *Firmer chisels* have long, strong blades that may be mallet driven to perform heavy cutting. *Butt chisels* have short blades, allowing them to be used in places inaccessible to longer blades. Chisel blades range in widths from ⅛" to 2".

Types of cutting points include straight cut, beveled,

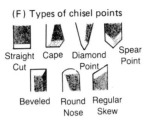

4-10.
Types of chisel points

cape, round nose, diamond point, regular skew, and spear points (figure 4-10).

Gouges

A gouge is a chisel with a concave blade. Gouges are held in the same fashion as chisels, but in contrast to chisels, cutting across the grain with a gouge allows better control. The bevel can be on the inside or outside of the blade.

To whet a gouge, use a wedge-shaped slip stone kept wet with oil. First whet the bevel, then the flat side of the gouge, to remove any burr that may have formed. In whetting a concave surface, move the gouge with a slight rotary motion. To regrind an outside bevel gouge, use a wet grindstone and move the gouge across the wheel's perimeter with a rolling motion. An inside bevel gouge is ground on a cone-shaped grinding wheel. In general, follow the instructions for grinding chisels.

DRILLING TOOLS

Centering Tools

You can use these tools to make a guiding hole in the material so that the drill bit will not jump out of position as you begin drilling.

Dot punches have 60° points and are best for locating small holes. After applying the dot indentation, increase it in size with a 90° punch.

Automatic center punches are good for precise punching. They have a spring that pushes the point into the surface to be marked.

Bell punches or *self-centering punches* precisely locate the center of the end of a bar.

Drill Holders

Bit braces (figure 4-11A) allow a great amount of pressure to be exerted in the making of ⅛″ to ½″ holes. Its ratchet device allows the brace to be worked in confined spaces where it would be impossible to turn the tool a full 360°. The brace holds tapered or round shank bits.

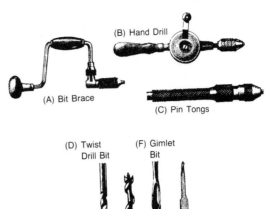

4-11.
Drills and bits

Hand drills (figure 4-11B) or *wheel braces* are for small hole drilling. Twist drill bits of up to ¼″ in diameter can be used in these. The breast drill, a larger version of the hand drill, takes twist drill bits of up to ½″ in diameter. A large amount of thrust can be directed through the drill by leaning on the end plate. *Automatic push drills* have sliding sleeves that, when pushed back and forth, turn the drill.

Pin tongs (figure 4-11C) are chuck-type instruments for holding small round tools and work. *Pin vises* are similar to, but larger than, pin tongs.

Drill Bits

Twist drill bits (figure 4-11D) are for drilling small holes in metal, plastic, and wood, and they may be used in both hand and power drills. Twist drills must be used slowly, however, or they will not be cleared of chips and will, therefore, become hot. They usually come in ¹⁄₃₂″ increments from ¹⁄₁₆″ to ¾″ and in many smaller sizes. Some have square shanks for use in bit braces. Special taper shank bits have tangs (base ends) that fit into drill press spindles. Carbon tool steel drill bits can be used for hand and low-speed power drilling.

Tempered bits can be used to drill soft metals. High-speed steel bits used for high-speed drilling have the longest life expectancy. Never use twist drill bits on hardened steel.

To select the best drill bit for a particular material, check the drill point angles given in table 4-1. These angles correspond to the tightness of the wind of the fluted portion. A looser wind is desirable for wood because sawdust tends to compact and clog the bit. For

Table 4-1. Best Drill Point Angles for Various Materials

Material	Angle
Wood, fiberboard	30°
Plastic	30°–45°
Soft cast iron	45°
Copper	50°
Heat-treated steel	62°

drilling metal, a bit with a tightly wound flute can be used. When drilling hard material or using very small drills, withdraw the bit periodically to clear it.

The factory-made point angle of a twist drill is usually 59°, a compromise angle that works truly well only in brass. Anyone contemplating extensive drilling of other materials may want to have some specially modified bits.

Larger drill bits have number designations stamped on them. Smaller bits must be identified by measuring them in a drill gauge. Extremely small drill bits have to be measured by micrometers. To eliminate constant measuring, keep your drill bits in a numbered stand.

Auger bits (figure 4-11E) are used in bit braces and electric drills for drilling medium- and large-size holes in wood. They come in $\frac{1}{16}''$ increments, from $\frac{1}{4}''$ to $2''$. Their identification numbering system is based on sixteenths of an inch: a No. 1 bit has a $\frac{1}{16}''$ diameter, so a No. 2 bit has a $\frac{1}{8}''$ diameter, etc. Augers have an end screw that makes contact with the wood first, then draws the bit into it. Screws are designated by their pitch: fast (for end hole drilling and for use in resinous wood), medium, and slow (for the smoothest hole). Spurs (nibs) at the front of the bit score the circumference of the hole, cutting a cleaner one than is possible with a twist drill. Single twist or straight core (solid center) auger bits are used for hard or gummy woods, and double twist auger bits for soft woods. Augers were not designed for end-grain drilling.

Gimlet bits (figure 4-11F) are used in bit braces for boring screw holes into wood. They come in $\frac{1}{32}''$ increments, from $\frac{1}{16}''$ to $\frac{3}{8}''$.

Screw bits (figure 4-11G) are used in hand and electric drills for simultaneously cutting the pilot, and clearing and countersinking holes for screws. Other large-hole drill bits that are better used with power drills are described on page 39.

Drilling

Gripping the fluted portion of a drill in a chuck may cause it to snap. Before starting to make a hole, test the drill for straightness. Small work must be clamped down, or the drill will cause it to rotate. Thin sheets, when drilled, will climb, so they too must be clamped down.

When the drill is hand-held without the aid of a drill press stand, make sure that the bit is going into the work at a 90° angle. Test with a try square or sight by eye from two positions: at a point when the drill rests on the material and at a point after it has gone in a short distance. Make a cardboard guide when drilling at a slight-to-moderate angle. When the angle is considerable, bore a similar-size hole into a wood guide block, saw off the bottom of the block at the proper angle, and clamp it to the work. Then make the final hole into the work through the guide. Use a power tool for holes smaller than $\frac{1}{16}''$ because hand drilling tends to bend or break the bits.

If the drill squeaks, it may be clogged, it may have been fed too fast, or it may simply be dull. Overheating results in fast dulling and may even cause the tool to lose its temper. In general, small bits should be turned and fed faster than large ones.

To start a hole in wood, draw intersecting lines and punch the center of the intersection. In metal, repeat the process and then, using an inking compass and layout ink, draw a circle the size of the drill bit's diameter. Use the punched depression as the center of the circle. If the drill starts to drift off center, retract it and punch a center hole opposite to the drift. This should reposition the drill and compensate for the inaccuracy. If holes are to be drilled in a great number of similar pieces, make a template with the hole cut into it. Clamp the template over the work and use the hole as a guide.

Drill a pilot hole first when drilling through rough metal, when working with wood whose grain pulls the drill off center, or when using large twist drill bits.

For large holes in wood, drill from both sides to prevent splitting the wood around the exit hole. This can easily be done by having the first hole slightly puncture the exit side of the wood. This hole should be used to start the drill from the other side.

For extremely deep holes, drill from both sides of the work or buy an extension drill. Both techniques enable you to drill holes that are about twice the length of any given drill bit.

Holes may be drilled into the sides of dowels by inserting the dowel into a wooden block that has been pierced by a hole that will position the drill on its pass through the dowel.

When drilling plaster, frequently withdraw the drill to clear it of chips. Wet plaster should be removed from the drill with a piece of wood.

Lubricate your drill bit when drilling metal. Use kerosene for steel and white paraffin for aluminum or brass

CARVING TOOLS

Carving tools or lino cutting tools are similar to chisels and gouges but are used for fine carving instead of for cutting. Their blades taper toward the tang (the tapered end fitting into the handle) instead of being parallel to it. Cutting edges may be square or oblique to the long axis of the tool. Blades may be straight or bent.

Carving tools are identified by the cross-sections of their blades. *Parting tools* have V-shaped blades with obtuse, medium, or acute angles. *Veiners* have U-shaped blades that are deep and narrow, while *fluters* have large blades. Blades that are curved are called *quicks* if the curve is almost U-shaped, *mediums* if their curve is the shape of a quarter moon, and *flats* if the curve is almost flat. *Firmer* or *corner chisels* have perfectly flat blades.

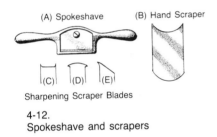

(A) Spokeshave   (B) Hand Scraper

(C)   (D)   (E)

Sharpening Scraper Blades

4-12.
Spokeshave and scrapers

Spokeshaves (figure 4-12A), used to make chamfers and curved edges, should be held with both hands and pulled forward.

Scrapers are employed to remove small amounts of material—wood, plaster, acrylic, or polystyrene. They are used after planing and before sanding. Some scrapers have beveled cutting edges and are used for smoothing wood surfaces. Scrapers should be gripped with both hands. They may be pulled or pushed, but should always be inclined at a 75° angle toward the direction of travel. Unlike the blade edges of the plane, the chisel, or the gouge, the scraper's blade edge does not do the cutting. Instead, cutting is done by hook edges that are adjacent to the blade. When the blade loses its hook or becomes damaged, it must be sharpened.

Hand scrapers (figure 4-12B, C, D, and E) have flat, concave, or convex overall shapes. Their cutting edges may be square or beveled.

Cabinet scrapers resemble spokeshaves. Their beveled blades produce smooth cross-grain cuts, but they do not cut soft wood well. If the blade produces dust instead of shavings, it is dull and must be burnished.

To sharpen a square edge scraper or a cabinet scraper:

1. Clamp the blade in a vise and square file the cutting edge with a smooth mill file.
2. Whet the edge on an oilstone.
3. Lay the scraper flat on its side on the stone and remove any burrs that may have formed.
4. Lay the scraper flat on the workbench and draw the edge with a few strokes from a burnisher.
5. Clamp the scraper in a vise and turn the edge with a few strokes of the burnisher. Hold the burnisher at a 90° angle to the side of the blade for the first stroke and slowly decrease the angle until it is 85° at the last stroke. Oil the scraper during burnishing.

A bevel edge scraper is sharpened in the same general way, except that Step 4 is omitted and, in Step 5, the burnisher is held for its first run at an angle slightly greater than the angle of the bevel. This angle is increased to 75° by the last burnishing.

SANDING TOOLS

Sanding should be done *after* planing and scraping because the abrasive particles left behind after sanding will dull blades. For maximum material removal, sand at a 90° angle to the grain. For smooth finishing, sand with the grain. Clear the abrasive of sanding dust by slapping it against a hard surface. Otherwise the dust will prevent the abrasive from working effectively.

The surface of wood should be rubbed with a damp cloth before the final sanding. This will raise the grain, which, after it has dried, can be sanded smooth.

Use a constant application of soap and water as a lubricant for wet sandpaper, and keep the surface being sanded free of residue by sponging it clean.

Files

The thousands of files available are identified by their tooth cut type (figure 4-13A), by cross-section (figure 4-13B), and by coarseness. *Single cut files* or *mill files* are used for a final finish and for lathe work. *Double cut files* are used to remove large amounts of material. *Rasp cut files* are used on wood and other soft materials. *Curved tooth files* are used on sheet metal.

The different degrees of coarseness are: dead smooth, smooth, second cut, bastard, coarse, and rough. Small files are numbered 8 (finest) to 00 (coarsest). Some files have edges without teeth; these are called *safe edges*.

Small jeweler's files or *Swiss pattern files* have single

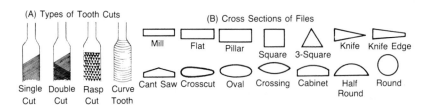

4-13.
Files

Table 4-2. Files for Various Materials

Material	File
Plaster	Rasp cut
Wood	Rasp cut
Aluminum	Special purpose aluminum rasp for heavy removal; special purpose aluminum file for smooth finish.
Copper, brass	Special purpose brass file
Soft steel	Double cut file for heavy removal; single cut mill file for smooth finish
Die castings	Special purpose die-cast file

and double cut teeth, come in most cross-sections, and may be used on metal and acrylic plastic.

A good selection of files to start with would include a 6″ or 8″ wood rasp; and some 6″ metal files with flat, round, and triangular cross sections and fine and coarse cuts. The best files for particular materials are listed in table 4-2.

To file, clamp the work in a vise. Keep your eye level with the surface of the work that is to be cut. Place the file in your right palm, and hold its tip in your other hand. The file must be held level throughout the stroke. If it is not kept in firm contact with the work on the cutting stroke, it will wear out quickly. Filing is done on the forward stroke only. Lift the file on the back stroke to prevent excessive wear. When filing soft metal, rub the work on the back stroke to clear the teeth of the file. Fine filing should be done perpendicular to the grain; rough filing at a 30° angle to the grain.

To apply a smooth finish to metal, use a smooth file, but do not use one with a short-angle cut. Hold the file at a 90° angle and draw it back and forth along the long axis of the surface being filed.

Files should be cleaned with a stiff wire brush (file card). Very clogged teeth may be cleaned with the point of a scriber. Covering the file with chalk or turpentine before use helps to prevent clogging and removes oil.

Storing files on a rack will protect their teeth from damage. Never store them in such a way that their teeth are in contact with other files or with metal.

Abrasives

When possible, abrasive paper should be mounted on a block backing that will hold it in the shape that is to be imparted to the work. Block shapes used for sanding can be flat, slightly concave, convex (in varying degrees), or dowel-shaped.

For heavier work, the abrasive paper should be mounted on or held by hand around a hard wood block. Ready-made block sanders are also available. When sanding flat surfaces, avoid blocks that are made from flexible materials because they will deflect under pressure. If you are sanding a large flat surface, place the paper on top of the workbench to create a flat contour. For sanding slightly curved surfaces, sandpaper can be mounted on a rubber block.

There are two systems for grading the size (and thus the coarseness) of abrasives. The system used for flint and emery paper runs from 8/0 (the finest) up through 3½ (the coarsest). There are, however, some slight variations in the actual coarseness of same-number papers put out by different manufacturers. The system used for aluminum oxide and silicon carbide papers runs from 600 (the finest) to 12 (the coarsest). This system is based on the number of openings per inch in the smallest screen through which the grit used on the paper can pass. Garnet paper is graded by both systems. Abrasives for various materials are listed in table 4-3. Experimentation will determine which grit size will produce the best finishes on various materials.

Table 4-3. Abrasives for Various Materials

Material	Abrasive
Hardwoods, aluminum, copper, steel, plastics	Aluminum oxide
Hardwoods, softwoods, composition boards, plastics, paper	Garnet
Glass, acrylic, finely finished paint	Silicon carbide
Plaster, paint removal	Flint
Acrylic, soldered joints	Emery

The following materials are the ones most commonly used as abrasive papers.

Flint (buff-colored), while not effective for sanding wood or metal, may be used to sand plaster and paint, whose tendency to clog the abrasive disallows their being abraded with more expensive substances.

Garnet (orange or red) comes in a wide variety of grit sizes and grit spacings, and in wet or dry types. It performs well on wood, and its longer life offsets its higher cost.

Aluminum oxide (reddish brown) is used mostly on metal, but it also performs well on wood.

Silicon carbide (bluish black) has a very hard grit and is good for fine-sanding paint finishes and acrylic plastic.

Emery is made with a natural abrasive. It has been superseded by some of the more effective synthetic abrasives.

Crocus uses iron oxide as the abrasive and is good for fine sanding and metal polishing. *Steel wool* can be used to polish metal and to finish the edges of acrylic sheets and blocks. *Cutters*, used for fast material removal, are block-shaped sanding tools whose faces are covered with steel teeth that are somewhat similar to those found on a food grater.

CLAY-WORKING TOOLS

For cutting heavy blocks of clay, use a carving knife or any of the knives made for troweling. For lighter cutting and smoothing, use a stiff high carbon steel putty knife.

Wire-end modeling tools are about 8″ long and come with square, pointed, round, asymmetric, and oval ends. Square ones can be used to square off small surfaces; and pointed ones, to clean up intersections. Thin line tools are smaller versions (5″ long) of the wire-end tools.

Boxwood or *Duron modeling tools*, used to impart textures and to cut clay, come with serrated, plain, curved, and flat edges.

Polyethylene film and *wax paper* are good wrappings in which to store clay and scraps.

5:Power Tools and Their Use

A good supply of power tools, while not indispensable to the making of precise models, produces great savings in muscle and time. Before purchasing a power tool, follow these steps:

1. Make a list of the types of operations to be performed. Take into account any conceivable future jobs.

2. List the tools that can perform these operations either with or without special attachments. Abilities of various tools are outlined in table 5-1.

3. Obtain and carefully consider information about all the tools you are thinking of purchasing. Since power tool functions often overlap, a comparison of the two

Table 5-1. Abilities of Various Tools

Tool	Operation	Shaping and cutting, light	Shaping and cutting, heavy	Saber sawing	Circular sawing, light	Circular sawing, heavy	Band sawing	Jig sawing	Drilling, light	Drilling, heavy	Orbital or reciprocating sanding	Belt sanding	Disc sanding, light	Disc sanding, heavy	Drum sanding	Grinding, light	Grinding, heavy	Buffing and polishing	Lathe turning, light	Lathe turning, heavy	Planing	Routing	Engraving	Paint mixing
Small hand motor tool (portable)		C		C				C					C	A	C	C			C			C	C	C
Circular saw (portable)					C																			
Saber saw (portable)								B																
Scroll saw (portable)				A				A																
Circular saw (bench-mounted)				B	A			B																
Radial arm saw (bench-mounted)		A	A	A	A				A				A	A					A	A		A		
Band saw (bench-mounted)							A																	
Jigsaw (bench-mounted)		A	A	A				A			A													
Electric drill (portable)		C	B	B					C	B			C	A		C	C	C	B				C	C
Drilll press (bench-mounted)		A	A						A				A	A		A	A	A	A	A		A		
Orbital sander (portable)											A													
Belt sander (portable)												A				A								
Belt sander (bench-mounted)												A				A	A							
Disc sander (bench-mounted)														A		A								
Grinder (bench-mounted)																	A							
Lathe (bench-mounted)									A							A	A	A	A	A				
Jointer planer (bench-mounted)																					A	A		
Router (portable)																A					A	A		
Router shaper (bench-mounted)																A					A	A		

Key:
A: tool adequate with proper cutter; however, some models may not be adequate for all operations
B: tool adequate with adapter.
C: tool adequate hand held with proper cutter, or as bench-mounted if stand is obtained.

ists may reveal that many operations can be accomplished with a basic tool and its attachments.

Tool power or capacity must also be considered. Roughly, there are two basic tool sizes with which the modelmaker must be concerned. To make baseboards, carrying boxes, hardwood and Plexiglas block models, as well as highly machined Plexiglas models, bench-mounted or portable power tools usually found in the average home craftperson's workshop are required. To cut thin sheet material and stripwood used in hollow models and to fabricate furniture and other small assemblies, small hand-held power tools and tools with small stands that can be set up on a worktable are required. These are designed for the amateur model-maker and may be obtained from hobby shops.

ACCESSORIES

Motors

Since some bench-mounted power tools are sold without motors, it is a good idea to be familiar with various facts about electric motors.

Motor sizes required by various tools are as follows: grinder and jigsaw, ¼ h.p.; small jointer, drill press, and lathe, ⅓ h.p.; and band saw, table saw, belt sander, disc sander, and shaper, ½ h.p. There are two types of motors: the split-phase motor used in tools that do not draw a great starting load (sanders, grinders, drill presses); and the capacitor-type motor used where a heavy starting load is encountered (saws, shapers, jointers). Tool speeds are determined by the motor speed and by the pulleys used both on the motor and on the machine. The formula for computing tool speed is: diameter of motor pulley times motor speed divided by diameter of machine pulley equals the machine speed.

A motor speed control is useful because tools require different machine speeds for different materials. Wood is drilled and cut at higher speeds than those that should be used on metal or plastic. Large holes are drilled better at slower speeds. Speeds for band sawing, jig-sawing, drilling, and lathing are shown in tables 5-4, 5-5, 5-6, and 5-8. Paint mixing must be done at slow speeds to reduce splashing. Soldering temperatures differ according to metal used. Incandescent light intensity for photography should be controlled.

Since most inexpensive power tools have only one speed, some sort of speed-controlling device is probably needed. Figure 5-1 shows a minimal control that can be fabricated quickly. By changing the wattage of the

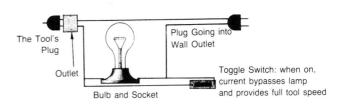

5-1.
A motor tool speed control device

bulb, the tool's speed can be altered. More sophisticated devices will vary tool speed from 0 rpm to the maximum factory-rated speed. Electronic variable speed controls also automatically feed more voltage when a motor starts to slow down under the load. These controls work only with the small motors of portable power tools and with resistance soldering irons.

The capacity of speed controls is rated by amperes. A 7.5-ampere model is sufficient for use with portable tools. If three 500-watt photo bulbs are used, a 15-ampere capacity control is necessary. If overheating occurs at low speeds, disengage the tool and turn the speed up to maximum. The tool's fan will increase to its maximum speed and quickly cool the tool.

Miter Gauge and Rip Fence

Two of the most useful (even indispensable) accessories are the miter gauge and rip fence. The best *miter gauge* is shaped like an adjustable protractor mounted on a long arm running in a track on the table with the power tool. Material held against the protractor may be squarely pushed into the blade for an exact cutting angle. The stock must be held firmly against the gauge to prevent pivoting created by the thrust of the blade. Facing the gauge with sandpaper will increase traction. Miter gauges are found on good circular, cut-off, band, and radial arm saws, and on bench-mounted disc and belt sanders.

The *rip fence* or *rip guide* is an adjustable tool table stop placed parallel to the cutting direction of the blade. It is adjustable to any distance from the blade so that material pressed against the fence will be cut to the desired width. This allows multiple cutting of exact measurements. Rip fences can be found on good circular, band, portable saber, cutoff, and radial arm saws, router shapers, and jointer planers.

Other useful accessories include a *tilting table* for bevel cuts and *tool bench casters* for mobility when working on unusually large material.

POWER TOOL CARE

Tools (screwdrivers, wrenches, and so on) will be needed to disassemble and maintain power tools. All bench-mounted tools should be checked periodically to adjust the relationship between the blade, table level, rip fence, and miter gauge. Miter gauges and table-tilting apparatuses must be tight and must not vibrate out of position during operation. The greasing schedule suggested by tool manufacturers should be posted in the shop and followed.

Do not overload tools by feeding the work too rapidly. If a tool stalls, back it away from the work until its motor resumes running at full speed. On the other hand, if not enough pressure is applied to the tool, it will skim across the work, eventually dulling the blade.

POWER SAWS

Portable Circular Saw

This saw (figure 5-2A) is used to make straight cuts in heavy wood and other materials that cannot be worked on a table circular saw. It can also make rabbet and dado cuts. Its use to the modelmaker is generally limited to construction of baseboards and carrying boxes.

Saws are rated by the diameter of their circular blade, usually running between 4″ and 8″ for shop saws. A 6¼″ blade is sufficient for making a 45° cut through 2″ material. Various blade types are listed in table 5-2.

The depth of cut of the saw can be adjusted by raising or lowering the shoe of the tool. Buy a tool equipped with a shoe that may be tilted (for bevel cutting), a miter gauge, and a rip guide. Some saws have a safety

Table 5-2. Circular Saw Blades for Various Materials

Material	Blade Type
Wood, cross cutting	Crosscut
Wood, cutting with grain	Rip
Plywood	Plywood
Soft composition board	Fine-tooth
Plastic, up to 1/16″	Fine-tooth (8 to 14 teeth per inch); blade 1/16″ to 3/32″ thick
Plastic, 1/4″	3 to 3½ teeth per inch; blade 1/8″ to 5/32″ thick
Metal	Cutoff wheel (an abrasive disc)
Miscellaneous	Combination

clutch that stops the blade from turning when it kicks back from the work. Another good safety feature to look for is a telescoping blade guard.

The smoothest cuts are made by hollow-ground blades, but these may burn your stock if not projected at least ¾″ beyond the other side of the cut. When cutting, always keep the good side of the material facing down. Piercing cuts can be made by resting the front of the saw's shoe on the work and lowering the spinning blade until it cuts through.

To make a perfectly straight, long cut in places where the rip guide cannot be used, clamp a stick to the work and use it as a guide for the saw. Due to the shape of the cut made by the circular blade, interior corners must be finished with a hand saw. Rabbet cuts may be made by means of two passes of the circular saw. To cut into a narrow edge, clamp a piece of scrap wood along it to give a wider surface on which to rest the saw's shoe. Dado cuts may be made by running the saw several times across the cut until the required material has been removed or by buying a dado cut attachment for the blade.

CIRCULAR SAW ACCESSORIES. A *saw guide* is a steel straightedge with an adjustable T-square head mounted on one end. By placing this guide on the work and running a cutoff or portable saber saw along it, you

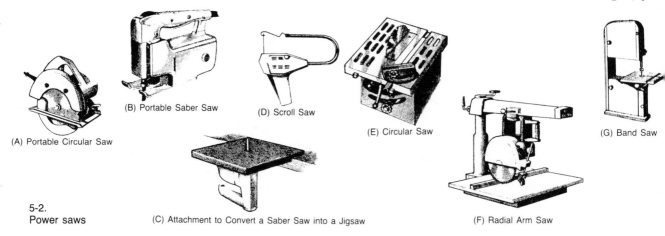

(A) Portable Circular Saw

(B) Portable Saber Saw

(C) Attachment to Convert a Saber Saw into a Jigsaw

(D) Scroll Saw

(E) Circular Saw

(F) Radial Arm Saw

(G) Band Saw

5-2.
Power saws

can make straight cuts at any angle to the edge.

Tables that convert a circular saw to a table saw are also available.

Portable Saber Saw

Saber saws (figure 5-2B) are used to make straight and curved cuts in fairly heavy material. One with a rip fence can be substituted for a cutoff saw to make baseboards and model cases. If possible, purchase a saw that has a tilting base (for bevel cutting), a rip guide, and the ability to cut wood at least up to 2″ thick.

Saber saw blades (table 5-3) have ends that are pointed to allow the piercing of sheet stock without having to drill an insertion hole. Because saber saw blades may cause splintering along the cut, cover the cut line with transparent tape before cutting, keeping the good side of the material facing down.

SABER SAW ACCESSORIES. A *jigsaw conversion*, as its name implies, converts a saber saw into a table jigsaw (figure 5-2C). A table that converts a portable saw into a bench-mounted saber saw is called a *saber saw conversion*.

Table 5-3. Saber Saw Blades for Various Materials

Material	Teeth per Inch
Softwood, up to 2″	7
Softwood over 2″	7 (extra long teeth)
Hardwood and composition board	10
Plywood	10 (taper-ground)
Nonferrous metals	14

Portable Scroll Saws

These saws (figure 5-2D) are used for cutting intricate curves in thin (up to ¾″) material. Because they are portable, they may be taken right to the model to cut out windows or area ways, for example. It is fairly difficult to make long straight cuts with this tool. The scroll's function is similar to that of the jigsaw.

Bench-Mounted Circular Saw

These saws make straight cuts in heavy wood and other materials (figure 5-2E). Useful in fabricating baseboards and model cases, they can also cut out pieces for wood and plastic solid block models. Some saws have tilting tables or blades that can make bevel and chamfer cuts. All may be used to make dado cuts. Saws are rated by blade diameter, usually running between 7″ and 12″. The table size also is an indication of the tool's capacity. Some machines have extender arms that increase the holding capacity of the table. Purchase a saw with a miter gauge, a rip fence, and, if possible, a hood guard (to go over the blade). A circular saw may be converted into a disc sander by mounting a sander disc in place of the saw.

Circular saws usually come from the factory equipped with a combination blade, but for the various blades that may be used on this saw, see table 5-2.

Keep the good side of the material facing up when cutting. Make sure that the stock has good support and do not let it bind the blade. Use a pushing stick to feed the work through the saw whenever you are making a narrow cut. When crosscutting, do not stand in line with the cut.

CIRCULAR SAW ACCESSORIES. These saws have two major accessories: dado blades and molding heads.

Dado blades are a sandwichlike grouping of three blades. The inside and outside are cutting blades, with the center blade acting as a chipper to remove the material between the two cutters. Rabbet cuts may be made with dado blades. Two passes of the saw are required—one with the stock on its edge.

Molding heads are held in the arbor of the saw in place of the saw blade. They are used to cut grooves and other shapes for moldings.

Radial Arm Saws

These are combination tools (figure 5-2F) that will saber and circular saw, cut miters, rout coves, shape, disc and drum sand, grind, buff, drill, and make tenon, dado, and rabbet cuts. The tool's motor and cutter, movable in all directions, are mounted on an overhead arm. The saw is useful in making baseboards, carrying boxes, and large block models. Some models have lathe attachments and variable speed controls.

Bench-Mounted Band Saws

Used to make curved and straight cuts in heavy material, some bench-mounted band saws (figure 5-2G) will even cut 8″ thick stock. Band saws are very useful in cutting the large blocks of wood and acrylic that are used in solid block models. The saw's throat depth determines the depth of maximum cuts. The best purchase would be a saw that has a tilting table (for bevel cutting), a rip fence, and a miter gauge. Since the blade is in the form of a continuous loop, piercing is impossible. Forcing the work will cause the blade to bow, producing a cut that is not perpendicular to the table.

To cut a tightly curved object with a wider blade, make a series of radial or tangential cuts. To make sharp interior corners, cut holes at the corners by drilling, then saw up to these holes and use them to maneuver the saw around to cut the next side.

BAND SAW ACCESSORIES. Blade width determines the tightness of the minimum radius cut. A ⅛″ blade will cut a ¼″ radius; a ½″ blade, a 1¼″ radius, and so forth. Band saws usually run at speeds of 2,000 to 4,000 feet per minute. This speed must be slowed down to 250 or 350 feet per minute for ferrous metal. Other speeds for different materials are given in table 5-4. In general, faster speeds produce smoother cuts, slower speeds are for heavier work, coarser blades should be used on thick materials, and finer-tooth blades are for thinner material. Blades with the smallest amount of set give the smoothest cuts, but are harder to maneuver through curved cuts.

Raker set blades, in ⅟₁₆″ to 1″ widths with 6 to 24 teeth per inch, can be used to cut thick ferrous material. Also available are *wavy set blades* of from ⅟₁₆″ to 1″ widths, with 8 to 32 teeth per inch; *hook tooth blades* of from ¼″ to 1″ widths, with 2 to 6 teeth per inch; and *skip tooth blades* of from ³⁄₁₆″ to 1″ widths, with 2 to 6 teeth per inch.

Table 5-4. Band Saw Blades for Various Materials

Material	Teeth per Inch	Tooth Style	Speed (Ft. per Min.)
Softwood	3–6	Hook or skip	4,000–5,000
Plywood	4–6	Hook or skip	3,500–4,500
Hardwood	3–6	Hook or skip	3,000–4,000
Fiberboard	6–8	Raker or wavy	500–1,000
Masonite	3–6	Hook or skip	1,000–2,000
Acrylic	3–6	Hook or skip	3,000–4,500
Polystyrene	4–6	Hook or skip	3,000–4,000
Copper tubing	14–18	Wavy	250–500
Steel tubing	18–32	Wavy	125–200
Paper, cardboard	3–4	Hook or skip	2,500–5,000

Bench-Mounted Jigsaw

These saws make intricate cuts in sheet material (wood, cardboard, metal, and plastic), and cut lengths from thin strip material. The cut depth capacity of the jigsaw is limited by the distance between the blade and arm support. Some machines, however, have swiveling blades that can be set sideways to give an unlimited depth. Try to buy a saw with a tilting table. Some jigsaws will accept files and sanding drums placed in their lower jaws and perform as saber saws. Many saws are equipped with a removable arm. By detaching it and fixing a saber saw blade in the lower chuck, you can increase the machine's capacity to cut bulky material.

The blade of the saw should be kept at a tangent to the line of curved cuts without forcing the cut or twisting the blade. Internal cuts can be made by drilling a hole in the material, passing the unseated saw blade into the hole, and reattaching it into the saw's chucks. This procedure is called piercing.

When cutting metal, use beeswax as a lubricant. Sandwich very thin sheets of material between two sheets of scrap wood to prevent fluttering by the blade. Keep in mind that too much blade tension will cause the blade to snap.

JIGSAW ACCESSORIES. Blades come in many thicknesses (0.01″ to 0.03″), many widths (0.025″ to 0.25″), and with many teeth per inch counts. In general, the thicker the material being sawed, the heavier the blade and the slower the saw's speed; the narrower the blade, the tighter the curve it is possible to cut; and the greater number of teeth per inch there are, the smoother the cut. Use a wide blade when making straight cuts. See table 5-5 for more information on jigsaw blades.

POWER DRILLS

Portable Hand Motor

This tool and the jigsaw are the two most useful power tools needed for the construction of simple models. You can use the motor tool for drilling, circular sawing, sanding, buffing, polishing, paint mixing, grinding, engraving, turning, shaping, and routing if you have the accessories shown in figure 5-3. Some of these operations can be facilitated by the use of an accessory table to position the work accurately. But, in general, the operations require only the insertion of a different cutting tool into the motor's chuck.

HAND MOTOR TOOL ACCESSORIES. Buy the following cutting and sanding accessories only as needed—large sets often include tools that are rarely, if ever, used.

Cutters, sometimes called *rotary files* or *rasps* (figure 5-3A, B, and C), are used for cutting grooves, shaping, inlaying, and concave routing. Small ones can be used for engraving (figure 5-3D) and scribing, although they are not strong enough to be used on hard metal. Large ones may be used on wood, plastic, and metal. Tungsten carbide cutters may be used on hard steel as well as on softer materials.

Emery cutting wheels, made of thin stone, are for cutting and grooving metal and wood. Diameters range up to 1½″.

Saws (figure 5-3E) cut thin plastic, soft metal, wood, or cardboard and are also used for grooving and dovetailing.

Routing cutters (figure 5-3F) are used for routing, inlaying, and mortising metals.

Emery wheels (figure 5-3G) are used for shaping and sanding. In grinding soft materials, a little candle wax

Table 5-5. Jigsaw Blades for Various Materials

Material	Quality of Cut	Teeth per Inch	Blade Type	Speed (rpm)
Wood, up to 1/16″	Very smooth	20	Thin, fairly narrow	1,600
Wood, up to 1/8″	Very smooth	18	Thin, fairly narrow	1,600
Wood, 1/8″ to 1/2″	Very smooth	14	Thin, fairly narrow	1,500
Wood, 1/8″ and up	Medium	15	Medium-thick, medium-wide	1,200
Wood, 1/4″ to 2″ (for most saws)	Rough	7	Thick, wide	750
Fiberboard, 1/8″ and up	Medium	15	Medium-thick, medium-wide	1,200
Plastic, up to 1/16″	Very smooth	20	Thin, fairly narrow	1,600
Plastic, 1/16″ to 1/8″	Very smooth	18	Thin, fairly narrow	1,600
Plastic, 1/8″ to 1/2″	Very smooth	14	Thin, fairly narrow	1,500
Nonferrous metal and mild steel, up to 1/16″	Smooth	30	Thin, medium-wide	1,200
Nonferrous metal and mild steel, 1/16″ to 1/8″	Medium	20	Medium-thick, medium-wide	950
Nonferrous metal, 1/8″ to 1/2″; mild steel, 1/8″ to 1/4″	Medium	15	Medium-thick, medium-wide	1,200

(A) Rotary Files and Burrs:
shown at 1/4 size

(B) Rasps:
shown at about 1/3 size

(C) Regular Cutters

(D) Small Engraving Cutters

(E) Saw (comes in two thicknesses)

(F) Routing
Cutters

(G) Emery Wheels

(H) Silicon Grinding Points

(I) Steel
Brush

(J) Bristle Brushes

(K) Felt Polishing Tips

5-3.
Hand motor tool accessories

on the wheel can prevent its pores from being filled. Wheels may be cleaned and reshaped on a dressing stone.

Silicon grinding points (figure 5-3H) shape and grind steel and other hard materials.

Cloth-backed abrasive discs remove flash from castings and are used for cutting. The nonrigid disc depends on centrifugal force to stiffen it for cutting.

Abrasive drums are drum-shaped mandrels over which abrasive-coated cloth skirts are slipped. These drums are used for sanding wood, metal, and plastic.

Wire brushes (figure 5-3I) remove rust and excess solder, and produce a wire-brushed finish on metal. *Bristle brushes* (figure 5-3J) clean and polish metal.

Felt polishing tips and *wheels* (figure 5-3K) screwed into mandrels are used for polishing metal and plastic. They are used with polishing compound.

Other motor tool accessories can also be used to modify motor performance.

Collets allow for the use of a wide variety of tool shaft diameters in a motor. *Mandrels* are shafts that hold the emery-impregnated polishing wheels, sanding discs, felt polishing wheels, and saws in the motor's chuck. *Flexible shafts* allow for working in tight places.

Rheostats can be ued to lessen a tool's speed when working on plastic or drum-sanding wood (the tool's high speed might otherwise melt or burn these materials).

Universal stands (figure 5-4A) hold the motor, freeing both hands for work. The stand may be adjusted up or down. *Shaping tables* (figure 5-4B) may be raised or lowered to regulate the depth of the cut. *Drill press stands* (figure 5-4C and D) will hold the motor tool in a vertical position. The material being drilled can be clamped to the table below it, and the table can be raised or lowered.

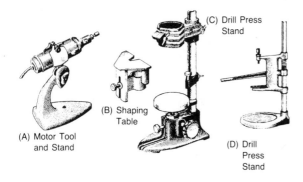

(C) Drill Press Stand

(B) Shaping Table

(A) Motor Tool and Stand

(D) Drill Press Stand

5-4.
Motor tool stands and tables

Portable Electric Drill

This is a larger version of the small hand motor tool. Its motor's power is rated by the largest drill it can efficiently drive into a steel plate. Motors come with ¼″, ⅜″, and ½″ ratings. The ¼″ size, whose maximum speed is between 1,500 and 2,500 rpm, is of most use to the modelmaker. More expensive models have variable speeds.

There are three common types of electric drill chucks: hand chucks (tightened by hand) will easily loosen up under the bending loads imposed by certain accessories; chucks tightened by hex-keys are stronger; geared chucks, however, are the most highly recommended.

PORTABLE ELECTRIC DRILL ACCESSORIES. Cutting and sanding attachments include the following:

Rotary files and *burrs* are used for cutting grooves, shaping, and routing. *Rotary rasps* shape and rout. *Rubber discs* hold sheets of sandpaper and polishing bonnets. *Sandpaper discs* are mounted on rubber discs. *Carborundum wheels* are used for shaping and sanding.

Air-inflated pads are used to hold polishing bonnets. Their flexible surface will not burn or leave rings or whirl marks on a fine finish. *Polishing bonnets* are attached over air-inflated or rubber pads and are used for buffing. *Grindstones* include a buffing wheel and arbor. *Ball-jointed disc sanders* sand flat surfaces without the necessity of holding the drive shaft of the drill perpendicular to the surfaces.

Compass cutters cut large circles if one end of the beam is pinned to the center of the desired circle and the drill is fitted on the other end. *Roto-forms* are used for heavy shaping. *Router-drills* or *hole saws*, if moved laterally, rout away material after a hole is cut.

You may also need the following accessories:

Speed reducers mechanically lower a tool's speed and increase its torque. This often becomes a necessity in drilling hard materials. Drill speeds for wood and metal are shown in table 5-6. *Flexible shafts* allow greater maneuverability, enabling cutters to reach otherwise inaccessible places. *Drill guides* steady a drill for perpendicular cutting. *Horizontal bench stands* convert a drill into a grinder or sander. *Drill press stands* change a drill into a drill press. *Cut-off saw attachments* are excellent for converting a ¼″ portable electric drill into a cut-off saw. The attachment includes a tilting shoe and rip guides, and is adjustable for depth of cut. *Electric hand planes* convert a drill into a plane.

Bench-Mounted Drill Press

This tool combines highly accurate drilling, routing, carving, shaping, grinding, polishing, buffing, mortising,

Table 5-6. Drill Speeds for Wood and Metal

Operation	Speed (rpm)
WOOD	
Drilling up to ¼″ diameter holes	3,800
Drilling ¼″ to ½″ holes	3,100
Drilling ½″ to ¾″ holes	2,300
Drilling ¾″ to 1″ holes	2,000
Drilling greater than 1″ holes with twist drills and large hole drills	Slowest speed
Routing	Highest speed
Carving	4,000–5,000
Mortising hardwood	2,200
Mortising softwood	3,300
METAL	
Grinding	3,000
Fine wire brushing (slower speed for coarse brushing)	3,300
Buffing soft metal with a cloth wheel (slower speed for hard metal)	3,800
Drilling large holes with hole or circle cutter	Slowest speed

rabbeting, tenon cutting, milling, paint mixing, rotary planing, and disc sanding. Its capacity is rated by its throat depth (the distance from chuck center to support column).

Many bench-mounted drill presses are equipped with tables that can be raised and lowered. Tilting tables allow angle drilling. Another important feature is adjustable speed. This allows proper drilling and routing of all types of material. Many presses have a speed range of from 400 to 5,400 rpm (table 5-6).

When the drilling speed cannot be adjusted, use a high-speed steel twist drill bit that will resist excessive speeds. Bits with threaded tips should not be used unless the press is slowed down enough to match rotation and to feed speeds to the screw's thread. With large tools, the work must be clamped to the drill press table. Use a special chuck to hold those cutting tools that develop side thrust.

DRILL PRESS ACCESSORIES. Cutters that can be used with the bench-mounted drill press include the following: *Mortising cutters* have a drill inside a square chisel. The drill removes most of the wood and the chisel squares off the edges of the cut. Long mortises are made by a series of cuts. Mortising cutters may also be used to cut open side mortises. *Rotary planer discs* can form tenons and rabbets.

Electric drill and drill press large-hole bits and cutters include the following:

Extension or *expansive bits* (figure 5-5A) are adjustable in size—one bit can cut holes of from ½″ to 3″ in diameter. *PTI bits* (figure 5-5B) come in diameters of ⅝″ to 2″ and are for drilling holes in wood. This type of bit requires no pilot hole. *Forstner bits* (figure 5-5C)

come in 1″ to 2″ sizes and are also used for drilling holes in wood. They produce very smooth holes and are especially good for boring end or thin wood. They may be used to drill overlapping holes and to rout out wood and plaster objects. *Hole* or *fly cutters* (figure 5-5D) are used to drill holes in wood and metal. They are adjustable so that the smallest model cuts holes from ⅝″ to 2½″ in diameter and the largest cuts holes from 1¼″ to 8″ in diameter. *Rotary hacksaws* (figure 5-5E) are for drilling holes up to 3″ in diameter in thin wood and metal. Smaller rotary hacksaws may be used in a breast drill. Some can be adjusted to cut a variety of hole sizes. *Circle cutters* (figure 5-5F), used for drilling holes in wood or steel, are adjustable. Small circles may be cut out with a breast drill. *Spade bits* (figure 5-5G) are for drilling holes up to 1¼″ in diameter. *Bit gauges* limit the amount of penetration of a drill or bit.

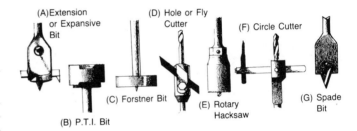

5-5.
Large-hole drill bits and cutters

SANDERS

These are useful for finishing baseboards, model cases, and solid block models. Bench-mounted disc sanders may also be used to perform various shaping and finishing operations on hollow built-up models.

Portable Sanders

Orbital sanders (figure 5-6A) are for the removal of a moderate amount of material and for sanding to a finish. The sander has a sandpaper pad that moves with a slight orbital motion (the size of the sander is usually measured by the area of its sanding pad). The orbital sander is constructed to go right up to obstructions. It is important to apply the correct amount of pressure to this tool—too little will result in no sanding action. Some models have a built-in vacuum action and dust-collecting bag.

Reciprocating sanders are similar to orbital sanders except that the pad moves back and forth and produces a smoother finish. Some move in both an orbiting and reciprocating motion.

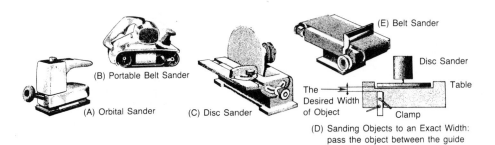

(A) Orbital Sander (B) Portable Belt Sander (C) Disc Sander

(E) Belt Sander

Disc Sander

Table

The Desired Width of Object

Clamp

(D) Sanding Objects to an Exact Width: pass the object between the guide stick and the sanding disc

5-6.
Power sanders

Belt sanders (figure 5-6B) are for the fast removal of material from large surfaces. The size of this machine is specified in terms of its belt width, which runs between 2½″ and 4″. Some portable sanders come with stands that can be used to convert them into bench-mounted belt sanders. Since a great deal of wood dust is usually produced, a dust collector is always a useful accessory. Most good models have provision for mounting one.

When using a belt sander, first contact the work with the rear of the belt, then bring the rest of the belt down onto the work. The sander must be kept constantly moving or a depression will be sanded into the object. Too fast a belt speed will burn the material. For smooth, satin finishes, use a canvas belt covered with a mixture of powdered pumice and paraffin oil. Also, paint the surface to be sanded with a 1:2 mixture of paraffin oil and kerosene.

Bench-Mounted Sanders

Disc sanders (figure 5-6C and D) can be used to sand flat surfaces and to square corners on large- and medium-sized objects. They are especially handy for squaring partitions, walls, and floors and are best for use on end grain.

The disc sander should have a tilting table (for bevel sanding) and miter gauge. Because the disc sands more rapidly at its edges, you must move the work across the disc's face. Hold the work on the down rotation side of the disc; otherwise, it will be flung off the table. To sand perfect circles, drill a hole in the center of the piece, attach it with a bolt to a piece of scrap wood, and clamp the scrap to the sander's table. To sand a number of objects to the same width, clamp a guide stick to the table. Abrasive discs (table 5-7) can be attached to the sander's disc with rubber cement.

Belt sanders (figure 5-6E) are used for grinding and for the fast removal of stock. They give fine, one-directional sanding not possible with the rotary action of the disc sander. Some machines come with a tiltable

Table 5-7. Abrasive Discs and Belts for Various Materials

Material	Abrasive	Grits for Rough to Fine Sanding
Softwood	Garnet	40–100
Hardwood	Aluminum oxide	50–180
Nonferrous metals	Aluminum oxide or silicon carbide	36–220
Plastics	Silicon carbide	80–400

vertical table and a miter gauge. Others do not have a table, only a stop to prevent the work from being carried off the belt. The sanding belt of most machines may be positioned in a vertical (for edge and end sanding) or horizontal (for surface sanding) position. To sand inside curves, place material over the sander's idler drum (the drum that is not powered).

Bench-mounted combination disc and belt sanders are available.

LATHES

Lathes can be used for turning, boring, drilling, and sanding. Lathe capacity is measured by the maximum-size stock that can be turned on it and expressed by the length (center-to-center distance) and diameter (swing) of the work.

Tools that are carbide tipped may be used on non-ferrous metals. Jeweler's files and small carving tools are used when turning small objects mounted in a hand motor tool or in other small improvised lathes.

In general, the larger the work, the slower the turning speed (table 5-8). Rough abrasive paper should be used at a slow speed; fine paper at a high speed.

Because most small objects needed by the modelmaker can be turned on a drill press, with a portable electric drill, or even with a small hand motor tool, the lathe is superfluous to all but the best-equipped shops.

Lathe chisels come in the following shapes: skew (for general smoothing, detail cutting, forming tapers, trim-

Table 5-8. Lathe Speeds for Various Materials

Material	Speed (rpm) for		
	Sanding	Shaping	Finishing
Wood, up to 2″ diameter	900	2,500	4,200
Wood, 2″ to 4″ diameter	800	2,100	3,500
Nonferrous metals, up to 2″ diameter	600	1,300	3,000

ming ends and shoulders, forming beads, and making V-cuts); round nose (for making long curves and coves, and forming concave grooves in faceplate-mounted stock); gouges (for rough cutting and for heavy stock removal, for forming coves, and for smoothing); parting tools (for forming small Vs, shoulders, and tapers, sizing cuts, and cutting off end stock); and square nose (for fast removal of material, cutting square shoulders, forming tapers as well as recesses and bands, making V-cuts, and smoothing convex forms). Blades should be slowly and steadily fed into the work. They should be held by placing the left hand on the blade (directly behind the lathe rest) and the right on the handle.

Wood lathes have a range of speeds—from as low as 200 rpm in some models to as high as 6,400 rpm in others. Most tools, though, have a much narrower range of speeds. Metals and plastics may also be turned on wood lathes.

Metal lathes have speeds that range from as low as 20 rpm on some tools to a high of 7,200 rpm. Metal lathes can also be used to mill and cut threads.

Working on the Lathe

There are two ways to turn work on the lathe.

Spindle turning is achieved by attaching the stock material between the two centers of the lathe. First locate the center of both ends of the stock. Push the spur center (on the lathe's headstock spindle) into one center. Make a seat with an awl in the other end of the stock and attach it to dead center of the lathe. Adjust the pressure of the center and oil it to allow the stock to turn freely. Draw the position of various details on the stock and cut them roughly with a parting tool. Finish the object by using cardboard templates to check its shape.

Faceplate turning has the work attached to a faceplate, which, in turn, is attached to the headstock spindle of the lathe. Center the stock and mount it on a faceplate with screws, or, to avoid marring the object, paste it to the faceplate. Attach the faceplate to the lathe's headstock spindle. If the work is small, you could screw it into a device called a screw center, which goes in the lathe's spindle.

BENCH-MOUNTED JOINTER PLANERS

These jointers are used to flatten wood surfaces and to make rabbet, bevel, chamfer, recessing, and taper cuts. They are of extremely limited use to the model-maker since they are needed only in the construction of baseboards, model boxes, and solid block models—functions satisfactorily performed by other tools. Jointers are rated by the width of the material that they can plane and also by the length of their table.

ROUTERS

Portable Routers

These tools (figure 5-7A) can perform the same operations on heavy wood as bench-mounted routers can. Blades, which are adjustable for various cut depths, must be held perfectly flat on the surface of the work or the cut will be ruined. A guide used in making grooves or dadoes will keep the line of cut parallel to the edge of the material. If the cut is too far in from the edge to allow using the guide, clamp a straight board to the work and run the router along it. Circular grooves can be cut by building a pivot into the router. A portable plane attachment can be purchased to convert the router into a power plane.

(A) Portable

(B) Bench Mounted

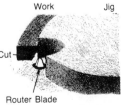

(C) Jig for Routing Curved Shapes

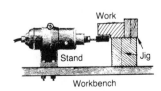

(D) Hand Tool Used as a Router

5-7.
Routers

Bench-Mounted Router Shapers

Router shapers (figure 5-7B) are used to rabbet, dovetail, groove, and plane, and to make coves, chamfers, dadoes, and round edges in wood. These tools are for working wood of the size that would be used in baseboards, model boxes, and larger plastic and solid wood block models. Their adjustable cutting blade, mounted on a vertical spindle projecting through a table, turns at about 20,000 rpm, producing smoothly machined surfaces. Straight surfaces are shaped with the aid of the tool's fence. Curved material requires a guide of scrap wood (figure 5-7C). A shaper can also be converted into a drum sander.

A light router (sufficient to shape the thin pieces of plastic and wood used in hollow built-up models) may be improvised from a small portable motor tool (figure 5-7D).

MULTIUSE POWER TOOLS

These tools combine many functions without duplicating basic components, such as the motor and table. In this way, they conserve on shop floor space as well as on cost. Converting from one tool to another usually takes a matter of minutes.

Multiuse Bench-Mounted Tools for Light Work

These can be bought from power tool suppliers. One such tool combines the features of a lathe, grinder, drill press, and portable drill, and is useful for light, highly accurate plastic, wood, and metal machining. Another example of a combination tool is basically a jigsaw with flexible shaft, grinder, and shaper attachments.

Multiuse Bench-Mounted Tools for Heavy Work

These combine a 9″ circular saw, an 8″ disc sander, a grinder, and a polisher. Additional accessories can make the tool into a jointer, 36″ lathe (a motorless lathe is needed), horizontal drill, saber saw, and drum sander. They can be used to construct baseboards and model boxes, to cut heavy, solid block models, and to perform operations on hollow built-up models.

Multiuse Portable Tools for Heavy Work

For a multiuse tool based on the ¼″ portable drill, use the many accessories available for the drill. It can then be made to perform the functions of a portable drill, portable router shaper, drill press, bench-mounted grinder, portable cut-off saw, portable saber saw, and portable orbital sander.

6:Materials: Paper, Clay, and Plaster

A professional modelmaker, noted for the speed at which he produced high-quality models, once commented: "I'm not a fast worker. I construct models rapidly because my shop is well organized and I know most of the materials that exist and how to work with them. This allows me to select those which can save me huge amounts of time."

The advantages of a well-organized workshop and planned selection of tools have already been discussed in previous chapters. This chapter and the next describe the materials most commonly used in modelmaking and the various ways of working with them. If you are a beginner, a complete knowledge of available materials and proven techniques will greatly help you develop your modelmaking skills. With practice, and experimentation with new techniques, you will be able to use those materials that most successfully represent your particular architectural projects.

Your choice of the materials to be used should be governed by: the object being modeled; the handling given the model and its desired life expectancy; your skill in working with various materials; the tools that are available; and the availability of the material.

Using materials that are readily available will save you a great deal of time in both planning and constructing the model. File current catalogs of material suppliers and always refer to them as the need arises. The materials you need might have to be obtained by mail so allow for extra time when planning for the models if you have not established a stockpile of hard-to-locate materials.

Also, after purchasing new materials, lay aside samples with the manufacturer's name and address written on them. Paste flat samples and ads for interesting new materials into a loose-leaf binder. When shopping for materials, carry an architect's scale to measure their exact scale dimensions. Materials meant for model railroad constructon are often out of scale and must be checked carefully.

The throwaway office and household objects that can sometimes be improvised into model parts are another source of potential model material. These include architectural samples, broken toys and jewelry, scraps of cardboard and paper, and so on. Some modelers save all the odds and ends that cross their path, but you will find, after years of junk collecting, that precious few of these things are ever used. Certain architectural samples (especially fabric, wall coverings, and other flat materials) will, however, be of use. Mount samples of these in a scrapbook along with the name of local suppliers who will sell (or sometimes give) a square foot or two of the product to the modelmaker.

Because many models are built on a rush basis and on weekends, it is better to start their construction with an oversupply of materials to compensate for material that will be wasted through cutting, making mistakes, and experimentation.

The professional modelmaker will at some time encounter a section of the work that requires a technique for which he or she lacks either tools or experience. Truly difficult techniques not meant for eleventh-hour experimentation are metal casting, milling, vacuum forming, electroplating, engraving, and photoprinting. This work can be subcontracted to another modelbuilder or to a fabricator. The occasional modelbuilder should know and make use of outside services.

Finally, here is a bit of advice-by-example for modelmakers who are sometimes overtaken by an uncontrollable urge to construct a model or part of a model out of real materials.

The first example involves a college student who made the ground slab of a ¼″ = 1′ scale house out of a rough-texture cardboard that was painted. He then decided to remake the slab, using concrete and reinforcing bars. After taking inventory of available materials, the student compromised somewhat and used plaster of Paris with two sizes of sand as the concrete and aggregates, and piano wire for the reinforcement. The result, although rather good for this type of exotic experiment, took a long time to achieve; the error of his undertaking was fully impressed upon him when he was complimented by several classmates on the cardboard slab, which—while it did not resemble concrete, they said—did have a look to it that was unlike anything they had ever seen.

The second example involves a client of a leading professional modelmaker, who insisted that the plaza to be constructed in front of his building be modeled in real stone. After it was machined, at great cost, the stonemason announced that its 1,000-pound weight did not allow it to be placed into the model in any other way than at an exactly vertical position. Since he wanted a plaza, not a monolithic headstone, the client had to abandon the slab.

BONDING MATERIALS

Adhesives

Adhesives and cements are, by definition, substances capable of holding material together by surface attachment. The types that are commonly used for making models and furniture are listed in table 6-1. Notice that cements having an animal, fish, or casein base are sometimes called *glue*. Cements made of flour or some other vegetable base are called *pastes*.

When using any of the adhesives described below, be sure to follow the directions provided by the manufacturer of the specific brand.

Cellulose cement is a quick-drying, clear, waterproof, flexible cement in liquid form and is packaged in tubes, in which it lasts indefinitely. Its solvent is acetone. Both model and airplane cement and slower-drying household cements are examples of this type of adhesive.

Cellulose cement may be used on most porous materials; however, its rapid drying speed often prevents it from thoroughly penetrating these types of surface, so when cementing porous objects, coat each side of the joint, allow the cement to dry partially, then put on a second coat and press the joint together by hand, or clamp, until dry. Cellulose cement shrinks on drying and can distort thin objects. Cellulose cement can also be used on some nonporous materials if the solvent is allowed to evaporate. Nonporous objects need only one coat of the cement.

Contact cement is a quick-drying, water-resistant, thin liquid made of neoprene and naphtha or toluol. It is also available in a noninflammable water-base variety. Some contact cements are sold in cans, others in spray bombs. Contact cement is of rather low strength

Table 6-1. Adhesives for Various Materials

Adhesive	Paper	Cardboard	Fabric	Light Wood	Heavy Wood	Metal	Foam Plastics[1]	Plastics	Plaster
Cellulose cement (model airplane and household)	X	X	X	X		X		X[2]	X
Contact cement (neoprene base)	X	X	X	X		X	X	X	X
Rubber cement	X	X	X	X		X	X		X
Rubber adhesive (nitrile base)	X	X	X	X		X		X	X
Casein glue				X	X				X
White glue (polyvinyl acetate resin)	X	X	X	X	X			X	X
Epoxy cement			X	X	X	X	X	X	X
Resorcinol resin glue	X	X	X	X	X			X	X
Plastic resin glue (urea base)				X	X			X	X
Acrylic resin glue				X	X	X		X	
Aliphatic resin glue	X	X	X	X	X				X
Hide glue	X	X	X	X	X				X
Solvents of various plastics								X	
Resin of various plastics								X	
Solder						X			
Liquid solder						X			

1. Test the cement or glue on a scrap of the plastic before using.
2. Use when cementing celluloid and acetate to other materials.

(household cellulose cement is almost seven times as strong). A joint covered with contact cement will adhere on contact without clamping.

Apply a coat to both surfaces, allow it to dry, apply a second coat, allow this to dry thoroughly (30 to 40 minutes), and join the objects within 3 hours. When the surfaces are pressed together, they will adhere on contact without the need of clamping. If the second coat is not allowed to dry thoroughly, the joint will open when heated (by sunlight, for example).

Rubber cement comes in tubes and cans, is flexible, and can be used on anything. Its bonding quality is low in strength and even less when applied under conditions of high humidity. Rubber cement is especially good for use on paper and fabric and on materials having dissimilar expansion rates. It does not wrinkle paper or other thin materials.

When making a temporary bond, coat one surface and join the pieces while the cement is still wet. On nonporous materials the cement should be allowed to dry and then heated before joining. For joints of greatest strength, apply cement to both pieces, allow to dry, then join. Excess dry cement may be removed by rubbing it off when it has dried. The solvent is methylethyl ketone.

A special type of rubber cement, called one-coat rubber cement, remains tacky indefinitely. Use it to create pressure-sensitive materials that can be pressed into place many days after coating.

Synthetic rubber adhesive (nitrile base) is a waterproof, flexible adhesive and can be used on many different materials. Coat both parts to be joined with adhesive, allow them to dry for 2 minutes, then press the assembly together. This adhesive dries in 5 minutes. Any excess must be removed with acetone solvent. Joints may be heat-cured for additional strength.

Casein glue is water-resistant and a good gap filler. It has a shelf life of over two years. Casein is best used to glue heavy wood assemblies and most other porous and nonporous materials to wood. When gluing oily woods (yellow pine, for example), wash the wood first with a strong solution of alkaline household cleaner.

The glue should be mixed, applied, and cured at a temperature of 70°F. Casein in powder form should be mixed one part (by weight) glue to one part water that is at 50° to 70°F. Stir until the mix becomes pasty, let stand for 10 to 15 minutes, then stir again until the mixture becomes smooth. Apply an ample amount with a stiff bristle brush. Clamp the joint and, with a damp cloth, wipe off any excess. Set starts in 10 to 15 minutes. Retain clamps on softwood for 2 or more hours and on hardwood for 5 or more hours. Some woods are stained by regular casein glue; these should be cemented only with nonstaining casein.

White glue (polyvinyl acetate resin) is water soluble, dries clear, and is fast drying. It comes in ready-to-use liquid form in bottle or plastic containers. White glue is not compatible with lacquer solvents. Use it on wood, paper, and cloth, but not on metal.

Clamp until the glue has set, about 30 minutes (it attains full strength in 3 days). Clean off the excess with a damp cloth before it sets. The shiny residue that sometimes remains is hard to sand off. Mix the glue with an equal part of water to make a transparent joint.

Epoxy cement usually comes in two parts and sets by chemical action, not by solvent evaporation. Epoxy will bond almost any material and can also be used on all plastics as a body cement. Its shelf life is about a year. Epoxy does not shrink on setting and is waterproof. Contrary to popular belief, it is not as strong as household cellulose cement.

Mix the epoxy on a piece of glass or other disposable surface. Apply to both surfaces to be joined (roughen nonporous surfaces first) and press the parts together (no clamps necessary). Epoxy must be used within about 2 hours after it has been mixed. It dries in 3 hours and completely cures in 18 hours. Infrared heating will shorten this time to 1½ hours. (One instant epoxy, available in a hypodermiclike applicator, hardens in a minute). Remove excess with denatured alcohol before it sets. Clean hands with nail polish remover or denatured alcohol immediately to prevent dermatitis.

Resorcinol resin glue comes in two parts, liquid resin and powdered catalyst, and is used on wood and paper. Apply at 70°F or higher and keep clamped for 10 hours or longer. It sets in 8 hours and attains full strength in 6 weeks. It is waterproof and will keep indefinitely on the shelf.

Plastic resin glue (urea base) bonds wood. It comes in powder form and is water-resistant when dry. Mix the powder in cold water: two parts (by volume) powder to one part water. If you want the glue to set rapidly, use only half as much water. Apply glue to one surface only and clamp for 5 to 6 hours. Joints must fit perfectly.

Acrylic resin glue is usable on almost any surface and is a good gap filler. It comes in two parts and setting time can be varied depending on the proportions of the mix.

Aliphatic resin glue comes in a powder (which may be precolored with water soluble dyes) or in liquid form. It is a good gap filler and is water-resistant. This glue has a shelf life of up to 1 year. Light work requires 2 minutes of clamping; heavy work, 45 minutes.

Solvents of various plastics, and the uses of solder are described in chapter 7. The use of resins for laminating fiberglass is described on page 134.

WORKING WITH ADHESIVES. Cement must wet the surfaces of a joint and come into molecular contact with as great an area as possible. For this reason, cements must be in a liquid form when they are applied. They are liquefied by being dissolved in water or solvent, heated, or mixed with a catalyst that solidifies by chemical action. They should be used as soon after they are purchased as possible.

Cement must penetrate porous surfaces, or else the bond will be poor. Quick-drying cements often harden before they have a chance to infiltrate pores deeply. End-grain wood, foam plastics, and porous plaster are materials that often cause trouble.

Cements that harden by evaporation usually have little filling capacity. When this type of cement contracts, a crack will develop if the objects being glued do not move together. To prevent cracking, the pieces constituting the joint must fit together tightly and must be clamped in such a way that they are pushed toward the cement line.

When mixing cements, use paper medicine cups with gradations printed on the insides.

Pick applicators with care. They should not spread cement beyond the desired area. Brush applicators are generally best for rubber cement and plastic solvents, syringes for cellulose cements, and metal ladles and spreaders for heavy wood glues. A toothpick can be used to apply cement to a very small area.

Masks of tape may be used to prevent cement from flowing onto parts of objects that should remain uncoated. Make certain, however, that the solvent in the cement will not eat through the tape.

Apply cement to both surfaces in such a way that, when clamped, only a small excess will be squeezed out of the joint. To prevent too much excess from being squeezed onto the surrounding material, do not spread the cement to the edges of the pieces being joined. Also, do not attach too many parts to an assembly at one time. Let one application of cement set before attempting to attach new pieces.

With a cement that requires clamping, care must be taken to apply pressure evenly along the pieces. If it is impossible to clamp the work, a cement that does not require clamping should be used. Contact cement, rubber cement, and epoxy cement are such adhesives. When making complicated joints, impossible to hold together with clamps, all joints except those that require maximum strength should be cemented with fast-drying cellulose cement and hand-held until they set.

Small work should be cemented on a sheet of glass. A double-edged razor blade that has been broken lengthwise can then be worked under the joint to cut it loose. Place large work (baseboards, for example) over sheets of wax paper while the joints dry.

Use a clean, dry rag or one dipped in the solvent of the adhesive to remove any excess cement dripping out of the joint while it is still wet. Rubber cement, however, is easiest to remove after it has dried. Areas covered with plastic solvents are another exception since they should not be touched while wet.

FASTENERS

Pins serve several purposes in modelmaking. They may be used to pin together balsa, stripwood, and other materials that are being glued and may be inserted into joints (in small assemblies) to act as miniature nails. Modelmaking pins come in sizes of from ½″ (No. 8) to 1⅞″ (No. 32) long. Escutcheon pins are available in hardware and dressmakers' stores. Bank and satin pins are available at dressmakers' supply stores.

Finishing nails have brad heads that can be driven ¹⁄₁₆″ into the wood with a nail set and then concealed with putty, plastic wood, or sawdust mixed with glue. They are often used on baseboard and carrying boxes or wherever an exposed nail head would be objectionable.

Nail sets, *taps*, or *brad awls* may be used with finishing nails or to drive nails into places a hammer cannot reach.

Brads are small versions of finishing nails and are used for the same purposes. In addition, they hold the carcasses of built-up models together. Brads can be obtained in lengths as short as ⅜″.

Common nails have flat heads and diamond-shaped points. They are used whenever a visible nail head would not be objectionable. *Wire nails* are small versions of common nails. *Fiberboard nails* have about the thinnest shafts of all.

To increase holding power, use nails that have barbs, screw threads, or rings along the shafts or nails coated with adhesive cement. The latter can be applied to nails as short as 1″ long; the other devices appear on nails 2″ long and longer. The holding power for any given nail is greater in hardwood and side grain than in softwood and end grain. Splitting in wood is caused by the shape of the nail's point and by its diameter in relation to the thickness and type of wood. It can be prevented by using thinner or oval cross-sectioned nails. Sharp nails tend to split hardwood.

Corrugated fasteners are for holding two pieces of wood together side by side. Use saw edge fasteners on softwoods and plain edge fasteners on hardwoods.

Wood screws are identified according to their head style, length, and diameter. Length is measured from the tip to the place at which, fully driven, they intersect the top of the wood. To prevent the wood from splitting and to create greater holding capacity, drill holes to start wood screws. First drill a "lead" or "pilot" hole to direct the screw and to hold its threaded part, then drill a "body" hole for the shank of the screw and, if the screw is to be countersunk or counterbored, a third hole to take its head. In hardwood the pilot hole should be the full length of the screw; in softwood it should be half the length of the screw.

Countersink bits are used on electric drills and are adjustable to any depth. When fastening two pieces of wood together, the screw threads should grip only the lower piece. The top piece should be drilled entirely through with the body hole. Wood screws are easier to drive if soap has been rubbed into the threads. When a part is to be held by several screws, first drive all of them snugly into place, then go back and tighten them up.

Screws may be concealed by wooden plugs obtainable in many diameters at boat supply stores and some hardware stores. To make your own, use a plug cutter. Match the wood of the object and cut so that the grain runs across the end of the plug, not lengthwise through it. Glue the plug into place and trim off any excess to make it flush with the top.

Machine screws are used for working in metal. They come in a variety of head styles including flat, round, and oval. The screws are specified in terms of their material, type of head, outside diameter, and length, as well as the number of threads per inch. Follow standard tables for the recommended tap drill to use with each size screw. The diameter of the tap drill runs a bit larger in diameter than that of the central shaft of the screw, so screw threads must be cut into the tap hole. This is done by screwing taps into the hole. Taps may be purchased in hardware stores or hobby shops. Dies (or thread chasers) used to cut threads into rods are also available. A drop of oil or a little graphite on the threads will simplify the driving of machine screws.

PAPERS AND BOARDS

Paper and cardboard are the most useful, versatile, and inexpensive of all easy-to-work materials. Complete models can be made from these materials using only a razor or knife, clamps, a straightedge, and glue. There is no limit to what can be constructed: walls, floors, roofs, partitions, laminated ground contours, and lightweight baseboards are just a few examples. Curved surfaces can be wet-formed from some types of cardboards or laminated from layers of thin Bristolboard. Extremely intricate objects may be built, as can strong and durable models, some of which have outlasted the buildings they depicted (figure 6-1 shows a cardboard and paper model that remains in perfect condition, half a century after it was built). Industrial designers even use cardboard for the construction of fullsize mock-ups of objects as large as computers and gasoline pumps.

Boards come in various surfaces and many require no further finishing. With a little ingenuity, any type of opaque material may be simulated with paper and

6-1.
Temple of Apollo
Modelmaker: Hans Schlief
Scale: 1:200
Materials: cardboard and paper

This model, which is on display at The Metropolitan Museum of Art in New York, remains neat and unwarped after more than 50 years. Walls, roofs, and stadium seats were made from illustration board and columns from wood dowels. The small statues are made from paper, large ones from clay. Windows and decorative details were inked on board and ground contours were constructed of plaster. (*Photograph courtesy of The Metropolitan Museum of Art, Dodge Fund, 1930*)

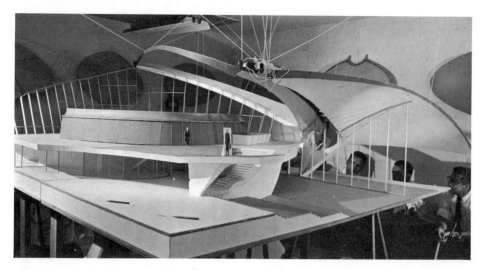

6-2.
TWA Airline Terminal, Kennedy Airport, New York City
Eero Saarinen & Associates, Architects
Ammann and Whitney, Engineers
Modelmakers: members of the architects' staff
Scale: ¾″ = 1′

Models were used in all design phases of this complexly shaped building. The overall shape of the shell roof was studied on small cardboard models. These were then torn apart and rebuilt as aesthetic and engineering considerations were amalgamated, until three basic designs were chosen. Shown is a rough study model of the interior. Because it was built at a large scale, it was possible to analyze the interrelationship of the building's many shapes. (*Photograph by Baltazar Korab*)

board. Keep in mind that heat and sunlight can cause most boards and paper to crack, warp, or become brittle, although cold has no effect on them. For fingerprint-free paper and board, cover your fingers with French chalk (obtainable at art supply stores) while you are working.

Available Papers and Boards

Knowing which kinds of papers and boards are available will help you speed up your construction time and produce more realistic cardboard models. Suppliers and manufacturers, some of which are listed in Appendix 1, usually publish catalogs from which you can order. Some manufacturers channel their papers and boards to supply houses and retail outlets, which then stamp their own brand name on the material. Many papers of potential use to the modelmaker can be obtained from artist supply outlets or from gift wrapping and wholesale paper suppliers. Artist supply stores also carry boards. To learn who, in a given city, carries a specific type paper or board, you might have to write to the manufacturer.

Papers and boards are available in black, white, grays,

silver, gold, and a wide range of colors. Textures can be matte, semimatte, glossy, and semiglossy. Very smooth finish is like plaster at ¼″ scale. Smooth finish is like concrete at 1/16″ to ¼″ scale. Boards with rough finish are somewhat coarser. Boards can be from 1/6 to ⅛″ thick.

Strawboard cannot be folded and bent. Its extreme absorbency makes it swell when adhesives are applied. Thus, it should not be used for building surfaces that are exposed to view. It may, however, be used as reinforcement. Shellacking makes it waterproof and increases its strength.

Chipboard is a medium gray/brown uncoated cardboard used frequently for contour models, massing models, and even presentation models (figure 6-3).

6-3.
Cincinnati Residence
Gwathmey Siegel & Associates, Architects
Modelmaker: Gustav Rosenlof
Scale: ⅛″ = 1′
Materials: chipboard and Plexiglas

Chipboard was used for wall and roof construction, as well as for the ground cover in this model. It was even used for curved surfaces; the board was scored and bent and then adhered to a wooden core. Windows and skylights are Plexiglas, with tape representing the mullions. While chipboard is used most frequently for massing studies, its use in this final detailed model is very successful. (*Photograph by Louis Checkman*)

6-4.
Methodist Family Practice Center, Gary, Indiana
Schmidt, Garden & Erikson, Architects and Engineers
Modelmaker: SG & E
Scale: ⅛″ = 1′
Material: Strathmore board

This model was built for a study of the interior layout of the building. Walls, constructed out of white Strathmore board, have cut-out windows and are glued together. Curved surfaces were scored first for easy bending. Paper strips along the top edges help keep the curve. Color boards were used for some walls and for the base cover. (*Photograph by SG & E*)

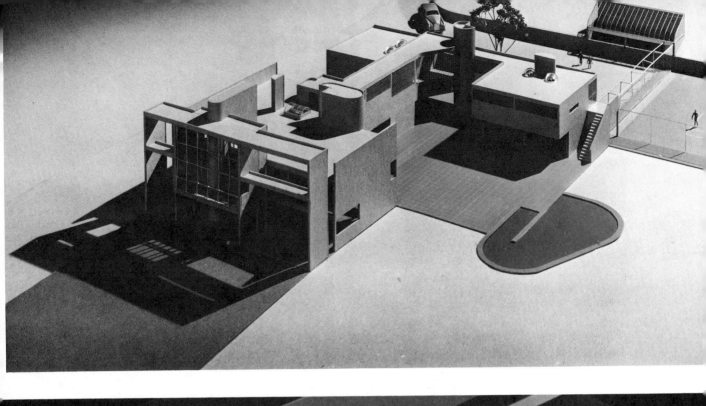
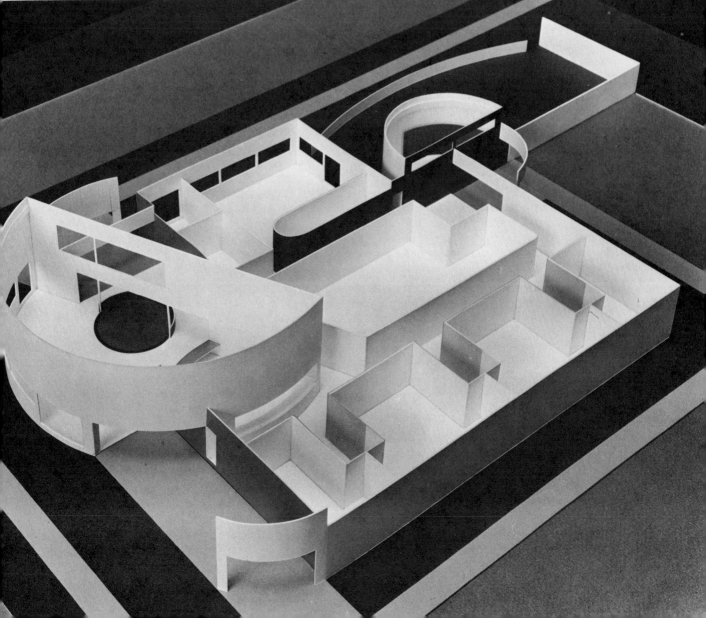

6-5.
San Francisco Executive Office
    Park
Hellmuth, Obata & Kassa-
    baum, Inc., Architects
Modelmaker: Stan Teng
Scale: 1/16" = 1'
Materials: foam board and
    Plexiglas

This simply constructed model
was useful for studying one
possible atrium design of an
office building. Walls and floors
were made from foam board,
with openings cut out with a
mat knife. The skylight was
made of Plexiglas and has
scored and taped mullions.
(*Photograph by Peter
Henricks*)

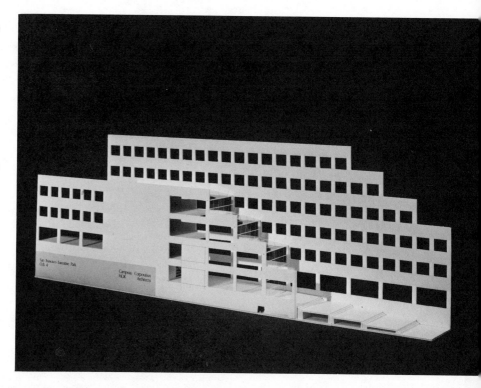

Strathmore board is a thin white illustration board that is useful for quick study or temporary presentation models (figure 6-4). Its cutting edge is a consistent white, and it is available in thicknesses of 1/32", 1/16", and 3/32".

Foam board has a layer of polystyrene foam sandwiched between two paperboards and comes in thicknesses of 1/8", 3/16", and 1/4". It is especially useful because it is a sturdy material for building wall and floor assemblies (figure 6-5) and for contour laminations (see figure 16-1), yet is easily cut with a mat knife.

Bainbridge board is made of layers of facing papers, with one side a fine quality medium surface. It is best used for base covers. Use contact cement to apply it to Masonite. It also serves as a good cutting surface for worktables.

Corrugated cardboard is easy to cut and useful for forming curved, fairly thick surfaces.

Bristolboard allows some of its ply to be stripped down to form recessed areas. The strength and ease with which it bends makes it the best thin board.

CUTTING PAPERS AND BOARDS. Use a razor blade or thin-bladed knife. The shearing action of scissors will cause curling cuts in thin strips of paper and in medium and heavyweight board. Knives with thick blades create wedge-shaped cuts. A paper cutter guarantees long, straight cuts. By setting the material against the top cutting guide, perfect 90° corners can be made. When cutting with a blade or knife, place the material on hard (plywood or Masonite) cutting surface. A soft cutting surface may produce a ragged cut on the bottom face of the paper or board or cause a fin to be depressed along the length of the cut. Cut material that is heavier than three-ply Bristolboard with several strokes. Use a metal straightedge to guide the blade when making straight cuts. To cut outside curves, use scissors on thin material. Cut thicker board with a blade and then sand with an emery board or with abrasive paper mounted on a sanding block. For inside curves, cut with a razor blade and then sand with abrasive paper mounted on a dowel or wood strip.

To cut clean inside corners (when cutting out windows, doors, etc.), pierce the corners with a pin. Cut from the pin prick toward the center of the cut to avoid overcutting the corner.

All identically shaped objects should be cut out together (one over the other), with the sheets temporarily clamped or tack-cemented together. If the pile of boards is too thick to cut out in one operation, use the first object cut (not subsequent ones) as a die to lay out the remaining ones. Place it on the stock and transfer its corner with a series of pin pricks.

To drill clean holes, sandwich the board between sheets of plywood. Punches can be used to make holes 1/10" to 1" in diameter.

BENDING AND SHEET FORMING. To make curved surfaces with thin board and paper, first score halfway through with a scriber, and then bend it to shape. Thicker board should be partially cut through on the outside of the bend, and then bent. To make cylindrical shapes, roll paper or thin board around a dowel, bevel its edges with a 30° bevel cut, and then lap glue the seam. Cones, coned discs, and bullet shapes may also be made out of paper and board. Accurate patterns for these shapes can be perfected through experimentation.

To form extruded shapes, use dowels and stripwood for the male molds. Build up the extrusion with several plies of Bristolboard. For best results, steam the paper over a kettle of boiling water. Tight or intricate bends may require both a female and a male mold. Put the steamed paper into the female mold and press it into shape with the male mold.

To form complex curved shapes, use gumstrip (parcel tape) or paper placed over a male mold, or wet straw-board (cardboard) pressed into a female mold. Press the strawboard into the mold with a ball or file handle.

6-6.
World Financial Center, New York
Cesar Pelli & Associates, Architects
Modelmakers: George Awad; R.M. Hurwit Associates
Scale: 1/50" = 1'
Materials: Plexiglas and laser-cut paper

The buildings of this final presentation model were constructed mainly out of Plexiglas. Existing surrounding buildings were lacquer sprayed. The reflective surfaces of the Center's buildings are represented by adhering mylar paper to the Plexiglas walls. Paper with laser-cut window openings was then applied to the mylar, as seen in the lower portions of the buildings. This model was also used in a promotional film by the leasing agent. (*Photograph by Kenneth Champlin*)

6-7.
Khulafa Street Development Project, Baghdad, Iraq
The Architects Collaborative, Inc., Architects
Modelmaker: TAC
Scale: 1/16″ = 1′
Materials: foam board, Strathmore paper, and posterboard

This study model was graduated to a presentation model. Close-up buildings were built of Strathmore, poster, and foam boards of various colors. The curved walls were scored in back for easy bending and then glued to roof and bottom plates. A professional modelmaker constructed the neighboring buildings with wood blocks. (*Photograph by Sam Sweezy*)

After the board has dried, remove it from the mold and waterproof it. Even tightly curved articles can be fabricated in this fashion.

To laminate medium and large objects with paper, construct a male mold out of plaster or wood. Apply five or more coats of shellac to the mold, and sand each coat so that the last one will have a glossy finish. Wax the mold and cover it with a layer of wax paper (if gumstrip is used, a layer of wet rag-tissue may be substituted for the wax paper). Apply the paper strips—gumstrip, strips of two-ply Bristolboard, or bond paper held on by liberal amounts of cement—and slightly overlap adjacent ones. At least three plies of paper should be used on the smallest objects, and up to ten plies on objects measuring several feet. Each of the first four layers should be at an angle of 45° to the preceding ply. The final layers may all run in the same direction. To prevent warping, allow the assembly to dry out thoroughly after a few layers have been applied. Care should be taken to prevent air bubbles from forming between plies. When the object has dried thoroughly, pry it off its mold. The shape may be sanded smooth and its inside and outside surfaces sealed with paint or sanding sealer. Handled properly, gumstrip may be bent into curves with as small a radius as 1/32″. The more intricate the shape, the narrower must be the gumstrip or paper.

INTERNAL BRACING. The secret of strong and long-lasting paper and cardboard models is internal bracing. Walls, floors, and roof will mutually brace each other, but additional bracing is needed for the large unsupported areas between these intersections. Brace joints either with a fillet of cement (test the adhesive for warpage as it dries on scrap), or a strip of wood laid along the joint. See figure 6-8 for some of the many possible ways to position bracing strips on typical surfaces. Cardboard models should be braced across the grain. The grain can be found by bending the cardboard in both directions—the grain runs parallel to the direction of the more flexible bend.

BONDING. Before bonding parts, assemble them and check all corners with a square. Butt joints may be used with thicker boards. Pressure-sensitive tape may be used on rough models to strengthen joints. Thinner materials must have flap joints. On flap joints that are not visible, use staples for added strength.

For *bonding cardboard to cardboard*, use a slow-drying cellulose cement. Quick-drying cement will harden before it penetrates the material's surface. Avoid water-based cements; white glue can be used. Rubber cement or white glue, while not producing a hard joint, may be used where excess cement must be easily removed. Cellulose cement may cause joint warpage in some instances. Place the cellulose cement as quickly as possible. Figure 6-9 shows two placement diagrams. If properly located, the cement will spread out to cover most of the board when clamping pressure is exerted. Learn by experience how close you can place the cement to the edges and corners and how thick a bead of cement you should use. Press flat assemblies under books for about one-half hour, or roll them with a photographic roller and spot clamp. Exert fairly even pressure throughout the entire length of the assembly.

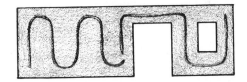

Cement

6-9.
Applying cement to sheet laminations

For *bonding paper to paper or cardboard*, use rubber cement, according to the following steps:

1. Coat the two surfaces to be joined with an even layer of rubber cement, using a 1″ × 6″ scrap of illustration board as a cement spreader.
2. Inspect both surfaces and level any thick concentrations of cement. Let the cement dry.
3. Lay the heavier material on your workbench with the cemented side up.

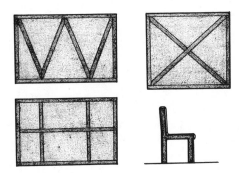

6-8.
Internal bracing of surfaces

4. Cover the cemented surface with a sheet of tracing paper, allowing a ⅛"-wide strip of cement-coated material to protrude from under the paper.

5. Have an assistant hold the second sheet that is to be joined above the first sheet, with the two cement-covered surfaces facing one another.

6. Carefully lower the top sheet so that it contacts the ⅛"-wide strip of exposed cement in the exact position in which it is to be attached. If a mistake in positioning has been made, pull apart the narrow cement line and start all over again.

7. If the sheets are positioned correctly, pull the tracing paper back from between the two sheets with one hand and have an assistant drop more of the top sheet on the bottom sheet. With the other hand, press the already-attached part of the sheets with a photographic roller or with a roll of tracing paper.

8. When the two pieces are completely mounted, inspect their surfaces and roll out any minor blemishes that may have appeared.

9. Give the entire surface a final hard roll.

Dry mounting is of use to modelers who make a number of built-up models. While dry-mounting presses are quite expensive, they do make it possible to adhere printed simulated building materials and colored paper to the cardboard perfectly and rapidly. Even embossed paper can be dry mounted, but first test to see if the embossing is compressed by the mounting pressure. Often, it is still presentable even though somewhat flattened. Some embossed or flat plastic sheets may be dry mounted, but this will depend on the temperature of the press and on the melting point of the plastic. To test, place two layers of brown wrapping paper on either side of the plastic and cardboard assembly and put it in the press for two seconds. Remove and note how much the plastic has melted and how well the dry-mounting tissue has adhered the plastic to the cardboard (in two seconds the tissue probably has not melted). Then gradually increase the time in the press.

When mounting a new type of paper or board, perform a test on scrap material to determine the degree of the warps that are caused.

To dry mount:

1. Preheat the backing board and the overlay material to remove any moisture.

2. Tack-mount (using a small heated tacking iron) a sheet of dry-mounting tissue to the overlay material. Trim the tissue to the outline of the overlay.

3. Place the overlay/tissue sandwich on the backing board and insert the entire assembly into the dry-mounting press. Put a protective sheet of brown wrapping paper on top of the assembly.

4. Close the press for the amount of time recommended in the instructions for that thickness. Try to heat the work as little as necessary to achieve a good bond. Too much heat, or prolonged heat, may cause blisters to form in the work.

5. Remove the work from the press. Before cutting it into small pieces, or cutting out windows, or assembling the materials, allow it to reabsorb a normal amount of humidity. This will take one or two days. This step, while obviously a nuisance, will help prevent warping.

Dry-mounting sheets are commercially available. These have pressure-sensitive adhesive on both sides and do not require heat.

Stapling is a quick way to fasten paper pieces together for rough study models. Make tabs to join adjacent parts.

SEALING AND WATERPROOFING. Remove all blobs of cement with a razor blade. This is especially important if oil paint will be used eventually. Seal the material with sanding sealer; one coat is enough for average finishes, with up to three coats for a fine finish. Sand each coat of dried sealer with fine abrasive paper. Give the ends of boards extra coats of sealer or primer.

Most boards can be waterproofed with one or more sprayed coats of French polish, cellulose varnish, or cellulose lacquer. These substances render the board resistant to water or poster paints. In addition, French polish will stain the board yellow. So if a water-based paint must be used, first paint the board, and then apply one of the cellulose-based chemicals.

Simulated Building Materials

These are simulations of various building materials (brick, siding, shingles, etc.) printed, embossed (figure 6-10), or milled on paper, wood, or plastic in flat image or low relief. They are available primarily through hobby stores and come in ⅛" = 1' or ¼" = 1' scales.

At ⅛" = 1' or ¼" = 1' scales, you can draw building paper that compares favorably in cost (but not quality) with commercially obtainable papers. Some suppliers of simulated building materials are listed in Appendix 1. In addition, some manufacturers will custom-emboss patterns to your order.

Since less detail is required at scales under ⅛" = 1', you can make your own building material paper. The pattern can be simplified; for instance, brick need only be represented as horizontal lines. A good draftsperson can turn out building paper rapidly and economically by drawing or scribing patterns on paper, wood, or plastic.

6-10.
One Main Place, Houston, Texas
Hellmuth, Obata & Kassabaum, Inc.,
    Architects
Modelmaker: HOK
Scale: $\frac{1}{32}'' = 1'$

This massing model is an example of
solid block construction. It was made entirely out of basswood, which was then
wrapped with embossed metallic papers.
These papers were applied with transfer
tape. The embossing simulates the spandrels and glass areas. (*Photograph by
HOK*)

At larger scales (½″ = 1′ and up), the problem of making your own paper is much more complicated. It is often easier to have a metal die cut by a local producer of embossed stamps and to use this die in an inexpensive hand press for thin Bristolboard or polystyrene sheet.

PAINTING. If the embossed material requires a mortar line, paint the material the basic color first. Use lacquer or oil paint, first testing a scrap of the material to see if the paint you have chosen will work well. When the basic coat has dried, apply a water-based paint the same color as the mortar lines. Wipe the still-wet coat from the top surface of the embossing, allowing it to remain in the mortar lines. Mortar lines can also be produced with white pencil.

Embossed wood must first be sealed carefully with thin coats of wood sanding sealer. Before the sealer dries, brush as much of the liquid from the embossed joints as possible to prevent them from being filled.

Printed paper sometimes has a rather pristine look. To add a bit of irregularity, apply a thin transparent coating with artist's oils thinned with turpentine, or with thinned watercolors or poster paints. Apply the paint with a large wad of cotton, making sure that enough cotton lies between fingers and work surface to prevent streaking with finger pressure. Paint with a circular motion. Sometimes the effect of the paper can be improved if individual bricks, stones, or slates are selectively brush painted.

Drafting and Embossing Materials

All types of building materials and details may be draw on thin Bristol or other boards. If you want color, sele colored board or paper; or use watercolors, transpare photographic oil paints, or dusted-in pastels to color pattern drawn on white material. The harder you pre when drafting, the more three-dimensional the patter will be.

Time can be saved by drawing the texture on draftir paper and reproducing it by the black-, blue-, or brow on-white process. The resulting prints can then k mounted, or colored and mounted. Photographs ca also be used (figure 6-12).

The scribing of board (figure 6-13) or polystyrer

6-11.
Yale University Beinecke Rare Book and Manuscript Library,
New Haven
Skidmore, Owings & Merrill, Architects
Modelmaker: SOM model studio
Scale: ⅛″ = 1′
Material: foam board

This preliminary study model was built out of foam board covere with black line prints. The base is a wood frame covered wi Bainbridge boards. Trees are sprayed steel wool and wire. (Ph tograph by Louis Checkman)

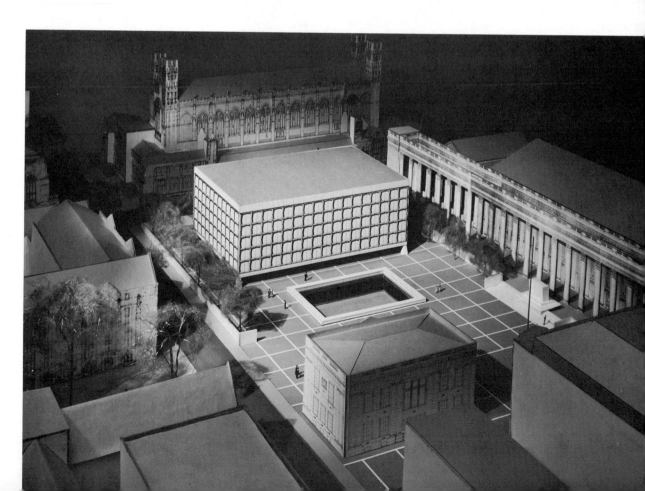

6-12.
Untitled
Nathaniel Lieberman
Dimensions: 19″ H × 36″ L

The brick walls in this model were represented with black-and-white prints mounted on wood-braced Masonite walls. The construction was then photographed in an actual grass setting, to which a leaf and an apple were added. (*Photograph by Nathaniel Lieberman*)

6-13.
Cutler Ridge Showroom, Miami, Florida
SITE Inc., Architects
Modelmaker: SITE
Scale: ⅛″ = 1′
Material: Bainbridge board

The brick-textured surface of the Bainbridge board walls was created by scoring the board with a dull knife. The model was then assembled and painted in layers of black, white, and gray. Plexiglas was used for the doors and wood dowels for columns. (*Photograph by SITE*)

may also be used. Choosing a board whose texture matches the prototype material will equal all but the most realistic ready-made product. Spray-painted sandpaper can be scribed to make realistic brick, block, stone, or roofing. A multiline scribing tool can be improvised, or use devices like a heavy comb (to emboss corrugated metal and pattern on foil).

Large patterns with pronounced three-dimensionality should be vacuum formed against a pattern.

APPLYING. If possible, lay out the desired shape on the back of the material, since pencil marks are difficult to remove. Because of the danger of splintering, cut with a single-edge razor, using extremely light runs in embossed and milled woods.

Bond simulated materials with regular paper, plastic, or wood cements. Orange shellac may be used to hold thin paper on cardboard, but the paper must be quickly applied to the brushed-on shellac. Dry mounting may also be used if it will not ruin the embossing or melt the plastic. Embossed plastic should be glued with a filler cement that will not attack the plastic. Apply cement to the simulated material, not to the understructure. Use tweezers to position small pieces. Be careful to keep the courses of brick, siding, and so on parallel to the bottom of the building and to line them up between adjacent sheets.

Embossed simulated building materials (and all embossed papers) should be tested to see if they will withstand an application of cement without wrinkling. Brush on several thin layers of adhesive to strengthen the material, allowing each coat to dry before applying the next. When the embossed paper has achieved sufficient rigidity, it may be cemented in the usual way.

Small objects (chimneys, columns, etc.) should be completely covered, with paper overlapping one side (figure 6-14B). To turn corners, first cement one side in place, leaving a ⅛″ excess. Then bevel cut the paper with a razor guided by a bevel-edged steel straightedge. Bevel cut the paper that will cover the second side before it is cemented in place. Cement this piece, making sure that the beveled joint is tight, without a visible seam. If a crack is visible, carefully fill it with sanding sealer, or balsa dust and cement. Sand it smooth to alleviate any shadow caused by the crack, and touch up the joint with paint. Bevel cutting is difficult to master, but it will produce better results than lap or butt joints.

Attempt to cover a surface with a single piece of simulated building material, even if it means a certain amount of wastage. If the material to be used is not large enough, carefully plan where the seams will fall. See figure 6-14A for the best location of seams on a wall with windows, doors and other openings. If possible,

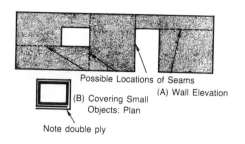

Possible Locations of Seams
(A) Wall Elevation
(B) Covering Small Objects: Plan
Note double ply

6-14.
Covering with overlay material

run all seams along a natural line in the paper (the horizontal mortar line of brick, the line between two pieces of siding, or the like). This is usually easy to accomplish with horizontal seams. Vertical seams require a delicate matching of material. Brick, tile, and similar material may be laboriously matched by cutting out individual members along the two sides of the seam and by fitting the resulting crenulated pattern together.

Window and door returns should be covered with material. This can be done by folding the material back into the opening if it is paper or by making a miter joint in plastic or wood. Sills and frames can be made from stripwood. If the scale of the model is too small to allow for covering the returns, they may be painted the color of their prototype material. Paint them first and then cover that side of the model with the simulated building material.

Overlays and Tapes

If the textures you need are not available in embossed papers, review the catalogs of various manufacturers for the overlay that most closely approximates the desired pattern. If you cannot find an overlay for a particular texture, try to visualize what combination of overlays might meet the requirements. Overlay papers are made in various shades of gray and colors, and are translucent or opaque. Another way of adding color to the texture is to place the overlay on colored board. Plan the construction of the model so that colored board is substituted for white board where this is required.

Pressure-sensitive overlays are attached to a backing sheet. To apply the overlay, place the sheet over the area to be covered and burnish the backing sheet lightly with a plastic or bone burnishing tool. The overlay can then be given a final burnishing. *Dry-transfer overlays* are removed (like a decal) from their sheet of backing paper, positioned, and burnished.

Tapes may be used to represent plaza patterns, mullions, moldings, and similar prototype parts. They can be applied conveniently with a tape pen guided along

straightedge. For curved patterns, use thinner tape
rawn along a French curve. Burnish the tape lightly
fter applying.

Tapes, like paper, are available in a variety of colors,
ncluding gold and silver. Their finishes are matte or
lossy, and they are opaque, transparent, or fluorescent.
apes come in widths of from 1/64″ to 2″.

Striping may also be achieved by applying thinned
aint with a ruling pen or with a striping tool. The
atter applies the paint by means of a wheel receiving
continuous flow of paint from a small reservoir. Wheels
ay be obtained in various widths from artist supply
tores.

6-15.
Copley Place Development
The Architects Collaborative, Inc., Architects
Modelmaker: TAC
Scale: 1/16″ = 1′
Materials: foam board and posterboard

Cut foam board was used for floor plates around which posterboard
walls were attached. The reflective glass window areas were represented with Mylar tapes and thin, scored Plexiglas was used
for the skylights of the entrances. (*Photograph by Sam Sweezy*)

6-16.
Governor's Palace
Le Corbusier, Architect
Modelmaker: Alex Gorlin, Cooper Union School of Architecture
Scale: ⅛″ = 1′
Materials: paper board, Plexiglas, and wood

This model is a detailed study of a Le Corbusier building and was reconstructed from plan and section drawings. The exploded view shows the many sections of the model; these can be disassembled and examined individually. Paper boards were used extensively in building this presentation model, which demonstrates the versatility and durability of this material. Paper, skillfully used, equals the quality that can be achieved with wood or plastic, but has the added advantage of being lighter and more easily cut and assembled.

-17.
his close-up of one of the levels seen in
gure 6-16 shows the interior space ar-
angement. Curved and straight walls are
aperboard, which was painted before being
lued in place. Clear walls are plastic. Col-
mns are solid basswood strips with corners
otched on a table saw.

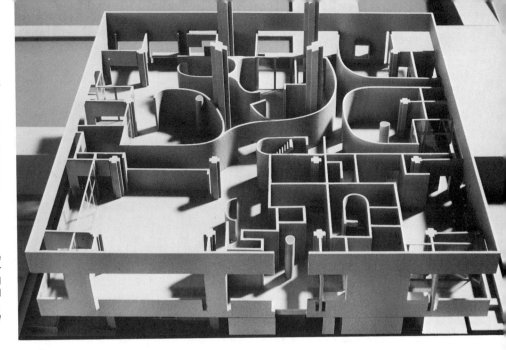

-18.
he completely assembled model of the
Governor's Palace is reflected in the upper
ool, which was simulated with a backpainted
Plexiglas sheet. The base was constructed
ut of wood. *(Photographs (figures 6-16,
-17, and 6-18) courtesy of Cooper Union
School of Architecture)*

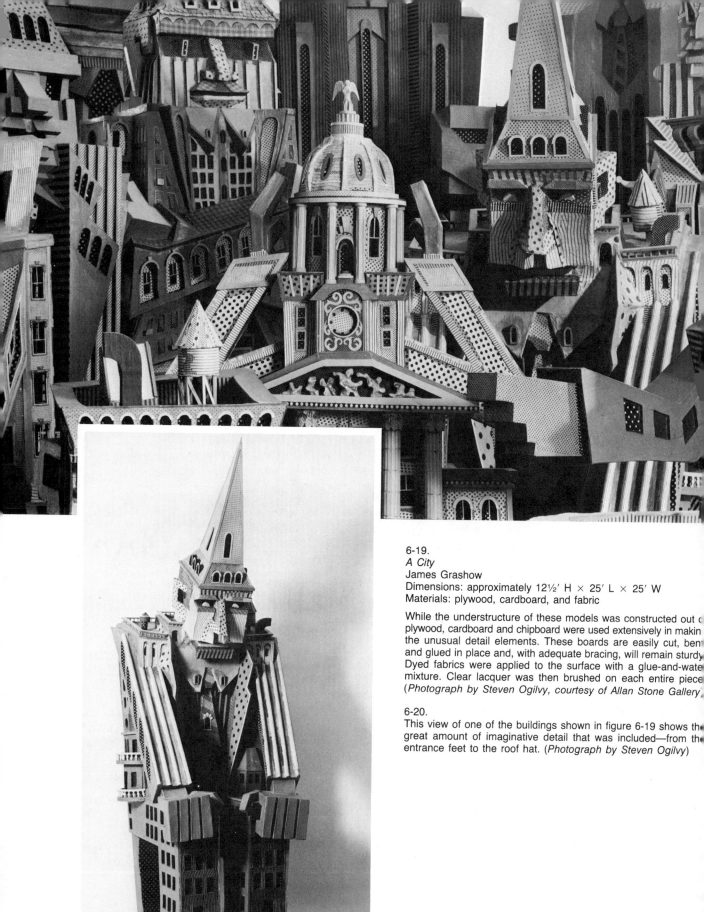

6-19.
A City
James Grashow
Dimensions: approximately 12½′ H × 25′ L × 25′ W
Materials: plywood, cardboard, and fabric

While the understructure of these models was constructed out of plywood, cardboard and chipboard were used extensively in making the unusual detail elements. These boards are easily cut, bent and glued in place and, with adequate bracing, will remain sturdy. Dyed fabrics were applied to the surface with a glue-and-water mixture. Clear lacquer was then brushed on each entire piece. (*Photograph by Steven Ogilvy, courtesy of Allan Stone Gallery.*)

6-20.
This view of one of the buildings shown in figure 6-19 shows the great amount of imaginative detail that was included—from the entrance feet to the roof hat. (*Photograph by Steven Ogilvy*)

NONHARDENING PLASTICINE AND AIR-DRYING CLAY

There are many uses for clay and plasticine in model-making. They can be used not only for rough massing models but also for highly detailed designs, shapes, and patterns for casting.

Nonhardening plasticine is available in a variety of colors and can be purchased in artist supply stores. Plasticine is made from kaolin, gypsum, and oil. If it should dry out, it can be made pliable again with the addition of glycerin. Plasticine may be painted with oil paints, Krylon spray, or acrylic lacquers, but not with water-base colors.

Clay comes in a wide variety of firing temperatures.

6-21.
Metropolitan Opera House, Lincoln Center, New York
Wallace K. Harrison, Architect
Ammann and Whitney, Consulting Engineers
Modelmakers: members of the architect's staff
Scale: ½" = 1'
Material: plasticine

The curved ramps and stairs of the grand staircase of the Metropolitan Opera House were studied in rough models. Plasticine was shaped on chicken wire, to which wood was added for the flat surfaces. People were painted on boards. (*Photograph by architect's staff*)

6-22.
Beach House
Sanford Hohauser, Designer
Modelmaker: Sanford Hohauser
Scale: ½" = 1'
Materials: clay and rocks

This design and presentation model was constructed in a rather unusual way. Since the exact final shape of the building was to be created only after the model had been studied and modified, it was decided not to make the model from mesh and plaster. A high firing temperature clay was used instead. The rough exterior shape of the building was modeled in the clay, which was studied and modified. The shape was then partially hollowed out; wood props prevented it from collapsing. When it became difficult to remove any more material without causing the external contour to sag, the clay was allowed to dry. Additional material was then removed with a scraper. When it became obvious that further thinning would cause the model to crumble, it was fired at around 2,000°F. The resulting hard, porcelainlike material was then scraped and sanded to its final thin wall dimensions. The room divider was carved from balsa and filleted to the fired clay wall with plastic balsa. Rocks were cast by placing lumps of clay into a gunny sack, flexing the sack, allowing the clay to dry, and, prior to its removal, breaking it into suitable sized pieces with a hammer. The baseboard was ½" plywood on a 1" × 2" pine strip frame.

These range from 250°F (done in an ordinary kitchen oven) to those requiring up to and over 2,000°F firing temperatures. Firing transforms the chalk-dry clay into a hard material. Industrial clays (used by industrial designers to make full-size mock-ups of autos, etc.) are first heated or mechanically kneaded into plasticity and are then modeled into rough shape. Precise detailing and final surface finishing are done after the clay has cooled and hardened (they do not require firing). This type of clay may be machined and extruded to extremely close tolerances and finished to a polished surface.

Clay shapes may be built solid, or on armature wire or wood forms. Unsupported clay cannot be fabricated into thin shapes, but if it is partially cut down to its final dimension while wet and allowed to dry, it may be carefully sanded and scraped to the desired dimension. Cover clay with a wet cloth to keep it from drying out between work sessions.

6-23.
Gate of Souls
Charles Simonds
Dimensions: 15″ × 30″ × 30″
Materials: clay, sticks, and
   sand

The landscaping in this model was made out of clay blocks that were modeled into a continuous ground contour. Sand was applied to the top surface. For the building, clay was first rolled out in thin layers and then cut into small strips and blocks; these were stacked piece by piece. (*Photograph by Eric Pollitzer, courtesy of Rosa Esman Gallery*)

6-24.
Metropolitan Opera House,
   Lincoln Center, New York
Harrison and Abramovitz,
   Architects
Ammann and Whitney, Con-
   sulting Engineers
Modelmakers: members of the
   architects' staff
Final presentation model:
   Thomas Salmon
Scale: 1/32″ = 1′
Materials: plasticine; final pres-
   entation model: acrylic

Many rough plasticine massing models of early design schemes for the Metropolitan Opera House were sculpted for close study.

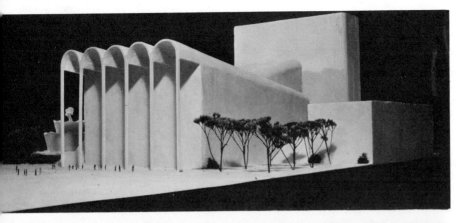

6-25.
Once several design choices had been made, the crude masses of these models were replaced by carefully cut plasticine blocks on which major details were simulated: glass was shown with a rough comb-scraped finish; important panel lines were scribed or shown with thin stripwood; arches were pressed from sheets of plasticine on rough carved wood forms. These models were mounted on rough plywood bases.

6-26.
In a later phase of the design, models of surrounding buildings were made out of cardboard covered with plasticine. The final design had now been selected and a rough model was replaced by a cardboard and plaster one.

6-27.
The final presentation model ($\frac{1}{16}'' = 1'$) was built by a professional modelmaker. Walls, roofs, and windows are of acrylic; columns are cardboard; vaults were carved from Hydro-Stone; elevated walks are sheet metal, and railings and figures are cast metal. *(Photographs (figures 6-24 through 6-27) by Ezra Stoller)*

FILLET AND OTHER CARVABLE MATERIAL

Fillets too large to be constructed with a heavy application of filler cement often must be specially built. Since the fillet usually must be sanded into final shape, it is important that it be made with a material easier to sand than its surrounding construction (table 6-2). If it is not, there will be a tendency to cut into the surrounding areas while attempting to sand the fillet. Fillet material may also be used to fill cracks and holes in material.

Apply fillet material to a surface that has been cleaned and roughened. Some fillet materials may be applied to surfaces painted with only certain paints. Check product instructions for which paint may be used.

Plastic wood, plaster, and gesso can be used as fillet materials. Since some plastic woods shrink, put wood plugs in large holes and use plastic material around them. Sand and other aggregates can be mixed in with gesso to create various textures. Gesso should be used to build up thick shapes.

Liquitex modeling paste is an acrylic putty pigmented with finely ground marble. It may be used to build all sorts of shapes and, if Liquitex Gel medium is added, the objects will remain flexible permanently. Modeling paste takes a day or longer to dry and harden. Once dry, it can be carved, sanded, and delicately tooled. The addition of gel improves the modeling characteristics of the paste and prevents shrinkage, but complicates sanding of the dried mix. To prevent excessive shrinkage and cracking, the paste should be applied in a series of layers $\frac{1}{8}''$ thick. Modeling paste can be applied to any nonoily surface and can be painted with oil, enamel, casein, or tempera paints.

Epoxy paste (ren shape) can be carved with woodworking tools. It comes in cans and tubes and, once mixed, has to be applied within 15 to 30 minutes. It can be machined at the end of about 45 minutes. Epoxy paste will adhere to many materials and is used by patternmakers to repair molds and construct fillets.

Epoxy metal compound is a very hard filler—like cold solder in appearance—and its preparation is similar to that of epoxy cement. Large shapes made from epoxy metal may be built on a wire armature. Deep fillets should be built up from several layers. Many epoxy metals will adhere to wood, metal, and plaster. While still wet, it can be worked with clay-modeling tools. Once hardened, it must be cut, or ground, with power tools, filed, or sanded. Denatured alcohol or acetone should be used to clean epoxy off tools before it hardens. Once dry, this material may be painted with enamels, lacquers, or waterpaints. Its natural metal finish may be burnished to a high luster.

Sculpt stone is an easy-to-carve natural stone widely used by artists. Modelmakers can sometimes use it to carve large curvilinear shapes. The material can be cut, drilled, turned, filed, scraped, sanded, and polished. It comes in many colors, some translucent.

Sculpt metal is an air-hardened, puttylike aluminum compound that adheres to metal, wood, and plaster. It may be used by modelbuilders to form curvilinear shapes. Worked like clay, thick masses should be built up of $\frac{1}{8}''$ layers. Each layer should start to dry before the next one is applied. After the entire object is completed, it must be allowed to dry from six hours (for $\frac{1}{4}''$ thick objects) to two to three days (for massive pieces). Infrared heat will speed hardening. Build up domes and similar objects on $\frac{1}{8}''$ metal screening. Hardened material may be cut, sawed, carved, filed, sanded, buffed, or burnished to a high luster. Sculpt metal may be painted with lacquers, synthetic enamels, and oil-base paints.

PLASTER

Plaster is often totally excluded from the repertoire of modelmakers. The fact that it is a wet material, requiring mixing and a certain amount of dexterity to apply, discourages people from using it, and in most applications, it can be replaced with other materials. In the past, however, plaster was a major modelbuilding material used almost as universally as wood was a generation ago or as acrylic is today. Highly detailed baroque and renaissance buildings were modeled, in all their detail, exclusively from plaster. Slabs with end dimensions as small as $\frac{1}{100}''$ were cast on linen and other reinforcements. Roof tiles, friezes, and other relief surfaces were also cast. Figure 6-28 shows a modern facade with a repetitive pattern that is entirely plaster cast.

Plaster may be used in the making of open molds if the object to be duplicated has no undercuts; or for

Table 6-2. Fillet for Various Materials

Material	Fillet
Cardboard	Plastic balsa wood, gesso, or barbola paste
Balsa, softwoods	Plastic balsa wood
Hardwoods	Plastic wood or cement and fine sawdust
Acrylic	Dichloride and acrylic chips
Polystyrene	Automobile metal filler or polystyrene body putty
Metal	Sculpt metal or solder
Plaster	Plastic wood, French putty, or crack filler
Miscellaneous	Hard wax

6-28.
Alcoa Building
Harrison and Abramovitz, Architects
Modelmaker: René Chamberlin
Scale: 1/16″ = 1′

This facade texture study model was made from cast plaster slabs assembled on a wood frame.

6-29.
Lincoln Center Ballet Theater, New York
Philip Johnson, Architect
Modelmaker: Joseph Santeramo of architect's model shop
Scale: 1/2″ = 1′

Columns, arches, and ceilings of this study model were made from cemented Masonite. Curved areas were built up from plaster. People are represented with twisted tin foil. (*Photograph by Louis Checkman*)

two or more pieces, in closed molds that cast certain types of undercuts. It is useful in making curved structures such as domes and large fillets in casts and ground contours.

Plaster can be finished smoother than most types of clay. Its homogeneous texture makes it easier to carve than wood. Different types of plaster vary in hardness, strengths, and ways of working with them.

Plaster selection should reflect the use to which it will be put. In general, soft plasters (those with low strength) are easiest to carve, although finer detail may be cut into slightly harder material. Plasters used for wet modeling or running of shapes should have a long period of plasticity. All plasters will cast into intricate shapes, so, for casting, select a plaster for its strength or expansion qualities.

6-30.
Memory Form—House with Seven Gardens
Lorna McNeur, Architect
Material: plaster

The base of this model was made by pouring plaster into a box mold. After it had set, it was cut and sanded to shape. The back portion of the ground level was chipped away. The buildings' facades are plaster slabs made by pouring plaster into shallow frames. Blocks of wood were placed in these frames where the windows and doors were to be located. After the slabs had hardened, they were removed from the frames and assembled with glue. Fresh plaster was added along the edges. These corners were sanded smooth in the final step. (*Photograph by Anne Turyn*)

Gypsum plaster can be divided into the following types: plaster of Paris is fast-setting, soft, and brittle; molding plaster, a finely ground grade of plaster of Paris, is used for fine molding work; gypsum wall plaster and patching plaster are both crude grades of plaster of Paris and have retarder added. *Wood-fiber plaster* is comparable to gypsum wall plaster, but has wood fibers added to reduce cracking.

Working with Plaster

Perhaps one of the reasons modelmakers resist using plaster is the many types of defects that can occur. The list is almost endless. Pinholes form if the plaster is not soaked long enough in the mix water or if the mixing is too vigorous. Voids may also occur because of these factors, or because the plaster was too stiff when poured, or because an air pocket was trapped during pouring. Hard spots develop if the plaster is not soaked long enough in the mix or if the object is not dried properly. Efflorescence occurs if the plaster becomes contaminated or is not dried properly (evaporation should be through the back of the object). If the plaster mix is not creamy enough or if the plaster is of too coarse a grade, the result is a rough finish. Deterioration occurs if the plaster is of a low quality or contaminated: possibly the mixing procedure was not carefully followed, the plaster was not soaked long enough in the mix water, was mixed too vigorously, or was not dried properly.

With the proper preparation and procedures, however, all these problems can be avoided, or solved, so be sure to follow the guidelines given here for best results.

EQUIPMENT. You will need a ready supply of water when working with plaster. Although bottled water may be sufficient for less extensive plaster work, the repeated use of plaster requires running water. Sinks should have a plaster trap or strainer to prevent plaster from blocking up the drain.

The other provisions you will need for extensive plaster

work include: a glass, marble, or slate work surface; a mixing bowl, rubber mixing spatula, and scoop (which can be made out of cardboard); trowels and putty knives to clean up bowls and work surfaces and to apply small quantities of plaster); file cards; Italian rasps for filing hardened plaster (these come in beavertail and knife shapes); hand-forged steel tools for modeling and re-touching (chisel, spear, hook, pointed, and beavertail shapes, some with serrated edges); brushes (to apply the separator and to dust off sawdust); and either a sanding block or steel scrapers (saw-toothed or smooth-edged) to finish flat surfaces (concave surfaces should be finished with an aluminum or zinc scraper).

Plaster will rust tools if it is not removed quickly, so they should be kept clean and well oiled. Plaster also quickly dulls cutting tools.

MIXING PLASTER. Mix plaster in either a flexible bowl (when cleaning, twist the bowl so that hardened plaster residue pops loose) or a Pyrex bowl (it will not cake the plaster and is readily cleaned). Slowly pour the powdered plaster into a bowl filled with water (*never the reverse*). Stir with a rubber cake-mixing spatula until the mixture assumes the consistency of thick cream and is completely free of lumps. A mixture that is too thin will result in weak plaster. Too thick a mixture is hard to pour and may not fill all the extremities of a mold. If the plaster does not combine readily with the water, two or three drops of liquid household detergent may be added as a wetting agent. (Commercial plaster containing retarder has a wetting agent already mixed into it. Besides hastening mixing, wetting agents will reduce lumping and bubbles and will help the plaster to bond with adjacent dry plaster).

The exact proportion of water to plaster will vary with the type of plaster being mixed and the use to which the mix will be put. For plaster that can be used for smooth finishing coats, the mix should contain 10% more water. For a stiff plaster to be used as the first coat in bulk applications, use a mix with 10% less water; as layers of normally mixed plaster are added, the bulk coat will absorb some of the water from the subsequent coats, creating a stronger interlayer bond. If mixing by eye rather than by exact weight, mix the plaster to the ideal thick cream consistency, then add 10% more water for a thin mix or 10% more dry plaster for a thick one.

Do not stir the mixture too vigorously because this will force air into it. Also, do not continue stirring the plaster after it has started to harden because the result will be a soft, powdery material. And, finally, do not add more plaster to the mix once you have stopped stirring.

To maintain a supply of plaster for an extended plas-tering operation, fill a shallow pan with water, and then pour a mound of plaster into the center of the pan. The top of the mound should be well above the top of the water. The water will be slowly drawn up into the mound by capillary action. Use plaster that has mixed itself to the correct consistency. In time, the bottom of the mound will set. Despite this, the system will provide a supply of fresh plaster for a much longer period than if prepared in the standard way.

APPLYING PLASTER. Plaster may be applied by pour-ing, troweling, or even by spraying. This last procedure requires a special spray gun (which may also be used to spray mold-making rubber and plastic resins) that eliminates the possibility of pinholes and air bubbles forming. Vibrating the plaster as it is being poured will also lessen the possibility of pinholes. Remove hardened plaster from tools by soaking them until the plaster dissolves.

DRYING PLASTERS. Most types of plaster take about one-half hour from wetting time to initial set, and, in general, another ten minutes to reach final set. About an hour after setting, plaster achieves about 45% of its final strength. Drying parts must be supported for some time because their own weight may warp them. Place slabs on a level surface and prop other shapes up as well as possible.

For faster-setting plaster, stir faster or longer, mix with warm water (160° to 180°F), or add an accelerator (potassium sulfate or pulverized set plaster added to the mixing water). You can also make an accelerator by mixing a pound of plaster with a gallon of water and continuing to stir this mixture through its set (half an hour); this will prevent it from hardening. One cup of this mix added during the mixing of 50 pounds of plaster will accelerate set by 5 to 10 minutes. Accel-erators used in excessive amounts can cause efflores-cence, however. If plaster seems to set slower than usual, it may be because it is getting old.

To slow the setting action of the plaster, mix size, vinegar, or cream of tartar into the powdered plaster. Cold water (50° to 60°F) added to the mixing water will also extend the setting time.

To create a harder plaster, immerse the cured object into a strong solution of borax, and gradually heat it. Bone emulsion may also be used, and other packaged hardeners are commercially available. This treatment results in plaster that will be hard enough to polish.

REINFORCING PLASTER. Placing a layer of plaster-impregnated scrim (an open canvas mesh) over a layer of poured plaster will reinforce it. Finish the reinforce-ment by pouring a thin layer of plaster onto the scrim. Another way to reinforce is to mix sisal or hemp fiber into the wet material before it is applied. Make fiber

by cutting hemp rope into short lengths, then untwisting the fiber. Edges of thin slabs may be reinforced with brass or aluminum rods (steel or iron ones are not used because they may rust). If these rods are projected from the slab, they may be used to anchor the finished slab in place against adjacent material.

Reinforcing mesh, tied inside molds with thread, may also be used. Run the thread out of the mold and tie it to the workbench. Complexly curved thin-walled shapes may be built up on a wire armature covered with galvanized screen mesh, copper mesh, buckram, or similar reinforcement materials. A low-expansion plaster should be used with mesh reinforcement. For constructing large curved surfaces, such as topographical contours, use ¾″ lace wire, a refined version of chicken wire, which is easy to work with because it is very soft and malleable.

6-31.
Ghost Parking Lot
SITE Inc., Architects
Modelmaker: SITE
Scale: ½″ = 1′

The wood frame base of this model was covered with cardboard that had been shellacked for waterproofing. Model cars were glued to the base and covered with layers of tissue and plaster. The model was then painted with black, white, and gray latex paint. (*Photograph by SITE*)

CONSTRUCTING PLASTER SLABS. The easiest procedure for building up a slab or strip of plaster is as follows:

1. Cut four pieces of stripwood that are as thick as the intended slab or strip.

2. Assemble the strips in a frame the inside dimensions and thickness of which correspond with the dimensions of the desired plaster shape.

3. Cut several canals from the inside to the outside surface of the wood frame. The excess plaster will flow through these apertures.

4. Lay a sheet of glass on the workbench. Put the wood frame on the glass.

5. Place a mound of mixed plaster in the center of the frame. Allow the plaster to thicken enough so that it will not run too freely when a second piece of glass is put in place.

6. Press a second sheet of glass down on the plaster hill. Squeeze the glass down until it comes in contact with the wood frame.

7. After the plaster has set, remove the top piece of glass and fill any voids.

EXTRUDING PLASTER. Parts can be extruded from wet or dry plaster, and circular dish and cylindrical shapes can be run in it. Complexly shaped assemblies may be built up with parts made from several types of extruding or running operations. Join the parts with fresh plaster, using clay to mask and protect surfaces that have already been finished. Four different types of running operations are described separately below.

1. Plaster may be extruded into many shapes with detail on one side. For instance, a long strip may be run, the cross-section of which resembles the end view of a small home with a sloping roof. Cut this strip into small blocks, each one representing a house for a model of a residential development. The same procedure may be followed with large moldings and cornices, odd-shaped columns, and so on. Thus, for certain shapes, plaster running can be an efficient substitute for plaster casting.

The extruding of plaster is basically the running of a metal template through a mound of wet, stiffish plaster. The template should be made of 16-gauge steel, or 27-gauge half-hard brass or zinc (if the object to be run measures 6″ × 3″ or larger). Use thinner metals on smaller extrusions. File the scraping surface of the template to a bevel (figure 6-32B). After cutting the template with snips or a jeweler's saw mounted on a spiral blade, attach the template to the template board with nails. The cutout in the board should be about ¼″ larger than the cutout in the template (figure 6-32A). The running assembly should be constructed from hard stripwood or lumber of adequate thickness to make it rack-free.

Work on a surface made of a fairly thick piece of wood. Protect it from absorbing water, and from warping, by cementing aluminum foil to it or by giving it several coats of shellac. Anchor the wet plaster to the wood with small lumps of clay or half-driven brads. Grease the wood under the template board, outrigger, and slipper board, but not the surface on which the plaster will rest. The plaster must be of a consistency that is thick enough to hold the shape and yet be moldable. Run the template over the plaster, keeping it in a straight course by pressing it firmly against the guideboard. Add more plaster to any voids that form on the

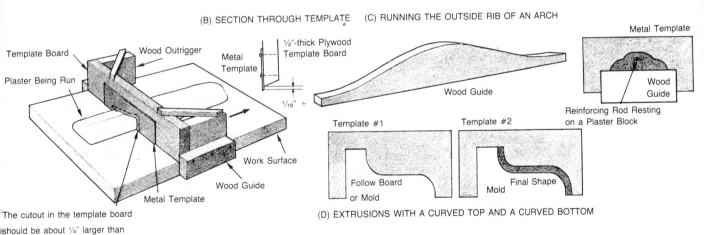

(B) SECTION THROUGH TEMPLATE   (C) RUNNING THE OUTSIDE RIB OF AN ARCH

Template Board
Wood Outrigger
Metal Template
½″-thick Plywood Template Board
Metal Template
Plaster Being Run
1/16″ +
Work Surface
Wood Guide
Metal Template
Wood Guide
Template #1
Follow Board or Mold
Template #2
Mold
Final Shape
Metal Template
Wood Guide
Reinforcing Rod Resting on a Plaster Block

The cutout in the template board should be about ¼″ larger than the cutout in the metal template

(A) RUNNING A LONG EXTRUSION

(D) EXTRUSIONS WITH A CURVED TOP AND A CURVED BOTTOM

6-32.
Running plaster

extrusion. Make additional runs only in one direction. Frequently remove the plaster that has collected on the template or it will scuff and damage the extrusion.

If the plaster hardens before it can be precisely shaped and the template starts to pit and tear it, apply another normal-mix batch of plaster. If the first layer of plaster has hardened into glaze, the second coat will not adhere unless the surface of the first layer is scraped off.

To finish an extrusion, pour a thin mix of plaster over the roughly shaped object and immediately run the template. After the extrusion has dried, give it another pass of the template.

2. You can also run extrusions that have detail on both sides. Do this by running a plaster follow board or mold, which will impart the shape to one side of the extrusion, and then run the final extrusion on top of the follow board (figure 6-32D). After running the follow board, give it several coats of cut shellac to seal it, and a coat of parting agent. Take the template used to run the follow board and retrim it to the dimensions of the top surface of the extrusion.

3. Square or rectangular objects may be extruded, and their ends also run. Mount the wet plaster on a baseboard that conforms in shape to the plan view of the object. Then run template or templates from all sides of the baseboard.

4. To run an extrusion with an arched underside, make a wood guide ramp with the intended curve of the arch. Shellac the ramp and grease all the surfaces that the templates must slide over.

Setups for running patterns with repetitive lateral or vertical undulation may also be created.

TURNING PLASTER. Domes and flat circular objects may be turned on the device shown in figure 6-33A.

Columns and other cylindrical objects may be turned on a homemade lathe, such as the ones in figure 6-33B and C.

DRY-FORMING PLASTER. Plaster can be turned or run when dry as well as when wet. The complete procedure for making a part such as a saucer dome is:

1. Cut a plan-view template of the dome out of cardboard.
2. Cement it to the side of a block of plaster thicker and larger than the desired object.
3. Cut the plaster block to the desired plan shape.
4. Make a running template out of metal, sharpen its cutting surface, and attach it to a back-up sheet of wood.
5. Run the curve, holding the template at a 90° angle to the edge of the disc. If the angle is not held throughout the scraping, the section run will not be even.

Plaster may also be dry turned on a lathe. Wood-turning tools, files, and scraping templates may be used. A drill-press-mounted homemade scraper can rout various shapes into plaster. Solder this scraping template in a slot cut into a brass or steel rod and hold the rod in the chuck of the drill.

JOINING PLASTER. You can cement wet plaster pieces together with cut shellac. The procedure is as follows:

1. Mix one pound of flake-orange shellac with one gallon of grain alcohol.
2. Fill a dish with 1″ of the mixture and set it on fire.
3. Stir while the mixture burns, and when bubbles cover half of the surface of the liquid, snuff out the fire.

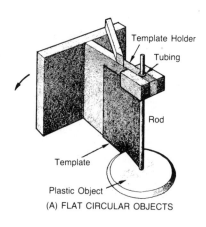

(A) FLAT CIRCULAR OBJECTS

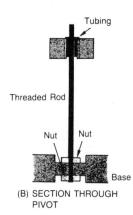

(B) SECTION THROUGH PIVOT

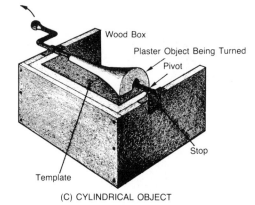

(C) CYLINDRICAL OBJECT

6-33.
Turning plaster

4. Let the mix cool and remove the surface skin.

5. Paint the burnt shellac on the plaster joint that has been primed with several coats of cut shellac. Press the joint together and let it dry one or two days.

Dry plaster parts may be cemented with white glue, casein, cellulose, or contact cements, or they may be welded by wetting the area around the joint and filleting the parts together with fresh plaster. The pores of plaster parts must be closed before the object can be cemented or have a parting agent applied. This is accomplished by painting with one or more thin coats of cut flake-orange shellac diluted in grain alcohol. The mixture must be thin enough to sink into the surface of the material.

To nail plaster, first drill a pilot hole that is 1/16″ smaller than the diameter of the nail. Screws do not work as well as nails in plaster. Use nails that will not rust. The plaster is less likely to crack if the nails are driven into wet plaster. A line of nails will provide a stronger joint if they are driven in a staggered, not a straight, row.

Large plaster parts may be doweled together for added strength. Use brass or aluminum, not wood, dowels, since the moisture in plaster will make the latter swell. Nails with cutoff heads may also be used. To make the dowels invisible, sink them below the plaster surface and fill the ends of the holes with plaster.

To form a right angle intersection with plaster slabs, use the doweling technique or use brass reinforcement rods (figure 6-34A). First, cut the edge of the slab (which is horizontal in this case) so that there will be a 1/16″ crack between it and the vertical slab. Drill or gouge holes in the slabs into which the reinforcements will be inserted. Roughen the plaster around the joint. Assemble the parts and dampen the joint. Fill the crack and reinforcement holes with a wet mix of plaster. When dry, sand the joint smooth.

When *joining wet plaster to wood*, take into account the expansion properties of the materials. If the plaster is even slightly wet when it is joined to the wood, it will cause the wood to expand. When dry, the wood will shrink away from the plaster, causing a crack to form. To prevent this, when pouring plaster on wood, shellac the wood to prevent it (at least partially) from absorbing moisture; then drill holes into the wood and moisten it before pouring the plaster. The plaster will infiltrate the holes and be less likely to separate from the wood. Rubber-cement a layer of aluminum foil to the wood and drive flathead nails partway into the wood before pouring on the plaster. The nails will help anchor the plaster, and the foil will tend to prevent the transfer of moisture from the poured plaster.

To anchor half-dried plaster parts to wood, first drive nails that have had gauze flaps placed under their heads through the plaster and into the wood part. Roughen the plaster area under and around the flap and apply a thin layer of fresh plaster over the flap and nailhead.

Heavy plaster and wood parts may also be attached with bolts (figure 6-34B). First drill a hole into the plaster and set in the bolt. Fill the hole with wet plaster and attach the part to the wood.

When *joining plaster to metal*, drill holes in the metal and allow the poured plaster to infiltrate, or insert screws or bolts in the metal and pour the plaster around the projecting shanks.

PATCHING AND FILLING PLASTER. The pores of plaster parts must be closed before the object can be cemented or have a parting agent applied. This is accomplished by painting with one or more thin coats of cut flake-orange shellac diluted in grain alcohol. The mixture must be thin enough to sink into the surface of the material.

PAINTING PLASTER. Color pigments may be added to the mixing water of the plaster before the plaster powder is introduced. These pigments create a dull finish.

Plaster is sometimes difficult to paint because of its porosity and tendency to form small surface cracks. The prime and sealer coat must cover these irregularities as well as bond together any loose surface particles. The prime coat should be shellac thinned with denatured alcohol (use a 1:1 or 1:2 mix) or wood sanding sealer. You can also soak the plaster in boiled linseed oil to which a little turpentine and dryer have been added. Sand the prime coat with calcium carbide or garnet paper in the range of Nos. 220 to 280, using water as the sanding lubricant. Before priming, release agents must be removed from plaster casts with alcohol.

Paint plaster with tempera. A glossy finish may be obtained with a finish coat of white shellac, clear glaze, clear lacquer, or varnish. See page 172 for a description of other plaster dyes and paints.

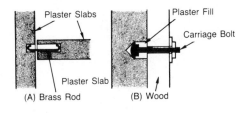

6-34.
Joining plaster slabs

6-35.
Shelter for Battered Women
Rosemary Maurer, Cooper Union School
  of Architecture
Materials: plaster, paper, and cardboard

Plaster casts of different parts of the body
were used to study the proposed building's
various shapes.

6-36.
The plaster forms (see figure 6-35) were
covered with newspaper and paint and incorporated into this preliminary study model.
The walls on either side are laminated layers
of chipboard, held in place with four metal
rods. The base is poured plaster that has
been painted.

6-37.
This is another study model for the Shelter for Battered Women. It measures 4″ × 10″ and was constructed with the plaster forms and wood, cardboard, laminated drawings, and photographs.

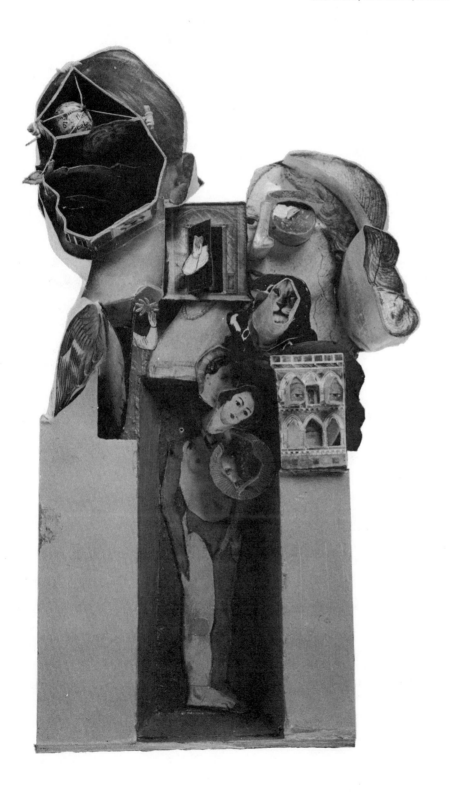

7:Materials: Wood, Metal, Plastics, and Fiberglass

WOOD

Woods with excellent properties for the construction of walls, roofs, and other flat objects include basswood, lime, satin walnut, sycamore, white chestnut, and obechi. They can be easily finished, are warp-free (if they are properly sealed) (figure 7-1), and require only slightly more sophisticated tools than those for balsa. Thin strips may be cut from dry selected pine, birch, spruce, mahogany, beech, basswood, and obechi.

Carved objects may best be made out of obechi; yellow pine, beech, and lime are almost as good. Use beech or sycamore for small, highly detailed, carved objects. Most of these woods can be obtained from lumberyards that specialize in uncommon wood and in stores that sell veneers and inlaying wood. Basswood, spruce, and mahogany are obtainable from mail-order model supply houses.

Basswood

Basswood, the easiest wood (after balsa) to obtain, is soft and easy to carve because of its uniform texture, and it will cut in any direction. Its greater density and strength make it superior to balsa for the construction of beams, columns, mullions, space frames, and furniture legs. Many fairly rough models have been beautifully constructed from unpainted basswood.

CUTTING BASSWOOD. Because basswood is a hardwood, it should be cut with power tools. First cut stock pieces close to the dimensions needed on a power saw. A crosscut blade should be used for cutting against the grain and a ripping blade for cutting with the grain. If the piece is higher than the blade, raise the blade to slightly more than half the height and run the piece through. Then lower the blade and cut the piece on the reverse side.

See the tables in chapter 5 for the various tools and blades to be used with wood.

7-1.
Funerary Model of a Residence Taken from the XI Dynasty
  Tomb of Mehenkwetre, Thebes, Egypt
Scale: approximately 1:20
Dimensions: 84 cm × 42.5 cm × 39.5 cm

This 4,000-year-old model was made entirely of coniferous wood covered with gesso. The base block originally had the same length and width as the outside walls, but it has shrunk with age. Walls were mortised and tenoned to the base and mitered to one another. Doors, windows, and columns were carved. The pool (in the center of the courtyard) was lined with copper sheet, evidently to allow it to be filled with water. Trees were wood covered with gesso; branches, leaves, and fruit were carved separately and doweled together. Cracks were filled with gesso. (*Photograph courtesy of The Metropolitan Museum of Art, Museum Excavations 1919-1920; Rogers Fund supplemented by contribution of Edward S. Harkness*)

Angles can be cut by adjusting the miter gauge to the required angle. Smaller pieces can be sanded down to the angle on a belt sander. Use a jig to keep the piece in the right position and a line drawn on the wood to guide you.

If a number of wood pieces are to be positioned together, buildings on a block, for example, have the grain showing on top and running in the same direction, for the best effect.

BONDING BASSWOOD. Use white glue to bond together pieces of basswood. It may be necessary to glue very large pieces to obtain a width greater than is available in stock. They should be clamped together, with scrap wood protecting the surfaces. Small pieces should also be clamped to make the joining line almost invisible. Very small pieces can be held in place for a few minutes, or taped together.

PAINTING BASSWOOD. The wood should be sanded to a smooth finish and then sealed. You may need to sand it again after a light coat of paint has dried. Build up layers of paint instead of applying one strong coat.

Balsa Wood

Balsa wood is probably the easiest wood to use for modelmaking. Its credits are many, but so are its shortcomings. It is the easiest wood to cut and shape, to bend, and to cement; but it is relatively hard to give balsa a good grain-free finish, and the wood scars on impact. To offset its faults, buy as hard a balsa as can be found, especially if it is to be carved. Avoid using even hard balsa in prominent places and on models that must have a hard, glossy finish.

Balsa's density ranges from 3 to 50 pounds per cubic foot. Often a small plank will have a given density at one end and up to three times that density at the other. If you buy balsa from a mail-order firm that grades the wood, mark samples with these weights and keep them for reference. Use samples of weights that have worked well in the past and try to match them when buying new supplies. Balsa may be used to make entire models, or to construct walls, floors, roofs, partitions, or internal bracings. Blocks of balsa may be carved to form furniture, people, cars, molds, and solid models, and sheet material may be bent into such curved objects as vaults, etc.

CUTTING BALSA WOOD. There are three common ways to cut wood (figure 7-2). Each is described below.

1. *Tangential to the growth rings.* Planks and sheets cut in this way have a broad grain pattern and are flexible across the grain. They are appropriate for making objects that involve cross grain curves (tubes, curved walls, etc.). These parts must be reinforced across the

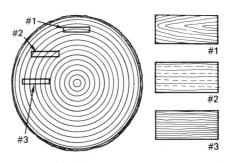

7-2.
Cuts of wood

grain, or the balsa may eventually split along it.

2. *Between the tangential and the radial cuts* (or quartersawed). This is the strongest of the planks. Its grain has tiny golden flake or curl markings.

3. *Radial to the grain.* These planks and sheets have narrow, closely spaced grain and are very stiff. Since this cut of wood is prone to splitting if it is curved, it should be used only for flat objects. When reinforced across the grain, this cut becomes quite strong.

To cut balsa, use a razor or sharp knife, making a series of light strokes rather than a heavy one that might tear the wood if the cut is across the grain. A very fine-tooth saw without set may also be used.

Incidentally, strips of exactly the same length should not be cut from stripwood, because this often results in some length variation. Instead, cut a sheet with a width equal to the length of the strips and then cut the strips from this sheet.

BENDING BALSA WOOD. Only thin sheets may be bent. First try to bend the wood when it is dry. If this does not work, soak it in hot water or steam it over a kettle. Pin and clamp the wood in place on a bending die or male mold. Allow it to dry, then cement it to the rest of the model. To build up very tight curves, use a lamination of thin sheets rather than trying to bend a single thicker plank. These suggestions can also be used with basswood and other woods.

BONDING BALSA WOOD. Balsa wood and small parts made of other woods are best cemented with quick- or slow-drying cellulose cements. White glue may also be used. Use the double-coat technique with cellulose cement to increase the joint's strength up to eightfold (with balsa) over the strength of a single coat. Parts may easily be pinned together until dry. The pinholes can be filled and sanded smooth as part of the sealing and finishing step.

7-3.
Gate Keeper's House to a Suburban Cemetary
Jeffrey W. Kusmick, Architect, New Jersey Institute of
  Technology
Scale: ⅛″ = 1′
Materials: balsa wood, matboard, and H/O scale plastic house kit

The facades and roof came assembled in the plastic house kit. These were cut away with a mat knife to expose the interior. The wood framing members were the most difficult aspect of the model construction. Each stud of the house was hand cut from ¹⁄₃₂″ balsa wood sheets and then individually glued into place. The electrical wiring running through the stud walls was accomplished by using a needle and thread and carefully passing it through each stud. Junction boxes, to which the wiring was connected, were then added. Trees were represented by natural twigs. (*Photograph by Jeffrey W. Kusmick*)

Dowels may be glued into holes by first rounding their ends and by cutting a small air vent groove along the length of the dowel that will be buried in the assembly.

PAINTING BALSA WOOD. When painting balsa, take special care to fill and to even out the grain. For the first coat, use sanding sealer that also acts as a prime coat. Allow it to dry thoroughly, then lightly sand with 0 grade emery paper, working up to 000. One coat of sealer is usually enough for matte paint or small intricate objects; elsewhere, use two or three coats.

Use sanding sealer if intending to paint with a cellulose-base paint. Use shellac as a filler for enamel painting. Sand the shellac with wet abrasive paper.

Scale Lumber, Structural Shapes, and Trim

Many of the formed wood, plastic, or brass shapes that are extremely helpful in the construction of detailed models are commercially available. In addition to these, you may fabricate your own shapes out of laminated

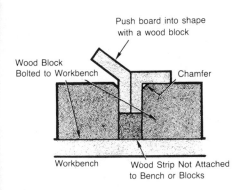

Push board into shape with a wood block

Wood Block
Bolted to Workbench

Chamfer

Workbench

Wood Strip Not Attached to Bench or Blocks

7-4.
Forming structural shapes from wood or board

basswood, bent brass, bent or laminated Bristolboard, and bent or laminated polystyrene sheet. Forming jigs (figure 7-4) can build up almost all shapes, from moldings and angles to double-latticed girders. Almost any shape may be ordered custom-fabricated out of brass, but these pieces are quite expensive, costing up to eight times as much as basswood shapes.

MAKING STRUCTURAL SHAPES. Shapes can be made out of bent Bristolboard, metal, or strips of polystyrene as well as out of wood. Most structural shapes are built up from combinations of cemented or soldered angles and flat plates. *T*s and *Z*s are made from two angles; channels, from two angles and a plate; I-beams and H-beams, from four angles and a plate. If the structural shapes are unsupported, they will warp when subjected to varying temperatures. To prevent this, make them out of acrylic.

Moldings, cornices, and other trims can be fabricated from quarter-rounds and from strips of basswood, or sheets of Bristolboard or polystyrene cut into strips.

CUTTING STRUCTURAL SHAPES. Cut stripwood and shapes in a small miter box using a razor saw (figure 7-5). Cut shapes by inserting stripwood between the webs and flanges to prevent the shape from crumpling under the pressure of the saw or knife. Always use moderate pressure to achieve a cut. Use a zona saw to

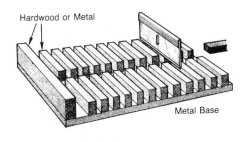

Hardwood or Metal

Metal Base

7-5.
Cutting stripwood to even lengths

cut metal shapes and razor or fine-toothed saws to cut plastic and wood shapes. Wood shapes must often be sanded, preferably with sanding blocks.

Plywood

The warp-resistant quality of plywood makes it useful in several aspects of modelbuilding. Model bases and carrying boxes can be made from ⅛″ to ½″ material. Wood with an outer ply of pine is usually satisfactory. For natural wood finish, see what the local lumberyard offers.

Walls (figures 7-6 and 7-7), roofs, and other flat members of the actual model may also be made from plywood. For these parts, use materials that are ¼″, ³⁄₁₆″, ⅛″, ³⁄₃₂″, ¹⁄₁₆″ or ¹⁄₃₂″ thick.

Avoid using inferior-quality plywood or plywood with unequal laminations that will warp and come apart at the edges, especially along cut lines.

CUTTING PLYWOOD. Cut ³⁄₆₄″ and thinner plywood with a knife; for thicker material, use a fret saw or some equivalent tool. It is not advisable to work the edges of plywood more than necessary. Try, therefore, to make a fine, accurate cut requiring the least possible finishing. It is difficult to cut strips narrower than ¼″ wide in ¹⁄₃₂″-thick plywood, ¾″ wide in ⅜″-thick plywood, and so on, because the plies may separate.

BENDING PLYWOOD. Curves may be bent into up to ⅛″ plywood, but in only one plane. When making tight curves, see that the outside grain of the wood runs perpendicular to the bend. The minimum radius per plywood thickness is 1″ (¹⁄₃₂″), 2″ (¹⁄₁₆″), 6″ (⅛″), and 15″ (¼″). If the grain runs in any other direction, the minimum radius of the bend will be about double. Wetting or steaming will allow a tighter bend.

FINISHING PLYWOOD. Plywood panels of any appreciable size should be supported by frames to prevent warpage. Thin plywood should be cemented with a slow-drying cellulose cement. Locate nails a distance of at least four times the thickness of the sheet from the edges to prevent splitting. Since it is hard to finish plywood smoothly, many coats of sanding sealer are required to close the grain. Panel ends must be filled with plastic wood and sanded smooth. Pine or birch plywood is generally the easiest to finish.

METAL

Sheet metal is not used often in model construction. In simple models the use of metal is usually relegated to the modeling of railing and furniture legs. But from time to time, the need may arise for the high strength-

7-6.
A Secret Base Somewhere in the West (front view), 1981
Ed Kerns
Dimensions: 22″ × 24″ × 24″
Material: carved wood with pencil

The artist began making constructions like this one while waiting for his paintings to dry. Everything is made of wood, except for the glue and nails that secure the pieces together. The base is a wood frame covered with ¼″ plywood. The wall, car, and cactus, also made of plywood, are cut and sanded to shape. The wall is held vertical by wood blocks supporting it at its bottom edge from behind.

7-7.
This is the back view of the model shown in figure 7-6. It is apparent that the plywood floors and stairs were glued to the wall, since the only nails seen in the front view are those that go into the wood blocks at the bottom edge. All the other elements in this scene, including the space shuttle, rockets, tanks, computers, tables, beds, and people, were carved out of hardwood. Detail was drawn in pencil. (*Photographs (figures 7-6 and 7-7) by Eric Pollitzer, courtesy of Rosa Esman Gallery*)

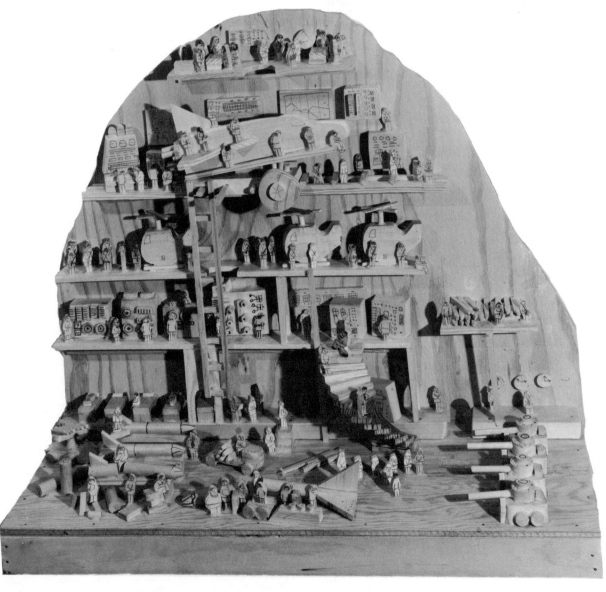

7-8.
The Bliss Doll House
R. Bliss Company

The Bliss Company manufactured this
dollhouse in the late 1800s. It is made out
of wood and covered with paper printed
with such details as shingles and wood
siding, doors, and some of the windows.
Lace curtains can be seen through the
porch and upper story windows. By looking at the seam in the wood on the porch
overhang, you can tell that the left portion
of the house could be swung open to reveal the inside. Unlike later dollhouses,
the back is not open. The wrinkling of the
paper on the side wall could have been
caused by the type of glue used to adhere
it to the wood. More likely, however, it
was caused by exposure to humidity and
temperature changes. (*Collection of the
Newark Museum*)

7-9.
The Zanzabar, 1982
Michael C. McMillen
Dimensions: 50″ × 33″ × 10″
Materials: wood, plaster, and metal

Great effort was taken to create the dilapidated state of the structure
represented here. The weathered effect was achieved by roughly
breaking, chipping, charring, and painting wood stock pieces. Dust
clearly presented no problems. The wood was glued together and
covered with plaster, which was cracked away in certain areas
after it set. It was then painted and smudged with charcoal pencil.
Plaster was also used to make the foundation. Small elements
like the broken chair on the third landing and the broom outside
the front door were made of wood, while the heater, pipes, and
antenna were made out of metal. Rather than sitting on a base,
the construction is attached to the wall with hooks. (*Photograph
by Douglas M. Parker Studio, courtesy of Asher/Faure Gallery*)

7-10.
Two Stories with Porch (for Robert Cobuzio)
Donna Dennis
Dimensions: 126″ × 120.5″ × 85″
Materials: wood and glass

Standing 10′ tall, this construction is larger than a typical model, yet clearly smaller than the house it represents. Basic carpentry and housebuilding construction techniques were used to build the wooden structure. Glass was used for the windows and door. The exterior was painted with acrylic and enamel paint. Cellulose compound was used to represent the stonework along the bottom and side edges. An actual mailbox hangs by the front door. The light on the porch and second story window are incandescent bulb and the vacancy sign is neon. (*Photograph by D. James Dee courtesy of Holly Solomon Gallery*)

o-thickness ratio that only metal provides for the con-truction of mullions, space frames, plaster and plastic crapers, light baffles, hammer-formed domes, vaults, nd other complexly curved thin-wall objects. Metal is ometimes etched with acid to form small-scale facades nd larger-scale railing, as well as wall and floor textures.

METAL LAYOUT. When it becomes difficult to see pen-iled layout lines on metal, use blue layout dope. This hemical, available in hardware stores, should be sprayed n the metal and lines inscribed into it. When the work s finished, the dope may be removed with alcohol.

CUTTING METAL. Reducing stock sheet metal to the esired shape requires either sawing or cutting with nips (tables 7-1 and 7-2).

When using snips, place the top blade on the line of he planned cut to ensure accuracy. Insert the metal s far back between the blades as possible. Blades must e held perpendicular to the metal to prevent a beveled ut. Do not bolt blades together too tightly or they will hew the metal as well as worsen the distortion caused y the shearing action of the cut. Oil the pivot occa-ionally. If a cut requires a great amount of pressure, lamp one of the snip's handles in a vise and use both ands on the other handle.

Regular pattern snips have a straight blade for making traight cuts and for making curved cuts of large radius.

Combination snips, such as duck bill and hawk's bill nips, are for straight or curved cuts.

Aviation snips are for straight or curved cuts. They ave a compound lever action that can cut thicker metal.

When cutting thin material with a saw, make sure hat the blade is fine enough that at least three teeth ome in contact with the work in order to prevent the blade from being damaged. If the thickness of the metal is less than the distance between teeth, the saw will bounce in the cut, tear the metal, and possibly damage the blade. When starting a cut at a sharp corner, hold the saw at a small enough angle to a flat side so that at least three teeth come in contact with the work.

Mount metal in a vise with jaws close to the cutting line to eliminate sawing vibration. While cutting, fre-quently reposition the metal to keep the cut line close to the jaws. To cut thin sheet metal, clamp it between two pieces of wood to give it rigidity. For cutting tubes, first file a notch for the blade to follow.

While in use, the saw should be held parallel to the ground or with its handle slightly elevated. If a blade snaps and the new one, not being worn down, does not fit into the cut, start a new cut on the opposite side of the work and try to make it run into the first.

To cut an opening in sheet metal, drill away as much of the material as possible, then enlarge the hole with a triangular file and finish the corners with a file that has a knife cross seciton. Saw from corner hole to corner hole.

When using *jeweler's, coping,* and *fret saws* to cut metal, be sure to select a blade hard enough to perform the task. A blade meant for wood will also cut aluminum. Never use these saws on hardened steel.

Hack saws can cut plastics and metal. Their replace-able blades have 14 to 32 teeth per inch.

Use high-speed steel blades on hard steel, and low-tungsten steel blades for mild steel, brass, copper, alu-minum, and so forth. Hard blades break more easily than flexible ones do. Coarse blades have a standard alternate set to their teeth. Fine-tooth blades have an undulating set.

The saw's frame can be adjusted to take blades 8″, 10″, or 12″ long. Blades can be adjusted to pointing down or sideways. Teeth should point away from the handle.

ETCHING METAL. Etching is used to cut entire facades or minor details, such as metal railings, safety treads, etc., or to make molds into which objects like railings may be cast. Metal can be etched in low relief (to a depth of about 15/1,000″) from one side, or it may be etched from both sides and cut through completely.

Etching is accomplished by covering the metal sheet with a thin layer of acid-resisting wax and then scribing the desired pattern through the wax with an etching needle. The plate is then etched with acid to the required depth.

DRILLING METAL. Locate the drill hole with a fine center punch. Use a sharp drill and work on a hard surface to prevent a raised rim on the hole. See table 5-6 for drill speeds to use with metal.

Table 7-1. Tools to Cut Sheet Metal of Various Thicknesses

Tool	Brass and Copper	Aluminum	Steel
Snips	Up to ¹⁄₁₆″	Up to ¹⁄₁₆″	Up to ¹⁄₃₂″
Jeweler's, coping, or fret saw	Up to ⅛″	Up to ³⁄₁₆″	Up to ¹⁄₁₆″
Hacksaw	Any thickness	Any thickness	Any thickness

Table 7-2. Blades for Various Metals

Metal	Teeth per Inch	Type
Sheet metal or tubing up to ¹⁄₁₆″	32	Flexible
Sections ¹⁄₁₆″ to ¼″ thick; wire tubing with walls over ¹⁄₁₆″ thick	24	Flexible
Tool steel, brass or bronze sheet, sections ¼″ to 1″ thick	18	Hard
Solid pieces of aluminum, soft steel or copper over 1″ thick	14	Hard

7-11.
Indiana Tower in White River Park
Cesar Pelli & Associates, Architects
Modelmaker: Kenneth Champlin (CP&A)
Scale: $\frac{1}{32}'' = 1'$
Materials: etched brass, lacquer paint, and printer's ink

Each side of the tower was made of three layers of $\frac{12}{1,000}''$ brass laminated together with solder. The mitered edges were hand filed. The pieces were sent out for photographic etching to make the tower openings. They were then assembled by running a bead of solder down the edges. The surfaces were filed smooth. Lacquer paint was used for the main background color. The outline color of the windows is printer's ink applied with a hard vinyl silkscreen roller. The surrounding buildings were made of spray-painted chipboard and wood and the realistic water in the foreground, of very thin acetate. (*Photograph by Kenneth Champlin*)

7-12.
The School
Lauren Ewing
Material: etched metal

Here we see the two buildings of *The School* being constructed by the artist and her assistant, Larry Jasi. The exact dimensions of the roof, wall, and floor pieces were determined by making paper templates. These included edge tabs that could be overlapped at the corners. The paper templates were then given to a machinist who reproduced them in metal. After the metal was cut, the artist covered the templates with a protection solution, except where the window openings would be. An acid solution, which etched through the metal to create the openings, was then applied. The metal pieces were joined in the same way as the paper templates. Figure 7-13 illustrates how the overlapping tabs were screwed together. These screws were countersunk and filed smooth. The two buildings were lacquer sprayed. Small metal shapes with bells in them were placed in each corner roof top—cubes for the boys' building and circles for the girls'.

7-13.
The School (rooftop detail)

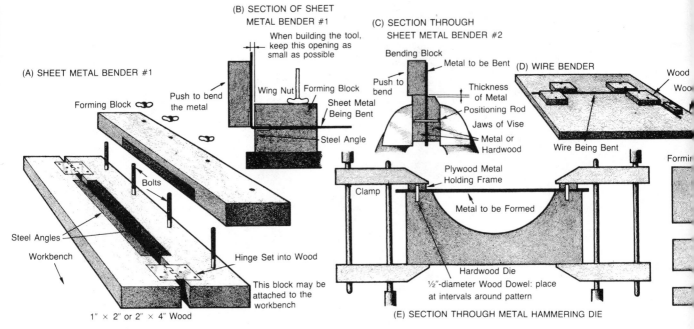

7-14.
Metal forming

BENDING METAL. When a specific radius is required, bend cold or heated wire on a properly sized wooden dowel. Bending a number of identical pieces may warrant a bending jig. For a kink-free bent tube, first insert a snugly fitting wire.

Bending jigs (figure 7-14) should have plywood sheet bases. Bends must be made a few degrees more than the intended final angle because of the wire's tendency to spring back slightly when it is removed from the blocks.

Wire bending dies (figure 7-14D) are held in a vise or screwed to the workbench. They can bend wire of up to ⁵⁄₃₂″ in diameter.

Pliers and *nippers* may be used to grip, bend and nip thin metal objects.

For long bends in sheet metal, some sort of bending tool is needed. To bend medium lengths of lightweight stock, use the tool in figure 7-14C. When bending with hand pressure, use a pushing block the full length of the material. When hammering a bend, move the block from one end of the material to the other and gradually hammer it into shape with light blows.

For really long bends and for bends in heavy metal, construct the tool shown in figure 7-14A and figure 7-14B. To compensate for the tendency of the metal to spring back after pressure is released, bend it slightly more than the desired angle; the forming block should be slightly beveled. Metal of up to 16 gauge can be bent to 90° with these sheet benders.

SHEET METAL FORMING. Metal is easily hammered into almost any curved form. Construct a hardwood female mold and a clamping frame for the metal (figure 7-14E). Carve a set of hardwood (oak or maple) bumping or forming tools in the shapes shown in the illustration. Use annealed (soft) aluminum sheeting of 0.01″ to 0.02″ thickness—it is about the easiest metal to hammer form. Clamp it over the mold and tap it gently into shape. Hammer the bumping tools with a light cellulose-faced mallet; use light blows to depress the metal gradually down into the mold. Make several circuits around the perimeter of the mold and gradually work the tool toward the center, moving it in circles of ever-decreasing diameter. Be careful not to allow the metal to wrinkle too deeply. Use the largest tool to smooth out the wrinkles that will inevitably form. Use the smallest one to shape the tightest curves. When the material has been worked to the bottom of the mold and smoothed out, remove it from the mold. If there are wrinkles on the outside of the shape, return it to the mold and continue hammering. When the shape is finally smooth, trim off the excess metal with shears.

Soldering Metal

Soldering can be one of the most frustrating construction techniques. To solder successfully (figure 7-15), it is absolutely necessary that the soldering iron, flux, and solder be of high quality and meant for the job at hand.

7-15.
New York Convention Center
I. M. Pei & Partners, Architects
Modelmakers: architects' model shop headed by
George Gabriel
Scale: 1/16" = 1'
Materials: brass dowels, Plexiglas, and wood

This is a close-up photograph of the presentation model and shows the entrance to the building. The structural truss work was made with metal rods precisely cut to length and carefully soldered together. The floors, walls, and stairs were made of 1/8" Plexiglas bonded with acrylic solvent, sanded smooth, and lacquer sprayed. The pattern on the floor was first painted a base color, then covered with protective tape that was cut with a mat knife along the lines of the pattern. Alternating sections of the tape were removed and the floor was resprayed with the second color. The tape was then totally removed to reveal the resulting pattern. Hundreds of painted cast metal figures were added to show the great activity expected at the Center. (*Photograph by Nathaniel Lieberman*)

Unlike many other techniques, soldering will not allow the substitution of skill and perseverance for incorrect tools and materials.

Soldering, by definition, is the holding together of metals, using the surface adhesion of the solder as the binder. Unlike welding, where the metals to be joined are fused, the soldered pieces are not melted—only the solder becomes molten. The strength of solder, which is low, diminishes as it ages in a joint that is under stress.

TOOLS AND MATERIALS FOR SOLDERING. Solder comes in two basic types: soft and hard. Soft solder may be melted with matches, electrically heated irons, or blow torches. Hard solder usually requires a torch.

Soft solder is compounded of tin and lead. It melts at low temperatures (under 700°F) and adheres well to copper, brass, tin, and steel. The more tin in the solder,

Table 7-3. Properties of Common Solder Alloys

Type	Ratio of Tin to Lead	Melting Temperature
Slicker solder (tin-lead solder with the lowest melting point)	66/34	356°F
Standard solders	48/52	360°F
	25/75	545°F

Table 7-4. Soldering Irons for Various Types of Work

Iron	Work
Pencil Iron	
6 to 20 watts	Miniature parts, very small bulbs
Iron or Gun	
50 watts	Small parts, electrical connection
60 watts	Medium-size parts
100 watts	Medium-size parts (speed)

the more easily it melts and the less brittle it will be (table 7-3). The more lead that the solder contains, the longer it will remain in its melted state. The ratio of solder metals commonly used in modelmaking ranges from 40 parts tin/60 parts lead to 70/30. Solder comes in bars (for heavy work), ribbon or wire form. Ribbon or wire solder comes in a solid state or cored with flux. There are several solders on the market especially prepared for the soldering of small parts.

Hard (silver) solder, often called braze or filler metal, is an alloy that can contain lead, tin, bismuth, copper, gold, or silver. It has a higher melting temperature and greater strength than soft solder does. Hard solder comes in rod or wire form. Some solders are flux covered. A torch must usually be used to reach the hard solder's melting temperature. The following are some of the available torches and their maximum temperatures; alcohol lamps (2,100°F) and Bunsen burners (1,400°F), both usable only on small joints; propane torches (3,600°F), good for small and medium-size work; acetylene (5,500°F) and oxyacetylene (6,300°F), torches required for heavy and very heavy work. Those silver solders that contain cadmium should be used only in a well-ventilated area, or by a worker wearing a respirator. Prolonged exposure to cadmium fumes can cause illness or death.

Liquid or *cold solders* do a reasonably good job of adhering to metal. They are applied like cement and require no heat. Their disadvantages include shrinkage and the long time they take to dry; make sure you compensate for their contraction. Apply the first coat to a clean surface, let it dry five minutes, then apply a second coat and press the joint together. Allow the solder to dry before loading the joint. Cold solder should be used only where the heat from an iron would damage the work or on assemblies that do not have to be overly strong.

Soldering irons should be properly selected (table 7-4). An inexpensive iron will soon wear out. An iron of the wrong size can overheat, damage the work, and unsolder adjacent joints, or it may not be able to create sufficient heat.

An iron must be matched in size to the work un-

dertaken. It should be able to produce a temperature of about 100°F, above the flow point of the solder.

Irons come with fixed or interchangeable tips; the latter naturally provide greater flexibility. Some irons come with an on-off switch, eliminating the need to disconnect the plug after finishing a job. Rest soldering irons in a holder when they are not in use.

Tinning the soldering iron means the tip of the soldering iron must be tinned or covered with a thin coat of solder. Otherwise oxidation will form and prevent the iron from transmitting its full heat. To tin an iron

1. Sandpaper all oxidation from the tip.
2. Heat it until it starts to darken.
3. Rub it with solder covered with flux or with flux-core solder. An easy way to do this is to melt a little solder in a tin can and dip the iron into it.
4. Wipe off the excess.

If the iron overheats, black scale, or a bluish color will form on the tip. This must be sanded off and the iron retinned. Hooking a thermostat to the iron will prevent this from becoming a frequent occurrence. This device will cut off the electricity when the iron reaches its optimum temperature. Some more expensive irons are constructed with a built-in thermostat.

Soldering torches are used when a very high temperature is needed, as in silver soldering or brazing or when a large area must be heated. For these purposes a torch is better than an iron. Torches may also be used for spot welding of various metals.

Torches vary in type of fuel used, fuel supply, temperatures reached, and kind of tip. Butane and propane are the most common fuels. The fuel supply can be half an hour for small torches and up to two hours for a larger one. Temperatures range from 2,000°F to as high as 5,000°F. Hold small work in position during torch soldering or it may be blown out of line by the flame.

Light-duty welders, which can perform brazing, soldering, metal cutting and soldering, and fusion welding, can reach 11,000°F. Thicker metal may be worked with these welders, but it takes great skill and effort (figure 7-16). Some torches also have interchangeable tips. These an be either soldering-iron-like or ones that produce open flames.

Flux forms an oxidation-preventing film over the joint to be soldered. This is necessary because heated metal rapidly oxidizes, which interferes with the holding ability of the solder.

Flux is usually a rosin or acid compound in paste form. It can be purchased in cans or cored into ribbon or wire solder. Corrosive flux should not be used on electrical connections or on fine parts.

Rosin flux is noncorrosive and nonconductive. It comes in lump or powdered form and may be applied as a powder or dissolved in alcohol and brushed on. Rosin works best on tinned metals, electrical connections, brass, copper, lead and small parts. After being applied to the parts to be soldered, rosin must be heated until it vaporizes into smoke. For fine soldering, dissolve the rosin in alcohol and brush it onto the work. Rosin core

wire solder may be used on tinned metals, brass, or copper.

Zinc chloride flux is corrosive. It must be washed off the finished joint with a solution of soap, washing soda, and water. Store zinc chloride flux in a container that, along with its stopper, is made of plastic or glass. Apply it with a special rubber bristle brush. Zinc chloride should be used on copper, brass, bronze, zinc, and steel. Soldering salts are a crystalline form of zinc chloride and must be dissolved in water before use.

Soldering paste flux is usually zinc chloride mixed with Vaseline, palm oil, or ceresine wax. It is corrosive and is used on the same metals as is zinc chloride.

Tallow and stearine flux is noncorrosive and may be used on copper and lead. It comes in the form of a candle that must be scraped into shavings and applied to the joint.

Muriatic acid flux is extremely corrosive. If this flux

7-16.
Bronze Poet Series V
Ernest Trova
Dimensions: 20½″ × 26″ × 15″
Material: bronze
The architectural details, figures, and furniture in this piece were made from cast and welded bronze. (*Photograph by Al Mozell, courtesy of The Pace Gallery*)

comes in contact with your hands and clothing, wash them immediately, following the instructions on the package. Use at full strength on zinc, steel, stainless steel, brass, copper, and tin.

Stainless steel flux is extremely corrosive and also must be immediately washed off hands and clothing.

SOLDERING TECHNIQUES. Metal must be free of rust, paint, dirt, grease, and oxides for solder to adhere. Clean the joint thoroughly with emery cloth or steel wool. Do not polish the metal, since minute scratches will give the solder a better grip. Clean oily finger prints from the joint with a weak solution of sulfuric acid, then rinse in water.

Do not rely on the solder alone to make the joint strong. Where possible, let the metal do some of the holding work by using interlocking joints. When joining electrical wires, first wind them together. Joints must not move while soldering is in progress. Hold pieces in position with wire, clamps, or magnets. If clamps or magnets tend to conduct heat away from the joint, they must be insulated with newspaper. Allow the iron to heat for about a minute before starting to work.

Apply a thin, uniform coat of flux with a piece of scrap wood or a brush. Never dip the soldering iron into the flux can. To solder a large area (with an iron), tin the surfaces to be joined in the same manner as tinning iron. This is necessary because it is impossible to run the solder under large pieces, as you can under small objects.

Solder tends to flow into fluxed and heated areas. Thus, if flux and heat are properly applied, molten solder can be led to where it is needed. If the solder line is too broad, too much flux was applied or it was spread over too wide an area. Only experience will show how much to use. Large objects may have to be preheated with a torch.

There are three possible explanations for why molten solder may form into balls on the work: the metal does not take that type of solder; the wrong type of flux is being used; or the work is not sufficiently clean.

For mass production of many similar joints, use hardwood positioning jigs. Metal jigs should be avoided because they conduct heat away from the objects being soldered.

To solder with a torch: clean the joint; apply flux; heat the joint until it is hot enough to melt the solder; apply more flux; heat again; and then remove the flame and apply solder to the joint. The metal must be hot enough to cause the solder to flow freely into the joint.

If the area to be soldered is extensive, preheat with a torch or Bunsen burner and then apply the solder with an iron.

Match soldering is an improvised technique that shou be resorted to only when soft soldering electrical co nections or other joints that will not be scrutinized t closely. Place a spliced wire joint on a small sheet aluminum foil, with a piece of tape or wire solder restin on the joint. Hold a match below the joint and hop that the solder will run into the joint.

Soft soldering is used for small and long, narro joints. Hold the iron so that it contacts and heats bot pieces (figure 7-17). Put some solder on the joint, me it, and draw the iron across the joints so that the solde flows between the two members. If very small piece are to be soldered, it may be possible to run the iro along the sturdier of the pieces at a distance of a fractio of an inch from the joint. Heat can thus be conducte to the joint without the danger of the iron's pressur pushing the pieces out of alignment. The procedure called sweat soldering: The solder is melted by hea conduction rather than by direct contact by the iro on solder (figure 7-18).

Do not carry the solder to the work on the iron. Hea the work with a flat side of the iron's tip and place th solder on it so that the solder is melted into the join rather than just being deposited on it in a melted state After completing the joint, wash it clean of flux. Us water on most metals. A solution of soapy water an washing soda is best on bronze and brass.

Silver or *hard soldering* involves the following steps

1. Clean and flux the joints.
2. Clamp together the pieces to be soldered. Sinc brazing metal (hard silver solder) melts into a thi

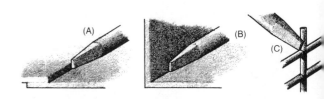

7-17.
Positioning the soldering iron

Tin wires, then set them into position and sweat solder

7-18.
Sweat soldering

quid that will not fill gaps, the parts that form the
int must fit together tightly.

3. Place a length of solder on each joint.

4. Heat the solder slowly in the torch's flame. When
.e flux starts to melt, increase the heat until the solder
elts and flows into the joint. If the brazing metal does
it flow evenly after the joint has been heated to pink-
hite, it may be because the joint is dirty. Once the
lder starts to melt, remove the flame immediately.
o much heat will adversely affect the metal.

5. Clean off the flux. If the object is bronze, brass,
copper, immerse the joint in a 1:50 solution of sulfuric
id and water, then wash it in water. Flux should be
moved from steel with a bath of plain water.

6. Smooth off the joint with emery cloth and a metal
e.

Soldering many joints simultaneously—on a single
ece of work or on several, or when soldering a joint
extensive that it would be impossible to heat it all
once with the iron (situations encountered when fab-
cating a complex metal grille, several metal furniture
gs, railings, and so forth)—involves the following
chnique:

1. Obtain a frying pan (an aluminum pan will do for
ft soldering; otherwise use a steel or stainless steel
e).

2. To prevent ruining the pan, line it with a sheet
f aluminum (or stainless steel if hard soldering is being
erformed). When this sheet becomes marred, it can
e sanded clean.

3. Clean and flux all joints.

4. Apply solder in one of three ways:

   a. Heat each part individually and tin its joint with
lder, then join the parts together in the pan and
heat it; this will cause the joints to sweat together.

   b. Place all parts in the pan, put bits of solder on
ach joint, and then heat the pan; this will cause the
lder to melt.

   c. Assemble all parts in the pan, heat the pan, and
en touch each joint with a length of wire solder.

The pan may be heated with an electric hot plate.
ry to limit, both in duration and intensity, the amount
f heat that is used. To do this, the entire object must
e evenly heated. A tin can with an end removed and
laced over the work will concentrate and more evenly
istribute the heat.

When making several soldered connections that are
ear already-soldered joints on one object, try the fol-
wing technique with soft solder:

1. Position a large piece of metal against the object
being soldered. Place it between the new joint and the
finished connection. The metal will draw the heat from
the object so that it does not attack the old connection.
Beryllium-copper clips, called heat sinks, can be purchased to perform this chore.

2. Keep finished connections wrapped in wet rags.

3. Use a blowtorch; its high temperature, but low
Btu output, may not affect nearby finished joints.

Using silver solder allows objects to be reheated
without affecting already-soldered joints (this cannot
be done with soft-soldered objects). Thus, complicated
jobs can be silver soldered one joint at a time.

Soldering copper is easy. Its melting point is 2,000°F.
Any solder or flux may be used. Most convenient are
acid core solder or all-purpose rosin core electrical solder.
When hard soldering, use braze metal and borax flux.

Soldering bronze and brass is also simple. Their melting points are over 2,000°F. Use any tin-lead solder
and rosin or zinc chloride flux. If using a flame, be
careful not to overheat the metal. After soldering, wash
off the flux with soapy water and washing soda. For
hard soldering, use braze metal and borax flux.

Soldering tin is difficult because of the metal's extremely low melting point (450°F). Use a special tin-
lead-bismuth solder (alloy of wood) and muriatic acid
flux. Tin cans and other tinned iron and steel objects
can be soldered with tin-lead solder and rosin flux.
Brazing is not recommended.

Soldering lead is easy, but its low melting point (621°F)
dictates that a cool iron be kept in motion over the
joint. Use a solder with a low melting point. Oridinary
tallow is the best flux, though rosin may also be used.
Hard soldering may be done with lead solder without
a flux.

Soldering iron and steel requires tin-lead solder, aluminum solder, silver solder, or stainless steel solder,
and aluminum, zinc chloride or muriatic acid flux.

Soldering aluminum is not easy. It has a 1,200°F
melting point. Use aluminum brazing alloy (solder) and
special aluminum flux. Carefully clean the joint and
scrape all aluminum oxide from it. Immediately cover
it with flux (aluminum oxidizes extremely rapidly and
failure to remove the subsequent deposit will make
soldering impossible). An iron that can reach a temperature of at least 500°F must be used. Place the iron
on the joint. When the flux starts to smoke, apply
solder to the iron and let it run into the joint. The same
procedure can be followed with a torch. When soldering
aluminum to another metal, use aluminum solder and
flux.

Soldering stainless steel requires stainless steel solder and flux. Apply the solder when the flux flows freely from the heat of the iron, or use silver solder and flux. Apply the solder when the heat turns the flux to a clear red liquid.

Soldering dissimilar metals involves the use of a solder and a flux that will work on both metals. This is why iron or steel can be soldered satisfactorily only to copper or bronze.

Soldering rods or wires requires large overlaps (figure 7-19) for strong joints. To solder, simply clean the material that is to be joined, apply solder to each piece, place the pieces together, and sweat the joint.

Soldering electrical connections involves the following steps:

1. Remove all insulation and clean the exposed wire.
2. Wind the wire ends together and bend them back.
3. Hold a length of rosin core wire solder to the top of the joint. Apply a moderate amount of heat from a small iron held below the joint. Too much heat will destroy the flux or weaken the wire. Use a 60:40 tin-lead solder.

Soldering sheet metal in which there are to be extensive joints can be accomplished only if a large lap is provided, the joints are tinned, and a lock joint is constructed.

Painting and Finishing Metal

The natural luster of brass, copper, or aluminum may be retained if a coat of clear lacquer or paste wax is regularly applied. Metal that has become dull must be cleaned with a commercial metal polish or cleaner before lacquer or wax is applied. Wipe off all traces of polish or cleaner with a solvent.

To finish metal, file and sand it. See table 4-2 for the types of files to use on various metals. Sand metal with aluminum-oxide paper and roughly polish it with crocus paper.

A microscopic film of oil, greasy fingerprints, soldering flux, metal shavings, or dust on metal can prevent paint from sticking, so first clean the metal thoroughly. Sand off any rust or corrosion, then cleanse with any of the following cleaning agents: naphtha, benzine, carbon tetrachloride, or dilute hydrochloric acid. Commercially prepared cleaners are also available.

Other cleaning methods include: bathing the metal in a warm solution of water and synthetic detergent followed by an application of lacquer thinner that then wiped from the metal; or boiling it in a stron solution of soda water, followed by a rinse in hot wate and then a rinse in acetone or lacquer thinner.

Once the metal is clean, it should be etched to conve its smooth surface into one that will hold paint. Etchin is needed most on brass, aluminum, or die-cast metal The etching solution may be white vinegar mixed int water to the ratio of 1:10 or 1:20 or crystalline etche (purchase this in a hobby store) mixed with water.

To clean soldered assemblies, use a white vinega bath; or boil them in soapy water followed by a scrubbin and then a washing in hot water; or clean them wit either alcohol, lighter fluid, carbon tetrachloride, c printer's naphtha.

Priming is also very important, especially if you inten to paint by brush. Use a lacquer thinner as the prim coat if lacquer is to be used. For oil paints, use a regula metal primer. To make a water-base paint adhere t metal, mix a little glycerin into it. Since this will slov the drying of the paint, bake the painted object at abou 225°F.

Sharp corners and edges are hard to paint, and eve when the paint has finally been placed, it is easily wor off. To prevent this, use several coats.

PLASTICS: GENERAL

Selecting plastics for use in models gets more difficul as new materials become available. Often a modelmake will use a type of plastic simply because he or she like one or two of its characteristics and is accustomed t it. A more scientific analysis of plastics would be ben eficial, as would obtaining a few scrap pieces of eac new type for testing as it is marketed. As new plastic are invented, obtain information about them directl from their manufacturer.

Machining Plastics

Follow general instructions given later in this chapte for power cutting acrylic and for attaching plastic wit screws. Thermosetting plastics—acrylic, acetate, poly styrene, and so on—should be cooled during machining Water, plain or soapy, or a solution of water and water-soluble oil may be used. Subjecting plastic to excessiv heat can cause color change, distortion, or fusing togethe

(A) Hook Splice   (B) Branch Tip    (C) Telegraph Splice    (D) Temporary Splice

7-19.
Splices

7-20.
Universal Theater
Frederick Kiesler, Architect
Dimensions: 72″ × 48″ × 58″

The roof and side walls of this model were made of aluminum hammered to shape on a wooden form. The stepped seating, also out of metal, was bent on a jig. The pieces were soldered and welded together. The base is made of Plexiglas. (*Photograph courtesy of André Emmerich Gallery*)

7-21.
Theater for Mannheim, Germany
Mies van der Rohe, Architect
Modelmakers: members of the
    architect's staff
Scale: ⅛″ = 1′

Roof trusses, mullions, and columns were made from milled brass sections assembled on wooden jigs, soldered together, and then nickelplated to represent stainless steel. Glass walls were represented by gray acrylic. Models with exposed structural shapes may also be constructed out of glued milled basswood. The result, while not as superb as this model, will take much less time. (*Photograph by Hedrich-Blessing*)

7-22.
The Library
Lauren Ewing
Material: metal

The metal pieces of this model were m
chined and constructed in the same way
the artist's *The School,* (figures 7-12 and
13). The metal base was soldered togeth
as was the grid work in the doorways. T
columns are made out of metal pipes a
the opening in the roof is lined with a me
strip bent into shape.

7-23.
The Library
Lauren Ewing
Full-size construction
Materials: wood, pvc pipes

The proposed material for this structure w
metal, as shown in the model in figure 7-2
but it proved too costly to build. This preser
an unusual example of a model built in ti
actual material and the building built in wh
would otherwise be model materials.

Table 7-5. Characteristics of Common Plastics

Characteristic	Acrylic	Nylon	Polystyrene	Acetate
Tensile strength (psi)	8,000–11,000	10,000	5,500–7,000	4,500–8,000
Impact strength (120 D) ft.-lbs./in. notch	0.4–0.05	1.0	0.26–0.6	1.0–3.0
Flexural strength (psi)	12,000–17,000	13,800	8,000–19,000	6,000–10,000
Compressive strength (psi)	11,000–19,000	4,900	11,500–15,200	18,000–25,000
Heat distortion temperature (°F)	150–210	300–360	176–194	130–160

of the cut. Be careful when lubricating plastic with water or a water-and-oil solution. The lubricant must not be allowed to drip into the motor or electrical wiring of the tool, an especially serious problem when working with portable electric drills or small hand motor tools. If it does, a dangerous shock can occur. Be sure to hold the tool above the work or use a flexible shaft attachment.

Sheet Forming Plastics

Sheet thermosetting plastics may be heated to correct warps in the sheet or to form them into complexly curved shapes. Acrylic plastic is easily molded. Regular acetate is difficult to mold into deep shapes and will become white if the temperature is not high enough while it is being stretched. Special acetates made for pressure molding and polystyrene are workable. Each desired shape presents its own problems for determining the forming system to be used. Possible systems are: vacuum forming on male or female molds; forming in a tight-fitting male and female mold; forming on a precise male mold, using a loosely fitting female mold; and forming on a precise male mold, using manual pressure to press the plastic into shape.

Male molds give greater sharpness of detail on the inside surface of the object and are simpler to build than female molds, which create sharpness of detail on the outside surface.

When determining the dimensions of the male mold, take into consideration the thickness of the plastic. The dimensions of the mold plus the thickness of the plastic should equal the desired size of the object.

When forming objects that have curves in two directions, the plastic will have to be stretched: the final object will therefore have a wall thickness less than the thickness of the original sheet.

Molds may be made of cardboard, hard balsa, patternmaker's wood (mahogany, sugar pine, etc.), or plaster. (Balsa will suffice only for molding thin plastic.) To save material, build large hollow molds and reinforce them with internal partitions. If plaster, they should also be reinforced with hemp fiber. Small details may be added to the mold by using wire or Bristolboard. If detail is to be scribed into the plastic, it should be done before the plastic sheet is formed. The mold's finish should be as smooth as possible. Use synthetic resin, high-temperature varnish, or casein paint to close the grain. Shellac or ordinary paints and varnishes will not be able to withstand the heat of the molding process. Covering the mold with a sheet of soft (billiard table), felt, imitation chamois, or suede-covered rubber will also help to impart a smooth finish to the plastic.

HEATING. Plastic sheets may be heated with one or more infrared lamps held about 18″ above the material. A thermometer should be used to gauge the temperature. There are several types of ovens that can be used for this process. An air oven can be constructed by building one or more electric heaters inside a box and hanging the plastic through a slit in the top of the box. A fan placed inside will circulate the heat.

Figure 7-25A shows an electric heater used without a surrounding box. Electric heating elements can be purchased in large drugstores or hardware stores. Two or more elements providing the necessary area of heat should be hooked up in series. An electric kitchen oven may also be used if it is equipped with a heat control. Infrared radiant ovens can be made hot enough to soften plastic of up to ¼″ thickness.

The most important consideration—whatever type of heater you use—is that it heat the plastic uniformly. Allow the heater to warm up before placing the plastic under it. Experiment with a scrap piece to determine the necessary heating period. If the plastic is too rigid to form or if it tears on the mold, it has not been heated enough. If the formed plastic shape cools with a rough or bubbly surface, it has been overheated.

Since plastic, especially thin material, cools rapidly, you must work with it as soon as it is removed from the heater. If the work does not progress quickly enough, it may be necessary to heat the mold as well. First, test any material covering the mold to make sure that it will withstand this heating.

To avoid leaving fingerprints on heated plastic, handle

7-24.
Lincoln West
Kohn Pederson Fox, Architects
Modelmaker: Jeffrey W. Kus-
    mick (KPF)
Scale: $\frac{1}{16}'' = 1'$
Materials: Plexiglas and wood

The curved facade was made of
$\frac{1}{32}''$ Plexiglas, softened in a
kitchen oven and shaped on a
wood mold. When the Plexiglas
hardened, the edges were
trimmed and frosting was
sprayed on the back. The rest
of the building was made of
basswood blocks covered with
Strathmore paper. Columns are
wood dowels. The front of the
base was made out of foam
board. (*Photograph by Jack
Horner*)

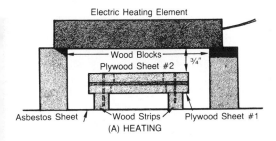

Electric Heating Element

Wood Blocks
Plywood Sheet #2   ³⁄₄″

Asbestos Sheet   Wood Strips   Plywood Sheet #1

(A) HEATING

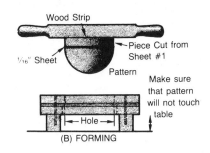

Wood Strip

¹⁄₁₆″ Sheet   Piece Cut from Sheet #1

Pattern

Make sure that pattern will not touch table

Hole

(B) FORMING

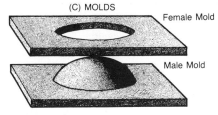

(C) MOLDS

Female Mold

Male Mold

7-25.
Sheet forming plastic

t with clean, soft, cotton gloves. Double-thickness (for heat insulation) cotton gloves are available in many novelty or hardware stores.

Hot plastic may be cut to shape with shears. Once formed, plastic must be allowed to cool evenly or internal strains that can cause crazing (fine cracks) or splitting will develop. A fan may be used to hasten cooling, but should not blow directly on the plastic.

FORMING ON ONE MOLD. There are several ways to avoid making two molds. The heated plastic may be drawn down manually onto a male mold, or the mold may be pressed into plastic held in a frame. Both processes draw the plastic out to roughly half its original thickness. The following is the procedure for forming a shape by pressing the mold into the plastic:

1. Make a male mold out of balsa or hardwood (figure 7-25B).
2. Out of ³⁄₈″ or thicker plywood, cut two sheets the size of the base of the object, with a 1″ to 2″ addition in all directions. Trace the outline of the base of the object onto these sheets.
3. On the first sheet, measure a distance from the outline (traced in Step 2) equal to the thickness of the plastic. Draw a new outline that represents the base of the object plus the thickness of the plastic, and then cut the plywood according to this line.

4. On the second sheet of plywood, measure a small distance from the outline (traced in Step 2). Draw a new outline that represents the base of the object plus this small dimension, and then cut the plywood along this line.

5. Set the two plywood sheets one above the other and drill two or four (if the sheets are large) dowel holes through the sheets. Cement dowels into the first sheet and, when the cement has dried, place the second sheet on the dowels, testing the fit and alignment of the system.

6. Cement the piece of wood cut from the second plywood sheet to the base of the male mold. Trim the plywood piece flush with the sides of the mold.

7. Cement a strip of pine to the underside of the mold assembly. The strip should be of sufficient strength to withstand the pressure of the plastic-forming operation; it should also be long enough to provide a good handgrip.

8. Heat and form the plastic.

It is ready to form when it starts to sag in the heating frame. This will require approximately two seconds of heat for every ¹⁄₁₀₀₀″ thickness of plastic. If the plastic seems hot enough but requires great pressure to form the hole, the first plywood sheet may not be large enough.

If the mold has a complex pattern with several facets, drill small venting holes through each facet up, through, and out of the plywood mold backing.

See figure 7-25C for another setup that requires only one mold. It is not as reliable as the assembly used in figure 7-25A and B, but it is much easier to make.

To form shapes by manually drawing the plastic down onto a male mold, the following procedure should be observed:

1. Heat the plastic.
2. With the aid of an assistant (if necessary), grip all four corners of the plastic and stretch it over the mold. Hold it in place until the material cools or use a soft cloth or thin metal sheet to press the plastic against the pattern.
3. Trim the edges with a hacksaw and file smooth.

FORMING BETWEEN TWO MOLDS. Sheet plastic may be formed between two close-fitting molds (figure 7-26). First make a plaster or wood male mold, then construct the female mold. To allow for the thickness of the plastic,

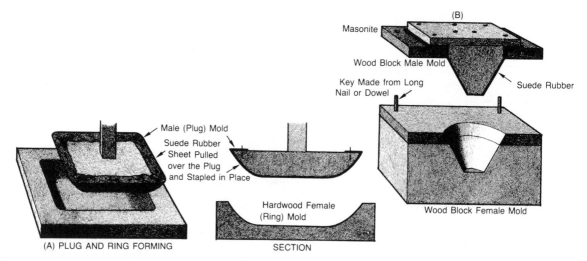

(B)

Masonite

Wood Block Male Mold

Key Made from Long
Nail or Dowel

Suede Rubber

Male (Plug) Mold

Suede Rubber

Sheet Pulled
over the Plug
and Stapled in Place

Hardwood Female
(Ring) Mold

Wood Block Female Mold

(A) PLUG AND RING FORMING

SECTION

7-26.
Sheet forming plastic between two molds

cover the male mold with a sheet of self-adhesive or regular patternmaker's wax, the thickness of which should equal the plastic. If using patternmaker's wax, lacquer the male mold and, while the lacquer is still wet, apply the wax. To cover complicated surfaces, make the wax pliable by softening it for a few minutes in hot water. Cast the female mold in plaster. The molds must be brought into contact with the plastic at a steady speed. If forming is attempted too quickly, the material will tear; if too slowly, the plastic will cool before it is shaped.

VACUUM FORMING. Vacuum forming is a molding system that uses air pressure to force the plastic sheet against a mold or to blow it through a frame. The latter technique limits the variety of shapes (hemispheres, etc.) and the preciseness of their dimensions. Vacuum suction can be obtained from an ordinary vacuum cleaner, an air compressor, or a water-tap-activated aspirator. Figures 7-27 and 7-28 are examples of shapes that may be vacuum-formed.

Vacuum forming against a mold may be done in several ways. Snap-back forming takes advantage of plastic's tendency to return to its original form when heated. To perform this technique, blow the sheet into a dome, introduce a male mold under the blown plastic, and reheat the plastic. When reheated, the plastic will try to drop back to its original sheet form; it will press against the mold, assuming its shape.

You can also construct a pressure chamber that can accomplish various techniques of vacuum forming. Make the pressure head (figure 7-29A) at least 4″ wider in both dimensions than the size of the largest object to be formed. Clamp molds securely at all corners of the

head and along all the sides (figure 7-29B and C). Use a sufficient number of clamps to prevent a pressure leak. This may require as many as four large wood clamps (or twice as many C-clamps) if your pressure head measures about 1′ × 1′. To form the object:

1. Heat the plastic and the female mold. The plastic must be evenly heated or it will blow into an uneven shape.
2. Start the compressor. As air is forced behind the plastic, it will be blown against the mold.
3. When the form is fully blown, idle the compressor so that the air pressure behind the plastic is kept constant.
4. After a few minutes, open the compressor to full pressure for a minute or so. This will compensate for any shrinkage that the plastic may have undergone.
5. When the material has cooled, remove it from the mold, cut off the rim of excess material, and finish its edges.

Figure 7-30 shows another easily fabricated, and more verstile, pressure chamber. Part C shows a section drawing of a female mold (metal in this case) in place. Note that the vacuum hole cut into the mold is at the lowest point of the mold. Part D shows a process called drape forming; this produces an object whose wall thickness is more constant than that produced by the other systems illustrated. Note that the mold has four air holes (two show in the section), each one at a low point in the form. If the object being formed were to have many low points, a vacuum hole below each point would be required.

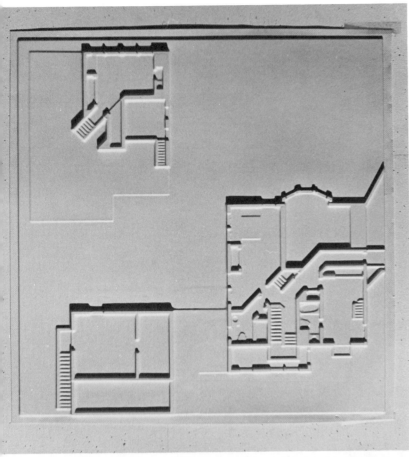

7-27.
House Near New York
Moore Grover Harper, Architects
Modelmaker: William H. Grover, AIA
Scale: ⅛″ = 1′
Material: polystyrene

This is a vacuum-formed plan of a segment of the first floor, done on a vacuum press designed by the architect. The raised plan made it possible for the client, who had lost his sight, to feel the layout of the house.

7-28.
New Jeddah Haj Terminal, Saudi Arabia
Skidmore, Owings & Merrill, Architects
Modelmaker: George Awad
Scale: ¹⁄₁₆″ = 1′
Materials: polystyrene, Plexiglas rods, and
    metal

The tent-shaped roofs were made out of vacuum-formed polystyrene, to which were added the thin strips of polystyrene. They were attached by plastic rings to columns made out of turned plastic rods. Metal wires were strung from the tops of the roofs to the tops of the columns. The buses and cars were made from solid Plexiglas pieces sanded to shape. Figures are cast metal. The base is a wood frame covered with polystyrene. (*Photograph by Jack Horner*)

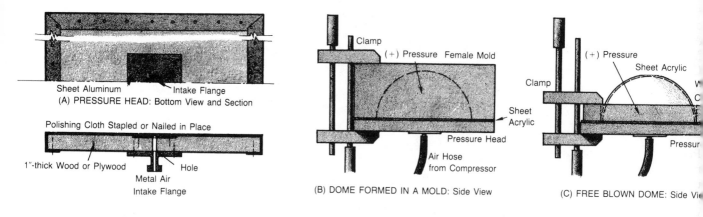

Sheet Aluminum   Intake Flange
(A) PRESSURE HEAD: Bottom View and Section

Polishing Cloth Stapled or Nailed in Place

1"-thick Wood or Plywood   Hole

Metal Air
Intake Flange

Clamp
(+) Pressure Female Mold

Sheet
Acrylic

Pressure Head

Air Hose
from Compressor

(B) DOME FORMED IN A MOLD: Side View

(+) Pressure
Sheet Acrylic

Clamp

Pressure

(C) FREE BLOWN DOME: Side View

7-29.
Vacuum forming plastic

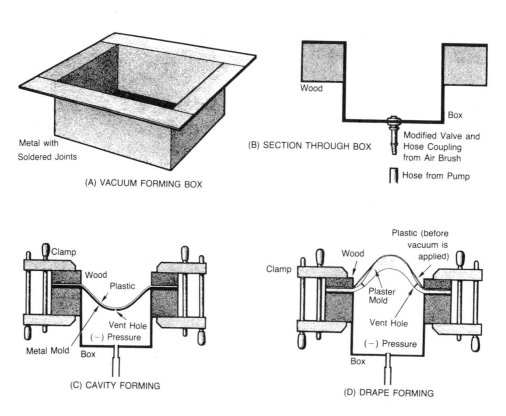

Metal with
Soldered Joints

(A) VACUUM FORMING BOX

Wood   Box

(B) SECTION THROUGH BOX

Modified Valve and
Hose Coupling
from Air Brush

Hose from Pump

Clamp
Wood
Plastic

Vent Hole
(−) Pressure

Metal Mold   Box

(C) CAVITY FORMING

Plastic (before
vacuum is
applied)

Clamp   Wood

Plaster
Mold

Vent Hole

(−) Pressure

Box

(D) DRAPE FORMING

7-30.
Pressure chambers for vacuum forming
plastic

Another version of vacuum molding useful in the forming of shallow objects is blowup vacuum reverse forming. A sheet of hot plastic is draped over the pressure chamber and the compressor is turned on to create positive pressure, billowing the plastic up into a dome. A heated male mold is pressed into the hot plastic dome from its outside and is held there until the plastic cools. Use auxiliary infrared lamps to heat the molds and to keep the plastic soft when working with pressure chambers.

Bonding Plastics

Plastic may be bonded to itself in three ways. First, resin from the plastic (mixed with a hardener) may be used as a cement. Second, solvents that dissolve a thin layer of the plastic may be used to weld the joint together when they evaporate. Third, "body" cements (also used to bond plastics to other materials) may be used to bind objects together by flowing into the irregularities of each surface. Epoxy makes a good body cement for most plastics.

Thick filler cements, with the ability to fill cracks in joints as well as to bond, may be made by mixing chips of a plastic with its solvent. The mixture may then be applied like glue.

Since solvent will mar the finish of the plastic, it must be deposited only where the pieces will be joined. Opaque plastic is easily refinished, but transparent or translucent plastic will often have to be replaced since refinishing clear material is extremely difficult.

Painting Plastics

Be careful to use paint the solvent of which will not craze or dissolve the plastic. If in doubt, experiment with a small piece of scrap.

ACRYLIC PLASTIC

Acrylic was initially used by modelmakers to represent transparent materials. In recent years, however, there has been an almost universal trend among professional modelbuilders to construct most solid block and hollow built-up models entirely out of this type of plastic. This trend away from plywood and hardwood is easily explained when the magnificent and often unique properties of acrylic are studied.

1. It is strong and fairly lightweight.
2. It is almost as workable as wood and, with the correct power tools, it is less costly to fabricate.
3. It may be machined with standard metal or woodworking tools.

4. It may be readily machined to close tolerances (some modelmakers hold to a 0.001″ tolerance).
5. Since it has no grain, it does not require the laborious filing and finishing that wood does.
6. It does not warp with changes in humidity.
7. An extremely fine finish can easily be achieved.
8. It may be formed into three-dimensional shapes by the hot forming of sheet material or by injection-compression molding of its powder.
9. Clear acrylic has light-transmission characteristics comparable to those of optical glass.
10. It can be obtained in transparent or opaque stock, in a variety of colors and in thicknesses of from 1/16″ to 1/4″.
11. The great versatility of acrylic allows it to be used in the making of complete models; in the modeling of columns, mullions, roofs, floors, walls, and partitions; in glazing; in the carving of furniture, lighting fixtures, glassware, and other furnishings; in the making of covers for display cases; in such heat- and pressure-formed objects as domes, vaults, and skylights; and in many other applications.

Acrylic does have a few unfavorable qualities, however.

1. Proper machining requires a shop with extensive power tools.
2. Its soft surface is easily scratched.
3. At extremely low temperatures, acrylic models become fragile. Many have shattered when handled roughly in shipping. To prevent this, hollow built-up models must be constructed on a wood core.

Acrylic is available in sheets as well as blocks, rods, and tubing.

Sheet acrylic must be purchased carefully because fabrication techniques can result in variations of thickness between one end of a sheet and the other. Manufacturers admit that their sheet material may possibly be as far off from nominal as 30% (on 0.03″ thick sheets) to 6% (on 4″ sheets). The above tolerances are for class A commercial grade acrylic; classes B and C commercial grade acrylic are even worse. Premium grade class A sheets run from 20% off (on 0.06″ sheets) to 5% off (on 1″ sheets); classes B and C between premium and commerical grades in accuracy. Not all colors can be obtained in premium sheets.

Sheet acrylic comes with a protective paper cover that should be kept on the material as long as possible and certainly until all shaping and end finishing operations have been completed. The paper can be used for laying out parts by pencil on the sheet, an operation difficult to do on the smooth surface of the uncovered plastic. If the paper is hard to remove, dissolve it with kerosene or hexane. Do not use other solvents or cleaning fluids that might affect the surface of the acrylic. Protective paper that has become wet should be removed from the acrylic before it dries to prevent a residue from forming. Store exposed acrylic on a felt-covered board kept scrupulously clean of shavings, grit, and other objects that might mar the finish of the plastic.

Acrylic, even with its protective paper, must be protected when held in a vise. Make pinewood inserts for the jaws of the vise. Uncovered acrylic must be held in a vise the jaws of which are covered with pinewood plates that have, in turn, been covered with illustration board.

Clear acrylic blocks can be obtained in 5″ to 11″ by 6″. Special sizes are available through manufacturers. *Rods* and *tubing* come in a variety of diameters, as well as in half round and square shapes.

The brand names of acrylic are Lucite (DuPont), Plexiglas (Rohm & Haas), Acrilan (American Viscose), Midlon (Plastex Corporation) and Methaflex (Plax Corporation).

Machining Acrylic

CUTTING. To execute straight cuts by hand, score thin material halfway through the acrylic with several passes of a knife, put the scored line over the edge of the workbench, and snap the material off along the line. To make curved cuts or straight cuts in thicker material, use a fret saw with a fine blade.

Power cutting thin sheets presents some problems. Vibration shocks may be eliminated by clamping the acrylic to a plywood backing. Saw blades must be occasionally cleaned with acetone or trichloroethylene to remove plastic deposits. When cutting several sheets of thin material at once, insert an occasional sheet of oiled paper into the stack to aid in lubrication.

Straight cuts may be made on a 3,400 rpm-powered circular saw with an 8″ to 10″ blade that has alternately set, radially filed teeth. See tables in chapter 5 for the number of teeth and the blade thicknesses to use on various sizes of acrylic. (To find blade specifications to use on material of any thickness, interpolate the two surrounding material sizes given.) Carbide tip blades work better than steel ones. To prevent overheating during sawing, lubricate thick materials with a 10% solution of soluble oil in water and keep it constantly running onto the blade. Lubricate the blade with oil, tallow, or white soap when cutting all thicknesses of material to prevent the protective paper from sticking to, and dulling, the blade.

To make large radial cuts in acrylic sheets or to trim blocks, use a band saw. Blade speeds should be between 3,000 and 4,500 feet per minute if a 3 to 6 tooth per inch blade is used. If an 8 to 22 tooth per inch blade is used, its speed should be 1,000 to 1,500 feet per minute.

The short stroke of the jigsaw blade often does not give the plastic chips a chance to clear the blade. They fall back into the cut and are melted by the continuous friction, causing the plastic behind the blade to weld together. To prevent this, use a skip-tooth blade.

Take into account how much material will be lost because of the saw kerf and sanding. Be careful not to cut acrylic pieces too small, since it is difficult to build up this material to the desired dimension once a mistake has been made. Keep saw blades sharp and free from nicks and burrs. Cutting edges should scrape rather than cut and have no rake to chip the plastic.

If the rate of feed and the speed of the blade is correct, coolants may not be needed. But when using single-speed power tools, or cutting thick material or attempting a smooth cut, some provision must be made to lubricate the blade. A solution of detergent in water or a 10% solution of soluble oil in water may be used. Accurate machining should be attempted only under temperature conditions approximating those that will be encountered by the assembled model.

After a part is machined, it is advisable to heat and then cool it if it will be subject to stress. This process, called annealing, reduces the internal stress that has built up during the cutting and increases the dimensional

7-31.
One New Montgomery
Kaplan/McLaughlin/Diaz, Architects
Modelmaker: Architectural Models
Base: Douglas Symes
Materials: acrylic block with crescent papers

The building was constructed with stacked acrylic blocks cemented with acrylic solvent. Glass areas were masked for spray painting. The skylight atrium was built out of Plexiglas, with mullions represented by tapes. Spandrels are crescent paper cut and taped to the walls. Surrounding buildings were made out of painted Plexiglas. (*Photograph by Douglas Symes*)

7-32.
United Artists Theater, San Francisco
Kaplan/McLaughlin/Diaz, Architects
Modelmaker: architects' staff
Scale: ⅛″ = 1′
Materials: acrylic tubing, Plexiglas, and foam board

This model was used to study the structural elements of the building. The truss work was made out of acrylic tubing, cut to length and cemented together with solvent. The glass walls were represented with clear Plexiglas, to which wooden strips were glued to show the mullions. The core and rest of the building were constructed out of foam board. (*Photograph by Douglas Symes*)

stability of the part. It also prevents crazing when the part is cemented.

DRILLING. Standard twist drill bits with slow spirals and wide polished flutes may be used, but the best results are obtained with repointed standard twist drills. The bit should be reground to a cutting edge with a zero rake angle and an inclined point angle of 55° to 60°. This modification will cause the drill to scrape, rather than to cut, the plastic, allowing the drill to emerge from the acrylic without fracturing it. Larger holes can be cut with hole saws or fly cutters with zero rake angle.

Drill at moderate speeds and with light pressure to avoid fusing the acrylic. Lubricate with mineral oil. The correct combination of drill shape and speed will produce a continuous, equal-width spiral of waste material. When drilling, place a sheet of plywood back-up material under the hole. For holes that are not intended to go through the material, use a drill bit with a 90° point angle. If the hole is over three times as deep as it is wide (but is not meant to go through the material), use a bit with a 120° angle.

Transparent holes may be made by drilling a pilot hole, filling it with wax, and then redrilling the hole to its final diameter.

ROUTING. Acrylic may be routed at a speed of 10,000 to 22,000 rpm (when using 1½″ diameter, two- or three-fluted cutters). If router speed is lower than 10,000 rpm, use a cutter with more flutes, or with a larger diameter, to arrive at the optimum surface speed. Cutters should have a positive rake angle of up to 15°.

TURNING ACRYLIC ON A LATHE. Work with up to 2½″ diameters should be turned at about 700 to 800 rpm. Maintain a surface speed of 500 feet per minute on large work. Feed should be about 0.004 to 0.005 inches per revolution. Use water as a coolant.

Lathe tools should be held at or below the center line of the part being turned. Cutting tools should have a zero or slightly negative rake.

CARVING. Internal carving of acrylic is sometimes used in the preparation of modeled grilles. Carve with a hand tool mounted on a metal cutter. Insert the cutter into the acrylic sheet and then, if required by the pattern, move it sideways, thereby enlarging the hole into the desired shape. The resulting internal patterns may be painted, left clear, or filled with plaster of Paris.

SCRIBING AND INLAYING. Intricate scribing is possible in acrylic. Well-tooled modelmakers can cut such patterns as sidings, horizontal brick courses, etc., with a milling machine or by mounting several circular saw blades (separated by spacers) in circular or radial arm saws. If this equipment is not available, use the scribing techniques for cardboard. Regular acrylic will warp when scored on one side. To prevent this, anneal it (after it has been scored) or use "normalized" acrylic.

Many types of detail (such as mullions and projected brick courses) must be built up from the side of the model. Cut grooves into the acrylic and inlay strips of material in these grooves. Simply bonding a noninlaid strip in the underlay material will not produce a neat bonding line. The strips should usually be acrylic, but if material under 1/16″ in thickness must be used, it is advisable to work with metal.

Engraving may be done with a hand motor tool or with drill press mounting cutters.

Bending and Sheet-Forming Acrylic

Acrylic is a thermoplastic substance whose forming temperature (temperature at which the material becomes soft and pliable) is between 275° and 320°F. Heated acrylic may be bent or sheet formed over dies made of wood, plaster, or other materials. If a mistake is made in heat forming, the plastic may be reheated and placed to cool on a flat surface. This will restore it to its original flat state. Straight bends are made by heating the plastic over a strip heater (obtainable at many plastic distributors) that applies a line of heat. The plastic is then bent along this line. Simple shallow shapes, such as ceiling vaults or hyperbolic paraboloids, may be formed by placing a heated plastic sheet over a form, pulling it down manually, and holding it until the sheet has cooled. Deeply formed shapes, such as domes, are made by stretching the hot plastic over a form and clamping the sheet at its edges until it has cooled. Some shapes are best fabricated by one of the vacuum forming processes. Cold forming may be used only when the radius of curvature is over 180 times the thickness of the plastic sheet; build the plastic into a frame that permanently holds it in the desired curvature.

In general, follow the instructions for the sheet forming of miscellaneous plastics (page 95). Remove the protective paper and heat the plastic to between 250° and 300°F (Plexiglas I-A) or to between 340° and 360°F (Plexiglas II) for 15 minutes. Keep the plastic on a clean, flat, metal surface while it is being heat softened. The plastic should be heated to the upper limit of the heat ranges because it cools rapidly when removed from the oven. Overheating, however, should be avoided since it will mar the high-gloss finish. Material under ¼″ thick may be bent by hand over a male mold or by the other systems listed on page 97. Acrylic shrinks upon cooling; if the model must be accurate, the mold should compensate for this. Shrinkage runs about 1/16″ per foot (in Plexiglas I-A) and 3/32″ per foot (in Plexiglas II).

Use 1/16″ thick acrylic for molding objects that are the size of a fist. Experiment with molds (and vacuum equipment if using that system) to ascertain the proper thickness of material for each object.

For vacuum forming, use a compressor capable of producing at least 50 pounds of pressure (a good paint spray compressor will do). See figures 7-29 and 7-30 for drawings of various pressure chambers that may be constructed for vacuum forming and figure 7-33 for an example of what can be produced with this technique.

Laminating and Bonding Acrylic

Lamination is sometimes required in the preparation of thick sheet-formed shapes if a single thicker sheet cannot be molded. Laminating cement is a compound of 25% (by weight) Plexiglas VS-100 clear molding powder, or acrylic sawdust, and 75% ethylene dichloride cement. Dissolve the powder (or sawdust) in the cement until a syruplike liquid forms. Apply this to the surfaces being joined and clamp them together evenly until dry. Allow one to two days to elapse before attempting to sand the edges.

The acrylic to be joined should be smooth but not polished. Low-viscosity solvent cements cannot fill cracks, so the pieces of the joint must fit together tightly. Masking may be used to confine the solvent to the joint area. This is especially important in the dip application of solvent (figure 7-34A). Cellophane tape may be used, provided it is burnished down so that the solvent has no opportunity to run under it. Another method of masking is to use plasticized gelatin solution. It is made from seven parts (by weight) water, eight and a half parts dry hide glue, and seven and a half parts diethylene glycol or glycerin. Heat the mixture and coat the surfaces to be masked with a thick film. When dry, cut and strip the film from the areas that should be exposed to the solvent.

For strong, clear joints, bond acrylic by welding it with a solvent. (It is a good idea to keep solvent bottles in safety stands made from wood blocks with drilled holes the diameter of the bottles. This can prevent disasters caused by spilled solvent.) Solvent cements that may be used include Rohm and Haas Cement I-

7-33.
Giant Concrete Bowl
Raymond and Rapo. Architects
Modelmaker: Theodore Conrad
Scale: 1/8" = 1'
Material: acrylic

Only a quarter of this presentation was constructed. Its shell concrete roof was vacuum-formed acrylic. Columns, beams, seats, and ramps were also made of acrylic. Cars were stretch formed from acetate that had been softened with acetone. (*Photograph by Robert Damora, courtesy of The Universal Atlas Cement Division, U.S. Steel Corporation*)

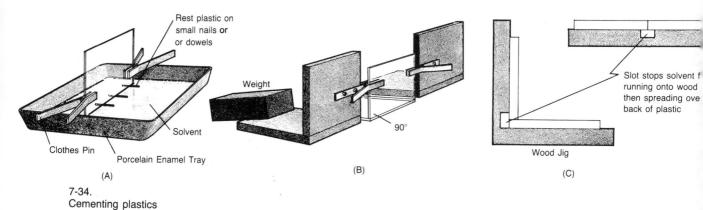

Rest plastic on small nails or or dowels

Clothes Pin

Porcelain Enamel Tray

Solvent

(A)

Weight

90°

(B)

Slot stops solvent f running onto wood then spreading ove back of plastic

Wood Jig

(C)

7-34.
Cementing plastics

A for very strong joints in Plexiglas I-A; Cement II for very strong joints in Plexiglas II or in cementing Plexiglas I-A to II; Cement I-C for joints of somwhat less strength in Plexiglas I-A; and ethylene dichloride for moderately strong, quick-drying joints in Plexiglas I-A. The first two cements require the addition of benzol peroxide (a catalyst) and a stabilizer before use.

Because of the ease with which it can be used, its quick-drying properties, and its strength, ethylene dichloride is the most convenient solvent to use. It sets in half a minute, dries in one hour, and is obtainable at all Plexiglas dealers. It may be applied to small areas with a brush, pipe cleaner, or eye dropper. Apply a light coat to each part, let it dry, apply another coat, and then press the parts together. This produces a low-strength joint.

A filler cement for acrylic can be made out of dichloride and acrylic chips. It takes two minutes to set and two hours to dry.

If, in the process of dissolving the material around the joint, the solvent tends to run over the surface that will be exposed, try dip applying the solvent (figure 7-34A). Place a felt strip in a porcelain enamel tray containing a little solvent. After the felt has blotted the solvent, touch the plastic to the felt.

For the strongest bonding of joints, soak both surfaces to be joined directly in solvent for two to three minutes if ethylene dichloride is to be used. The tray should be filled with just enough solvent to contact the lower edge of the object. Remove the object after two to three minutes (if objects are small and will not be under stress, they may be soaked as little as one-half to one minute) and allow the excess solvent to run off. Join the joint and clamp it together for five minutes (figure 7-34B). For extensive acrylic gluing, use several tray sizes to conserve solvent. For medium-strength joints, soak only one piece; then lightly hold the joint together for about 30 seconds. This allows the solvent to attack the unsoaked piece. Finally, apply full clamping pressure. When truing a 90° corner, use a square whose point is beveled so that it will not come in contact with the solvent line. Wooden jigs can be used to hold the pieces together without spreading the solvent (figure 7-34C). Lap and dado joints can also be made in acrylic to produce the strongest possible joint.

Pressure should be applied evenly and with a force of about 10 pounds per square inch. Too much pressure may cause the softened material around the joint to balloon out. Use clamps—weights, rubberbands, and spring clips—that will move the pieces together as the joint dries and shrinks. If the parts are allowed to separate because of shrinkage, the material around the joint will be drawn out and slight concavities will form. Heat lamps will hasten the drying of the solvent. Parts may be unclamped and handled in a few minutes if they are small and subjected to little load. Allow up to four hours to go by before handling large and heavily loaded parts.

Metal can be joined to acrylic if it is heated and fused to the plastic. To cement acrylic to wood, use ethylene dichloride, methylene chloride or vinyl trichloride.

When using screws to attach acrylic, select those with American standard coarse threads, not sharp V threads. Rounded grooves prevent cracking. Cut threads into the plastic with the standard tapping tools used on brass and copper.

In joining plastic to wood or metal, allow for the difference in lateral thermal expansion by elongating the holes in the part directly below the head of the screw. For any given temperature change, acrylic expands and contracts about ten times as much as wood or metal does. When attaching acrylic, do not tighten screws and bolts excessively or damage will occur to the threads of the plastic.

Filing, Sanding, and Polishing Acrylic

To smooth acrylic edges, use a file or scraper to remove rough cut marks. Finish with several grades of silicon carbide paper or emery paper. Start with wet grade 320 paper mounted on a hard felt or rubber block. Sand with a circular motion, then use, in progression, Nos. 360A, 400A, 500, and 600A. Wash the acrylic between sandings. If a large surface must be sanded, use ashing compounds on a powered buffing wheel. Use wet pumice or fine steel wool to remove any sandpaper scratches that may be left. Powered belt and disc sanders may also be used for sanding. Start with paper in the range of Nos. 60 to 80 to remove cut marks, then follow with finer grades of paper.

Polish by hand or with a powered wheel. Before polishing, peel the protective backing paper of the acrylic away from the edge to be polished. For hand polishing, use a piece of flannel that has been rubbed with buffing tallow or polishing wax. Follow with applications of white emery compound to the flannel and rub. Finally, wipe the plastic with a clean piece of flannel. For wheel polishing, use a powered muslin wheel dressed with tallow and revolving at 1,800 to 2,000 feet per minute. The wheel should be continually moved to prevent melting the plastic. Small acrylic parts and edges may be polished with a few drops of ethylene dichloride solvent. Too much solvent, however, will eat too deeply into the surface and roughen it. Polishing wax may be removed with alcohol. Final buffing is done with a clean, soft imitation chamois or flannel buff. The finished edge will be transparent. If a matte finish is desired, omit the buffing step.

If unpainted acrylic becomes severely scratched, it must be repolished. Hand polishing will suffice if the surface is small, but if it is extensive, power polishing is more practical.

Crazing in Acrylics

Acrylic has the tendency to craze when it is exposed to solvent cements. If the piece is to be painted, crazing does not necessarily have to be prevented, but if the joint is to be left transparent and is in a prominent place on the model, crazing must be precluded by annealing. Besides preventing crazing, annealing strengthens cement joints and increases the dimensional stability of the plastic. Cemented Plexiglas I should be annealed for 24 hours at 122°F after machining and immediately before cementing. Plexiglas II should be annealed for 24 hours at 158°F. Higher temperatures (up to 230°F) reduce the annealing time. To prevent crazing from appearing after cementing, Plexiglas must again be annealed for the same amount of time. Annealing should be done in a forced circulation air oven. After removing the plastic, allow it to cool slowly.

Cleaning and Painting Acrylic

Acrylic must be freed from an accumulation of static electricity before it can be cleaned. Spray it with anti-static aerosol spray or dab the surface with a facial tissue dipped in refined kerosene or hexane. Then remove the kerosene with dry tissues. Dust with a soft cloth or featherduster. If the plastic needs cleaning, use a soft cloth or chamois dipped in water or rubbing alcohol. The plastic may also be cleaned with a weak solution of any household detergent. Since this counteracts static electricity, the need for antistatic spray or kerosene is eliminated. (All these static combatant treatments last for a few months.) Dry the cleaned acrylic with a clean, damp chamois that does not build up a static electrical charge.

Waxing acrylic with commercial automobile paste wax will simplify future cleaning, fill in minor scratches, and help prevent new ones from forming. Rub the wax in with a dry, soft cotton flannel cloth. Deeper scratches must be removed by repolishing the surface, either by hand or by power tool.

Sanding wood sealer or shellac may be used as a prime coat for many paints. Lacquer may cause machined or formed plastic to craze because the solvent of the paint acts on the plastic. Use special acrylic-based lacquers, anneal the plastic, or use a protective primer to prevent this.

Translucent lacquers are also available. These should be spray painted on the reverse side of the plastic. Slow-drying enamels may be used, though they are less satisfactory than lacquers. Acrylic may also be colored with special dyes. A light transparent tint may be made by diluting the dye with water.

CELLULOSE ACETATE

Acetate is used to represent glass and other transparent prototype sheet materials. It may also be used for sheet forming fairly complex objects, such as domes, vaults, and curved furniture.

Cutting and drilling cellulose acetate is similar to working with polystyrene; follow the instructions given for polystyrene on page 108.

To bend and sheet form acetate, soften in a solvent and then mold over a smooth mold. To drape form, soften the acetate in a pan of hot water and form over a male mold.

Using a solvent is the best way to bond acetate to itself. Solvents used include acetone (the fastest acting), methyl cellusolve, and methyl cellusolve acetate. All are obtainable at plastic supply stores. Acetone sets in half a minute and thoroughly dries in fifteen minutes. Clear model dope may also be used as a solvent. Its setting and drying time is similar to that of acetone. Because of their toxicity, all solvents should be used with care.

A filler cement for use on acetate-to-acetate joints may be made from acetone and acetate chips. Cellulose cement can produce a fairly strong joint when it bonds acetate to other materials. Setting time for fairly quick drying cement is one minute and drying time is one-half hour. Extremely strong joints may be made with the very expensive Eastman 910, which can be used between acetate and polystyrene, wood, or metal.

To paint acetate, use a cellulose acetate-base lacquer. Apply only by spray.

POLYSTYRENE

Polystyrene is a material that has gained popularity in model construction. Its attributes include: low cost; the ease with which it can be cut, drilled, scribed, and finished; its lack of grain, and the facility with which it can be bonded and painted. It also is not affected by changes in temperature and humidity. Polystyrene is considered by some to be a replacement for paper and cardboard in the construction of walls, floors, and roofs. Strips of it may be used for mullions or combined into structural shapes. It may be bent in one direction into vaults or curved walls. Domes, complexly curved structures, or curved furniture can be die formed or vacuum draped. Very detailed moldings and mullions may be run from it. It also can be hot cast. Thus, polystyrene is a material of almost unlimited potential.

Polystyrene comes in two types: general-purpose and high-impact. *General-purpose polystyrene* is crystal clear and rigid but brittle. It should not be cut into sections with widths under 0.01″. This type is often used for window glazing. It starts to distort at temperatures above 160°F. Heat-resistant polystyrene, however, can endure high temperatures. *High-impact polystyrene* has three to five times the impact strength of the general-purpose variety. This allows it to be cut into much thinner sections. High-impact polystyrene comes in opaque semigloss colors only. It is more heat resistant than the general-purpose material. Use it for walls and roofs.

Machining Polystyrene

Cut thin polstyrene with shears or a paper cutter. For heavier material use a knife or a single-edge razor and a metal straightedge. Heavy sheets should be scored then broken along the score line. This produces better results than trying to cut all the way through. Saw with a fine toothed blade. Use a razor saw on all but the thickest material, on which you can use a hacksaw. Power tool blades must be continually cooled with oil to keep them from fusing the plastic. If the cut is rough, scrape it smooth with a knife blade or scraper. Clear plastic deposits from blades with solvents. Polystyrene is quite abrasive, and will rapidly dull tools.

When circular sawing, use a hollow-ground combination-type blade. Set the blade so that its top emerges slightly above the surface of the plastic. Feed the material at a rapid rate to prevent fusion by prolonged contact with the hot blade.

When band sawing, use fine-toothed blades at low speeds only. Skip-tooth blades should be used on heavy stock.

Drilling should be done at a low tool speed. Remove the drill from the hole frequently and clear it of plastic fragments. Keep the drill well lubricated with water or oil.

Scribing polystyrene is very easily done. Textures as fine as the grain of wood may be imparted at scales as small as $\frac{1}{4}″ = 1′$. All sorts of wall, floor, and roof textures may be scribed as can trim patterns, bas-reliefs, and cornices. Rivets and similar details may be embossed on thin material. Scribers can be made from nails, old drills or dental picks.

Turn polystyrene at slow speeds. Use tools without back rake, running them along the center line of the work. Improvised tools may be made from knives.

Carve polystyrene with a knife, chisel, or motor-powered burrs and shapers. Burrs and shapers should be frequently cleaned by immersion in gasoline.

Bending Polystyrene

Cold bending may be used to form polystyrene into objects that are gently bent in one direction. To allow it to spring back, bend the plastic on a form that gives it a slightly tighter bend than is desired. When bonding bent shapes, use as little solvent as possible. Too much applied at the site of the bend will cause splitting.

To make sharp bends, evenly heat the polystyrene with a soldering iron or strip heater, being careful not to form blisters. Then bend with hand pressure, using a wood block to form the desired angles. Because polystyrene is a thermosetting plastic, it will return to its original shape if reheated. All sorts of shapes may be made out of thin sheet in the same way as they are made out of Bristolboard, except that, when made of polystyrene, shapes are less susceptible to warping and do not require the finishing that paper demands.

Sheet-Forming Polystyrene

Polystyrene may be heated until it becomes soft (at about 200°F) and then pressed by a vacuum against a metal die. Use the same procedure as for vacuum forming acrylic (page 104), but pressure of only 20 to 25 pounds is required. Small vacuum-forming sets on the market have a capacity to form shapes of up to 3″ × 3½″, thus they are useful for making such diverse objects as patterned spandrel panels, bucket chairs, lighting globes, etc., in most scales. The vacuum is created by a hand-operated pump.

For die forming, carve a male pattern and cover it with the same thickness of patternmaker's sheet wax as the plastic sheet to be used. This will build up the correct separation between the two molds. Cast a female mold on this assembly. Place a sheet of heated plastic between the molds and bring them together.

Drape-Forming Polystyrene

For drape forming, stretch a heated sheet of plastic over a male pattern. The sheet should be hand held or tacked to a frame and kept in place until the plastic cools. Thin polystyrene shapes may tend to distort under their own weight. In certain instances, they may be stiffened by being filled with clay.

Small (up to 2″ × 2″) objects that are not too deep may be "cast" in carved metal or cast epoxy female molds. Squeeze the heated polystyrene into the mold; use a metal back-up plate and a vise, or press, to hold it firmly in place until it has cooled. True casting of polystyrene is sometimes used by professionals to make complexly shaped mullions, but many of them farm out this type of work to plastic fabricators.

Laminating and Bonding Polystyrene

Spread the solvent on one sheet with an eye dropper. Put the other ply in place and clamp both pieces together with weights evenly distributed over the entire surface. The speed at which the solvent will dry is determined by the width of the coated surface.

Polystyrene can be bonded to itself with any of several solvents. The three most common ones are: methylethylketone (mek, fastest drying); perchlorethylene toluene; and amyl benzene (slowest drying). These come in squeeze tubes and are sold in hobby stores. Amyl benzene comes in bottles with brush applicators. Be careful when using tubes since the slightest squeeze will send the solvent cascading over the work. Assemble the parts, then apply the solvent, which will be drawn into the joint by capillary action. Take care that fingers, clamps, or jigs are not in contact with the joint line or they will divert the solvent out of the joint and over the plastic. Apply just enough solvent to do the job. Too much will extend the drying time and will warp thin stock. If the solvent partially eats through the stock, the dried area will shrink and form a concavity on the outside surface of the plastic. Properly executed joints fuse together rapidly, but full strength is not reached for some time.

Since solvents are toxic, avoid prolonged skin contact and breathing their fumes.

To bond polystyrene to metal, use epoxy resin. To bond polystyrene to paper, use contact cement. To bond it to wood, metal, and other materials, use high-viscosity polystyrene cement, clamping the joint until it dries. If polystyrene must be fastened with screws, use a two-flute tap to cut the hole, lubricating it with light machine oil. Use only screws with coarse threads to minimize stripping. Wire parts can be fixed to polystyrene if the wire is held against the plastic and its other end is heated with a soldering iron. As the plastic starts to soften, press the wire into it.

Filling and Filing Polystyrene

Surface irregularities may be filled with automobile metal filler or polystyrene body putty (obtainable in hobby stores). Both are puttylike substances that are easily worked. Use ketone to clean automobile filler from the applicator. Slightly roughen the surface of the polystyrene with No. 400 abrasive paper before applying fillers. When building up large areas, apply several coats, allowing each one to dry before putting on the next. Final sanding can be done with No. 500 or 600 wet abrasive paper. To file, use a fairly coarse bastard-cut file. Clean it frequently on a file card.

Cleaning and Painting Polystyrene

Polystyrene may be cleaned with a 2% solution of household detergent in water. This will also help eliminate some of the electric charge that attracts dust to this material.

For painting, use the plastic paints available in hobby stores. Spray apply these paints, thinning them with ketone to make them stick more readily to the plastic.

Lacquer paint may be used on top of a prime coat. After the primer dries, lightly sand it down and rub it with a clean, soft cloth. "Dry" spray the lacquer since a wet spray or a brush application may detrimentally affect the plastic.

Enamel may be used also on polystyrene. Spray it on, allowing one-half hour drying time between coats. Dry rub with a rubbing compound to remove dust, hair, and other minor imperfections.

Casein and oil-base paints also work well with polystyrene. Water-base paints should be mixed with a small amount of acetone to make them adhere to the plastic.

FOAM PLASTIC

This superlight, easy-to-cut material has some application in modelmaking. It is used to make rough massing models as well as rough- and fine-ground contours. Foam may also be used in the carving of female patterns used in casting. This material comes in planks measuring up to 4′ × 8′, with thicknesses of ½″ to 17″.

Cutting Foam Plastic

A band saw with a fine-tooth or scalloped-edge blade can be used but leaves a rough finish. A special electric-powered hot wire cutting machine leaves a semirough

7-35.
Orchestra Podium, Interban, Germany
Frei Otto and Ewald Bubner, Architects
Modelmakers: members of the architects'
    staff
Scale: ½″ = 1′
Material: rubber sheet

The tent fabric was represented by a rubber sheet on which a grid had been drawn. A hanging attachment held a gauge that measured the height of the tent as it stood unloaded or with weights on it to represent wind or water loads. The plumb line attachment was connected to a pantograph machine which, when the plumb line was traced across the model, drew a contour map on the membrane. This drawing was used to aid the designer in laying out the canvas panels from which the final structure was built.

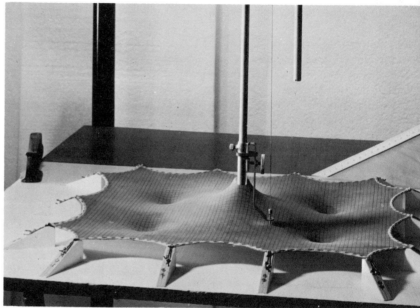

cut, the surface air spaces of which are fused closed. A wire cutter can be made by stretching a 0.004″ chromlux wire on a wood bow. The heat of the wire is governed with a rheostat. Accurate cuts are made with the aid of a plywood template.

Hand sawing may be performed with a coping or any fine-toothed saw. Foam plastics may be milled (on high-speed routers, drill presses, or milling machines) and may be lathe turned (if a sharp thin tool is used with a slicing, not a cutting, action). Cut rough contours with a soldering iron (to melt the plastic). The resulting rough surface may be finished smooth with an application of plaster. Use an electric pin to carve foam plastic. Foam may be sanded on power sanders or by hand. Its surface can be made more durable with a coat of sprayed paint or an application of plaster or epoxy.

Bonding Foam Plastic

Bond foam plastic to itself and to other materials with white or contact cement. Common adhesives tend to dissolve the foam immediately or over a period of time. Many of the jointing details of woodworking are usable in foam plastic construction. Planks may be dovetailed, rabbeted, and joined by plugs.

OTHER PLASTICS

Almost every year, new plastics are introduced in modelmaking. Two examples are vinyl plastic and nylon. *Vinyl plastic* is valuable for vacuum forming because of its ability to conform to highly detailed small molds. It has also been used for the construction of walls, doors, and other flat assemblies. *Nylon* is very easy to cut, machine, punch, and cement. Perhaps its best characteristic is that, unlike acrylic, it may be cold punched.

FIBERGLASS

If you need a complexly curved thin wall object of maximum strength, a large dome or shell structure, for example, the decision may be to make it out of fiberglass. This technique requires four materials: glass cloth, resin, catalyst, and hardener. The resin (with its catalyst and hardener) may also be used alone to cast thick sections. Casting resins are discussed in detail in chapter 8.

Fiberglass cloth is composed of drawn filaments of glass. Various manufacturers sell several types of cloth and fiber.

Plain weave fiberglass cloth has thread that is alternately crossed, making it the least pliable but dimensionally the most stable cloth. It comes in 0.013″, 0.022″, and 0.055″ thicknesses. Thick tapes are also available in 1½″, 3″, 6″ and 12″ widths.

Leno weave fiberglass cloth has threads that lock together to prevent shifting. It comes in 0.029″ thickness.

Most cloth comes in 38″ or 44½″ widths. Cloth may have different types of surface finishes to improve its draping characteristics or its adherence to the resin. Cloth with a silane finish should never be used with polyester resins. Some companies make cloth that is as thin as 0.002″, as well as a thin cloth called surfacing mat that is used where a high finish is required.

Milled fibers are used to make a puttylike mix to fill sharp corners of a mold.

Resins are available with several bases. Polyester resin is probably of greatest use to the modelmaker. Polyester resins include: artist resin, which is usually used with fiberglass, cures rapidly, is of medium viscosity and becomes clear and rigid upon curing; and flexible resin, which is for laminating objects with fiberglass, has medium-fast curing and a medium viscosity, and becomes clear and flexible upon curing.

Some form of catalyst is usually already mixed into the resin. Because of this, only the addition of the hardener is required to produce a workable mix. Overmixing will result in a shortened pot life.

Apply resin by brush or squeegee. Setting time, running about one or two hours, is determined by the percentage of hardener in the mix and by room temperature. It is usually good practice, no matter what type of resin is being used, to try for a lamination that is about half resin and half cloth.

After attaining its initial set, the object may be removed from the mold and allowed to cure fully at room temperature for several days. Curing time is affected by temperature and humidity—the higher the temperature, the faster the cure. Resin that comes in contact with the mold (or work surface) will harden, but the side that is exposed to air may not. To ensure hardening, wax may be added to the mix. Many brands of resin are manufactured with wax already included. If a surface is still tacky when it has cured, sand it down to solid material.

Resins have shelf lives ranging from a few months to about a year. Refrigerating them will increase this by two or three times.

Certain dyes can be mixed into the resin to impart an integral color. Filler mixed into the resin will turn the usually translucent fiberglass opaque. Some companies make their coloring agents in the form of powders. These should be mixed into the resin before the hardener is applied.

Separators, or release agents, are placed on a mold so that it is easy to remove the fiberglass lamination.

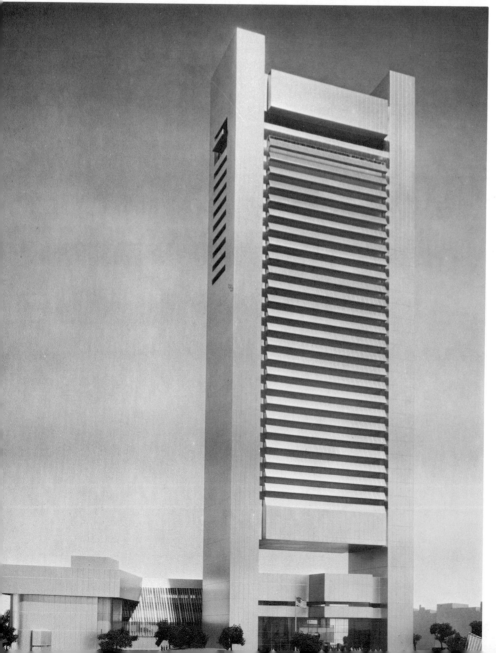

7-36.
Vanguard Office Complex, San Francisco
Hellmuth, Obata & Kassabaum, Inc.,
    Architects
Modelmaker: Richard Warner
Scale: ½″ = 1′
Material: Styrofoam

This study model shows a precast concret
panel system. It was made out of Styrofoam
blocks cut with a hot wire and glued togethe
(*Photograph by Peter Henricks*)

7-37.
Federal Reserve Bank, Boston
Hugh Stubbins & Associates, Architects
Modelmakers: F. W. Dixon Company
    (Walter Palladino)
Scale: ¹⁄₁₆″ = 1′
Material: acrylic plastic

This presentation model was made entirely
from acrylic. Walls were scored after being
cut to size. Edges were mitered for precise
corners and joined with acrylic solvent. The
model was then lacquer sprayed, with areas
to be left clear masked out with tape. The
base is contoured of high-density polyurethane foam with epoxy resin coating and
painted. (*Photograph by Robert D. Harvey
Studio*)

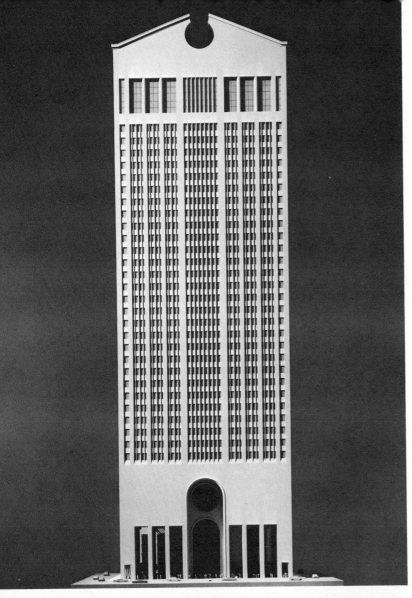

7-38.
AT&T Corporate Headquarters Building, New York
Johnson/Burgee, Architects; Simmons Architects, Associates
Modelmakers; architects' model shop headed by Joseph Santeramo
Scale: $1/16'' = 1'$
Material: Plexiglas

The facades are built out of three layers of Plexiglas to show the relief in the structure of the exterior. The glass was back painted with lacquer. Vertical bands were represented with $1/8''$ Plexiglas and horizontal spandrels with $1/16''$. The archway in the lobby was made out of a piece of plastic kerfed in sections and bent to shape. Figures and cars are cast metal. (*Photograph by Hedrich-Blessing*)

7-39.
Best Products Company
Urban Innovations Group, Architects
Scale: $1/8'' = 1'$
Material: mirrored Plexiglas

The facades of this project were built at varying angles. They were made out of various pieces of mirrored Plexiglas, cut to size and mitered at different angles to meet precisely at the corner. (*Photograph by Marvin Rand*)

7-40.
333 Wacker Drive, Chicago
Kohn Pederson Fox, Architects
Modelmaker: George Awad
Scale: 1/16″ = 1′
Material: mirrored Plexiglas

The Plexiglas wall sections of this model were scored with a cutter. All edges were mitered for clean, crisp-looking corners. T[ ] elevated train tracks were made of basswood strips. (Photogra[ ] by Jack Horner)

7-41.
Irving Trust Operations Center, New York
Skidmore, Owings & Merrill, Architects
Modelmakers: SOM model studio
Scale: 1/8″ = 1′
Materials: Plexiglas and wood

This began as a working study model but was later used for presentation. The walls were made of 1/8″ Plexiglas, with backpainted spandrels. Solar tint paper was applied to the inside of the walls to represent reflective glass. Chartpak tape mullions were shown on the exterior. The rounded corners were cut from plastic tubing, as was the core which runs through the entire height of the building as one piece. The floor slabs were cut from 1/2″ foam board and stacked on basswood columns. The middle section of the building was entirely open, so the floors were connected across the space with bridges made out of painted Plexiglas. The walls were cemented along the edges with acrylic solvent and glued with Sobo to the floor slabs behind the white spandrels. Because Sobo is a strong but pliable glue, when it was later decided to remove the walls to add to and photograph the interior, they were carefully pulled free of the slabs. Seating and tables are shown on the cafeteria level. This furniture was made out of Plexiglas rods, cut and sanded to length. Carpeting was represented by painted paper. Because the columns were glued down, the paper had to be cut and placed around each column. The entire structure above the cafeteria is an open truss system made of basswood sections, mitered and assembled with glue. The truss work can be completely lifted out of the model. All the pieces of this model were done quickly, in assembly-line fashion. Because it was disassembled often, it will not last as a final presentation model for any great length of time. But because each part of the model was cut precisely, it has withstood the constant changes, and in photographs will always appear as a well-crafted model. (Photograph by Wolfgang Hoyt/ESTO)

7-42.
Museum of Modern Art
Cesar Pelli & Associates, Architects
Modelmaker: Kenneth Champlin (CP&A)
Scale: 1/16″ = 1′
Materials: cardboard and Plexiglas

The inner structure of this model was made as a chipboard box covered with black pantone paper. The exterior was made out of clear 1/32″ Plexiglas with backpainted spandrels. Mullions were scored and filled with paint. The black paper is seen through the Plexiglas. Surrounding buildings and the base were built with matboard, which was then spray painted. (*Photograph by Kenneth Champlin*)

7-43.
Whig Hall Student Center, Princeton
    University
Gwathmey Siegel & Associates, Architects
Modelmaker: George Raustiala
Scale: 1/8″ = 1′
Material: Plexiglas

The entire model, except for the railing, was made out of Plexiglas. The curved walls are Plexiglas tubing, cut down to half or quarter round. The model was assembled and sanded smooth, then spray painted. (*Photograph by Louis Checkman*)

Table 7-6. Separators Used between Polyester Resin and Various Molds or Patterns

Mold or Pattern	Separator
Wood, Plaster	Separator may not be needed Wax polish Oil spray
Low-melting-point metal	Separator may not be needed Oil or graphite

Table 7-6 lists the separators to be used with polyester resins.

Working with Fiberglass and Resins

Since resins have great toxicity, it is important that the work area be properly ventilated and that prolonged contact between resins and skin be avoided. Never allow them to come in contact with eyes. Wash hands and tools with hot water and borax or household detergent. Wear protective gloves or use hand creams whenever possible.

If moisture gets into the hardener or resin, the plastic will be cloudy on hardening. Do not cast objects to thicknesses over ¾″ because heat caused by the chemical action may ruin them. Delamination of a fiberglass object is usually due to poor cloth wetting, air entrapment, interruption of the laminating process, or use of only partially gelled resin.

Porosity is caused by beating resin during mixing, the use of porous molds or patterns, the use of chilled materials, or the presence of moisture.

APPLYING A FIBERGLASS AND POLYESTER RESIN LAMINATION TO A MOLD OR PATTERN. Follow this procedure:

1. Make the mold or pattern from which the lamination will take its shape out of hard balsa, hardwood, or plaster. Sand the mold to a satin finish, using shellac to fill its grain. The side of the fiberglass or resin that touches the mold will have a smooth finish, provided the mold is extremely smooth. The other side will have to be power sanded for a good finish. Because of this, you may decide to mold a dome or other similar shape in a female mold to get the finished side on the outside.

Note that details may be cast into the side of the obje that faces the mold.

2. Treat the mold with one of the separators list in table 7-6.

3. Brush a coat of resin on the mold and allow it gel.

4. Brush on a second coat of resin and, while it still wet, place the first layer of glass cloth, coated wi resin, on it and press down. To eliminate wrinkles cloth that is curved in two directions, cut slits into t cloth. Make sure that no air bubbles are trapped ar that no wrinkles are allowed to form. Avoid bubbl by wetting all materials, including the cloth, and a embedded material, with resin prior to placing the Work out any trapped bubbles by stippling them wi the resin-applying brush. If the object must be uniform thick, the pieces of cloth making up one ply must laid with butt joints. If greater strength is desired, ar the object can have a varying thickness, use lap joint

5. Apply strips of chopped strand mats along th edges of the object to strengthen them. In genera only one layer of glass cloth will be needed on object up to 2′ large, especially if edges and other potentiall weak points are bolstered with strand mat.

6. When the resin has set, the object may be remove from the mold. Trim the edges of fiberglass into shap with shears.

7. If the object has been made on a female mold examine its outside surface for air bubble holes and fi them with resin.

8. Sandpaper the surface.

A system for forming fiberglass objects with wall of varying thickness is shown in figure 7-44. To determin how much any part of the object must be built up insert metal rods coated with a release agent into th pattern, allowing them to protrude a distance equal t the desired thickness at any given point. Then buil up the thinner portions of the object with additiona plies of cloth or mat. After the resin starts to harden remove the rods through the bottom of the mold. The same general system may be used with Celastic and plaster-impregnated cloth.

LAMINATING WITH EPOXY RESIN AND FIBERGLASS. This involves the following steps:

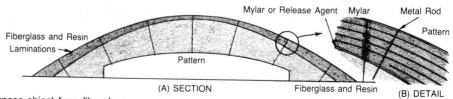

7-44.
Laminating a variable-thickness object from fiberglass

1. Apply a surface coat of resin to the mold with a
int brush. Do not brush it on—let it flow freely. Dab
on those areas whose fine detail must be reproduced.
ne coat should be $1/32''$ to $1/16''$ thick. Allow it to become
cky.

2. Fill sharp corners and projections with a mix of
e laminating resin and its hardener; then add glass
ers.

3. Apply the glass cloth plies. Either three or four
yers of lightweight cloth or one layer of heavyweight
oth will be needed to make a $1/16''$ thick lamination.

FORMING OBJECTS WITH TWO SMOOTH SIDES OUT OF
MINATIONS OF FIBERGLASS AND RESIN. Make a female
old and press down upon a lamination that has been
aced on a male mold. The pressure created will also
cilitate the forming of tighter curves.

Medium-sized objects with two smooth sides may be
rmed if these steps are followed:

1. Make a smoothly finished male mold and cover it
ith a release agent. Screw the mold to the workbench
ith its smallest end facing up.

2. Cut enough fibeglass cloth to go around the mold
vo or three times. Attach it to the mold as shown in
gure 7-45C. Use strands of fiberglass to tie the cloth
place. Cut tabs in the top of the fiberglass, trimming
nem so that when they are folded over the mold they
ill cover the end without overlap.

3. Brush on a sufficient quantity of resin so that it
oaks through all the layers of fiberglass.

4. Partially inflate a toy balloon and turn it upside
own over the mold. Press it down on the mold as far
s possible, then slowly let it deflate while continuing

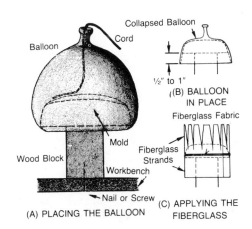

Balloon

Cord

Collapsed Balloon

$1/2''$ to $1''$

(B) BALLOON
IN PLACE

Fiberglass Fabric

Mold

Fiberglass
Strands

Wood Block

Workbench

Nail or Screw

(A) PLACING THE BALLOON

(C) APPLYING THE
FIBERGLASS

7-45.
Casting fiberglass objects with two smooth sides

to push it down (figure 7-45A). It is important that the
balloon be of the correct size and that it be made of
thick, high-quality rubber.

5. By the time all the air has escaped, the balloon
should be in the position shown in figure 7-45B. Cut
the neck off the balloon and turn the balloon inside out
on the mold. Do not worry if the rubber tears a bit
around the cut. The tightly fitting rubber will form a
smooth outer side to the fiberglass and will press it
firmly against the mold.

6. After the resin has hardened for about three hours,
remove the balloon and work the fiberglass off the mold.
Cut the excess fiber off the bottom of the object, and
file and sand it smooth.

EMBEDDING OBJECTS IN A FIBERGLASS AND RESIN
LAMINATION. Embedding may be used to make weak
sheet materials rigid. It may also be used to construct
models or screens, stained glass, fused glass murals,
and similar objects. Use a fiberglass cloth that can be
made transparent. Follow this procedure, working on
a flat surface that has been covered with glass:

1. Coat a sufficiently large area of the covered surface
with a transparent resin.

2. Place a layer of fiberglass on the resin.

3. Apply a second layer of resin, carefully working
out all air bubbles from the lamination.

4. Position the object that is to be embedded, taking
care that no air is trapped under it.

5. Lay down a second piece of fiberglass on the object
and soak it with more resin.

6. Place a sheet of common plastic wrap on top of
the sandwich and squeegee out all trapped air.

7. While the panel is still tacky, trim its edges.

8. When it has dried, remove the pieces of plastic
wrap.

If flat objects are to be laminated (such as a stained
glass photo transparency or delicate grille), or if the
sandwich is not required to have two smooth sides, it
will only be necessary to place a layer of transparent-
izable fiberglass on a sheet of plastic wrap, fix the
objects to be laminated, use one coat of transparent
resin to hold them in place, and transparentize the mat.

MAKING TRANSPARENT THIN-WALLED OBJECTS IN
RESIN. Follow these steps:

1. Make the pattern. Hollow it out to the desired
wall thickness.

2. Coat both sides with parting agent and allow them
to dry.

3. Cut a paper cup or other disposable container down
so that it is about $1/2''$ higher than the pattern. Position
the pattern upside down in the container so that its

bottom is even with the top of the container. Pour a mold-making resin around the object.

4. After this female mold has dried, fill the inside of the pattern with casting resin.

5. After the interior "plug" mold has dried, remove it, allow it to cure, and coat it with release agent.

6. Remove the pattern from the female mold, allow the mold to cure, and coat it with release agent.

7. Reposition the plug mold in the female mold. Fill the cavity with a clear casting resin.

8. When dry, remove it from its mold and cure. Do not remove it too soon or it will warp.

FILLETING AND CEMENTING FIBERGLASS AND RESIN OBJECTS. Fillet one fiberglass object to another by using strips of cloth or fiberglass soaked in resin. Resin objects can be glued to other materials with epoxy cement.

They may be joined to other resin objects by fir roughening the surfaces to be joined and then cementi these with an application of resin.

MACHINING AND FINISHING FIBERGLASS AND RES OBJECTS. To avoid chipping objects, first heat them 180°F water for about 15 minutes for small objects half an hour for large objects. Saw with a hand jig hacksaw, or use a hollow-ground blade with no set a power saw. Use lard oil, paraffin oil, or soap as lubricant.

Drill with a standard drill, using soap for the lubricar Withdraw and clear the drill frequently.

To remove the soft film that sometimes forms on to of the plastic, sand with coarse sandpaper. Use a le coarse paper to remove the scratches left by the rough paper, and a fine sandpaper to finish. All papers shou be of the wet variety. Polish with wax and a soft clot

7-46.
Assembly Hall for the University of Illinois
Harrison and Abramovitz, Architects.
  Ammann and Whitney, Consulting
  Engineers
Modelmaker: Leon A. Rosenthal. Model
  with roof by Alexander and Jones
Scale: Model with roof, ¼" = 1'. Model
  without roof, ¹⁄₁₆" = 1'
Material: laminated fiberglass

Model with roof: Segments of the dome were built of fiberglass on an acrylic pattern that was made of ¹⁄₁₆ of the dome. First, a female fiberglass mold was made and then the final, male mold was cast into it. Ramps, columns, windows, and buttresses were made from acrylic sheet. Mullions were drawn on. The model was built to show only half of the building. It was placed against a mirror to be photographed and was used as a pre-sentation model.

Model without roof: This model was also made of fiberglass laminations. Seats and ramps were made from acrylic. People were cut from paper and cars from wood. The baseboard and contours were constructed of illustration board, filled, and sprayed with six coats of lacquer. This model was used for design and presentation.

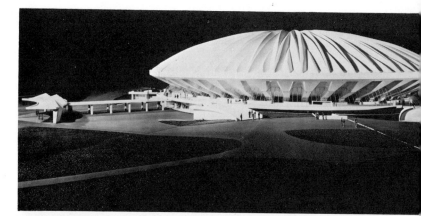

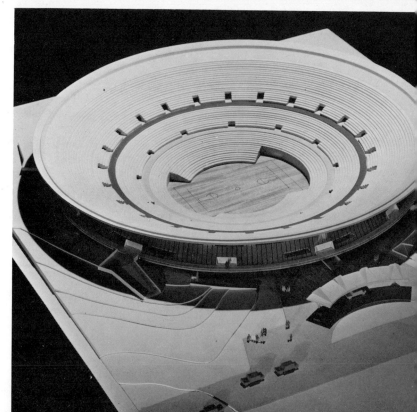

8:Construction Systems

SOLID BLOCK CONSTRUCTION

Models of many objects—from as small as parts of furniture measuring a fraction of an inch to as large as entire buildings—may be cut or carved from solid blocks of wood or plastic.

CUTTING. The elevations and plan of the object can be pasted or marked on the block as a guide for making the cuts (figure 8-1). These cuts are made on a band saw or, if the material is thinner than 2″, on a bench-mounted jigsaw. Even if you do not have these tools, you can still make solid block constructions in several ways. First, you can make them out of soft balsa and cut them out with a fret saw. Second, you can make them out of harder wood, which can also be cut with a fret saw, using a homemade guide to keep the blade cutting perpendicular to the surface of the wood (figure 8-1). Third, you can build the construction out of several plies of harder wood (see "Bread-and-Butter Construction"). This last method involves cutting each ply separately on a small power jigsaw or with a fret saw.

CARVING. Carve wood to its rough outside shape with a knife, spokeshave, or plane; smooth it with a plane or file; and finish with sandpaper. An electric drill or small hand motor-mounted abrasive paper discs may be used instead of hand tools. Acrylic objects should be hand-filed down or cut away with an electric drill-mounted rotary rasp. To prevent fusing of the plastic, constantly move the cutter and use oil as a lubricant. Acrylic objects may then be finished with files and abrasive paper.

Internal carving or wood hollowing should be done with a spoon gouge or an electric drill-mounted rotary rasp. Small objects may be hollowed out with a gouge or a small hand motor-mounted shaper. Acrylic objects can also be hollowed with the above power tools.

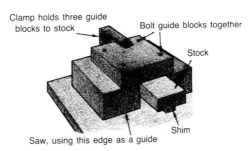

8-1.
Solid block cutting guide

Measure carving progress and the resulting wall thickness with calipers. If possible, hollowed out shapes with thin walls should be permanently braced internally. If this is not practical, temporarily brace them (a wood-strip or two is all that may be needed) while they are being painted. This will prevent them from being distorted by the drying paint. To keep the object from distorting with age, seal and paint both its inside and outside with the same number of coats.

Objects should be held securely during carving. Small shapes can be temporarily glue-mounted on wood scrap to ensure a better manual or vise grip. Large objects should be clamped down to the workbench. One of several possible clamping devices is shown in figure 8-2A. It allows the clamping of many shapes of blocks to the workbench.

BREAD-AND-BUTTER CONSTRUCTION

If thick blocks or planks of wood or plastic are unavailable or too expensive, objects may have to be built up out of thinner sheets. This type of lamination is known as

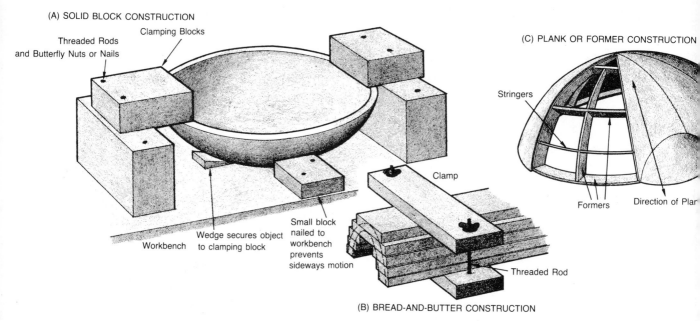

(A) SOLID BLOCK CONSTRUCTION

Clamping Blocks

Threaded Rods
and Butterfly Nuts or Nails

(C) PLANK OR FORMER CONSTRUCTION

Stringers

Clamp

Formers   Direction of Plan

Workbench   Wedge secures object   Small block   Threaded Rod
to clamping block   nailed to
workbench
prevents
sideways motion

(B) BREAD-AND-BUTTER CONSTRUCTION

8-2.
Three construction methods

bread-and-butter construction. For instance, if a 2'-long model of a hanger shaped like a barrel vault is being carved, considerable material can be saved by progressively laminating narrower plies from the base to the top of the vault (figure 8-2B). Plan the laminations on the drawing of the object and account for the thickness of the glue line. Cement the material together and securely clamp it until dry. Since many objects are too large for the clamping devices already described, you might have to devise your own clamp. Since the sides of a bread-and-butter lamination are rough, the elevations of the object cannot be pinned or transferred on to it. Instead, carve them by using templates of the elevations as guides.

PLANKED CONSTRUCTION

WITH FORMERS. When constructing large complexly curved objects (roofs, entire buildings, etc.) whose wall or ceiling thickness will be visible, use the planked construction technique (figure 8-2C) if you are unable to hollow out a carved solid block sufficiently. First locate the positions of the formers that will support the planking. Formers should be located where they will not block window, or other intended, openings. If the actual building has internal trusses or partitions, make

the formers correspond to their location. Cut formers out of wood sheet or make them out of segments of attached pieces of stripwood. Provide formers with sufficient strength to hold the bent planking. Formers should be held in position on the workbench with pins while they are being cemented together. When all formers are in position and dry, flex the frame by hand to be sure that it is strong enough to hold the planking. If it seems weak, add additional formers or stringers where needed. Stringers should bed into notches cut into the formers.

Next, apply balsa or basswood planking of about 1/64″ to 1/8″ thickness, depending on how tight a bend must be negotiated. Run the grain of the planks parallel to the curve that has the least curvature. Often the planks have to be cut into a pattern before they can be applied to the formers. In the dome shown in figure 8-2C, the planks are in the form of a triangle so that they may fit together closely. It is not necessary to plot geometrically the shape of the planks with great accuracy; it is much simpler to take a small representative area of the work and temporarily cover it with two or three roughly cut oversize planks held in place with pins and then trim them to exact shape. These planks may then be removed from the frame and used as cutting templates for the rest of the planking.

When all the planks are cut, cement them onto the frame and pin them in place until they have set. See instructions for wood bending in chapter 7. Areas of extreme curvature should be carved out of solid blocks of wood. If possible, these blocks should be notched to take the planks. Set the blocks permanently into the planking only after all the planks have been cemented in place. A complexly curved object may have to be built up of several areas of different planking patterns.

WITHOUT FORMERS. If the object is to be completely hollow and have no formers, first build the frame as previously described. Then cover the frame with overlapping strips of wax paper. Cut the planks as suggested above, but bevel their edges so that they can be bevel joined for additional strength. Cement the planks to one another and temporarily pin them to the formers. When the cement has dried, remove the planked skin it should come free of the wax paper without too much trouble) and give it several coats of sanding sealer on both sides.

In many cases, it will be necessary to build the planked skin out of several plies of thin sheet in order to form tight curves. Several plies will also be stronger if the joints of each layer are staggered so that no joint runs through all the plies. For even greater strength, run the grain of the second layer of planks at as near to a 90° angle to the grain of the first layer as is possible (given the curvature of the object). Another way to strengthen this type of construction is to cover the outside or the inside of the object with gauze impregnated in cement. A gauze-covered surface may be smoothly finished with several coats of sanding sealer or plastic balsa wood filler, each followed by a light sanding.

CONSTRUCTING COMPLEXLY CURVED OBJECTS

Almost every sheet material mentioned in this book may be bent into objects curved in one or more planes. Plaster-impregnated paper or cloth may be curved on a mold (male or female). Such plastic materials as sculpt metal, sculpt stone, clay, and plasticine may be applied to buckram, copper mesh, or galvanized metal wire held in shape on wood formers.

By using one of the casting systems outlined later in this chapter, you can simultaneously form curved objects and impart sharp details and textures to one or both of their surfaces.

Of the materials listed in table 8-1, all but wood, plywood, and acrylic may have details impressed upon them during their forming. These details, however, will be less sharp than those derived through casting.

PLASTER ON EGG-CRATE CONSTRUCTION

Large shapes may be built up of plaster on a skeleton of formers. This type of construction is most frequently used for building ground contours (see chapter 12). With some experience, you will be able to construct solid or nearly solid objects in this technique faster than you would be able to using the construction systems. Steps in this construction technique are:

1. Using section drawings of the object as guides, cut enough cardboard or wood formers to create an egg-crate pattern (see figure 12-8D).
2. Assemble them on a wood base.
3. Partly fill the area between the formers with crumpled paper or wood scrap.
4. Apply plaster slightly above the level of the tops of the formers.
5. Carve the hardened plaster to the accurate shape.
6. Fill the plaster with shellac and sand it to a satin finish.

CASTING

From time to time it will be necessary to produce many copies of a single object. Casting is one method of reproducing in great numbers such items as furniture, cars, people, cast-concrete columns, and moldings.

When making repetitive parts (whether casting them or not), carefully estimate the construction time. Since such a part may have to be reproduced 100 or 1,000 times (see figure 8-11), all attempts should be made to refine its construction, no matter how small the resulting saving in time per unit or step may be, since the saving will be multiplied by a large factor.

Before deciding to cast, determine what the effort in moldmaking plus casting will be in comparison to making each item individually. If it will be easier to make each item, the decision may still be to cast because the molds may be needed for future use, the objects must be identical in the smallest detail, or the object must be produced in a material that cannot be worked with the available tools.

Professional modelmakers often carve the pattern of an object in brass, or a similar durable material, and send it to a professional caster who makes the mold and does the casting. Even though this entire process may be expensive for a fairly elaborate small object (grilles, patterned facades, etc.), the general estimate is that this is more economical, even for a run of as few as six objects.

Table 8-1. Various Materials for Complex Curves

Material	Mold Requirement	Strength of Finished Object	Opacity	Requirements for a Smooth Surface	Notes
Paper	Male or female	Satisfactory	Opaque	Sealing and sanding	Simplest to make if tools are limited; walls can be of varying thicknesses; Bristolboard for curves one direction, gumstrip for complex curves
Wood	Male or female	Satisfactory	Opaque	Sealing and sanding	Simple to make but curve cannot be too tight in second direction; walls can be easily carved in varying thicknesses
Plywood	Male or female	Fairly high	Opaque	Sealing and sanding	Can only be curved in one direction
Metal	Female	High	Opaque	Smooth hammering and buffing	Highest strength and thinnest wall; a female mold is needed; requires special skills to hammer out a good finish
Acrylic	Male or female or both	Fairly high	Opaque, translucent, or transparent	None	Requires special tools, heater, and, possibly, a pressure chamber; a female mold may be needed; many integral colors are obtained.
Polystyrene	Male or female or both	Satisfactory	Opaque	None	Requires special tools, like acrylic; a female mold may be needed
Sculpt-O-Glas	Male or female	Satisfactory	Transparent	None	Fairly simple to use; walls can be of varying thicknesses
Celastic	Male or female	Fairly high	Opaque	Sealing and sanding	Fairly simple to use; walls can be of varying thicknesses
Plaster-impregnated paper or cloth	Male or female	Satisfactory	Opaque	Sealing and sanding	Fairly simple to use; walls can be of varying thicknesses
Fiberglass	Male or female	High	Opaque, translucent, or transparent	Grinding and sanding if one side is rough; otherwise only sanding	More complicated to prepare than Sculpt-O-Glas or Celastic; color is integral; walls can be of varying thicknesses

TERMS USED IN CASTING. Before reading the rest of this section, familiarize yourself with the following terms:

Blanket mold is a mold made of a flat object—wall or ceiling texture, for example.

Cast or *casting* is a duplication of the original object.

Closed mold is a female mold that is entirely closed. Casting material is poured into it through a casting channel.

Flash is a thin strip of casting material that leaks out between multipart molds. When dry, flash resembles a thin fin.

Key is the female or male identification built into the parts of multipiece molds that make the assembled parts fit together in perfect alignment.

Mold is the shape in or on which casts are made.

Open mold is a female mold that is open on one side. Casting material is poured into the mold through the opening. If the object to be cast has detail on both sides, it may be made in two open molds. The two resulting casts are then joined together.

Parting, release, or *separating agent* is a substance that is placed on a pattern to facilitate the removal of the mold or a substance placed on the mold to facilitate the removal of casts.

Pattern or *master model* is the original of the object to be duplicated.

Sprue, a channel through which the casting material is poured, runs from the outside of a closed mold into its cavity.

hrinkage and Expansion of Materials

objects must be cast to close tolerances, choose mold-
aking and casting materials whose expansion and con-
action relate to one another. If, for instance, a female
old is made out of a plaster that expands 2% on hard-
ning, the plastic or metal used for the casts should
so contract 2% on curing to produce casts equal in
mension to the pattern. Casting materials can: contract
s they solidify and cure; contract as they solidify, and
en expand as they cure; or expand as they solidify
nd cure.

Shrinkage and expansion are not simple problems.
arts of an object with different thicknesses will shrink
ifferent amounts, thus causing distortion. Also, as a
ot casting cools, stresses are created that might result
cracking. Since inside corners are especially prone
this, always use filleted corners to avoid this problem.

When casting the repetitive pattern of an exterior
mbossed metal panel wall or other texture finish, it
especially important to predetermine expansion and
hrinkage. If this is not done, the number of panels
ntended for casting will not cover the correct wall area.

Pattern Making

Patterns may be made out of almost any material. Highly
letailed objects may be carved out of hardwood or
acrylic blocks. Medium and large undetailed shapes may
be made from hard balsa, other woods, plaster, rapidly
ardening clay, and so on. Large wood shapes may be
ouilt up by the bread-and-butter or solid block carving
echniques; large plaster objects, by the plaster on egg-
rate method. Any surface air holes in plaster patterns
hould be filled with wet plaster and smoothly sanded
before molding is attempted.

When working with a mold from a pattern made of
light materials, anchor the pattern to the work surface
to prevent it from floating up through the mold material.

Pattern Materials

Wax comes in consistencies ranging from that of grease
to that of plaster. Melting points range from 100° to
300°F. Hard red pattern wax, which can be carved into
intricate forms, costs more than softer patternmaker's
wax. Wax is also available in sheet form, which saves
time when building up objects that have parallel sides.

Clay that hardens rapidly may also be used in making
patterns with extensive and fine detail. Excessive handling of the finished pattern, however, may deform it.

Woods upon which materials may be sheet-formed as
well as cast may be obtained for pattern making. The
desirable properties of such woods are lack of grain,

dimensional stability (when exposed to temperature and
humidity changes), and ease in carving. Mahogany meets
these requirements as does a resin-impregnated wood
laminate. Ren wood is a carvable, grainless plastic that
produces unbelievably good carving results.

Undercuts

Undercuts are protruding or indented details in the
surface of the object to be cast. These make it difficult
to simply lift the cast off the mold. The following techniques provide ways of dealing with this problem.

1. Use flexible molds that may be removed by
stretching them past all but the deepest undercuts.

2. Make removable undercut insertions in rigid molds.
Figure 8-3A shows an undercut form that is attached
to a male mold by means of a dowel in an oversize hole.
When the cast is removed, the form comes away with
it. Female molds may have similar detachable inserts.

3. When a large portion of the object is undercut,
make a male pattern that can be collapsed and withdrawn
from the cast.

If an undercut is too deep or large, you may have
to construct the mold in sections. If the object has deep
slender parts, make provision for the casting material
to flow into the mold to the end of these parts without
being blocked by trapped air. See figure 8-3B for a
typical air vent constructed to allow air to exit from
the end of the object. In general, each object presents
its own problems and undercuts must be planned
accordingly.

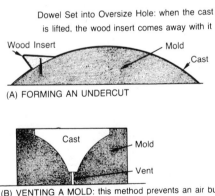

Dowel Set into Oversize Hole: when the cast
is lifted, the wood insert comes away with it

Wood Insert — Mold — Cast

(A) FORMING AN UNDERCUT

Cast — Mold — Vent

(B) VENTING A MOLD: this method prevents an air bubble
from forming in the mold's lower extremity

8-3.
Molds

Sealers

All patterns or molds made from porous materials must be fully sealed to prevent the casting material from being locked in place when dry. One sealing procedure recommended for porous objects used with casting epoxy is as follows:

1. Seal the mold with two coats of lacquer.
2. Apply two coats of polyvinyl alcohol.
3. Apply a generous coat of Epoxical Mold Sealer in a heavy paste (it may be thinned with white gasoline or kerosene).
4. After five minutes, remove any excess with a soft cloth. Casting must take place within one-half to three-quarters of an hour to prevent a repetition of the entire procedure.

Other sealers require less effort to use. They include sanding sealers and varnish. Some brands of sanding sealers will be attacked by the casting material and must, therefore, be tested prior to use.

Separators or Release Agents

Under each casting and moldmaking material mentioned in this chapter is a table that lists the release agents to be used with that material. If you are using a combination of materials that is not listed, an agent suggested for a similar combination may work. Keep in mind that very hot materials will cause some agents to boil off and some agents and materials chemically attack one another. Test the various separators on materials before proceeding with the casting.

Separators that will not mar delicate detail may be obtained from dental suppliers. These separators may be applied to plaster (and other) patterns that have not been sealed.

REMOVING MOLDS AND CASTS. Remove rigid molds from patterns and rigid casts from rigid molds in one of the following ways: by gently blowing them apart with compressed air; by evenly wedging the parting line with a sharp tool; by suspending one of the objects so that its weight, aided by light tapping, results in separation; by soaking them for a short time in warm water; or by using knockout pins (figure 8-5).

FLEXIBLE MOLDS FOR CASTING

Flexible molds make casting objects with undercuts possible. Ordinary flexible molds may be removed from patterns and casts that have slight to moderate undercuts. To make a mold with undercuts so deep that the rubber could not be stretched to release it, build release slits in the mold. Flexible molds may be made from several materials. Table 8-2 lists the two most common materials—*latex rubber* and *silicone rubber*—and some of their properties. *Synthetic rubber* (other than silicone rubber) constitutes a third possibility.

In addition to these materials, there are three others that are now almost obsolete. Molding gum is only good for one or two castings and must be used immediately after it has been molded. It shrinks rapidly and extensively during storage, is weak, and cannot be used with hot casting materials. Moulage, another material, must be melted over a fire, shrinks rapidly and extensively, and cannot be used with metal. Finally, gelatin must be soaked for eight hours and then melted. It, too, shrinks rapidly and extensively and cannot be used with metal.

Latex Rubber Molds

Molding rubber comes in two colors: black and white. The black is a bit tougher and works well on vertical surfaces. Both materials have a limited shelf life, so buy only enough to meet immediate needs.

Many materials may be cast in rubber molds. These include art plaster, artificial stone, hot wax, liquid mar-

Table 8-2. Flexible Moldmaking Materials

Mold Material	Relative Cost	Shrinkage during Storage	Resistance to Tearing	Materials To Be Cast in Mold
Latex rubber (black or white)	Low	Medium[1]	High	Wax, plaster, metals with melting temperatures below 300°F.
Silicone rubber	High	Low	Medium	Wax, plaster, metals with melting temperatures below 500°F.

1. Store in a sealed container after adding a teaspoon of water.

ble, low melting point metals, plastic aluminum, and epoxy metal compound.

MAKING OPEN MOLDS FROM LATEX RUBBER. The following steps are recommended:

1. Cement the pattern to a sheet of wood or plastic larger than the base of the pattern. Make sure that the base of the pattern is sanded absolutely flat.

2. Apply the appropriate release agent (table 8-3).

3. Use a soft brush to paint several thin coats of liquid rubber over the pattern. Let each coat dry about half an hour. Build up a total rubber thickness of about ⅛″ (approximately ten coats, although objects as small as 1″ to 2″ in height may only require eight coats).

4. Blow off or break with a pin any air bubbles that may form on the rubber. If they are allowed to remain, they will break and mar the surface of the mold.

5. When at least five coats of rubber have been applied, reinforce the base of the mold with one or more layers of gauze. A flange, from which the finished mold may be hung, can be constructed from gauze or extra layers of rubber and also placed around the base.

6. For additional support to the rubber around undercuts and other areas, build up these places with cotton flock filler mixed with liquid rubber (one part of each). Do not attempt to apply a coat of much over ¼″ in one application. The filler, which may be applied with a palette knife, is a sponge-rubber-like substance. It is obtainable from most of the companies that sell liquid rubber.

7. Allow the mold to dry. Remove it from the pattern.

8. To cure the mold, place it in a warm place for two or more days, or place it 3″ away from a 40-watt bulb for 24 hours. This will maintain a curing temperature of about 110°F.

Rubber has a tendency to shrink and pull away from large patterns. To prevent this, apply the first coat in the standard way and the second coat in a checkerboard pattern. Apply the third coat the same way as the first, and checkerboard the fourth coat on the areas not covered by the second. Repeat this procedure for the full ten coats. Between coats, keep the brush in soapy water to prevent the rubber remnants on it from hardening. Before using the brush again, shake it out. Apply the rubber to small patterns by dipping them into a vessel filled with the liquid. Rubber may also be spray applied.

BACKUP MOLDS. Backup molds or overmolds are sometimes required to stiffen large latex rubber molds that would collapse or become distorted under the weight of the cast-making material.

1. Place a topless and bottomless cardboard box around the completed rubber mold that has been filled with sand or some other light granular material. If the mold is small, a paper cup may be used. The container should be an inch or more larger than the mold in all directions.

2. Fill all undercuts (on the outside of the rubber mold) with clay or flock filler mixed with liquid rubber.

3. Coat the rubber mold with soap or an appropriate release agent.

4. Slowly pour a plaster mix into the box, being careful not to distort the shape of the mold.

5. Remove the rubber mold from the backup just as heat of crystallization starts.

TWO-PART LATEX RUBBER MOLDS. When objects have no flat side, you will have to construct a two-part mold.

1. Place the pattern into a block of modeling clay. Push it down until the top of the clay is at the level desired for the parting line of the mold halves. Make sure that the clay is tightly packed against the sides of the pattern.

2. Build a sprue by running a wood dowel from the pattern to the outside of the clay.

3. With another dowel, press cylindrical indentations into the corners of the clay block. The holes of the dowel must be absolutely perpendicular to the surface of the clay. Keys will be cast into these recesses. Molds for keys may also be made as a series of dents in the clay with a modeling tool.

4. Apply the liquid rubber coats to the exposed half of the pattern.

5. Make a plaster of Paris overmold. When it has dried, turn the assembly over and remove the clay from the bottom half of the pattern.

6. Make the second half of the rubber mold and the plaster overmold.

7. Pull the plaster overmold halves apart. Notice that it has keys cast into it.

8. Remove the rubber mold halves from the pattern.

Table 8-3. Separators Used between Latex Molding Materials and Various Patterns

Patterns	Separators
Wood (first seal the pattern)	Two coats varnish
Wax	Shellac or lacquer
Plaster, Hydro-Stone, Sculpt Stone (first seal the pattern)	Two coats varnish; shellac, lacquer, or banana oil If latex is vulcanized, no separator is necessary
Clay, Plasticine	Two coats shellac

9. Reassemble each rubber half in its overmold. Prepare to make castings. When pouring, hold the mold halves together with rubber bands.

MOLDS WITH RELEASE SLITS. If the pattern has deep undercuts, casting it in a mold that has release slits may be possible (figure 8-4A and B).

1. Rubber cement a sheet of aluminum along the side of the pattern running perpendicular to the base of the pattern. This finlike piece may also be attached by cutting a slot into the pattern and inserting an aluminum sheet.

2. Apply the liquid rubber to the pattern and to the fin. The release slit will be formed by the fin.

Fins may also be constructed with a clay wall perpendicular to the side of the pattern.

1. Paint one side of this wall with several coats of pearl essence lacquer. Allow each coat to dry before applying the next. Let the last coat dry overnight.

2. Pull the clay away from the lacquer, which has dried into a fin. Be careful not to rip the fin away from the pattern.

When casting with a slit mold, first clamp the closed slit to prevent casting material from entering it. A backup mold or a clamping frame are other possible ways of closing the slit.

CASTING IN A LATEX RUBBER MOLD. Use the following procedure to cast in a rubber mold:

1. Grease the mold with unsalted shortening, glycerin, or other appropriate release agent (see the separators listed in table 8-4).

2. Pour the plaster. Let it dry for about half an hour before removing it from the mold. Apply soap suds to the outside of the mold before attempting to lift it from the cast. Remove the rubber as if peeling off a glove.

Table 8-4. Separators Used between Latex Molds and Various Casts

Casts	Separators
Plaster	Liquid soap, glycerin, and wate Zinc stearate and alcohol
Casting rubber	Equal parts of water, liquid soa and Epsom salts
Low-melting-point metal	Oil or graphite A separator may not be neede

3. Before storing the mold, wash it in a mild detergen and rinse it in clean water. Rubber molds should be kept away from direct sunlight and from temperature of over 125°F.

Silicone Rubber Molds

In making flexible molds, the advantage of silicone rubber over latex is that silicone rubber will allow the casting of hot materials (up to 500°F melting point) and the mold will last for a much longer time in storage.

Materials that may be used in silicone rubber molds include plaster of Paris, modeling plaster, Hydrocal, low melting point metals (including lead, linotype metal), polyurethane foam, plastic resins, and wax.

The instructions in this section should be used with Dow Corning Silastic. They are, however, fairly typical of those used with other makes of silicone rubber.

1. Cement the pattern to a sheet of wood or plastic larger than the base of the pattern. Make sure the base of the pattern is sanded flat. Apply the release agent to the pattern (table 8-5).

2. Mix the silicone rubber and its catalysts, following the manufacturer's instructions, in a disposable vessel (a paper cup, for example). Stir gently to avoid the formation of air bubbles.

3. Pour the mix over the pattern to a depth of ⅛" or less. The formula of the chemicals will determine

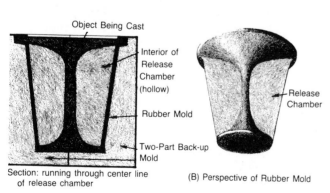

Section: running through center line of release chamber

(B) Perspective of Rubber Mold

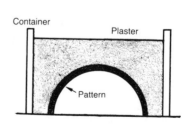

(C) Making the Female Mold

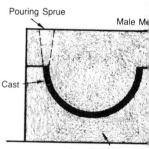

(D) Making the Cast

8-4.
Rubber molds

Table 8-5. Separators Used between Silicone Rubber Molding Materials and Various Patterns

Patterns	Separators
Wood (first seal the pattern)	Two coats varnish 5% solution of household detergent in water (this can be used on all except very complex, undercut patterns)
Wax	5% detergent solution (see Wood) A separator may not be needed
Plaster (first seal the pattern)	Two coats varnish 5% detergent solution (see Wood) A separator may not be needed
Hydro-Stone, Sculpt Stone, Sculpt Metal (first seal the pattern)	5% detergent solution (see Wood)
Clay, Plasticine	Two coats shellac 5% detergent solution (see Wood)
Acrylic plastic	5% detergent solution (see Wood)

their working and setting (curing) times. With Silastic, these can run from ten minutes to three hours for working and from half an hour to one day for setting. Silicone rubber cures at room temperature, but moderate heating will accelerate the process.

Build up the base of the mold, as well as other areas that will be subjected to constant flexing, with 20- to 25-mesh open-weave fabric. If the mold will be exposed to temperatures over 350°F, use glass fiber for the reinforcement. Place the fabric on the wet rubber and pour an additional layer of rubber over it.

Two-part molds may be constructed in the same way as for latex rubber molds (see page 125).

CASTING IN A SILICONE RUBBER MOLD. Apply release agents between the mold and various casts (see table 8-6). Heat the mold to a temperature of from 25° to 50°F higher than the casting material and pour the cast. Thin-walled objects (figure 8-4C and D) may be cast in the following way:

1. Construct the exterior mold by pouring the rubber into a container placed around the pattern. Carefully pour the mix into the corners of the container to prevent air pockets from forming.

2. When the rubber has set, remove the container and cut keys into the bottom of the mold.

3. Coat the inside of the pattern and the bottom of the mold with parting agent.

4. Turn the first half of the mold upside down and return it, with the pattern still attached, to the container. Fill the inside of the pattern with rubber.

5. After the rubber has set, disassemble the molds, remove the pattern and cut a sprue and the needed

Table 8-6. Separators Used between Silicone Rubber Molds and Various Casts

Casts	Separators
Plaster	Liquid soap, glycerine, and water Zinc stearate and alcohol A separator may not be needed
Low-melting-point metal	Oil or graphite A separator may not be needed

vent holes into the mold. Reassemble the two mold halves and begin casting.

Synthetic Rubber Molds

Several polysulfide rubber materials are available for moldmaking. Set up the pattern as for a latex rubber mold and apply separators listed in table 8-7. Carefully blend and stir the components of the rubber and brush these onto the pattern. Depending on the curative used, pouring life runs from 10 to 40 minutes, setting time from 1 to 3 hours, and curing time from 4 to 28 hours. At the end of the curing period, the mold can be stripped from the pattern. High room temperature and humidity hasten the curing. Because of this, a slower curative chemical can be used in hot, humid environments.

When applying rubber to the pattern, pour it slowly and in a thin stream. This will cause air bubbles to break as they pass over the lip of the pouring container. A stream of warm air against the poured, but still wet, rubber will cause any bubbles to rise to the surface. If the pattern is intricate, paint the rubber on.

Materials that may be used in synthetic rubber molds include plaster, polyester thermosetting resins (which can be cured at low temperatures), and epoxy resins.

LARGE BLANKET MOLDS. To make large blanket molds that require a long and dimensionally stable life, use Smooth-On FMC No. 300.

1. Set up the pattern and cover it with release agent (table 8-7).

Table 8-7. Separators Used between Synthetic (Polysulfide) Rubber Molding Material and Various Patterns

Patterns	Separators
Wood, Wax, Plaster, Hydro-Stone, Sculpt Stone, Sculpt Metal, Cardboard, Clay, Plasticine, Acrylic plastic	Vaseline thinned with kerosene Smooth-On Sonite

2. Brush on a thin coat of FMC No. 100. When it becomes tacky, brush or trowel on a ¼″ thick coat of FMC No. 300. Allow it to set. If all shrinkage must be avoided, apply a layer of burlap mesh to the wet FMC No. 300, making sure that no air is trapped beneath the fabric and that it is thoroughly saturated by the rubber. (If the mold is small and slight shrinkage is permissible, reinforcing is not necessary).

3. Make the plaster overmold by brushing a film of Smooth-On Sonite release agent on the rubber. Then pour or trowel on a layer of stiff plaster. Sisal or hemp fiber may be incorporated into the plaster for added strength. A lifting frame may be made from wood furring. The plaster may be permanently attached to the rubber by setting copper wool or chopped hemp into the still-liquid rubber. The plaster will grip the exposed strands and anchor itself to the rubber.

4. Apply a second coat of FMC No. 300 after the first one has set.

5. If desired, make an overmold as described in Step 3. Store the rubber mold in a cool, dark place.

If you intend to make castings from epoxy or polyester resins in a blanket mold, use FMC No. 302 for a first (⅛″ thick) coat and apply a layer of FMC No. 300 when the first coat has partially set.

CASTING IN A SYNTHETIC RUBBER MOLD. Before each casting of epoxy in a synthetic rubber mold, protect the mold by sponging it with a warm 1% to 2% solution of household detergent and water. After this has dried, brush or spray the mold with a film of polyvinyl alcohol. Allow the alcohol to dry and, taking care not to crack its film, spray the mold with one or two layers of fluorocarbon telomer dispersion.

Table 8-8. Separators Used between Synthetic Rubber Molds and Various Casts

Casts	Separators
Plaster	Equal parts of Vaseline and kerosene
Polyester resin	Smooth-On Sonite

RIGID MOLDS FOR CASTING

Rigid molds are made out of materials that harden. Unlike flexible molds, they cannot be stretched; this demands special attention to designing undercuts and to removing casts.

Plaster Molds

The materials most commonly used for rigid molds are plaster and epoxy. Although there are many problems connected with plaster, it is used fairly often and precautions can be taken to avoid difficulties. If the mold is cured at too high a temperature or for too long a time, it may crack or warp. Molds may warp if the plaster is of low quality or if too much parting compound has been applied. Chalkiness in molds is caused by curing at excessive temperatures. Softness may be caused by too much water in the plaster or by curing the mold at too high a temperature. If the mold softens after being used, it probably has not been sufficiently dried between castings. Mold hardness may be caused by an insufficient amount of water in the plaster mix. Rapid deterioration in molds may be brought on by the same factors that cause plaster to deteriorate (see page 68), or by not drying the mold before use. Molds that develop mildew must be thoroughly washed and dried.

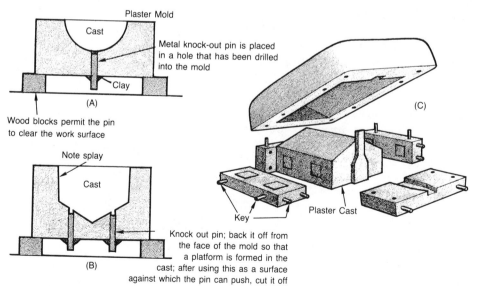

8-5.
Casting in plaster

Plaster Mold

Cast

Metal knock-out pin is placed in a hole that has been drilled into the mold

Clay

(A)

Wood blocks permit the pin to clear the work surface

Note splay

Cast

(B)

Knock out pin; back it off from the face of the mold so that a platform is formed in the cast; after using this as a surface against which the pin can push, cut it off

(C)

Key

Plaster Cast

Materials that may be cast in plaster molds include olyester resin, epoxy resin, low-melting-point metal, nd plaster itself.

PLASTER PATTERNS. These should be sealed with gum hellac thinned with alcohol (one part of each). Finely etailed patterns should be sealed with applications of numerous coats of soap dissolved in water; a surface finished in this fashion does not require a separator.

OPEN MOLDS. Molds must have splayed parts to permit removal of casts (figure 8-5A and B). Figures 8-6 and 8-7 show examples of open molds. To make a female mold:

8-6.
Elements analysis of Palazzo
   del Te
Cooper Union School of
   Architecture
Scale: $\frac{1}{16}'' = 1'$
Material: plaster

The pediment, niches, columns, and smooth stonework were plaster casts done in plaster molds. The patterns which are the original shapes from which the molds are made, were carved out of wood. A thin sheet metal mold was used for the textured stone because it could be hammered to create the rough surface.

8-7.
Classical Facade Study. Here we see the facade (see figure 8-6) partially reconstructed by first taping drawings of the elevations to a board and then gluing the plaster pieces to the drawing.

Table 8-9. Separators Used between Plaster Molding Material and Various Patterns

Patterns	Separators
Wood (first seal the pattern)	Oil Wax polish
Wax	Moldcraft 4H
Plaster (first seal the pattern)	If the pattern is large and without detail, wax polish may be used on plaster molds when casting most materials. Apply in a thin coat and polish with a soft cloth until a glasslike finish is attained Olive, raw linseed, light lubricating or white mineral oil 1 part melted soft soap in 5 parts water; apply several brushed-on coats to the pattern, wash off excess liquid, let dry, and oil 1 part beeswax, 3 parts paraffin, and 16 parts kerosene ¼ lb. stearic acid (stearin) cut into fine shavings and mixed with 1 part kerosene; boil to dissolve (overheating will cause it to burst into flames) Potters or neutral potash soap, rub several applications into the pattern and wipe any excess off with a clean sponge Russian tallow and olive oil Suet and paraffin melted to the consistency of cream Spirits of camphor (good on finely detailed patterns) 1 part Vaseline and 2 parts kerosene. Heat, mix, and brush on Wet mold with water until it stands on the surface of the plaster
Metal	Spray on a mixture of 10% S.A.E. No. 10 mineral oil, 2.75% bayberry wax, .25% Aerosol O.T., and 87% water
Clay, Plasticine	Powdered talc Soap jelly made from a solution of soap and water

1. Seal the pattern and apply the separator to it and to the surrounding work surface (table 8-9).

2. Pour the plaster over the pattern. If intending to cut down on the weight of a large mold, reinforce the first layer of plaster applied to the pattern with cloth; as the plaster hardens, gradually build it up to a 1″ thickness.

3. Allow newly made molds to dry before using. Molds that are 1″ thick require about a day's drying time; 4″-thick molds require three days' time. Prorate for other mold thicknesses.

4. When the plaster is dry, remove the mold, allow it to cure, fill any air bubbles or flaws, shellac, and sand to a satin finish.

To make a plaster mold for casting shallow metal

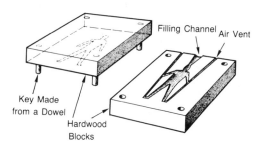

8-8.
Casting figures

objects such as screens, fences, or wall textures, tr͏y the following procedure:

1. Make a wood frame to enclose the mold. Pin it t͏o a woodworking surface.

2. Oil the frame and work surface.

3. Pour the plaster into the frame. When it has almos͏t set, draw a straightedge across it, leveling it with th͏e top of the frame.

4. When dry, remove the slab from its frame.

5. Turn the slab over and trace the elevation of th͏e object that is to be molded.

6. Carve the outline with a pointed instrument an͏d gouge out the depth of the object. To get an idea o͏f the progress being made, periodically press plasticine or clay into the depression, remove it, and study the detail and depth that has been carved.

7. Drill holes for keys in each corner of the slab.

8. When the female pattern has been completed, melt one part soft soap into five parts water and brush many layers of the liquid mix onto the plaster.

9. Wash off any surplus soap and allow the plaster to dry.

10. Oil the plaster, then immerse it in water for about ten minutes.

11. Make a new wood frame. This one should be the same size as the plaster slab but twice as deep.

12. Put the slab into the frame, pattern side up, and oil the slab and frame.

13. Pour plaster into the frame and, when the plaster is almost set, strike off the top of the slab as described in Step 3.

14. After the plaster has set, remove the frame and separate the two slabs. You will now have a positive impression of the object and four keys cast into the second slab.

15. Remove the positive impression of the object with a scraper and a pointed instrument, and incise the other side of the object into the second slab.

16. Cut air vents and a sprue into one mold half.

17. Place and clamp the two finished mold halves together.

18. Pour metal into the mold.

CLOSED PLASTER MOLDS. If undercuts or details on the sides of an object make one-piece open mold casting impossible, cast in a closed mold (figure 8-5C) of two or more pieces.

1. Determine how many mold pieces are required to clear all undercuts.

2. Make the biggest part of the mold first. Build fences to contain the plaster of the first mold piece. Fences can be made out of clay, with the exception of those that touch clay patterns (these must be made from sheet metal inserted into the pattern).

3. Cut keys into the fences.

4. Coat the pattern and fences with separator.

5. Pour the plaster. Remove the fence when dry.

6. Coat the other side of the pattern and the edge of the first part of the mold with separator and cast the second mold part. Repeat the procedure with the other mold parts.

To hold multipiece molds together for casting, cement the cracks with plaster. Chip this plaster off when disassembling the mold.

ONE-SHOT MOLDS FOR CASTING OBJECTS WITH UNDERCUTS. If sheet forming or casting an object that has undercuts, make the mold from Bestwall Breakaway Plaster. This restricts the mold to being used once. The material used for the cast must be able to withstand a temperature of 170°F.

Carve the mold out of plaster. To facilitate removal, make its walls as thin as possible. After casting or sheet forming the object, soak it and the attached mold in 170°F water until the plaster dissolves. It may then be removed with a spatula. Male molds can be carved into a mass of plaster that has been cast onto a wood plug. The plug is withdrawn before the disintegration of the plaster.

CASTING IN PLASTER MOLDS. To make plaster casts in a plaster mold:

1. Hold the bottom of the mold level (if it is not flat) on the work surface with lumps of clay.

2. Before casting, immerse the mold in water for about ten minutes. The liquid will fill tiny air holes and prevent air bubbles from later working their way into the casting plaster.

3. Pour the plaster into the mold and immediately pour it out, again to avoid trapping air bubbles. Many of the air bubbles will be swept out with the plaster.

Table 8-10. Separators Used between Plaster Molds and Various Casts

Casts	Separators
Plaster (first seal the mold)	Use any of the separators listed in the plaster patterns and plaster molding materials table (table 8-9).
Polyester resin (first seal the mold)	Wax polish Moldcraft oil spray
Epoxy resin (first seal the mold)	Smooth-On Sonite U.S.G. Epoxical Release-All
Low-melting-point metal (first seal the mold)	Moldcraft 2D Oil or graphite A separator may not be needed

4. Refill the mold a little at a time, jarring or vibrating the mold while pouring.

Never pour plaster across a pattern or mold. The turbulence may cause streak or flow marks to form and remain on the hardened plaster.

It is better to cast large objects with walls that have the same thickness throughout. Such an object will dry evenly, with less chance of cracking. Pour the plaster to a ¾″ thickness along the bottom of the mold, then build up a layer of stiff plaster to the desired even thickness along the sides of the mold.

REMOVING PLASTER CASTS AND MOLDS. Plaster expands as it sets. When making a plaster mold or cast, remove it from its mate while it is still hot. Final expansion runs from about 3% to as little as 0.002%. If slabs and other objects are not allowed to expand freely, they will warp. Female molds must have walls of sufficient thickness to resist the expansion of the casting material.

Remove plaster molds from their patterns and casts from the plaster molds by gently prying and tapping. If intending to make more than a few casts, avoid this procedure since, in time, it will damage the mold. Instead, use heavy (⅛″-diameter or more) brass or steel knock-out pins. Set them into a hole drilled in the center of the base of the mold (figure 8-5A). If, because of its size, the mold requires more than one pin, allow them to protrude an even amount from the mold so that when the mold is pressed against the workbench, the pressure against the pins will evenly push the cast out (figure 8-5B).

The first cast is always the hardest to remove—the more the mold is used, the easier the removal process becomes. Suction may make it difficult to remove a large plaster cast from its mold. To break this adhesion, place the mold under water and gently pry the cast from it. Dry the mold before using it again.

CLEANING PLASTER CASTS. If a cast that has been removed from its mold possesses damaged corners or pits, patch it while it is still wet.

Use a pointed tool to apply plaster to pits. Fill larger voids by applying the plaster with a wet palette knife. Broken corners should be roughly built up first and allowed to partially set. While the plaster is still wet, file and sand the corner to its final shape.

Remove flash with a flat file while the plaster is still wet. Since fine detail on plaster casts will not stand up as well under handling as will fine detail on casts made from metal or plastic, the material must be carefully worked.

Epoxy Molds and Casts

Epoxy resin has been used increasingly in recent years to make both molds and casts (including thick section casting). Its high strength and dimensional stability make it, in many instances, a more attractive material than plaster. Shrinkage of epoxy resin is low. Some surface coat resins shrink only 0.0001 to 0.0007 inches per foot. Compressive strengths of epoxy run from 10,000 to 22,000 pounds per square inch. The use of epoxy resin and fiberglass in the lamination of thin-wall objects is detailed on page 116.

Resins come in pint, quart, and larger containers, and have a storage life of about one year. When preparing to use them, you must mix them with a hardener.

The following uses of epoxy are of interest to the modelmaker. Instructions quoted and products named come from the various catalogs of U.S. Gypsum Company. Other firms also make useful epoxy resins. Many of the techniques for molds and casts outlined in the plaster casting section may also be used with epoxy.

SURFACE COAT RESINS. Some of those sold by U.S. Gypsum are noted in this paragraph. Epoxical Surface Coat 404 is a machinable, black, iron-filled gel-coat resin used with fiberglass laminations or for casts and molds and has good wear characteristics. It will not run off vertical surfaces and can be applied in thicknesses up to ½". Its pot life is 25 minutes, and it becomes firm in 50 minutes. Epoxical Surface Coat 405 is a thixotropic resin used for surfacing plaster molds or for applying fiberglass laminations. It will not run off vertical surfaces and will harden even if in contact with wet plaster. Epoxical Surface Coat 406 is a faster-setting version of No. 405. Its pot life is 9 to 13 minutes.

USING EPOXY TO FACE PLASTER MOLDS. Sometimes a plaster mold is prone to breakage, surface marring, or chipping because of its size, shape, or use. If lined with epoxy, however, plastic molds will be greatly strengthened and their casting life will be extended. The procedure is as follows:

Table 8-11. Separators Used Between Epoxy Resin Molding Material and Various Patterns

Pattern	Separator
Plaster, Wood (first seal the pattern)	Smooth-On Sonite / U.S.G. Epoxical Release-All / Coat with lacquer, wax, and then apply polyvinyl alcohol

1. Place the pattern in a box the dimensions of which will determine the size of the outside of the mold. Patterns (and molds) that may be used with epoxy include plaster, wood, metal, vulcanized rubber, and plastic. Seal plaster and wood with quick-drying automotive-type Duco Lacquer No. 1907, Tygon, or Epoxical Polyvinyl Alcohol Liquid Mold Release (table 8-11). The latter agent should be applied only after the pattern has been coated with lacquer; let it dry and wax it.

Wood with a really open grain should first be sealed with paste wood filler diluted with thinner or naphtha. Brush on the filler and let it dry. Wipe off any excess by rubbing the pattern across its grain and let it dry overnight. Apply a coat of DuPont No. 1991 Duco Clear Sealer, let it dry, and sand it. Apply several coats of Duco No. 1907 Clear Lacquer, let it dry, wax with paste wax, then polish it. Apply two spray coats of polyvinyl alcohol and one coat of Epoxical Mold Sealer-Separator.

2. Spray the pattern with Epoxical Mold Sealer Separator.

3. Brush on a face coat of Epoxical surface coat resin.

4. For extra strength (needed mostly in large molds), spray or flock on a ¹⁄₃₂" to ¹⁄₁₆" layer of copper, steel, or aluminum reinforcing slivers. Do not allow a buildup of metal in the corners of the mold. If the mold is not very prone to breakage, omit the metal.

No type of epoxy, except that made from thick section casting resins, must be cast in thicknesses over ½" to ¾". Thicker sections would be damaged by the excessive heat generated during setting. This heat would break down the parting agent, warp the plastic, and form air voids and bubbles in the surface.

5. After the epoxy has hardened, brush on a coat of Ultracal plaster.

Greater bonding between plastic and plaster can be achieved by allowing the plastic coat to become tacky, then brushing on a second coat of plastic, and, immediately after that, pressing wads of hemp into it. Fiberglass tape can also be pressed into the still-wet resin, and the form undulated like a multilooped serpent, with loops projecting ½" or more from the surface of the plastic.

6. While the plaster is still wet, pour on additional plaster to fill the box completely.

7. Remove the pattern and box just before drying the plaster (three to four hours from the start of its mixing).

Laminations of epoxy and fiberglass can also be backed up with gypsum plaster. This is sometimes done to provide additional strength in huge molds. Another way to back up epoxy and fiberglass laminations is to add U.S. Gypsum Epoxical Core Fill to it. Core Fill (five or six parts) is mixed with laminating resin (one part) and is applied after the last layer of cloth is in place. The hardened fill has a compressive strength of 2,000 to 4,000 pounds per square inch, depending on the hardener used.

CASTING THICK SECTIONS IN EPOXY. Molds and casts that are ½″ to 4½″ thick may be cast from Epoxical thick section casting resins (figure 8-10). Sections 8″ thick can be cast by adding aluminum granules to the resin. This also improves the dimensional stability of the epoxy. Additional thicknesses can always be added with a backing of plaster or a wood core insert. The intended thickness of the section should be estimated and the correct formula of thick section resin and two types of hardener then computed from tables (provided by manufacturers of epoxy).

Pour through sprues, made from tubing, when making all but the smallest objects. Fill the tubes to the top with resin after the object has been cast. This will create hydrostatic pressure to keep the mold or cast filled with resin as the resin sets and shrinks. Without this pressure, square corners may contract and become rounded. Cast objects should be allowed to dry overnight and then removed from their pattern or mold by wooden wedges, ejector pins, or air pressure.

Table 8-12. Separators Used between Epoxy Resin Molds and Low-Melting-Point Metal

Cast	Separator
Low-melting-point metal	Oil or graphite
	A separator may not be needed

METAL CASTS

Metal is most commonly used in casting figures, vehicles, and tree armatures. It can also be used for making truss sections (figure 8-13), detailed grilles and fences, and even entire models.

HIGH-MELTING-POINT METAL CASTS. Industrially produced, finely detailed castings are made in metal that has a melting point above that found in the Cerro alloys. Because of the relatively complex foundry equipment that is required for such casting, it is only used in the more elaborate professional model shops, although small foundry kits *are* available. These consist of a 2,400°F furnace (¾″ × 4″ capacity), blower, mixing vessel, and melting crucible. Smaller, lower-temperature furnaces, including a heater and metal ladle, are also available.

One interesting industrial metal-casting process that may be worth reviewing is lost-wax casting. This system is used to produce complicated objects with numerous undercuts in one cast. The alternative to this system is tedious several-part casting in a less precise, flexible mold. The latter system also limits the melting point and, therefore, the kinds of metal that can be used.

The steps in *lost-wax casting* are as follows:

1. Make a wax pattern.
2. Make a female mold from refractory plaster.
3. Melt out the wax.
4. Fill the mold with casting metal.
5. Break away the plaster.

Variations on this technique allow one to make the pattern in a material other than wax and then to produce it in many wax pattern copies. These copies are assembled on a wax tree (which also creates the pouring sprue). For dense castings free of surface flaws, the molten metal is often injected into the plaster mold in a vacuum chamber; or the mold and its still hot cast are swung on a centrifuge.

These systems, and the others possible with high-melting-point metals, are complicated by the danger inherent in working with molten metal. If the mold contains moisture, the hot metal may cause it to explode. It may be better to have a local jewelry-casting firm do the work. Metal casting can also be custom-made to specifications.

LOW-MELTING-POINT METAL CASTS. The major inconveniences of casting in hot metals can be eliminated by using low-melting-point metals. In this way, molds that would be destroyed by high temperatures may be used. Boiling water can replace a more elaborate furnace and the danger of the molds' exploding will be eliminated. Objects that may be cast include people, tree armatures, furniture, railings, and grille work.

Molds may be made of the usual mold materials (including rubber) as well as of cardboard or wood. A mold of a complex cornice made out of cardboard is shown in figure 8-13C, D, and E.

Casting with Low-Melting-Point Metal

1. Melt small quantities of the metal in an iron or stainless steel (not brass or aluminum) ladle suspended in a pot of boiling water. Melt large quantities in a pot.

8-9.
Yanbu Industrial City, Module 02, Saudi Arabia
3D/International, Architects. Master Plan: Dan Brents
Scale: 1:100 metric. Base: 10′ × 12′
Materials: acrylic and cast epoxy resin

The 19 different housing configurations in this project, one of which
is seen here, were built in acrylic. Since these few basic building
elements had to be repeated hundreds of times casting was the
logical solution for this model.

8-10.
Silicone rubber molds were made from the acrylic models and
1,200 units were cast with epoxy resin to assemble 14 different
cluster types. Public structures were constructed of solid acrylic
with 1/32″ acrylic facades.

8-11.
This is a view of the entire master plan. (*Photographs (figures 8-
9 through 8-11) by Judd Haggard of William M. Burwell, Inc.*)

Table 8-13. Separators Used between Low-Melting-Point Metal Molding Material and Various Patterns

Patterns	Separators
Wood, Hydro-Stone, Sculpt Metal, Cardboard, Clay, Plasticine, Acrylic plastic (first seal the pattern)	{ Oil or graphite { A separator may not be needed
Plaster (first seal the pattern)	Oil or graphite Moldcraft 2D (allow the pattern to dry before pouring the metal)

Table 8-14. Separators Used between Low-Melting-Point Metal and Plaster

Cast	Separator
Plaster	Spray on a mixture of 10% S.A.E. No. 10 mineral oil, 2.75% bayberry wax, .25% aerosol O.T., and 87% water

Take care not to overheat the metal or, when cooling, it will revert to a brittle crystalline form.

2. Pour into a cool mold. To fill a deep mold, pour the metal through a tube inserted into the bottom of the mold. Withdraw the tube while pouring.

3. Remove the casting from the mold as soon as it has cooled. If certain metals are allowed to stand in the mold too long, they will expand and tightly grip the mold.

Long objects cast in low-melting-point metal must be supported in the model or they may sag in time.

"BOLOGNA" CASTING WITH LOW-MELTING-POINT METAL. To cast very delicate repetitive objects (such as trusses, joists, or fences) that are needed in great numbers, a technique called Bologna casting may be used (figure 8-13A and B).

1. After precisely constructing the mold, preheat it by encasing it in aluminum foil and hold it over an electric heating element or place it in an oven.

2. When the mold is heated above the melting point of the metal, slowly pour in the molten metal. Hold the mold at a slant. If any air bubbles are forming, they will be visible through the acrylic mold top. If they do form, tap the mold to work them out. If a substantial number of air bubbles refuse to be worked out of the mold, wrap it in foil and reheat it, then resume the agitation.

3. After the entire mold has been satisfactorily poured and cooled, remove the acrylic and slice the metal and wood sandwich on a band or circular saw equipped with a fine-tooth metal cutting blade. Sections as thin as 1/50" can be made with these tools.

4. To remove the pieces of wood from the metal cast, position each wood piece over a hole cut in a sheet of wood and carefully push it out of the fragile metal frame.

If it is impossible to saw the sections thin enough, sand crudely cut sections to the desired thickness by first cementing them to a sheet of wood. Then cement strips of cardboard (whose thickness is equal to the desired thickness of the section) to the periphery of the sanding block. These strips will limit the amount that can be sanded off the metal section. Remove the sanded section from the wood sheet by pouring cement thinner over it.

8-12.
David Lloyd Kreeger House
Philip Johnson Associates, Architects
Modelmaker: Joseph Santeramo of the
    architects' model studio
Scale: 1/8" = 1'

The vaults of this presentation model were cast in polyester resin. Walls, flat roofs, screens, and columns were machined from acrylic. (*Photograph by Louis Checkman*)

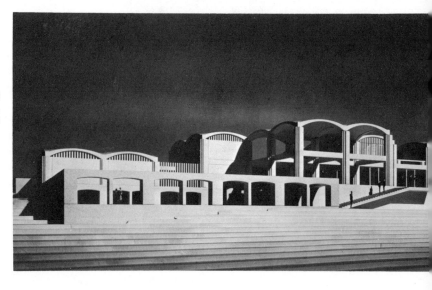

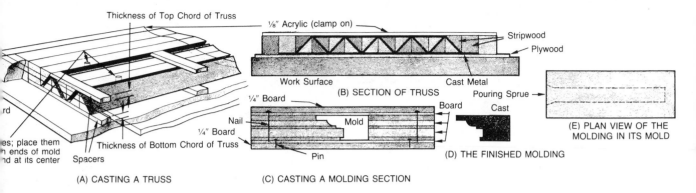

Thickness of Top Chord of Truss
⅛" Acrylic (clamp on)
Stripwood
Plywood
Work Surface
Cast Metal
(B) SECTION OF TRUSS
Pouring Sprue
¼" Board
Board
Cast
Nail
Mold
(E) PLAN VIEW OF THE MOLDING IN ITS MOLD
¼" Board
Board
Thickness of Bottom Chord of Truss
es; place them
h ends of mold
d at its center
Spacers
Pin
(D) THE FINISHED MOLDING
(A) CASTING A TRUSS
(C) CASTING A MOLDING SECTION

-13.
Casting with low-melting-point metal

COLD METAL CASTS. Two casting materials that serve as shortcuts to a finished mold are plastic aluminum and epoxy metal compound, both of which may be cast into latex rubber molds.

Plastic aluminum comes in tubes sold under various brand names. It may be formed into casts with fine detail. This material shrinks and warps badly, however, especially in castings that measure ¼" or more in dimension. Larger castings may be made in several pieces to lessen the warpage. Pack the liquid aluminum into the rubber mold with a palette knife.

Epoxy metal compound is a filler and sealer material that comes in two parts, mixed in the same way as epoxy cement. It may be cast in a well-oiled latex rubber mold.

RUBBER CASTS

Certain types of rubber may be used to make casts as well as molds. Casting rubber may be made into flexible or rigid hollow casts formed in female plaster molds. The amount of filler mixed into the rubber determines the rigidity of the cast. The mix is poured into the mold and allowed to stand for 15 to 30 minutes. The excess liquid is then poured out. Parting agents are not required. Cured rigid casts may be painted with oil, watercolors, lacquer, or enamel. Flexible casts must be painted with flexible rubber paints, which come in limited colors.

9:Various Shapes and How to Model Them

The table given in this chapter can be used as a quick reference guide for choosing ways to make various model shapes. When planning a specific shape, decide whether the object will be opaque or transparent and whether it can be a basic form or must be highly detailed. Finally, consider the number of these forms you will need. The materials and construction techniques suggested here are reviewed in chapters 3 through 8.

Table 9-1. Various Shapes and How to Model Them

Shape	Opacity	Detail	Number Produced	Construction Techniques
Simple solid blocks, all sides flat	Opaque	Rough	One	Rough cut: clay or plasticine, foam plastic, acrylic, or wood Laminate: several plies of board
			Mass-produced	Cast: plaster; for small shapes use metal, polyester, epoxy, or metal Press into molds: Clay or plasticine
		Precise	One	Wood, acrylic, plaster, or ren wood
			Mass-produced	Cast: plaster; for small shapes use metal, polyester, or epoxy
	Transparent	Rough or precise	One	Acrylic
			Mass-produced	Acrylic or cast polyester resin
Solid blocks curved in one direction (columns, drum shapes, etc.)	Opaque	Rough	One	Carve or turn: wood, acrylic, foam plastic, clay, or plasticine Rod or tubing: wood, acrylic, or metal Former and plank construction (for large shapes)
			Mass-produced	Press into molds: clay or plasticine Cast: plaster
		Precise	One	Turn: acrylic, wood, plaster, or ren wood Rod or tubing: acrylic, wood, or metal Former and plank construction (for large shapes)
			Mass-produced	Cast: plaster; for small shapes use metal, polyester, or epoxy
	Transparent	Rough or precise	One	Acrylic rod or tubing
			Mass-produced	Cast: polyester resin Acrylic rod or tubing

Shape	Opacity	Detail	Number Produced	Construction Techniques
Solid blocks curved in one direction and scalloped (fluted columns, decorations, etc.)	Opaque	Rough or precise	One	Fluted with tool: clay, plasticine, or foam plastic; wood dowel; acrylic rod or tubing Carve: wood or acrylic Bend on frame: Bristolboard or polystyrene Two-dimensional fluted drawn detail (if acceptable)
			Mass-produced	Cast: plaster, metal, polyester, or epoxy Press into molds: clay or plasticine
	Transparent	Rough or precise	One	Acrylic
			Mass-produced	Acrylic, cast polyester resin
Solid blocks curved in two directions (domes, etc.)	Opaque	Rough or precise	One	Carve or turn: wood, acrylic, or foam plastic Carve: clay or plasticine Former and plank construction
			Mass-produced	Cast: plaster Press into molds: clay or plasticine Ready-made domes, or cut from balls
	Transparent	Rough or precise	One	Acrylic
			Mass-produced	Acrylic, cast polyester resin
Solid, highly detailed objects (column capitals, moldings, small furniture, etc.)	Opaque	Rough or precise	One	Carve: acrylic, plaster, or wood
			Mass-produced	Cast: polyester, plaster, epoxy, or metal
Punctured, highly detailed objects (grilles, etc.)	Opaque	Rough or precise	One	Carve or machine: sheet acrylic, polystyrene, or metal Etched metal Two-dimensional drawn detail (if acceptable)
			Mass-produced	Cast: polyester, epoxy or metal. Two-dimensional drawn detail (if acceptable)
Simple slabs	Opaque	Rough or precise	One	Cut: illustration and other boards, sheet wood, plywood, composition board, acrylic, or acetate
			Mass-produced	Cast: metal, polyester, or epoxy
	Transparent	Rough or precise	One or mass-produced	Cut: sheet acrylic or acetate

Shape	Opacity	Detail	Number Produced	Construction Techniques
Punctured slabs or slabs with recessed or projected details (facades, furniture fronts, etc.)	Opaque	Rough or precise	One	Laminate: illustration or other boards, sheet wood, acrylic, polystyrene, or acetate Mill: acrylic Etched metal Two-dimensional drawn detail (if acceptable)
			Mass-produced	Cast: plaster, metal, polyester, or epoxy Two-dimensional drawn detail (if acceptable)
	Transparent	Rough or precise	One	Laminate: sheet acrylic or acetate Mill: acrylic
			Mass-produced	Cast: polyester resin
Complex slabs (folded plate construction, complex skylights, etc.)	Opaque	Rough or precise	One	Fold or bevel cut: illustration and other boards, sheet wood, or acrylic
			Mass-produced	Cast: metal, polyester, or epoxy
	Transparent	Rough or precise	One	Bevel cut and cement: sheet acrylic, or acetate
			Mass-produced	Cast: polyester resin
Slabs curved in one direction (vaults, curved walls, etc.)	Opaque	Rough or precise	One	Bend: illustration or other board, sheet wood, or acetate (softened with a solvent) Laminate: several plies Bristolboard, gumstrip, or fiberglass Wet-form against a mold: card or other board, or sheet wood Hammer or bend against a mold: metal Vacuum- or drape-form: acetate or acrylic
			Mass-produced	Cast: plaster, metal, polyester, or epoxy Vacuum- or drape-form: sheet acetate, acrylic, or polystyrene Run: plaster
	Transparent	Rough or precise	One	Vacuum- or drape-form: sheet acetate or acrylic Bend on mold: acetate (softened with a solvent)
			Mass-produced	Cast: plaster

Shape	Opacity	Detail	Number Produced	Construction Techniques
Slabs curved in two directions (concrete shells, domes, molded furniture, etc.)	Opaque	Rough or precise	One	Wet-form on a mold: cardboard and other boards Hammer or bend against a mold: metal Laminate: gumstrip or fiberglass Bend against a mold: sheet acetate (softened with a solvent) Vacuum- or drape-form: sheet acetate or acrylic
			Mass-produced	Cast: metal, polyester, or epoxy Vacuum- or drape-form: sheet acrylic or polystyrene
	Transparent	Rough or precise	One	Vacuum- or drape-form: sheet acetate or acrylic
			Mass-produced	Cast: polyester resin
Thick-walled structures curved in several directions, walls having various thicknesses	Opaque	Rough or precise	One or mass-produced	Carve: wood, ren wood, acrylic, plaster, air-drying clay, or sculpt stone Former and plank construction Mount on wooden skeleton: Celastic, plaster or plaster-impregnated cloth, mesh, or buckram

Shape	Opacity	Detail	Number Produced	Construction Techniques
Frames whose members have square and rectangular cross sections (framing models, sun shades, etc.)	Opaque	Rough or precise	One	Cut and cement: stripwood, strip illustration and other boards, strip acrylic, or polystyrene Solder: metal strips
			Mass-produced	Cast: metal, polyester, or epoxy Cut and cement: strip acrylic
Frames set against glass (exterior wall construction)	Opaque	Rough or precise	One	Cut and apply or inlay: strips of wood, illustration or other boards, acrylic, polystyrene, metal, or tapes Two-dimensional drawn detail or detail scribed into acrylic
			Mass-produced	Cast: metal, polyester, or epoxy
Frames whose members have thin, round sections (space frames, geodesic domes, etc.)	Opaque	Rough or precise	One or mass-produced	Cut and cement: metal, acrylic, or wood rod or tubing Construct egg-crate out of acrylic, and scribe or paint

Shape	Opacity	Detail	Number Produced	Construction Techniques
Frames whose members are tapered or curved in one direction (cast concrete frames, furniture parts, etc.)	Opaque	Rough or precise	One	Carve or sand: sheet wood, illustration and other boards, acrylic, or polystyrene Two-dimensional drawn detail (if acceptable)
			Mass-produced	Cast: metal, polyester, or epoxy
	Transparent	Rough or precise	One	Cut: sheet acrylic
			Mass-produced	Cut: sheet acrylic Cast: polyester resin
Frames whose members are curved or tapered in two directions (vaulting, decorative designs, cast concrete frames, etc.)	Opaque	Rough or precise	One	Carve: acrylic or stripwood Two-dimensional drawn detail (if acceptable)
			Mass-produced	Vacuum-form: sheet polystyrene or acrylic Cast: metal, polyester, epoxy, or plaster

10:Exterior Building Finishes and Elements

Wall, floor, and roof finishes may be shown in many ways and with a high degree of detail. When planning the construction of a model, you should consider how the exterior details will be represented. Elements such as moldings and cornices may be added to the exterior surfaces of an assembled model, as can certain simulated building materials. These materials include commercially available paper, board, or polystyrene sheets on which various patterns have been drawn, scribed, or embossed (figure 10-1). On the other hand, if you are making your own building materials, you may want to draw or scribe the patterns on the individual wall pieces before the model is assembled. Or you may want to cast (figure 8-6) or vacuum form (figure 7-27) certain details or textures to create a more three-dimensional effect. Building materials may also be represented with actual architectural products, but these will have to be converted for model use. The stock of samples from an ordinary office will provide additional materials that can be used directly or modified for finishing purposes.

EXTERIOR BUILDING FINISHES

Stone

Stone embossing is achieved in a slightly different way from that used for embossing regularly shaped materials. First, let a can of enamel of the desired color stand until much of its oil comes to the surface. Second, pour off the oil and trowel the remaining pigment onto illustration board or other sheet material. Third, after the paint begins to set, emboss the stone with a wood scribe. Gesso may be used in place of the enamel in this technique.

Large stonework can be made of wood or paper boards cut individually and applied (figure 10-2) or cast in plastic or plaster on a homemade pattern.

Marble

Many types of marble may be represented by marbelized paper. For example, white, opaque acrylic or alabaster can be used for white marble. However, hand painting is the technique many professional modelbuilders use to create marble, granite, and other patterned stones. To paint a marble texture, first apply the basic color of the stone. While the paint is wet, dab the other colors on with cotton balls. A feather may be used to smear the paint into realistic swirls and striations.

Complex plaza or floor patterns may also be masked and spray painted, made from tape, scribed, or penciled or inked in. To protect the more delicate of these effects, cover them with a thin sheet of acrylic or apply a coat of clear lacquer or varnish.

Shingles

Although you can use the usual drafting and scribing techniques to represent shingles and roof tiles, they may also be constructed in the following ways:

1. On thin wood sheets, illustration board, or thick Bristolboard, score the vertical lines lightly.
2. With a blade, heavily score the horizontal lines, making the cut at an angle to the surface of the board.
3. Lift the edge of each shingle with the blade.
4. Impart color to the shingles with thin poster color wash and warp them slightly for a realistic effect. For a more accurate three-dimensional effect, each shingle or tile can be cut out and applied individually (figure 10-3).

Large-scale siding can be cut in strips from two-ply Bristolboard. Cut the strips twice as wide as the exposed part of the shingles (tape graph paper to the cutting board as a guide for dimensions). Then mount the strips one over another to provide a highly realistic effect.

10-1.
Ready-made wall, floor, and roof finishes. This is a sampling of the wide variety of simulated building materials available from manufacturers and hobby stores. Brick, block, stone, siding, roofing, and paving are only some of the textures and patterns that are simulated on sheets of paper, plastic, and wood. These sheets come in many different sizes and thicknesses.

10-2.

Black Building with White Piano
Caroline Huber
Dimensions: 22½″ H × 10¼″ W × 10¼″ D
Materials: wood, glass, and paint

The thin wood sheets cut into stone block shapes were glued in rows on the walls, which were then painted. The building cornice and doorways are also made out of wood. Windows are shown with glass.

10-3.
Bently Avenue House
Modelmaker: Robert L. Duncan
Materials: balsa wood and Plexiglas

This model is constructed of 7¼-pound balsa wood. Its framed construction is covered with sideboards cut from thin sheets. The tower was made by bending wet balsa sheets around an oatmeal can and its cap was made of solid balsa turned on a lathe. Approximately 7,000 shingles were applied on the roof. The drains are made of brass tubing and windows are clear Plexiglas. No measurements were used in planning the model—all information was taken from photographs and visits to the site of the house.

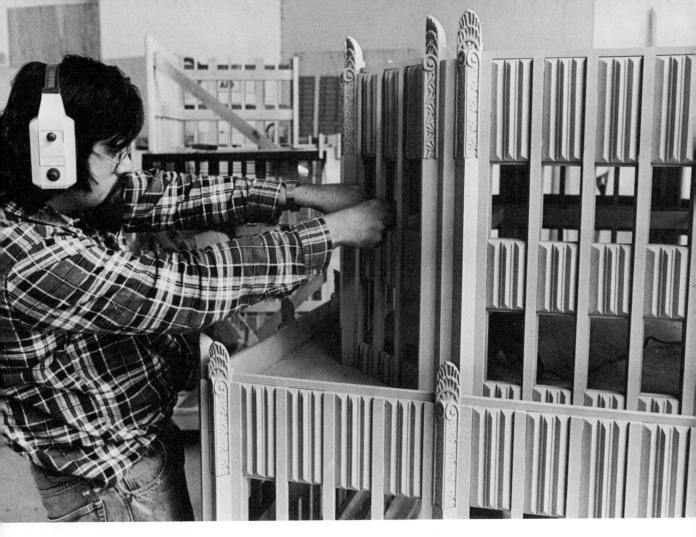

Spanish Tiles

One way to make Spanish tiles is to cut soda straws lengthwise in the proper dimensions, glue these in place, and paint. Another method is to press the curved patterns in thin Bristolboard between carved hardwood or extruded male and female molds. First, dampen the board; then clamp it between the molds.

Corrugated Metal

Scribe a corrugated metal pattern into a sheet of heavy metal foil. Use a sharpened wood dowel or hair comb as the scriber and coat the back of the scribed sheet with cement to stiffen it.

Wood Finishes

Wood may be approximately modeled with veneers at ¼", and larger, scales. Use mahogany, sapeli, makori, or other fine-grained tropical wood. The grains of quartered walnut, ribbon or quartered fiddleback mahogany, red Philippine mahogany, lacewood, white gum, redwood burl, or elm Flexwood will reasonably conform to 1" = 1'

10-4.
Blade Runner, detail of special effects miniature
Warner Bros. (A Ladd Company Release)
Special photographic effects: Entertainment Effects Group

This large hollow model has a wood frame construction. The exterior panel structure was made out of wood and assembled onto the frame. Windows were later set into the openings. The intricate Art Deco building details were plaster cast.

and larger-scaled models. Other species or scales of wood must be custom painted, or, in some instances, a fine grain veneer may be stained another color to approximate the wood needed.

EXTERIOR BUILDING ELEMENTS

Moldings and Cornices

All sorts of moldings may be built up from strips of thin Bristolboard or wood. Half-rounds may be molded from wet paper over a dowel. Larger moldings can be extruded from basswood or polystyrene if a reground

blade is used as a scraper. Scrapers may also be made out of small, old files or hacksaw blades. When using a saw blade, first remove its temper, file the desired cutting edge, and then retemper. The scraper may be hand held and drawn along a straightedge, or set into a hardwood guide and drawn along a workbench edge. It is best to cut the molding with a series of light cuts rather than trying to do it all at once.

Quite intricate moldings can be run or cast in plaster (figure 10-5), even in as small a scale as $\frac{1}{16}'' = 1'$. But high-quality results can be achieved with the above techniques in any scale.

There are many other materials that can be used to approximately represent moldings. Decorative tapes are available in many interesting patterns. A specific pattern can also be custom-made, but a minimum of 3,000″ is often required. Several lines of pressure-sensitive overlays also carry patterns for moldings.

10-5.
House in Entrance Room
George Grant

This is a wood frame construction coated in plaster. Different-color tile pieces were embedded in the plaster while it was still wet. The tentacles projecting out of the roof are wire wrapped in gauze that had been stiffened with plaster. (*Photograph courtesy of Betty Parsons Gallery*)

10–6.
A City, detail
James Grashow
Materials: plywood, cardboard, and fabric

To simulate exterior finishes on this building facade, fabrics of various colors and patterns were applied to the cardboard and plywood forms. (*Photograph by Steven Ogilvy, courtesy of Allan Stone Gallery*)

Grilles and Railings

Professional modelmakers often cast grilles or railings in metal by using flexible molds. The original patterns are machined from bronze.

You can sometimes find perforated metal or embossed plastic sheets that come close to your requirements. Perforated metal comes in many styles—round holes in various diameters, rectangular slots, oblongs, square holes, triangular perforations, among others—and common copper mesh can be used at small scales to indicate grilles. Plastic waffle patterns are also available from various manufacturers. To make your own perforated pattern in paper, use hole punches.

The Ozachrome process can be used to print a grille pattern on acetate, which then may be mounted on acrylic for additional stiffness.

Wrought Iron Ornaments

Wrought iron ornaments may be cut from thin shimmed brass that is sliced into very narrow strips and then burnished into curlicues. If it is not important that the exact pattern be represented—only some indication of a filigree effect—glue lace to a thin sheet of acetate and, when dry, cut out panels to the desired shape.

Gutter or Drain Pipes

These can be made from aluminum or brass tubing. Gutters are made by sanding half the tubing away.

Rivets, Nuts, Bolts, and Valves

It is sometimes necessary to represent these small objects on $\frac{1}{8}'' = 1'$ or larger-scale models. Exact scale replicas are commercially available in a variety of sizes and types. These should be used if you are constructing a piping layout model (see chapter 19) or a structural detail model. If these objects can be simply represented, make them yourself. Emboss rivet or bolthead shapes into Bristolboard, metal foil, or polystyrene sheet. Pour cement, glue, or shellac over the back of the sheet to make it better able to withstand handling. Valves can be represented with short lengths of wooden dowels or brass tubing.

11:Painting and Finishing

Painting is an extremely critical operation in model-making and other crafts. After spending laborious hours on a model, you may feel tempted to rush the final painting. The schedule may demand it or you may just desire to see the work finished and on display. Unfortunately, a rushed paint job will always look like just that and can easily ruin the skilled craftsmanship that is underneath. On the other hand, a good paint job can successfully complete the model, and even improve it, although paint should never be expected to cover sloppy construction or fully make up for lack of detail.

Painting takes more time than most people realize. Many builders of all-acrylic models estimate that painting and finishing take up to one-third of the total construction time.

Two secrets that will ensure a good paint job are to use good tools and materials and to be thorough in planning. Before starting construction, study all the model's parts to determine which must be painted before being permanently attached to it. Visible parts placed inside others must be painted before being assembled, as must parts painted a different color from surrounding areas. The only exceptions should be those parts whose paint lines are easily masked. When possible, try to obtain materials that are manufactured in the desired color, as is often the case with paper, cardboard, simulated building materials, acrylic, flock, etc. If you cannot get the desired color, paint these materials yourself. Be sure to paint stock material all at once to ensure a consistent color. Also, to prevent warping, cut the exact areas needed out of the already painted stock.

Painting should not be the final construction operation—it should be done in phases throughout the construction of the model. When painting small-scale figures, furniture, or other intricate objects, apply the largest areas of color first, then the smaller touches.

Paint thickness must be relative to scale. Too thick a finish can destroy detail and cause the model to look like a toy, not like a miniature structure. To preserve detail, it is best to select a paint that will cover with one moderately thin coat; if this is impossible, apply the paint in two thin coats rather than in one thick one. Sand lightly between the coats if possible. The problem of atmospheric dust marring the finish can be overcome by the use of a spray booth and quick-drying paint.

Models are usually displayed under artificial lighting, which provides less light intensity than the actual building would receive from natural light. To compensate for this, paint the model in slightly lighter colors than would be used on the actual building.

Some models have painted-in shadows so that they will not have to rely on display lighting to provide these accents. Of course, do not shadow paint models that will eventually be photographed under varied lighting conditions.

Large town-planning models that will be primarily viewed from one side as well as dioramas should be painted with some degree of aerial perspective. Colors farthest from the viewer should be muted and misty; those closer to the viewer, more chromatic and contrasting.

TYPES OF PAINT

Paint is composed of pigment, which gives color and opacity, and of vehicle, the liquid in which the pigment is suspended. When dry, vehicle bonds the pigment together. Thinner or reducer is sometimes added to paint to make it flow easily; more volatile than the vehicle, this evaporates first. Thinner may also be used to rejuvenate some types of dried paint.

Paint may be applied in several coats. The first or primer coat forms a bond between the material and the paint. Because the primer has a clinging tendency greater than that of most paint, it helps ensure that the paint will not peel or flake. It also helps to prevent paint from being peeled off when tape masking is used. Primers used on porous materials also seal the surface and are often called sealers.

After applying the primer, put on surfacer coats containing pigment. These coats fill pores or grain, impart some color, and produce an even surface for the final or top coat. Well-primed materials and those with a smooth surface do not require surfacer coats. Some paints are self-leveling—they have a tendency to flow into a level finish, eliminating brush marks and other irregularities.

Earlier sections of this book give painting instructions for balsa, building paper, metal, paper and cardboard, plaster, plastic, and wood. Many characteristics of the various general types of paints are enumerated there.

Oil Paints

Oil paints are very easy to apply by brush, but their long drying time limits their usefulness to the modelmaker. However, interesting rough finishes useful in the representation of stone, earth, etc., can be rendered with oil paint. Artist's oil paints come in about the largest color range of any paints, but keep in mind that their thickness can hide model detail and their finish is not abrasion resistant.

The vehicle for oil paint can be linseed, soybean, or tung oil. Oil paints are thinned with turpentine or mineral spirits. They come with high-gloss or flat finishes. The high gloss can be flattened if a greater quantity of turpentine is mixed into it, but it will not be as affected if mineral spirits are used. Turpentine also hastens drying; oil retards it. Thinners will not rejuvenate dried-out paint. If a paint skin has formed in the container, remove it whole. If parts of the skin get mixed into the paint, strain the paint through two thicknesses of gauze.

Both varnish-base and oil-base enamels are oil paints. Enamels are useful because, among their other attributes, they produce a higher gloss than lacquers do. Quick-drying enamels are self-leveling and dry in four hours. Enamels may be used over oil, lacquer, shellac, casein, and rubber-base and vinyl-plastic water-base paints. A sealer should, however, be used between water-base paints (other than vinyl-plastic ones) and enamels.

Japan colors are quick-drying oil paints that can be obtained in many colors. They dry in two hours to a really fine, flat finish. Mix them with quick-drying varnish for a satin finish.

Water Paints

Watercolors, because of their transparency, lack covering power. In general, this limits their usefulness in model making. However, interesting details can be rendered on a model built out of or covered with papers and boards made especially for watercolor painting.

Poster colors are of more use. One of their biggest drawbacks—the ease with which they can be marred—can be eliminated by giving them a finishing coat of crystal or spirit varnish. This will also increase their richness and depth of color and give them a gloss.

Texture paints can be used to color plaster ground constructions. They come in powdered form and may be applied by brush or spatula, depending on how thick they are mixed.

Plastic watercolors, also called polymer, vinyl, or acrylic colors, are a new type of water paint. They can be used in a thin wash, thick, or mixed with gesso. They dry to a semimatte finish, but may be mixed with a medium that produces a glossy finish. Dried paint is waterproof and must be removed with paint remover.

Lacquers

Lacquer is a term frequently applied to any quick-drying paint. True lacquer used to have a nitrocellulose base, but now some are being made with acrylic, vinyl, or other bases. These paints are quick drying. Thinners vary with different brands, although acetone, glycol ether, or amyl acetate can be used with most. Do not use more than one part thinner to one part paint. The same, or cheaper, thinner may be used as a paint remover.

Cellulose paints are opaque and inflammable and can be used on wood, composition board, metal, paper, and many plastics (including acrylic). Their rapid drying is ideal for spray application, but difficult for brush application. For extensive brush painting, use special brushing (slower-drying) cellulose paints or the regular paint mixed with a retarder. Apply them by brushing in one direction. Allow the previous coat to dry for one or more hours before applying the next. Use No. 400 wet sandpaper between coats.

Most top-coat lacquers dry to a mellow luster. For a high-gloss polish, apply a silicone car or furniture polish, or apply a coat of high-gloss clear lacquer. To reduce the normal luster, add a flattening agent to the paint. During warm and humid weather, moisture may retard drying time. A fan can help to rectify this. Extreme moisture may also cause the lacquer to turn a whitish color. Avoid painting under these conditions, or use a special summer lacquer thinner, or add retarder mix to the regular thinner. Lacquer cannot be applied over oil paints because it would dissolve them. Although lacquer dries rapidly, avoid handling freshly painted objects for several hours.

Industrial and automotive lacquers are used by many professional modelmakers on acrylic and other materials because they provide a flat finish and do not ruin detail. These lacquers must be spray painted. Some of the heavier lacquers of this type require between 60 and 70 pounds of spraying pressure.

Synthetic Enamels

These enamels have a high-gloss finish and may be used on wood, plaster, metal, paper, and other materials. Strain enamels to ensure that they will form an absolutely smooth coat. Synthetic enamels are best applied by brush and should be as thin as possible. Use a soft brush and, with even strokes, apply in one direction. Since they dry rapidly, work quickly. Do not run the brush over an area that has just been painted. Objects to be painted must be completely grease-free. Wood must be perfectly dry or the enamel will soon crack and peel. Use synthetic filler as an undercoat and also to fill wood. Sand with wet sandpaper. Synthetic enamels dry in about four hours, but allow twice this time before working on the surface again. Sand smooth with extremely fine, wet, abrasive paper, and, if you need a high-gloss coat, polish with metal polish.

Metallic Finishes

To get metallic finishes, use chrome or other metallic oil-base paints, lacquers, and enamels. Some are available in spray cans.

Aluminum, gold, brass, and copper colors come in powder form. Mix the powder with lacquer thinner and clear lacquer and then spray-apply it. To prepare the powders for brush application, thin them with turpentine or enamel thinner, using quick-drying varnish or bronzing liquid as a vehicle.

Cylinders of wax that contain metallic powder are also available. These can be rubbed into wood, metal, plaster, etc., and buffed to a luster. They are thinned with turpentine.

Of all the metal finishes, none can surpass actual foil or leaf for realism. Household aluminum foil makes good polished chrome. It can be stretched over complex curves and held in place with rubber cement or shellac. Use a wood dowel to roll the foil flat and to burnish it into place. To represent anodized aluminum, spray translucent colored lacquer over aluminum foil (or, for that matter, over surfaces painted with aluminum paint).

Gold and silver leaf can be represented by adhesive papers that come in those colors; or you can use aluminum foil sprayed with matte finish for silver leaf, and aluminum foil sprayed with yellow translucent lacquer for gold foil.

Real metallic leaf can be obtained from shops carrying supplies for the sign-painting and book-binding trades. Thin sheets of leaf are held in place with size or burnishing clay. The latter is mixed with warm water until it is the consistency of heavy varnish. Take care to stir the mixture until it is smooth and free of bubbles. Apply the mix to the surface to be gilded and allow it to dry. Then sand it with 7/0 sandpaper and dust it. Apply more mix, allow it to dry, sand it, and dust it. Next, wet the surface and make it tacky with a 10% solution of alcohol. At this point apply and carefully press down the metal leaf with cotton batting. After allowing the leaf to dry overnight, burnish it with agate burnishers. A coat of clear Leaf Lacquer or French varnish may be applied to the leaf to protect it and to prevent discoloration.

To avoid the complications that a truly effective metallic finish entails, some professional modelmakers send out wood, plaster, and plastic parts to a metalizing shop for spraying, or send metal parts to an electroplating shop for plating. Figure 7-21 shows brass that has been nickel-plated by an outside shop to represent stainless steel.

Shellac

Shellac is a natural gum that comes in flake form or, more often, already dissolved in denatured alcohol. Two types are available: natural (which is orange in color) and bleached (which is white). White shellac makes a good undercoat for objects that will be painted with translucent or transparent paints.

Varnish

A combination of resin, drying oil, drier, and solvent (turpentine or mineral spirits), varnish usually comes in a clear state and may be pigmented. It is best to spray varnish, since application with a brush often fills up detail.

PREPARATION FOR PAINTING

Inspect the surface of the object. Fill all cracks, holes, and end grain with filler. Sand it smooth, making sure that all saw marks, whiskers, or flash are also removed.

To protect work surfaces from dripping paint and spray, cover them with newspaper. Keep a supply of clean, lint-free cloths or soft paper nearby, in case of a spill.

Thoroughly mix all paints before starting to paint. A wire rod with a hoop end can be inserted into an electric drill and used as a power mixer. If there are lumps or other particles in the paint, strain it through gauze, or through a nylon fabric stretched over the mouth of a paint jar and held in place by a rubber band. Another strainer can be made by cutting the tip from a cone-shaped paper cup and plugging the hole with a pad of lint-free cheesecloth. Commercially made strainers are also available. From time to time, stir the paint. Keep two containers of paint remover on hand. One should be used to clean most of the paint from the brushes, and the second for a more thorough rinse.

Mix small test amounts of paint by the drop. Paint a test strip and allow it to dry before judging its color. Glossy paints usually become darker as they dry; flat paints become lighter. Some pigments (red, Prussian blue, etc.) become more vivid. To facilitate color matching, keep an exact record of all the ingredients mixed in a batch. When mixing larger quantities, convert the drop count into half-ounces, ounces, and so on.

Test each new type of paint on the material to be painted to be sure it will adhere to and not warp the material. If slight warps do occur, eliminate them by bracing the material internally or by using the paint in a drier state. If a test on a flat piece of material is inconclusive as to the degree of warpage, build a rough mock-up of the assembly and test for the amount of bracing required to prevent this condition.

Clean caps and paint bottle tops before closing paint containers. Paint bottles should be stored upside down to allow the paint to seal up the cap and prevent evaporation.

Paint may usually be removed with a cloth dipped in thinner. Since cardboard and paper models may warp from this procedure, lightly sand or scrape off misplaced paint on these materials and then, if necessary, respray the surface. Removing paint from metal parts can be facilitated by immersing them in thinner and by brushing the paint off with a toothbrush. In more severe cases, remove paint by giving the metal object a bath in a solution of caustic lye and water. Some plastics will be attacked by certain thinners. To prevent such an accident, first test the thinner on a piece of plastic scrap.

MASKING

There are several masking agents of use to the modelbuilder. In general, masks can be divided into two categories: those that are hand-held, and those that are temporarily attached to the surface being painted.

Hand-held masks are commonly used when painting one surface of the inside of a corner or a 90° intersection. These masks may be cut from acetate, stencil paper, cardboard, or some other thin, stiff sheet. Only simple borders (straight lines, etc.) should be attempted with a hand-held mask.

Masks attached to painted surfaces can be made from one of the following materials.

Pressure-sensitive tape and *paper*. This must be carefully selected and a scrap must be tested before use. Many spray-painted matte paints cannot be masked with tape without being damaged. Some painted surface (lacquer, for example) must be allowed to dry several hours before being unmasked. Electrical black tape can be stretched to mask curve lines, but it usually proves hard to remove. Never use a tape, transparent or otherwise, whose sticking tenacity makes it impossible to remove without damaging the surface of the work. If a recommended tape is hard to remove, its holding power can be lessened by pressing it onto, and then removing it from, window glass a sufficient number of times to kill some of its adhesive quality. After the paint has dried, remove tape by pulling it back from the surface at a 30° angle. Make sure that it is pulled straight back and not slightly sideways to prevent raising the surface of the underlying materials.

Striping tape. This should be used to mask extremely thin lines. It is available at hobby shops.

11-1.
Tower 49, New York
Skidmore, Owings & Merrill, Architects
Modelmakers: SOM model studio
Scale: $\frac{1}{16}'' = 1'$
Material: Plexiglas

The facades of the tower were built out of $\frac{1}{16}''$ Plexiglas and the floorplates out of $\frac{1}{8}''$ Plexiglas. The walls were backpainted with green car paint. On the exterior, silver paint was dabbed along the score lines with a rag. Once the lines were filled with the paint, the excess was wiped off with denatured alcohol. Acrylic solvent was used along the edges to assemble the model. Because of the backpainted interior, glue was used to cement the floor plates in place. Great care was taken to simulate the rich architectural detailing of the surrounding buildings on the site. Information was culled from photographs and elevation drawings of not only the front facades, but the sides and back as well. These buildings were made of Plexiglas, backpainted with gray spray paint. Windows on the exterior remained masked out until all details, such as moldings and cornices, were added on as basswood strips. In cross section these strips were angled, flat, and coved. These were cut individually and glued in place. The different buildings were then painted various shades of gray and beige, and the masking was removed. (*Photograph by Wolfgang Hoyt/ESTO*)

Friskets. These mask flat surfaces that require an irregular masking line. The procedure is as follows:

1. Cover transparent frisket paper with a thin coat of rubber cement.

2. While this coat is still slightly wet, lay the paper (cement side down) on the object to be masked.

3. Smooth the paper down with a straightedge, working from the center to the edges.

4. Cut the paper to the desired outline, being careful not to cut into the object.

5. Remove the unwanted part of the frisket and check its edges to make sure they are holding tightly.

6. If there is any rubber cement remaining on the surface to be painted, allow it to dry and then carefully remove it with the sticky side of a piece of drafting tape or with a rubber cement pickup.

7. After applying the paint, remove the frisket and clean any cement from the object.

Gum strip. This can be used for masking some hard, waterproof surfaces. To remove, soak it in water.

Liquid frisket. This can be painted on flat or irregular surfaces. Remove surplus frisket by rolling it off with your fingers or with a bit of art gum or by picking it up with a piece of masking tape.

When painting two colors up to a masked line, either mask twice, applying the two colors so that they butt up against one another; or (if the added thickness of paint is not objectionable) paint the entire object with the lighter color, mask the line, and then apply the second color.

Paint thickness along a mask barrier will generally relate to the thickness of the mask. To achieve a thin coat at this point, either use a thin mask (frisket) or spray the paint with a dry spray. Be careful, however, not to build up a paint ridge against the mask.

PAINTING TECHNIQUES

Brush Painting

Brush painting demands patience and skill if you want to avoid visible brush strokes, a deposit of hair on the model, or a loss of detail. The difficulty of brush painting is proportionate to the size of the surface that must be painted. (Whenever possible, spray the finish. The extra equipment cost will be amortized quickly by the savings in time, temper, and model.)

Dip the brush only halfway into the paint. Avoid getting paint into the roots of the bristles and do not accumulate too much of it on the brush. Brush paint on with long, even (in thickness and width) strokes

applied in one direction. Try to achieve even coverage. If irregularities or runs do occur, go back over them and smooth out high and low spots. Specks of dust or hairs should be removed immediately with a pin.

After painting, clean brushes by any of the following means: wiping off as much paint as possible; washing the brush in oil paint reducer (if painting with an oil paint), lacquer thinner (if using lacquer), alcohol (after using shellac), or liquid brush cleaner; or washing the brush in soap and water. The next time the brush is used, inspect it, especially the roots of its bristles, to be sure that it is clean. To return the brush to its original shape, moisten it and mold it with your fingers.

BRUSHES. Sable is the most durable (and expensive) brush. White bristle comes next in cost, but is much harder. Camel hair is soft and costs only a quarter as much as sable. Buy the best of each type to avoid the problem of falling bristles.

The shape of the brush is important. See figure 11-2 for the various available shapes of small and medium-size brushes. Use thin, pointed shapes for painting detail work; flat shapes for painting extensive flat surfaces and straight borders of large areas; and round brushes for painting moderately small objects and for reaching into corners. Brushes must carry enough (but not too much) paint to the work. Since fast-drying lacquers may dry on a very small brush before they can be deposited on the work, use a larger brush for this type of paint.

Spray Painting

Spray painting produces the best finish and is the easiest technique to master. Certain multifaceted objects (trusses, trees) can be practicably painted only by spraying. Spray paint also dries faster, is less liable to obscure detail, and creates a more uniform coat. A compressor or air cylinder system can also dust models and work surfaces with a jet of air. On the other hand, very small touches of paint cannot be sprayed easily unless complicated masking is undertaken. The time it takes to clean the equipment may make it more practical to brush paint these small areas. Masking is often required when spray painting.

There are spray instruments at almost every price level, but do not be overly economical and sacrifice results. If only the finest finishes will be acceptable, consider an artist's air brush (for painting fine and medium-size objects), or an air gun (for large area application); both are powered by an air compressor or a compressed gas cylinder.

SPRAYERS. The following sprayers provide an uneven air supply:

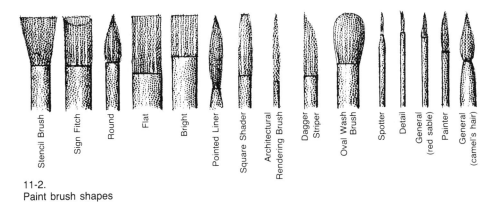

11-2.
Paint brush shapes

Stencil Brush
Sign Fitch
Round
Flat
Bright
Pointed Liner
Square Shader
Architectural Rendering Brush
Dagger Striper
Oval Wash Brush
Spotter
Detail
General (red sable)
Painter
General (camel's hair)

11-3.

Ruckus Manhattan, detail of Chase Manhattan Plaza
Red Grooms and The Ruckus Construction Company
Dimensions: 10'10" × 20'6"

This playful rendition of Chase Manhattan Plaza is a mixed-media piece that combines three-dimensional construction with two-dimensional illusion of space. The first five stories of the building's curtain wall were made out of clear vinyl sheets on which spandrels and mullions were painted. The wobbly columns spanning these floors are wire frame skeletons covered with fabric. The windows reveal interiors filled with people. The building continues above the windows, but only as a flat painted image. The figures crowding the foreground are painted directly on the plaza surface in forced perspective and this, combined with the slope of the plaza, creates the heightened sense of depth. The surrounding buildings are painted like backgrounds on a diorama, although the ones here do not follow the normal rules of perspective drawing. (*Photograph by Richard L. Plaut, Jr., courtesy of Marlborough Gallery, New York*)

Lung-powered spray tubes will suffice for spraying on fixative, and even thin ink and watercolor paint, if a highly spackled texture is acceptable. Sometimes this is just the effect desired for rough model ground contours.

Perfume and *throat atomizers* and *flit guns* can also be used to apply thin paints in a spackled finish. One disadvantage, however, is that the pumping involved requires quite a bit of work.

Pump-action sprayers have more finesse than flit guns and are held and pumped with the same hand.

Electro vibro sprayers are run by inexpensive vibrators, but their usefulness is diminished by the roughness of their spray.

Sprayers supplying air under a constant pressure include the following:

Paint bombs come in two types. One has the paint sealed into the pressure cylinder and the other has a detachable paint receptacle and disposable pressure cylinder. With the former, paint is already mixed. Both types of paint bombs have drawbacks, which include no control over the amount of air pressure or the shape and size of the spray cone, and a sometimes excessive air pressure. Too much air pressure will create a spray mist and produce a dry grainy paint finish. Paint bombs spray large quantities of paint, making extremely fir painting difficult. Their nozzles should be held abov 12″ from the work. Some small disposable pressur cylinders can be used with artist's air brushes.

Artist's air brushes (figure 11-4) can be powered b air compressors made especially for them, improvise compressors (vacuum cleaners, for example), compresse gas cylinders, and even (although not recommended spray tires and tire pumps. Most air brushes are mean to be used with the steady pressure of 20 to 40 pound per square inch that only an air compressor or ga cylinder can provide. To operate an air brush, fill it small reservoir, using a long-haired paint brush t transport the paint. First press down on the trigge

11-4.
Blade Runner, detail of special effects miniature
Warner Bros. (A Ladd Company Release)
Special photographic effects: Entertainment Effects Group

The setting of the film *Blade Runner* is a city in rapid decay. The models used to simulate its buildings had to show not only norma aging and weathering, but also exposure to acid rain. These effects were meticulously rendered in paint applied with an airbrush. Dyes and charcoal dust were also used to simulate soot and grime (*Photograph by Mark Stetson*)

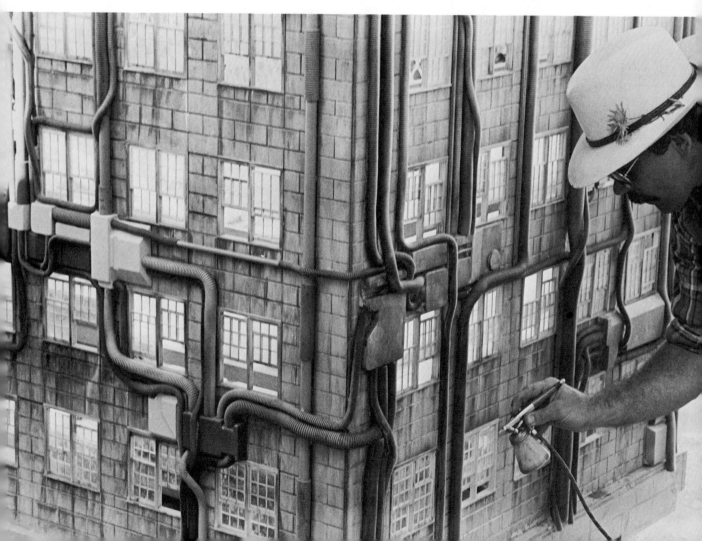

o start air flowing through the brush; then press down nd back to start the paint spray. The farther the trigger s pulled back, the greater will be the amount of paint hat will be sprayed. If the air brush can be adjusted o blow a lot of air but little paint, it can be held nearer o the work. This is useful when painting small multifaceted objects.

Garden-type hand pumps may be used with an air brush when attached to an air pressure regulator and gauge. The pressurized air is stored in a tank which dispenses a brief supply of nonpulsating air to the brush.

Compressed gas cylinders can be rented or purchased. Refills are inexpensive if only sporadic painting is done. For constant painting, it is more economical to purchase an air compressor.

Compressor systems come in two types. The first pumps air through a pressure regulator and supplies a constant flow of air through the sprayer (which must be a bleeder type). The other pumps air into a storage tank that is controlled by an automatic valve. This valve idles the compressor when the pressure in the tank builds above the desired level and starts the compressor when the tank pressure drops.

Spray guns are larger versions of the air brush. They are used for applying the heavier lacquers that are used to paint acrylic models and large areas. Paint is held in glass jars, not in the open reservoirs used by air brushes.

The following accessories may be useful when preparing for spray painting. *Viscosimeters* may be used to check the correct viscosity of the paint mix. *Air dusting guns* are for cleaning dust and shavings from the work. They may be run on a compressed air system. *Thickness gauges* are for measuring all types of adhesives and paints. Some measure wet films; others, dry.

GENERAL SPRAY TECHNIQUES. The following techniques should be used when painting with any sprayer. It is most important to use them with air brushes, spray guns, and paint bombs, however, since the results obtained with other types of sprayers are, at best, too crude to be improved by even the strictest adherence to technique.

Paint used for spraying must be of a thinner consistency than paint applied by brush. It should be the thickness of milk or water. Paint that is too thick may clog the sprayer, may spatter during application, or may not feed through the system. If the paint is too thin, it will run on the object being painted or require several coats to cover. In general, enamels require little thinning because they usually come from the container with enough oil. Lacquers, because of their fast evaporation, must be well thinned.

The optimum distance of the sprayer from the work will depend on the characteristics of the paint and on the sprayer. The proper distance between the spray and the surface also depends on the color being used: Light colors, for example, usually require more thinning than dark ones. In general, the paint should reach the object just before it dries.

As the sprayer is moved beyond its optimum distance from the work, the finish first becomes matte, then rough and sandy looking. Thus, a rough finish rather than a smooth one could mean the sprayer is being held too far from the work. If you want to produce textures, on the other hand, you can do so by varying the sprayer-to-object distance.

Since the sprayer may spatter on starting, aim it at a piece of scrap until its spray becomes uniform. Small objects should be secured in place with double-faced masking tape while they are being sprayed. Spray with overlapping strokes. Successive passes should overlap about half the width of the preceding stroke. The previous stroke should still be wet when it is overlapped. Otherwise, the paint will not flow together and may dry in streaks.

If attempting to spray a glossy finish, carry the paint strokes beyond the edges of the work before circling back for the next pass. If this is not done, the edges of the work will be less glossy than the center. This phenomenon occurs because the paint along the edges travels farther from the sprayer than the paint deposited at the center of the work does and so strikes the object when it is in a drier state, causing a matte finish. If the stroke is continued beyond the edge, however, the matte paint will not come in contact with the work. Another way to prevent this difference in degree of gloss is to hold the sprayer perpendicular to the work.

When sprayed too much in one place, paint sags, puddles, forms ridges, and, possibly, drips. To prevent sagging, hold the sprayer farther from the work, do not spray as much paint, modify the spray pattern so it leaves less overlap on each pass, or speed the movement of the sprayer across the work. Once sag has formed in enamel paint, it may be removed by leveling the ridges with a soft brush. Runs may be removed with lintless cloth dipped in turpentine or enamel thinner. To remove sag from lacquer, let the paint harden and then, with fine, wet abrasive paper, sand the ridges off. Or, while the paint is still wet, try to brush the ridges out with a soft brush dipped in thinner. When the paint has dried, brush strokes may be sanded off and the surface repainted.

If the correct amount of paint is being sprayed, but dribbles start to form as the paint dries, try changing the position of the object several times during the drying period and let gravity level the paint.

As in brush painting, it is better to build up a thick coat with several thin ones than to try covering with one coat. Allow each layer to dry thoroughly before applying the next.

To clean a sprayer, fill its reservoir with paint solvent and let some of it spray through the system. If using an air brush or spray gun, also place a finger over the nozzle while the spray is still coming out. This will reverse the flow of the thinner back through the sprayer. Next, remove your finger from the nozzle and let the spray continue in the regular way until there are no traces of paint in the spray. Clear the nozzle of an aerosol can by inverting it and spraying for a few seconds.

Dip and Smear Painting

It is also possible at times to sponge on paint to create a rough finish. This technique is especially useful when trying to paint ground or rocks realistically. Paint may also be applied by dipping the object into a thinned paint mixture. This is a time saver when painting complex one-color objects such as trees, cars, and so on. The object being dipped can be held on a pin or wire frame. After dipping, set it on a sheet of glass to dry. Stand the object so that the paint will drip toward the base.

Marble can be simulated by using cotton balls to dab various colors onto sheets painted with the base color.

Weathering

At times, some parts or all of a model must appear weathered (see figures 7-9 and 11-4). This is done to contrast old and new construction or to mute the colors of ready-painted automobiles, people, etc. A simple way to achieve a weathered finish is to dust the object with powdered charcoal or talcum powder (depending on the desired effect) and then to blow off the excess dust. Special paints, with whimsical names such as dust, rust, mud, and grime, are available through model train stores.

Flocking

Flock, a soft, woolly fiber, is widely used to give the impression of grass or moss to baseboards or to simulate certain types of upholstery fabric. Professionals apply flock with a special spray gun, but good results can also be achieved by first painting the surface with a coat of slow-drying paint the same color as the flock, then sifting the flock fiber on the paint and blowing off the excess when the paint has dried. Flock is available at many artist's supply stores, and inexpensive pump-action flock sprayers at many model train stores. For very evenly flocked surfaces, use a ready-made flocked paper, which is also available at artist's supply stores.

SAFETY CONSIDERATIONS

Spray only in a thoroughly ventilated room. Wear a respirator when using toxic paints. Be careful not to allow fire or electrical sparks to come in contact with the mist caused by quick-drying paints, the solvents of which are usually highly flammable.

Insurance companies usually require that you either have a spray booth or pay a much higher fire insurance premium. *Prefabricated paint spray booths* are available in various sizes. Small paint booths (2' × 1½' × 1½') make a good enclosure for light air brush spraying. Larger booths, constructed from metal partitions 7' high, come equipped with lights and a fan.

12:The Base

The base of a model, like the foundation of an actual structure, must be rigid. The fact that warpage must be avoided is obvious considering what it will do to the model resting on it. The base also must not rack and distort even if improperly lifted.

Small models may be safely constructed on a baseboard of ⅜″ plywood, or of ½″ cardboard, Celotex, or Homosote. When the dimensions of the model are greater than 2′ × 3′ or when the model weighs more than a few pounds, you should increase the thickness of these minimal materials. When the base is as large as 3′ × 4′, build a frame out of 1″ × 1″ or 1″ × 2″ lumber and nail and glue a thin baseboard to it. If the baseboard is plywood, run its exterior grain parallel to the longer edge. Celotex and Masonite can also be used. Because this under-framing stiffens the baseboard and keeps it from warping, it should be considered even for study models. The small extra effort required to build a framed baseboard is worthwhile, since it is unpleasant to work, even briefly, on a surface that is not warp-free. This baseboard can then be used for several models.

Bases of small models should be rectangular or square. Those that follow an irregular outline are hard to construct and pack and may present damage-prone corners.

If the model is large enough to make handling and shipping a problem, construct the base in several sections. These should be about 4′ × 8′ or some other convenient-to-move size. Just as some homemade boats have been built too large to remove from a cellar workshop, so too have some models been built too large for removal from the shop. When building a baseboard with two or more parts, have the joint between the sections follow a naturally occurring line—the side of a building, wall, or road, for example—not cutting across the structure. Join the base sections together with dowels or mortise and tenon attachments that can be easily taken apart. Screw or bolt the assembled baseboard together, locating the fasteners so that they are easily accessible for disassembly.

THE BASEBOARD

Framing the Baseboard

Framing members may be simply nailed together or, for greater strength, rabbeted or dadoed. Triangular plywood plates may also be used as reinforcements, as may metal angles.

Framing may be made from pine or Douglas fir. When selecting wood, make sure it is straight grained, free from knots and warps, and completely dry. It is worth a visit to the lumberyard to select so-called uniform wood strips personally; the actual dimensions of these strips are similar, but different enough that you may find that the variations make neat carpentry difficult. Place framing members along or under the edges of the baseboard, and, to prevent sagging, across the center of the board. Run these members across the shorter width.

The lumber used for framing or the internal bracing of large models or display stands may be bonded with casein, acrylic resin, or aliphatic resin glues. The latter two are good gap fillers; aliphatic glue is the fastest drying of the three. All these bonds can be colored to match the wood in order to prevent any excess squeezed out of a joint from leaving too noticeable a stain. Color the casein glue with water-soluble dye or alkali-proof dry earth colors that have been dissolved in water. Color the resin glues with soluble acid-fast dye.

Edging

Tape paper strips or glue hardwood strips to the edges of small baseboards. For a framed baseboard, glue and nail wood edging strips to the frame. Edging may simply be a fascia board, or it may be any of the trim moldings that are available at the local lumberyard. Rectangular strips, lattice strips, and squares are available in white wood, white pine, and, occasionally, in oak.

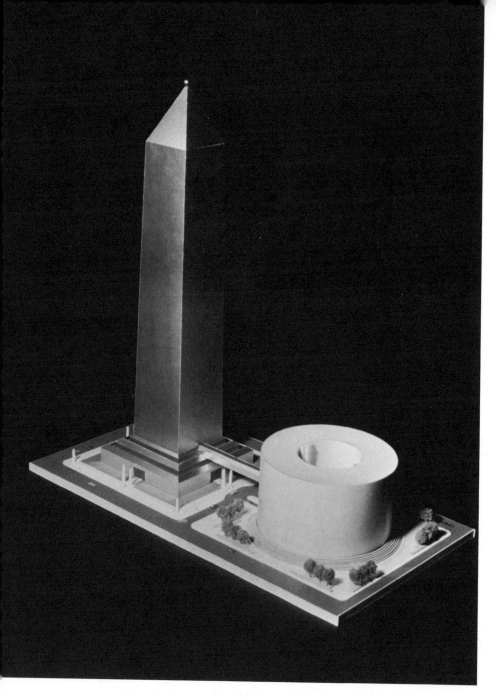

12-1.
Obelisk
Gresham, Smith and Partners, Architects
Modelmakers: Seab Tuck, Kem Hinton,
  and Mike Milo
Scale: 1″ = 40′
Materials: Strathmore board, matboard,
  and pantone overlays

This small, simple base was made by using
a matboard sheet braced with cardboard
strips. This provides enough support for the
buildings, which are light hollow constructions.
Pantone overlays were applied to the obelisk.
(*Photograph by Henry Schofield*)

For fancy edgings, use the following molding styles alone or in combination with one another: beads; coves; batterns; doorstops; quarter-rounds; back bands; and panel, fillet, conge, and floor moldings. Since these strips come in minimum widths of ¼″, they are of greatest use on fairly large models.

Simple edgings can also be cut from sheet stock with a bench-mounted circular saw. A router can be used to cut intricate molding shapes. Both tools enable you to work in mahogany and other attractive woods.

Edging for baseboards with irregular thicknesses due to a nonlevel ground line may be constructed after the contours, discussed later in this chapter, are all in place.

The edging may be made from ¼″ plywood or ¼″ pine trim. Place the uncut material along the side of the base and trace the uneven ground line on it. Cut the edging on a power or hand saw, allowing about ⅛″ excess material. This will later be sanded down to the tops of the contours.

For good results, miter the intersections of the edging. Screw or brad-nail the edging in place. The heads of these fasteners should be driven below the wood surface. The resulting holes can be plugged with dowels if you are using screws, or filled with plastic wood if brads are being employed. The edging may then be stained or painted.

12-2.
South Shore Harbour
3D/International, Architects
Modelmakers: 3D/I
Scale: 1:100. Base dimensions: 10′ × 10′

This model consists of four base sections measuring 5′ × 5′, stand skirt, and handrail. The water surface is made of backpainted acrylic sheet. All single-family housing is cast metal and all multifamily and commercial structures are solid acrylic. Trees were done with planting foam. (*Photograph by Lee Heald, Woodallen Photographers, Inc.*)

Finishing the Baseboard

If the model is on a level site or if there are extensive bodies of water around it, you may choose to have a baseboard that, uncovered or only stained, can abstractly represent the ground or water. Stained wood, Upson panels, Sheetrock, Masonite, Celotex, and flake board have all been effectively used in this way.

Plywood edging tape, a wood veneer with pressure-sensitive tape backing, may also be used. To apply, simply strip off the protective backing paper, press the tape into place, and run a warm iron over it. All these veneers may be lightly sanded and stained.

The base edging may be painted (figure 12-3), or if a natural wood finish is desired, stained and shellacked (figure 12-4). If reasonable care has been taken in its fabrication, the edging should be of the same quality as fine picture frames or furniture detail.

One great difficulty in painting wood is achieving a

12-3.
Untitled, 1981
Elisa D'Arrigo
Dimensions: 34″ H
Materials: painted wood and mixed media

Here, the base is as much a part of the overall design as the buildings that rest upon it. The patterns and colors of the ground continue along the base edge, just as the building stripes are repeated on the legs. (*Photograph courtesy of Rosa Esman Gallery, collection of Shaun Henderson*)

12-4.
Cement Plant Mixer & Hopper, 1979
Raymon Elozua
Dimensions: mixer, 24″ × 48″ × 18½″
          hopper, 24″ × 48″ × 21½″
Material: ceramic

Stained hardwood trim was used on the model bases. The display pedestals, which lift the models to a good viewing height, were built out of plywood and designed to follow the dimensions of the bases. (*Photograph by D. James Dee, courtesy of O.K. Harris*)

grain-free finish. Some paints can even raise the grain of the wood and thus add to the problem. If the paint being used does this, even if you have properly sealed and sanded the work, use wood sealer. For a smooth finish, fill in cracks and nicks with plastic wood. Sand this smooth and apply two or more coats of sanding sealer (sand between these coats, starting with No. 300 sandpaper and then changing to No. 400).

Work with the grain, frequently blowing the sanding dust from the work. Sanding sealers that can be used include various commercial sealers, shellac, thinned dope, regular dope, and clear lacquer mixed with talcum powder. Sealers can also serve as the primer coat. When the sealed surface is velvety smooth, it may be polished with a very fine steel wool. Paint the wood with dope, poster color, oil paint, or any other finish. Apply the paint with the grain.

To prevent pitch or sap from coming through the finish, shellac knots or other areas that could produce sap.

For natural finishes, use furniture polish (which comes in various wood colors) or wood stain directly on the sanded wood.

CONTOURS

Simplest Plot Plans

The simplest way to represent the ground and its contours is to cement an aerial photo or a black-and-white print of the plot onto the baseboard. Photographs are used mostly with very small-scale town-planning models. Plot plans may be used with models in all scales. Roads and existing buildings can be colored in on the print, and models of important buildings and trees cemented in place.

Laminated Contours

The simplest way to construct ground contours is to laminate them from sheet material. An interesting lamination pattern can greatly enhance a model's appearance (figures 12-5 and 12-6). While laminated construction is usually associated with less elaborate models, it has often been used on highly detailed, professionally constructed ones.

Lamination thickness should represent a significant increment of grade elevation. If the model is to aid in design, use a lamination thickness equal to the increment that is drawn on the plot plans.

Laminations may be made from such interesting-looking materials as cork sheet (for a rough earth look) or corrugated cardboard (on very rough models). More standard laminations can be finished by being painted, covered with flock, covered with green cloth (whose texture represents grass in a very interesting way), or even covered with a plaster coat to create a continuous contour. In all cases, try to use a material that is homogeneous instead of one constructed of plies of various compositions.

Constructing laminated contours is a three-step process. The first step is to make a map of the site, with the contours represented by continuous lines. This map should be reproduced to the scale of the model. The second step is to transfer each contour line to a sheet of the material being used. To transfer the lines, cover the bottom of the map with powdered graphite, place the map over the sheet material, and trace along the desired contour. If there will be many sheets laminated together, which will add unnecessary weight to the base, decide at this point what material underneath can be cut away. The best system to use is to leave a surface about 1″ wide for the next (higher) lamination to rest on. The third step is to cement the plies together. (If the assembly is in danger of sagging where the lower levels have been cut away, add support piers or columns. These may be permanently cemented into the model). Nails, pins, or brads may be used to strengthen the assembled laminations. They will also serve to hold the assembly together while the cement is drying.

Place buildings on laminated contours by excavating the shape of the building into the contours so that the building rests on the lowest elevation that intersects it. If only a few plies must be excavated, do this with a mat knife after the laminations have dried. If many plies must be cut or if you are laminating with tough material, lay out and cut the excavations at the same time as the contours.

One way to make contours is to place the contour plan on a thick board of wood and cut the board along each contour line. Reassemble the wood with adjacent boards depressed or raised to describe properly the contour heights.

Plaster Contours

Continuous contours are most easily constructed from plaster, wire mesh, and wood formwork. The construction procedure is as follows:

1. Tack a plot plan, the same scale as the model, on the baseboard (figure 12-8A). On it draw a 4″ or larger grid (4″ represents a very conservative spacing of supports for the plaster and may, on some models, be increased).

2. Cut 1″ dowels or 1″ × 1″ pine strips to lengths that correspond to the various heights that the wire mesh must be held above the baseboard at the intersections of the grid (figure 12-8A). Cut these posts carefully, so that they will stand squarely at 90° angles to the baseboard. Attach the posts to the baseboard with cement, screws, or nails. Another technique used to build the under support of the mesh is shown in figure 12-8C. Plywood or heavy cardboard formers are cut to the proper contour and then mounted on the baseboard. If the elevations vary greatly, it may be wise to build an egg-crate of formers (figure 12-8D).

12-5., 12-6.
Weyerhauser Company
Skidmore, Owings & Merrill, Architects
Modelmakers: SOM model studio
Scale: ¹⁄₁₆″ = 1′
Materials: chipboard and foam board

Plies of chipboard were cut and laminated to represent the site contours. The trees are made of lichen that was painted and glued to pins, which were inserted into holes drilled with a Dremel tool. The roads were painted, and a black plastic garbage bag was used to simulate water. (*Photographs by Louis Checkman*)

12-7.
San Francisco Executive Office Park
Hellmuth, Obata & Kassabaum, Inc., Architects
Modelmakers: James Fair, AIA; Andy Laguana and Stan Teng
Scale: 1/50″ = 1′
Material: plastic-backed foam board

This is a good example of a quickly constructed site contour model. Not only was the board easy to cut, but because of its thickness, fewer layers were needed to achieve the height of the hilly site. The buildings were constructed by stacking floor slabs made of the same type of board. (*Photograph by Peter Henricks*)

Quick contoured bases for study models can be made by cutting formers from corrugated paper.

3. Cut rough edging strips of plywood to go around the baseboard. These strips will support the wire mesh along the edges of the model.

4. Place galvanized iron wire mesh screening (chicken wire) over the posts. Hold the mesh in place with broad-head galvanized nails, carpet tacks, or staples; or notch the sides of the posts and wind wire through the mesh and around the notches. If, despite precautions, the plaster should rust the fasteners, producing a stain on the surface of the plaster, cover the stain with paint. Contours may be formed in the mesh by hand pressure. Abrupt changes in level, however, may require occasional cuts in the mesh. The material is then either overlapped or spread apart, and a piece of scrap mesh is wired in place over the resulting void.

Instead of using mesh, it may be better to pile crumpled paper and/or rock wool insulation around the dowels or blocks, up to within ½″ of the height of the desired elevations. Plaster or wood putty can be applied directly to the top of the paper and insulation.

5. If the base of the building, its areaways, and/or other subground construction are to be sunk into the plaster, they must first be boxed out with plywood or cardboard. Cut an opening into the wire mesh, place

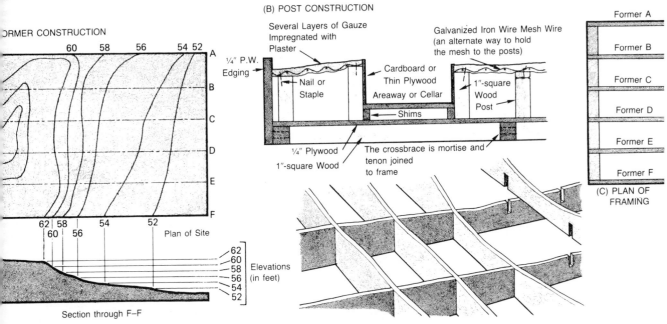

ORMER CONSTRUCTION

60   58   56   54 52

Plan of Site

62 58   54   52
60   56

62
60
58
56
54
52

Elevations (in feet)

Section through F–F

2-8.
Ground contour construction

(B) POST CONSTRUCTION

Several Layers of Gauze Impregnated with Plaster

Galvanized Iron Wire Mesh Wire (an alternate way to hold the mesh to the posts)

¼" P.W. Edging

Nail or Staple

Cardboard or Thin Plywood

Areaway or Cellar

1"-square Wood Post

Shims

¼" Plywood
1"-square Wood

The crossbrace is mortise and tenon joined to frame

Former A
Former B
Former C
Former D
Former E
Former F

(C) PLAN OF FRAMING

(D) EGG-CRATE CONSTRUCTION

he box, and then shim it up with balsa strips (figure 2-8B). Posts that would thrust through these areas must naturally be relocated, preferably so that they abut and help square up the boxed-out construction.

6. Trim any mesh hanging over the plywood edging strips. Hammer the edge of the mesh into the edge of the edging strips, being careful not to shatter the wood.

7. Mix a sufficient quantity of plaster to a heavy cream texture.

8. Soak wide strips of surgical bandage, muslin, scrim, or buckram in the plaster. Cover the mesh with several layers of this. (One alternative is to use strips of newspaper dipped in wallpaper paste or glue. These should be laid in a crisscross pattern on the mesh to a depth of about ten layers. Speed the drying of the paste with infrared bulbs. Once dry, give the assembly a surface coat of texture paint, which leaves it ready for color painting).

9. If the mesh still shows through, the plaster mix is too thin. Add more plaster to the mix for a stiffer consistency. With a palette knife, smooth on blobs of this new plaster to the gauze material that is already in place. Work the plaster with tools that have been dipped in water. The total plaster thickness should be ¼". Its top should be about ⅛" lower than or on a level with the top of the edging of the baseboard. Each ⅛" thickness that can be eliminated from the plaster will mean a 10-pound reduction in the weight of a 2' × 4' model, so try to hold the ¼" thickness.

10. Texture the plaster before it dries by studding it with rocks, pebbles, landscaping granules, sand, sawdust, or flock; or with brush strokes or tool working. Be careful not to leave trowel or finger marks in the plaster; but if you do, these marks may be removed by stippling the wet plaster with a brush. The texture imparted to the plaster and the materials placed in it should not be grossly out of scale. Often a matte colored finish is all the texture needs to represent grass, sand, or earth on a small-scale model. Also note that the earth or rocks should not be shiny or smooth. This lack of texture will impart an unrealistic, waxy look.

Nails may be inserted into the wet plaster at points where trees are to be placed. When the plaster has dried, remove the nails and place tree trunks in the resulting holes.

PLASTERS AND CEMENTS TO USE. Unlike casting plasters, those used to build contours need not be extremely dense or strong. The most important characteristics to be considered are texture, which should be compatible with the scale of the model, and the drying time, which should be sufficient to allow working with the top coat. When building the assembly with two or more coats of plaster, thoroughly wet the previous plaster layer before applying a new coat.

The plasters that may be used include *rough coat wall plasters*, which provides a subtle, textured finish; *patching plasters*, which give a smooth finish; and *scenic plasters*, which are model plasters and are sold in model train supply stores. To make your own scenic plaster, use four parts sawdust, four parts plaster, and one part library paste. Dissolve the paste in water, then add plaster and sawdust. This mix sets in about 15 minutes. By using the previous formula but increasing the library paste to two parts and adding a drop of glue for each pint of dry plaster and sawdust, the setting time of the mix will be extended to 8 hours. Mix the glue into the water before dissolving the paste in it.

High-temperature insulating cements have an extremely rough texture that may be used to create interesting effects. If you strain out some of its coarser fibers, you can modify this cement's texture. Casco powdered casein glue should be added to the dry cement to increase its binding ability.

Joint cements are used in construction to fill the joints between dry wall panels. They are slow drying and quite good for rock carving.

Texture paints produce a grainless imitation plaster surface. These paints, used by builders to finish gypsum wallboard, take about two days to harden, providing a long time in which to texture the surface. Fast-drying texture paint hardens in less time.

Plaster may be colored with water paints and flat oil colors. The latter soak unevenly into the plaster in a very realistic way. Apply paints with an inexpensive brush. Dry colors—for example, tempera—mixed into the wet plaster give a dull integral color.

Skin Contours

If you need a very light contour, or if the contour must be duplicated, build an egg-crate construction that will serve as a mold on which a skin contour can be shaped.

1. Tack a contour map, the same scale as the model, to the baseboard.
2. Draw a 2″ grid on the plan.
3. At each intersection of the grid, record how high the finished elevation will have to be. Start at the lowest grade with the minimum ground thickness that is desired, and work through other grades.
4. Cut a strip from ⅛″ thick wood or plywood for every line on the grid. Since the strip will be cut into a former for the grades that appear along that grid line, make it sufficiently wide to form the highest grade that will be encountered.
5. On each strip, draft the contour of the grid line that it represents. Also draw 2″ lines representing the intersections of the strip with all the strips perpendicular to it.
6. Using a jigsaw, cut the contour line in each strip.
7. On a bench-mounted circular saw, cut slots ⅛″ wide halfway into each strip centered on the 2″ lines. The slots should run from the top (finished grade side) halfway to the bottom on all the strips that run in one direction; and from the bottom halfway to the top or the set of strips that run perpendicular to the first set of strips.

8. Cement the strips together into an egg-crate.
9. From balsa, cut 1⅞″ × 1⅞″ × ¼″ or thicker blocks. Cement one of these into each cell of the egg-crate.
10. Carve the balsa to follow the contours of the egg-crate.
11. The skin contour can be made from Samcoforma, a material used in the shoe industry to stiffen shoes, or from Celastic. Place sheets of Samcoforma into a shallow enameled metal tray filled with liquid softener to make the sheets pliable.
12. Take the material out of the liquid and allow any excess to run off. Lay the limp sheet on the contour form. Slightly overlap adjacent sheets. The softener will cement the strips together. Additional layers may be added for greater strength.
13. Remove the skin contour from the form and finish its edges.
14. Cutouts for buildings and areaways may be sawed into the hardened material and boxed out with wood or cardboard.

Sheet Material Contours

Continuous contours may be made of "dry" materials if the site is fairly level. Build up the form of the contours from parallel plywood or heavy cardboard formers or from an egg-crate made of these materials. Then, cement sheets of ⅟₁₆″ cardboard, plywood, Sheetrock, or balsa on the form. Lastly, finish, paint, and landscape the surface, or waterproof it by cementing on muslin and then covering it with a thin coat of plaster, which can then be painted.

Styrofoam Contours

Contours may be quickly carved from lightweight Styrofoam planks (figure 13-14). Cut the plastic to its approximate shape with a sharpened putty knife or a serrated bread knife. Check the thickness of the remaining material by pushing a stiff wire through to the baseboard and measuring the height of the wire. The last ⅛″ to ¼″ of material can be eliminated by compressing it with hammer blows delivered through a block of wood. Individual rock outcrops may also be carved from Styrofoam.

Carved plastic may be: left uncovered or "landscaped" with a mixture of sawdust, flock, or granules and glue;

overed with a thin layer of plaster; or covered with a
kin layer of plaster, impregnated fabric, or Celastic.
A plaster or skin layer, usually incorporated on presentation medels, will protect the Styrofoam from abrasion. To be molded on Styrofoam, Celastic must be
softened with a special activator, since the regular one
will melt the foam.

Contours can also be milled from Styrofoam. They
resemble the stepped contours made by the laminating
technique. There are companies that will custom-build
contours to your specifications.

TITLE PLATES

The title plate of a model (figure 12-9) can range from
simple hand lettering applied to a strip of illustration
board to an engraved bronze plate. The possibilities
are almost unlimited.

Set letters made from plastic, wood, or plaster directly
on the baseboard or on plates made from wood, plastic,
illustration board, etc. Transfer or pressure-sensitive
overlay letters may also be used in the same way. If
an error is made, transfer letters may be removed with
a piece of cellophane tape.

Interesting effects can also be achieved by placing
transfer letters on an acrylic sheet and spray painting
the sheet, then carefully removing the letters and backlighting the sheet; or by backlighting transparent or
translucent plastic letters.

Avoid the dirt that eventually collects along the borders of pressure-sensitive letters (which must be cut
out and burnished in place) by using transfer letters
(those that, when burnished, come away from their
carrying sheet). Dirt may also be avoided by applying
cutout pressure-sensitive letters to a mock-up board,
then photocopying and using the resulting prints or
photostats on the model.

Attach title plates with cement, brass escutcheon
pins, fancy-head nails, screws, and so on.

Graphics in the form of keys (that explain symbols),
north signs, arrows to indicate flow of traffic, and name-
plates for individual rooms and buildings can greatly
enhance the appearance of a model and help to communicate facts about the project. North signs may be
cut from acrylic, illustration board, or paper, or salvaged
from compasses and inexpensive maps. For greater
protection against abrasion and dust, place north signs,
long verbal descriptions, and symbol keys under a sheet
of acrylic.

12-9.
St. Francis Hospital, Miami Beach
The Smith Korach Hayet Haynie Partnership, Architects
Modelmakers: model department of the firm

The title block is an important part of this model's presentation.
Here, pressure-sensitive letters were laid out and then photocopied.
The photocopy was laminated onto a board, which was then placed
on the baseboard. (*Photograph by William A. Pearson*)

KHHP
the smith korach hayet haynie partnership
architects   engineers   planners
175 fontainebleau boulevard-miami, florida 33172

east wing replacement facility
st. francis hospital
miami beach, florida

13:Landscaping

A modelmaker will often hurry through making the landscaping elements and adding them to the model, considering it a bothersome and unimportant last step. This is unfortunate inasmuch as proper care taken in representing the landscape will not only enhance the model but will also be a design aid for the architect. (This is true even with models that are intended strictly for presenting a building proposal.) Many last-minute landscaping problems become evident only with construction of a display model. Each modelmaker should therefore be aware of and use the techniques needed to rapidly present reasonably accurate facsimiles of each element of landscaping in the model.

Landscaping is one case in which you should use a combination of a great number of materials, so keep a good supply on hand. Using various bits and pieces of these materials, you can build an interesting, accurate, and authentic-looking landscape.

Exact model replicas of gardens and landscaping schemes are seldom made: making exact models of trees and bushes is a complex process and the budget allowed for such commissions is usually small.

Complex highway interchanges and road systems, on the other hand, are most easily presented and studied through the use of models. These allow the civil engineer to study sight lines and to plan signal and sign locations, something difficult to do using only drawings. Models aid the construction engineer in planning construction staging. They also show the owners of abutting properties how these will be affected by the road. Finally, they are used to generate public interest in projects and to aid legislative approval.

GROUND COVER

Earth, grass, and other ground cover items should be planned from a color photograph of the existing site conditions or, if these will change, from photos of other landscapes. In general, try to emulate the mottled texture and color of natural ground cover—slick-looking cover is not realistic. Mottling can be done by using granules or sawdust in different sizes or colors.

Paint

Oil paint should be used on plaster and other ground-simulating materials. It has a dull finish and the large range of available colors also simplifies the problem of mixing. Raw and burnt umber, Vandyke brown, and raw and burnt sienna may be used directly from the tube. Exact ground colors may be blended by combining two or more of these colors. Build the colors up carefully from several coats of thinned paint.

For grass colors, use pale green mixed from light chrome green and white; medium chrome green, light yellow, and white; or black or Vandyke brown added to either of the above mixtures. Medium green may be mixed from various combinations of green, yellow, red, white, and black. Dark green (the color of lush grass) is mixed from light chrome green, ultramarine, and white.

If the ground contours are made from plaster, they may be integrally colored and textured. Texturing is achieved by stippling the wet plaster with a stiff brush to produce a rough, eroded, earth effect.

Dry powdered pigments, or plaster coloring powder pigments as they are sometimes called, contain their own adhesive. To apply, spray set plaster with water and sift on the pigment. It may also be applied directly to setting plaster or to powdered plaster before water is added. Several applications of pigments may be used to create the effect of grass on soil. Certain pigments, calcimine and casein dry paint among them, will slow the setting of the plaster. Inert dry colors will not do this; use about half a cup with each gallon of dry plaster. Wet dye mixed into the water and used with pigment can create additional effects. Sawdust or flock may be mixed with dry pigment to represent coarse grass; small bits of lichen may also be added. If these large admixtures

13-1.
Untitled, 1982
Gifford Myers
Dimensions: 5″ × 5″ × 7″
Material: ceramic

The unusual material used in covering this small ceramic model was a dollar bill. Sections of the engraved floral pattern that border the bill were used for the ground cover and path. Other portions can be seen on the roof, windows, shutters, pediment, and columns. (*Photograph courtesy of Pam Adler Gallery*)

do not readily stick, spray the ground with gum arabic and water, matte spray, varnish, or clear lacquer. The pigment mixing formulas used to obtain various colors are:

Gray: mixture of burnt umber and the plaster. The proportion of pigment to plaster should be 1:20 to 1:10, depending on the shade required.

Reddish rock: three parts medium chrome yellow, one part burnt sienna, and fifteen parts plaster.

Yellowish grass: three parts medium chrome yellow, one part raw umber, two parts medium chrome green, and four parts plaster.

Bluegrass: three parts medium chrome yellow, one part raw umber, two parts medium chrome green, and four parts plaster.

The resulting color will be more realistic if pigments are not mixed together too evenly.

Fluid dye or *diluted India ink* may also be used to color plaster. Apply these by pouring or dabbing them onto the surface. Rough surfaces absorb more color than smooth areas do, and dye is absorbed by dried plaster much faster than by plaster that has been wetted down. If an area has been overcolored with fluid dye, bleach out the dye with a mixture of one or two drops of perchlorate bleach in two ounces of water.

Flock

Flock may be mixed into ground-representing plaster, which will whiten its color. If applying flock on top of plaster or other dry ground materials, use the adhesives recommended for dry pigments that have been mixed with granules. The flock should be sprinkled on the adhesive with a sieve. Spray shiny flock with matte fixative to dull it. Both flock and granules should be applied only to ground that has already been painted. No matter how carefully flock is applied, small areas of bare ground will show through.

Granules

Granules of many sizes, colors, and shapes are packaged for sale to the model railroad hobbyist. They are used to simulate almost all loose ground-covering materials, from grass to boulders. Granules may be combined with flock, real earth, sand, or colored sawdust to form additional textures and colors. One drawback of commercial granules, however, is their often unrealistically bright colors.

Since adhesives used with the granules will inevitably be visible, they must be transparent and have a matte finish. Among those that can be mixed into granules is powdered cement. Place the conglomeration on the model and spray it with water, or mix the cement with water and paint it on, sifting the granules onto the model last.

Casein glue may also be used. Paint the model with it, allow it to dry partially, and then go over it with water to thin it out. Sift the granules over the surface.

To apply granules, shake them out of a jar that has holes cut into its lid. A screw-on cover with two pieces may be modified by removing the center disc and replacing it with a section of wire mesh. Press the granules on the model, making sure they are in contact with the adhesive. Allow the adhesive to dry and then blow away the unstuck granules.

Landscaping Mats

Landscaping mats are available from several companies. These paper- or foam-rubber-backed sheets have granules already attached. Their textures range from fine to heavy pile. Cement mats with the same adhesives used for loose granules. Apply the adhesives to the ground and to the back of the mat with a 3″ brush or paddle, being careful not to let the excess squeeze out on the top of the mat. Press the mat down with a roller. Mats may be used to cover only relatively flat surfaces.

Other Materials

Sawdust or *small wood chips* may also be used for ground cover. Stain these with thinned oil paint and apply them to the model with the same cements used with granules.

Ground-up foam rubber, obtained in scrap pieces from upholstery shops, is also a possibility. Use latex or synthetic latex foam, not polyurethane, which yellows with age. Cut the scraps into grape-size lumps and color these with thinned oil paint or fabric dye. Grind the dried pieces in a meat grinder. Several textures can be produced: the finest can be used as grass or leaves, and the coarsest as clumps of small plants or even (on small-scale models) as shrubs.

Aerosol spray finishes are carried by some of the companies that sell granules. They come in earth, sand, and other textures. While some of these will create a satisfactory ground finish rapidly, others have a tendency to flow erratically from the can. Some come out dry and in short ribbons, others will not spray at all. Before purchasing these products, test individual cans at the store.

SAND, STONES, ROCKS, AND BOULDERS

Depending on the scale of the model, sand, pebbles, or small stones may be represented by any one of the several available white or gray commercial granules. White aquarium sand may also be used.

Larger rocks and boulders may be cast or built up from plaster. If the latter technique is used, mix retarder into the plaster to extend its working time. Roughly form the rocks with a knife blade. Detail imparted while the plaster is still plastic will lose sharpness before the plaster dries and give the rock an eroded appearance. After the plaster has hardened, cracks and rugged details can be sculptured with a knife or scribe. To increase the depth of an outcropping, build it up with softwood pieces or Celotex.

Boulders may also be made from natural stones, pieces of rough bark, foaming plastic, Celotex, vermiculite, hardened plaster, balsa, or hadite that has been crushed in a meat grinder. Cliffs may be represented by thin striated pieces of sandstone, other natural rocks, or cork bark. To make boulders, place wet clay in a burlap bag and knead it. When the clay is dry, remove it from the bag and break it apart into realistic shapes. For extensive boulders and cliffs (figure 13-3), preestimate their weight and use one of the lighter materials if there is a possibility that this weight may become excessive.

If the ground is made from plaster, all the above-mentioned materials may be embedded in it while the plaster is still wet. If the ground is made from a dry material, cement the rocks to it with household cement applied in double coats to both the rocks and the ground. To improve the appearance of rocks made from most of these materials, touch them up with wet plaster after they have been cemented in place. If using Styrofoam or other foaming plastics, apply plaster to close up the pores of the material, unless you want a stylized effect.

Shale is best simulated with Celotex that has not been touched up with plaster. Conglomerate rock formations (which in nature are boulders mixed with clay or silica) can be modeled by combining large and small granules or sand with real rocks. Cliffs and other areas of extensive rock outcropping should be shown with sufficient detail to look convincing. There is usually a scattering of boulders and pebbles at the foot of such a rock formation.

13-2.
The Tale of Two Cities, 1981
Chris Burden
Dimensions: approximately 600 square
feet

Nearly 3,000 toys, including cardboard buildings, tanks, and airplanes, were used to build these miniature cities. The installation, placed directly on the floor of a museum, can be viewed through binoculars. Sand, rocks, and two potted plants are used for the landscaping. (*Photograph by eeva-inkeri, courtesy of Ronald Feldman Fine Arts, Inc.*)

13-3.
Medieval Humanities Center
Lesley Gill, Cooper Union School of
Architecture
Scale: ⅛″ = 1′
Materials: plaster, acrylic plastic, wood,
and Styrofoam

The rock formations in this model were made by carving blocks of Styrofoam, which were then coated with plaster and painted. The formations look like they are carved out of solid plaster, but are much lighter. The building, which was made out of plastic, metal, and wood, was inserted into the site model. (*Photograph by Lesley Gill*)

13-4.
Hotel at Machu Picchu, Peru
Schweiker and Elting, Architects
Modelmakers: members of architects' staff

Walls, roof, and balconies of this presentation model were made from boards covered with gray and white paper. Ground contours and retaining walls were cut from sheets of coarse and fine cork. (*Photograph by Hedrich-Blessing*)

Various types of rocks may be represented by the following oil colors:

Basalt: dark gray to blue black

Brownstone: Vandyke brown plus a touch (5%) of orange

Granite: medium gray with small highlights of lighter gray blended into the darker areas

Blue granite: ultramarine and black

Gray granite: black with a translucent ultramarine overwash

Red granite: claret

Limestone: pale gray with areas of burnt sienna and ultramarine

Red sandstone: Indian red plus burnt sienna or Vandyke brown

Yellow sandstone: light chrome yellow and Vandyke brown or raw umber

Schist: pale olive

Shale: burnt sienna with bands of Vandyke brown

Roads, Paths, and Sidewalks

Paths and roads may be drawn or painted on the baseboard or earth contours (figures 13-5 and 13-6) or may be represented by flocking, granules, landscaping mats, colored paper, or painted sandpaper. All these techniques can also be used on stepped contours.

Use commercial mats to represent paths or parking lot paving. Gravel paths may be simulated by ballast mats, which can be found in model railroad hobby shops.

Paints used to represent paths and roads should be mixed with sand or talcum powder for a matte, textured finish.

Sidewalks should have their top elevations above those of roads or gutters. This gives a realistic look to models, even those as small as $1'' = 40'$. Make sidewalks from Bristolboard or spray paint them on the ground contour. To represent concrete sidewalk slabs on very small-scale models, crosshatch pressure-sensitive overlays. Make curbs from stripwood on large-scale models. Rule traffic division lines in white ink or, in large-scale models, represent them with white tape.

Highway Systems

A highway model is often constructed to a $1'' = 50'$ scale. The baseboard may be built from ½" plywood in $3' \times 4'$ sections for shipping convenience (transportation cases are often built for each section). Grades are built up by dowels or wood strips. Crumpled paper and rock wool insulation are piled around the dowels to within ½" of the final ground elevation. These rough materials are then covered with two layers of wood putty. The road is represented by 1/32" balsa sheet. Curbs, traffic islands, handrails, and so forth, are also made from balsa. Guardrail is usually made of wire mesh. The entire model is given a coat of shellac. Vegetation and houses are then added.

Bridges, Electrical Wire, Pylons, and Playground Equipment

These small, spindly objects may be made from soldered (hot or cold) brass strips and wires. Make large-scale models from Bristolboard. Use thin sheet acrylic for the sides of bridges and pylons. Score the plastic to represent the struts of the prototype. Rub paint into the scored lines and assemble the structure. Another

13-5.
Harry Lieberman—Ginivishov, Poland, Memory Map, 1973
Roger Welch
Dimensions: 4′ × 14′

As 93-year-old Mr. Lieberman described the village in which he grew up, the artist reconstructed a map of its major features on the plywood base before them. Wood blocks were used for key buildings and marker lines traced the roads and pathways.

13-6.
The finished map

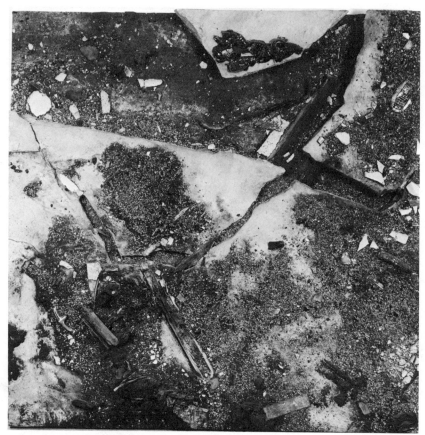

13-7.
*Shattered Concrete Study—Breakers Yard
Series, 1976–77*
Mark Boyle
Dimensions: 6′ × 6′
Materials: earth, glass, etc., on fiberglass

This piece looks as if a heavy 6′-square
section had been cut and lifted right out of
a road. It is actually a thin fiberglass base
on which the dirt, rocks, glass, and other
debris were fixed with resin. (*Photograph by
eeva-inkeri, courtesy of Charles Cowles
Gallery*)

technique requires carving the outline of the object into a block of clear acrylic. Polish the plastic and scribe the detail into its sides, then paint the scored lines. If the plastic is finished correctly, it will be almost invisible—only the scribing will be noticeable. If several objects are to be modeled, bending and gluing jigs will save time.

Parking Lots, Athletic Fields, and Farm Fields

Parking lots can be made of matboard or plaster (figure 13-8). Apply or spray paint on the surface; rule in white lines. Grassy fields may be simulated with green flock paper. In rough study models, show these areas on a black-and-white print made from the plot plan.

For small-scale farm fields, form a patchwork of green, yellow, and brown fields out of cemented-on granules, or flock. Pieces of different-color flocked paper may also be used.

For plowed fields, draw a coarse comb over the ground-representing plaster while it is still wet. Paint it with oil paints that have a high oil content to impart a wet look. If the ground is not made of plaster, cover it with a thin sheet of colored wax or clay with a heavy application of oil paint and emboss these materials with the comb.

Wheat and similar long-stem crops may be represented with binder twine, which is sold in lumberyards. Cut the twine to appropriate lengths, untwist the fibers, and paste their ends to the ground or set them into the wet plaster ground.

WATER

Water is potentially the most charming bit of entourage found on models. It may be simple, represented with single-ply materials; or, for greater realism, it may be built up of several layers. For an illusion of depth, use two levels of materials: one, representing the surface of the water, should be clear plastic; the other, representing the bed of the water course, can be the material of the contours with an overlay of scale pebbles and stones.

13-8.
Parking Lot Showroom
SITE Inc., Architects
Modelmakers: members of SITE
Scale: ¼" = 1′
Material: plaster

Metal wire mesh was shaped on a clay mold and thin layers of
plaster were built up on the mesh for this model. After the plaster
dried, the clay mold was removed and side walls added. The model
was then sprayed with latex paint in layers of white, black, and
gray. (*Photograph by SITE*)

The color of real water is influenced by three factors:
first, by the actual color, as modified by mud, algae,
and other material in the water; second, by the color
of the bottom, which is also dependent on the clearness
of the water and its depth; and third, by the light
reflected from the surface of the water. The latter two
factors should be represented by transparent colors.

Deep water under a clear sky is usually blue. Deep
water that is not reflecting the sun is green. Water
close to shore is greenish blue or greenish black. Muddy
water is brown. Other influencing factors are shallowness
and whether or not the bottom is sandy or strewn with
rocks. Banks of streams and other muddy spots should
be painted Vandyke brown. A top coat of varnish or
shellac will give it a wet look.

Ripples caused by the wind are usually more pronounced in the center of a body of water. Other ripples
may be formed by floating objects or by dripping water.
Wave formation and size should also change, theoret-
ically, as the waves get closer to shore. A collection of
color photographs of various bodies of water is a useful
reference.

Build the shoreline by overlapping the water-
representing material with the simulated ground material
(figure 13-9) rather than trying to cut the water material
to the exact shape of its bank.

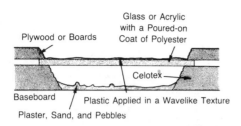

13-9.
Constructing bodies of water

To show reflections, paint the underside of transparent plastic a dark color (figure 13-10). Black acrylic has a good reflecting surface and can represent still water at night or under a dark sky.

If the ground contours are laminated, water may be represented by inserting a blue ply made from the typical lamination material or from blue acrylic. Pressure-sensitive overlays may also be used.

Represent frozen water with paraffin stained a pale blue green or with glass frosting sprayed on an acrylic sheet.

The whitewater of rapids and waterfalls may be represented by frosted cellophane. To simulate foam, use cotton that has been fluffed and pulled apart or fine steel wool painted white.

Real Water

While it can be extremely realistic when forming concentric ripples for photographic purposes, for example, real water is very difficult to work with. It should be used only if it will aid photography, and then only if extreme pains have been taken to waterproof the bed and banks of the water body.

Because of surface tension and other factors, water will appear to be out of scale. Mineral oil, on the other hand, forms ripples that are more realistic than those that can be made with actual water.

To provide a feeling of depth, apply real water over a painted bed or tint it. A half teaspoon of copper sulfate (sold in garden shops) added to each 2 gallons of water is a good tint. Miniature pumps may be used to agitate the water.

Rough Water

Rippled acrylic or cathedral glass are available in textures that represent water of various turbulences. Acrylic is preferable because it is much easier to cut and safer to use.

To represent fairly rough water in very small-scale models, mount smooth sheet acrylic over a layer of embossed paper or rough board. Acrylic may also be

carefully etched with solvent to form beautiful wav formations.

Sheet acetate can also be used. Soak it in aceton until it is almost dissolved, then remove it from th bath with a spatula and put into place. Stipple and wor the surface into the desired finish. Another techniqu is to slightly soften the plastic and form it on a roug wood form. When it is dry, remove it and place it o the model.

Casting plastic or water glass (sodium silicate) ma be applied to the model in one of two ways. The firs method is to apply it directly to a bed cut into th ground. This is best done when the ground is made ou of plaster. Model or stipple the wet plaster to creat the approximate texture for the top of the water. Ripple may be gouged into the plaster with a pointed too. The wet plaster will partially level itself, creating realisti waves. If the plaster does not level quickly enough hold the side of a revolving power tool under the base board and vibrate the plaster to a more level finish Next, paint the plaster; then apply the liquid plasti material.

For the second method, apply the liquid plastic to sheet of clear acrylic held above the bed. Place pebbles stones, and vegetation on the painted bed. Fix th acrylic sheet into the bank, and coat it with plastic o water glass. Allow it to set partially; then stipple an model it to shape.

Several layers of the liquid plastic will increase the illusion of depth, as will coloring it with dye. If applyin several layers, the first and second should be about $\frac{1}{16}$ thick and should be dyed. One layer should represen the color of the bottom and the other, the color of th water and the reflected sky. The top layer should b clear, with water flowers, boats, or other floating object embedded in it.

Animation may be achieved by mounting one or mor rotating, internally lighted drums under a translucen water-representing material. The drums, covered wit acetate on which a ripple pattern has been painted, wi simulate running water. Lights mounted behind rotatin discs into which windows covered with colored cellophan have been cut may be used instead of the drums.

Fountains

Use shiny steel or silver wire to represent fine wate sprays. If the fountain has a series of these, make then out of silver-colored mesh from which the wires running in one direction have been removed. Remove all bu the last few wires on one end of the sheet. Set tha end, which holds the assembly together, deep into the model. Fountains with a greater density of sprayed water may be built out of cellulose cement dripped ove an acrylic core.

13-10.
Redevelopment Project
The Hillier Group, Architects
Modelmakers: Todd & Chapin
Material: Plexiglas

Water and ground surfaces, as well as the buildings, were made of machined and painted Plexiglas. The base sections were covered with large backpainted Plexiglas sheets to represent the water. The land surface was then applied on top of this base cover. Rigid vinyl is used to show roads. The trees are made of polyurethane foam. (*Photograph by Leigh Photographs*)

Snow and Ice

For frozen water, use paraffin stained a pale blue green. Represent snow with any of the commercially available white granules. Many of the sprays found in stores around Christmastime may be used on larger-scale models. Before purchasing a spray, however, test it. Some products come out of the can too wet or in too rough a texture.

Icicles may be represented in larger scales by bits of twisted cellophane that have been dipped in a solution of sodium silicate (water glass).

TREES AND PLANTS

Because you may need to make dozens or even hundreds of trees for a model, you should devise ways of constructing them as quickly as possible. The most expeditious solution is to purchase ready-made trees in the middle scales ($\frac{1}{16}'' = 1'$ to $\frac{1}{4}'' = 1'$), as shown in figure 13-11, or armatures (on which to place foliage) in all scales.

A handy reference guide is a book of trees photographed in color. The proportion, color, and density of foliage of the prototype should be copied. Even hypothetical trees should be modeled with some species in mind. Basic tree colors are dark green and yellow for deciduous trees and dark green for conifers.

Trunks and Twigs

The skeletal structure of trees may be constructed from many materials. In all cases, the trees should be set into holes drilled in the model base.

Cast trunk and branch systems from metal in two-part molds. Surprisingly delicate limbs may be achieved if the molds are accurate. Several companies sell these parts ready-made.

Use thinly wound copper, or soft iron, florist's or picture frame wire to produce the trunk and branches of trees that are in $\frac{1}{32}'' = 1'$ and larger scales. Some experimentation will be necessary to determine how many strands will be needed to produce specific tree species. Some deciduous trees with many branches require as many as fifty or more strands to reproduce them in a $\frac{1}{8}'' = 1'$ scale. Use the following procedure:

1. Cut the wires to lengths that run from $\frac{1}{2}$ to $1\frac{1}{2}$ times the intended height of the model tree.
2. Place the wires together so that all the lengths are even at one end.
3. Use two pairs of pliers or a vise and a pair of pliers to twist the wires forming the trunk of the tree below the first branch.
4. Separate the strands above the twisted area into groups that represent major branches. Each group should have both long and short strands.
5. Twist each branch into shape, allowing the last fraction of an inch of each strand to stand alone. Additional short strands of wire may be added where needed to increase the number of branches.
6. The trunk may be finished with a coat of clay, plastic wood, or plaster. Clay, if applied wet, will create the effect of smooth bark. Plastic wood will be slightly rougher; if desired, paint with cellulose thinner to smooth it. Sand rubbed into any of the covering materials will give a rough bark effect. Patterned bark may be formed by scratching the cover of the trunk with a scribe. Knots, stumps, and other irregularities may be modeled in the covering material.
7. Paint the trunk with matte oil or cellulose paint if it is covered with clay or plastic wood, or with matte cellulose paint if it is covered with cellulose putty. If the tree is in a small scale, Step 6 may be omitted and the trunk dipped into thick, matte, latex house paint.

Multistrand copper electrical wire can also be used for trunks and twigs:

1. Strip away insulation above the place where the trunk would divide into branches.
2. Twist the thin wire strands into a realistic number of main branches.
3. Divide the main branches into smaller branches.
4. Cover the trunk and main branches with plaster of Paris, putty, plastic wood, or clay.

Less pliable wire may also be used for trunks. Cut it into strands of the appropriate length. Lash these together with fine florist's "hair" wire to form branches. Hair wire may also be used to hold together the strands that make up thicker branches and to create fine twig ends.

Conifers have a bottle brush construction. Continue the trunk to the top of the tree, thinning down the number of wire strands the higher it goes. Form the foliage by introducing sisal bristles into the twisted wire, trimming them with scissors. Dip the finished tree into dark green paint and sprinkle fine sawdust onto it while it is still wet.

Balls of natural cork, wood, or spherical or oval buttons (these are available in $\frac{1}{2}''$ to $2''$ diameters and are sold in beadcraft, knitting, and accessory stores) make interesting stylized trees, as do map pins or balls of foamed plastic. Small-scale tree trunks can be made from brads, pins, or lengths of metal rod.

13-11.
Ready-made trees. This sampling of trees, ranging in size from 5″ to 12″ high, can be bought assembled or unassembled. They include a wide variety of tree types, including apple, cedar, oak, poplar, silver birch, fir, and Scotch pine.

MATERIALS FOR PARTS OF TREES. Twigs of many natural bushes are of the correct size and form for model trees. (Notice that twigs should be shellacked or varnished prior to use.) Privet twigs are about the right size for ⅛″ and larger-scale trees. Baby's-breath stripped of its buds makes good branches, as do the twigs of many other bushes and trees. Use a twig from a tree as the trunk and cement baby's-breath to it, or bind several sprigs of baby's-breath together with thread. Apply a coating of plastic wood to cover the thread and to form a trunk of correct diameter. To represent pine trees, cement baby's-breath branches to long, straight twigs. The foliage can be made from cellulose sponge torn into realistic clumps.

Lichens are another natural material often used in making trees (figure 13-12). Coarse Norwegian lichen can be used as a filler material on the insides of large-scale trees. Fine ends should be saved for the outside, visible foliage of these trees and for small-scale trees. Mixed lichen comes in red, green, orange, rust, or natural color. Dixie-cup lichen, a plant similar to Norwegian lichen but finer, comes in light green and has occasional yellow buds. Raw lichen, and for that matter any natural plant, must be processed to prevent it from drying out, becoming brittle, and dropping from the trees. Commercially available packaged lichen has already been processed and much of it will remain pliable for over a decade. Raw lichen, however, is much less expensive than the packaged product. To process raw lichen, soak it in warm water for several minutes. Knead it to aid in water penetration. Next, remove it from the water and squeeze out all excess moisture. Place it in pickling solution for 24 hours or more. The solution can be made from 1 quart of glycerine, 1 quart of acetone, and 2 quarts of denatured alcohol. This will produce 1 gallon

13-12.
Forest Building
SITE Inc., Architects
Modelmakers: members of SITE
Scale: ⅛″ = 1′

The building was made of Bainbridge board. The trees are welded metal trunks on which lichen has been glued. The lichen was dipped into and sprayed with plaster to stiffen it. The entire model was then spray painted. (*Photograph by SITE*)

of solution, enough to pickle 1 to 2 bales of lichen. Remove the lichen and spread it on newspaper until it has dried. It may then be dip or spray painted with dyes or artist's oil colors diluted to a souplike consistency. Lichen may also be dyed while it is being pickled. Add 1 ounce of aerosol or Unox penetrant (both are sold in drugstores) to each quart of pickling solution. Dried-out lichen may be rejuvenated by soaking it in water and then dipping it into a mixture of one part glycerine and four parts water.

Loofa is a dried fiber sponge and is coarser and drier looking than lichen, which it roughly resembles. It is sometimes used plain or covered with a cemented-on mixture of sawdust, very small wood chips, and plastic wood.

Cellulose sponge, natural sponge, foam rubber, wire wool, underlying felt, wire mesh, or looped thin wire may be arranged realistically on trunks to form interesting middle- and large-scale trees. Rubberized horsehair, dried tea leaves, or short lengths of wool yarn may also be used as foliage.

Small wood chips, coarse sawdust, and plaster may be mixed to form realistic foliage for small-scale ($\frac{1}{32}''$ = 1') trees. Place the wet mix on trunks made from nails.

Many of these materials may be combined to create a greater articulation of form.

MATERIALS FOR ENTIRE TREES. There are several natural plants whose small buds and leaves are suitable for use as stylized model trees in $\frac{1}{32}''$ and larger-scale models (figure 13-13). A few of these plants are sold in large florist shops, but most may be obtained from the great outdoors. They are best picked in autumn, when they have dried out. Soak them half a day in glycerin to preserve them, or spray them with matte spray. Natural plants can be colored with fabric dyes or sprinkled with flock or sawdust for extra detail.

Baby's-breath (*Gypsophila*) has many small blossoms and a detailed twig system; it makes realistic-looking fruit trees and birch foliage. Baby's-breath may also be used to represent other species stylistically. Its delicate stem may be reinforced with plaster-coated twisted wire. Some florist shops sell it in assorted colors.

Yarrow or milfoil (*Achillea millefolium*), has dense $\frac{1}{4}''$ diameter buds and a detailed twig system, which make it a good material to represent underbrush or pine needle clumps.

Spirea has a shape resembling poplar trees. Asparagus fern resembles the boughs of cedar and fir trees. Gorse has very small leaves that make a good representation of pine. Millet seed sprays (used as bird food) may be threshed to remove the seeds, and then may be used as foliage.

Other usable natural plants are straw flowers, sumac, burning bush, fine leaf cedar, and sprigs of small evergreen needles.

Make evergreen trees by cementing asparagus fern into holes that have been cut in tapered splinters broken off cedar or ash stakes. You can also use balsa; turn the wood on a drill to create an evergreen shape. For a barklike texture, sand with rough sandpaper. Use wound wire for trunks of very small pine trees, and, for their foliage, insert a great number of thin wires into the trunk, in much the same way as a bottle brush would be constructed.

Palm trees are difficult to model accurately. Small ($\frac{1}{16}''$ scale and under) palm trees can be made from wire. Wind several strands to represent the trunk. The ends can then be left loose to create somewhat stylized leaves. Loosely twisted, fine wire can be added below the leaves to represent the fronds. For larger-scale palm tree trunks, use thin straw or dowels wired together along the length of the trunk. One end of the material can be unwired and spread in a natural leaf arrangement. You can also cut leaves from wire mesh and mount them on a rod or dowel trunk, or they may be cut from paper.

When the model has a scale so small that the inclusion of tree trunks and limbs is unnecessary, large groups of trees may be represented by clumps of lichen, cellulose, natural sponge, or fine wire wool. The grouping may also be cut out of a rough acoustical tile, foamed plastic, wire mesh, several plies of cardboard, or plaster.

Hedges and Bushes

Almost all the techniques suggested for making trees can be used to simulate hedges and bushes. For very small-scale models, sprinkle granulated cork, colored sawdust, or fine wood chips on cement-covered areas of the ground.

Foliage

Foliage may be fabricated from one, or a combination of several, of the following materials: cellulose sponge, lichen, commercially made granules, sawdust, bird seed, flock, paper, and drops of glue or paint. Flat or regular surfaces should be pulled apart or torn (not cut) to form the irregularities that are found in nature. Some types of foliage material (most notably sawdust and other small granules) should be applied to a bulk-creating underlayer of steel wool or lichen. Foliage may be affixed to model twigs by dipping the latter in shellac or, better yet, in a rubber-base adhesive and then sifting on the foliage. If you use an underlayer of steel wool or lichen, attach the top foliage layer with thinned liquid latex.

13-13.
Purchase Park
Hugh Stubbins & Associates, Inc., Architects
Modelmaker: Trip Tech Models, Inc.
Scale: 1/40" = 1'
Materials: cork and acrylic

The ground contours are layers of cork sheets cut and laminated
together. Dry natural plants, which fit the scale of the model, are
used for trees. These were hazed with spray paint and then inserted
into holes drilled in the cork surface. The buildings were constructed
with acrylic plastic. (*Photograph by Edward Jacoby/APG*)

When two different types of foliage materials are to
be used in one tree, place spots of glue on the first
material and sprinkle the second onto it.

PAINTING FOLIAGE. Spray painting or dip dyeing is
recommended since it is impossible to reach all of the
recesses of the foliage with a paintbrush. Spray painting
produces a more realistic, uneven effect. Highlights can
be brushed on or foliage of different colors combined
on each tree. Always use matte colors. To dye foliage
material, place it in a bag folded from a piece of loosely
woven fabric; dip the bag into a can of water dye; and
then take the foliage out and allow it to dry on a
newspaper.

The following are the oil colors used to represent
various species of foliage:

Autumn leaves: four parts ochre, two parts red
Elm leaves: five parts green, one part light yellow
Maple leaves: eight parts red, one part ochre

Oak leaves: four parts ochre, two parts burnt umber,
one part red
Pine needles: six parts light green, one part burnt
umber, a touch of light yellow

You can also used latex paints or flat lacquers.

13-14.
Johns-Manville World Headquarters, Colorado
The Architects Collaborative, Inc., Architects
Modelmakers: TAC
Scale: 1/16″ = 1′
Materials: Styrofoam and plastic

Solid Styrofoam blocks were glued together, leaving an excavated
area where the building could be inserted. The stepped elevations
were then carved out. These contours are accentuated by the
dramatic lighting.

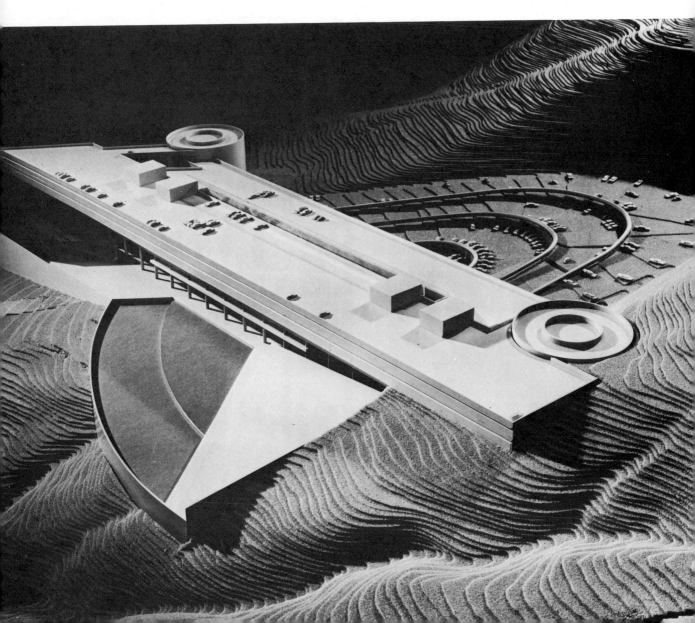

Flowers and House Plants

To make large-scale flowers, dip-paint little pieces of cellulose sponge or use small bits of lichen sprinkled with commercially made granules or drops of enamel paint. For smaller-scale flowers, use commercially made granules.

Flower beds may be represented by areas of Casco glue or cellulose cement on which green, coarse sawdust (to represent leaves), and multicolored birdseed, commercial granules, and flock have been placed.

Ivy may be represented by coarse, green sawdust or granules cemented to the walls of the model. Use steel wool that has been spread out, painted green, and cemented in place. Another method is to use small bits of lichen attached to strands of thin, flexible wire.

Make fallen leaves out of appropriate granules or brightly colored lichen cut into very small pieces and cemented to the ground.

Large-scale plants (1″ and 1½″ = 1′) are often used in detailed models of interiors. As with other forms of vegetation, each plant should conform to a recognizable prototype. Sometimes reasonable facsimiles may be obtained from real plants and bushes. More often it will

be necessary to make the model, leaf by leaf, from colored paper, applying this to wire stems. Sansevierias are made by cutting individual spikes from paper. Paint in the tiger stripes with green and yellow paint. Aloes and grasslike plants can be represented by rolling paper tightly into a cylinder. Slice it vertically and peel it back into an authentic-looking configuration. Ivy and other trailing plants are made by gluing dried tea leaves on stems made from thin wire. Spray paint them green. Large leaf plants are made by cutting leaves individually and gluing them to stems made from multistrand wire.

13-15.
Sunset Mountain Park Community Development
Daniel, Mann, Johnsons & Mendenhall, Architects
Modelmakers: DMJM
Scale: ¹/₁₆″ = 1′
Material: painted Plexiglas

To depict the proposed project realistically, a photograph of the building model was superimposed on a photograph of the actual site. The effect is due, in large part, to the skillful construction of this complicated model. Both the floor levels and the various grades on which they were situated were built on a mock-up of the site contours. (*Photograph by DMJM*)

14:Scale-Imparting Elements

Miniature people and cars are not simply elements of decoration on models. If properly used, they can aid in the visualization of a prototype by imparting an overall feeling of scale to the model (building) and giving some idea of the actual crowd of people and vehicles that will surround the completed design or travel through it.

PEOPLE

As with other articles of entourage, miniature people should complement, not compete with, the architectural portion of the model. In general, they should not be painted garishly or improvised in a bizarre fashion, unless this is the style of the design (see figure 14-1). Extra care must be taken in the case of rough models, where ill-chosen figures will distract the viewer's attention.

Whenever possible, buy ready-made figures. There are so many on the market in the $\frac{1}{50}'' = 1'$ to $\frac{1}{2}'' = 1'$ scale range that it makes little sense to attempt making your own, unless the figures need to be stylized for a particular effect. When it is necessary to fabricate these models, however, try to select a simple technique. Time spent on making people does not benefit the modelbuilding—the actual goal. The only exception is when the figures are to be reused or when you are constructing casting dies to make many models.

To show people naturally grouped on the model, have them standing, walking, or sitting in groups of twos and threes; the groups should also congregate around entrances and other places of naturally high traffic. They should not be evenly distributed along all sidewalks and paths, unless this will be the prototype condition.

Ready-Made Figures

In many scales, unpainted, ready-made figures are less expensive than beautiful hand-painted ones (figure 14-2). At large scales, these figures are more realistically de-tailed (figure 14-3). It is not possible to cast or carve a figure that economically compares with a ready-made one, but it is possible, by using shortcuts and mass-production techniques, to paint ready-made figures at a substantially lower cost than that of ready-painted ones.

Many professional modelmakers cast figures and vehicles in metal and will sell these castings to designers. A short search will unearth the name of a local modelmaker who could supply your needs at most scales up to $\frac{1}{2}'' = 1'$ for figures and up to $\frac{1}{8}'' = 1'$ for vehicles.

When working with commercial figures, the production procedure should be as follows:

1. Clean all casting flash from the plastic or metal figures. Scrape off major irregularities from plastic figures with a single-edge razor and smooth off the casting lines with a small jeweler's file.

2. Paint all flesh areas.

3. Mix and brush-paint all other colors, singly, proceeding from one figure to the next, spotting in the color where it is needed. Use a flat finish. If it is acceptable, the figures may also be spray painted one color. This saves time and does not detract, at $\frac{1}{16}'' = 1'$ and smaller scales, too badly from realism, especially when several colors are used and the figures are mixed together when mounted on the model.

4. To mount the figure, place a drop of glue onto the pedestal and insert it into holes drilled in the model floor or base. Paste figures without pedestals to the ground, using drops of epoxy glue or acetate cement. If you have trouble making the figures stand while the cement is drying, paste them on small pieces of clear, thin acetate and then paste the plastic pedestal to the model. Wood blocks with holes cut into them can be used as positioning jigs for holding the figures upright while the cement is drying.

Care must be taken to select ready-made figures that are accurately scaled. Some manufacturers are not very

14-1.
Ruckus Manhattan, detail of the Woolworth Building
Red Grooms and The Ruckus Construction Company
Dimensions: 15′ H
Materials: mixed media

The figures in this model do not play the usual role of defining scale simply because they are not in any one scale. The window washer peering down at the serpent stands three stories tall. The man under the umbrella dwarfs the crowd on the sidewalk. These comical figures add a narrative quality to this piece, something not ordinarily found in models. (*Photograph by Richard L. Plaut, Jr., courtesy of Marlborough Gallery, New York*)

14-2.
Ready-made figures. The figures shown here are only a sampling of those available through various manufacturers and hobby stores. These figures are made of wood or plastic, and range in scale from 1/32″ to 1/4″. They can be purchased painted or unpainted and come in many different lifelike poses.

careful about the height of their figures, and many have the tendency to cast heads that are out of proportion (an adult's head should be 1/7 to 1/8 of the total height).

Making Individual Figures

Because the number of people that must be fabricated will probably be large, the production system selected should have the fewest possible steps. Following are some techniques that can produce adequate figures.

Perhaps the simplest way to make figures is to cut them out of board. Fold the arms, legs, and torsos into a natural standing, sitting, or striding pose. If the figures are not folded, they tend, when viewed from the side, to look like random objects protruding from the sidewalk. Make figures out of colored paper or paint them. Or use photographs of people, printed at the proper scale. These can be pasted on boards and inserted into the model (figure 14-4). They can also be superimposed on

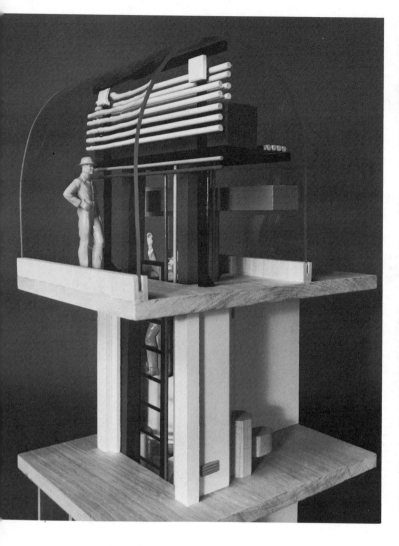

14-3.
Lewis County Jail
The NBBJ Group, Architects
Modelmaker: John Palewicz
Scale: ¾" = 1'
Materials: plastic and wood

This model was built from final mechanical and electrical plans to illustrate the complexity of the location of pipes and duct work. Wood was used for the floor and wall construction, with wood dowels used for the pipes, and the ceiling was made with a transparent plastic sheet, heat formed into shape. The two ready-made plastic figures add the element of scale needed in the model. (*Photograph by Niranjan Benegal*)

photographs of the model; photocopy the composite and make prints from the copy negative.

A rather whimsical technique, used in the 1964–65 New York World's Fair, consists of projecting a motion picture of actual people onto a model. This, naturally, would work only in a large-scale model displayed in a fairly dark room. The results, as can be imagined, are quite spectacular.

Two-dimensional figures, suitable for use on diorama models, may be made by using rubber stamps. These are available at various scales and show different styles of people. Stamp the appropriate scale figures into Bristolboard or double-faced illustration board, cut them out, and mount them on the model. A semiabstract three-dimensional figure may be made by using rubber stamps on prefixed acetate (or other transparent bendable plastic that will take ink). Cut out the figure, bend it into a natural pose, and mount it on the model.

14-4.
Christiana Mall
RTKL Associates, Inc., Architects
Modelmakers: RTKL model shop personnel
Scale: ¼″ = 1′
Materials: cardboard and wood

The figures in this model are photographs, reduced to scale, of RTKL employees. These images were cut out and mounted on chipboard. The model was constructed so that it could be effectively illuminated with photographer's lights through the skylights. (*Photograph by David Whitcomb, RTKL*)

For figures made from wood strips or dowels, a simple carving sequence should be devised so that the result is a reasonably convincing figure with a minimum number of cuts. Arms and legs should be splintered away from the torso and glued back in a natural position. Paint the figures, following the procedure outlined for ready-made figures.

The next two techniques are rather tedious, but can result in superb figures. It is perhaps best to use these systems for larger (over ¼″ = 1′) scales and in instances when relatively few need be made. Crude figures can be built up in clay or sculpt metal. More detailed figures can be made with wax or plaster.

To make *wax figures:*

1. Bend a soft wire armature into a natural pose.
2. Heat the wax (candle wax, beeswax, or the hard wax used in electroplating) to a temperature just a bit

higher than its melting point (too high a temperature will delay the hardening of the wax).

3. Use a cheap brush to apply the wax to the armature, and build up the figure in successive layers. Allow the wax to dry between coats. Water applied by finger will hasten drying time. Fine detail may be carved into the wax at this point.

4. Prime the finished figure with white liquid shoe polish, then paint with poster or model railroad oil colors and apply a coat of flat finish.

To build up *figures made out of plaster:*

1. Make a soft wire armature; bend it into a natural pose.

2. Mix plaster of Paris to the consistency of cream cheese and apply it to the armature. Hasten setting by baking under a 100-watt bulb.

3. Build up the final shape and details with thinly mixed plaster applied by brush.

4. Paint the finished figure with model railroad oil paints or poster colors.

ABSTRACT FIGURES. Even abstract figures should have accurate height and width proportions, especially for scales larger than $\frac{1}{32}'' = 1'$. There have been so many unfortunate instances in which the figures were so abstract that they were unrecognizable.

Pins without heads made very realistic figures at scales under $\frac{1}{32}'' = 1'$. The pins should be held with pliers as they are driven into the baseboard. Small wood strips or dowels may also be used. Map tacks, nails wound in wire or fabric, and twisted tinfoil are also effective for $\frac{1}{16}'' = 1'$ scale. Caraway seeds, pasted on end, may be used at approximately $\frac{1}{64}'' = 1'$ scales.

Casting Figures

Before undertaking the complications of casting, determine whether the number of figures needed warrants this technique. See chapter 8 for a review of some of the considerations.

ROUGH FIGURES IN METAL. Because of the flexibility of lead, it is possible to cast a basic figure that can then be bent into various postures and filed into modified shapes. The following technique is acceptable for making people above a $\frac{1}{16}''$ scale (at $\frac{1}{16}'' = 1'$, noses and other small details are impossible). At $\frac{1}{4}'' = 1'$ and larger scales, it is possible to cast cuffs, belts, ties, and so forth. In larger scales, make separate dies for men and women.

1. Carve the front of the figure in a hardwood female mold. Use a gouge to hollow the wood and then finish with sandpaper. Place a second block of wood on top of the first. Drill two or four holes for the keys (which can be nails or dowels). The style of the figure should be one that lends itself to modifications of many poses and physiques. Make the figure at a scale of about 6'3" tall, since some leg length will be bent under to make feet. Making several dies will expedite casting.

2. Remove the second block, and spread graphite powder on the carved first block. Press the blocks together, transferring the outline of the cut to the second block. Hollow out the second block. Gouge out the air vents and filling channel.

3. Clamp both finished mold halves together in a vise, or with clamps.

4. Melt some lead in a ladle and pour it into the filling channel.

5. Remove the casting from the mold. Cut off the metal that has been cast in the filling channel and air vents and any flash that has formed along the mold intersection.

6. Using pliers, bend the ends of the legs to form feet. With a fine file, shape the shoes with a few strokes.

7. File the excess metal from the figure.

8. Using a square jeweler's file, flatten out the face on both sides of the nose and shape the chin.

9. Flatten out the ends of the arms to form hands.

10. File the figure to give it a natural form. Bend it into a walking, sitting, or standing position.

11. Paint and flat finish.

FINE FIGURES IN WAX, METAL, OR EPOXY. Use the following procedure for casting fine figures:

1. Carve the figure out of Plexiglas, using fine burrs mounted on a light electric-powered hand drill. The figure must be formed so that it can be easily removed from the female mold—legs must be together and arms must lie close to the torso to prevent undercuts.

2. Cast a mold in plaster of Paris or rubber.

3. Remove the Plexiglas original from the female mold.

4. Cast the final figures in wax, epoxy, or lead. For better detail, or when cutting extremely small figures, cast in Zamac metal.

5. Once removed from the mold, the legs and arms of the figure may be cut apart and bent to various positions.

VEHICLES

As in the case of modeled figures, it is best to buy ready-made products whenever they are available (figure 14-5).

14-5.
Ready-made vehicles. Cars and trucks can be bought assembled and painted, like those shown here, or unpainted and partially assembled. These range in scale from 5/64″ to 1/4″, but other vehicles are available in even larger or smaller scales.

Ready-Made Vehicles

Unlike cast vehicles, ready-made ones are usually hollow and have internal detail and see-through windows which may be important at large scales (figure 14-6). They are sold in model railroad stores at 1:152 to 3/32″ = 1′ and, in an unbelievable profusion, at 1/8″ = 1′ to 1/2″ = 1′ scales. Although they are usually assembled, it is sometimes necessary to buy a kit for a specific type of car at some of the larger scales.

Some ready-made cars, notably those sold as toys (as opposed to those sold by hobbyists or to architectural modelmakers), do not have scales stamped on their boxes. When purchasing these brands, it is best to go to a store whose staff has a rough knowledge of the lengths of several types of cars or measure the models to determine scale before purchasing them.

The same procedures that were listed for cleaning and painting ready-made figures should be followed for vehicles.

Making Individual Vehicles

There are several ways to simplify the forms of individually made small-scale vehicles. One method is to cut hard stripwood or foam board to proper length (figure 14-7). By using wood of several different cross sections, you can represent enclosed cars, convertibles, buses, and trucks fairly convincingly at 1/32" and smaller scales.

If time permits and a more detailed representation is desired, cut the outline of the passenger compartment into the sides of the strips. Other more detailed techniques involve cutting the silhouette of the vehicle's wheels into the strip; or cutting a small bit of material away from both sides of the window parts of the passenger compartment; or sanding the corners of the strip. More complex shapes can also be built up from two or more pieces of attached stripwood.

Casting Vehicles

Vehicles may be cast in almost any of the casting materials listed in this book. When making smaller-scale vehicles, however, avoid plaster and other porous materials. Small-scale vehicles may also be vacuum formed from the polystyrene sheet.

14-6.
Neurotic Transformations of a Suburban Facade No. 2
Jeffrey W. Kusmick, New Jersey Institute of Technology
Scale: 1/8" = 1'

This view of the final presentation model shows one of a series of facades that were built out of balsa wood. The fact that these walls were in a constant state of reconstruction is reinforced by including various cranes, trucks, and workers on the site. The size in which these scale elements and the prefabricated plastic window assemblies were available determined the scale of the model. (*Photograph by Jeffrey W. Kusmick*)

14-7.
U. S. Insurance Group
The Grad Partnership, Architects
Modelmakers: David Zugale, RA; and Robert Krause, RA
Scale: 1/16" = 1'
Materials: foam board, cardboard, and color papers

Foam board was used to represent the cars and to make the building levels in this study model. The edges and structural support elements were made of cardboard. Colored papers cover the parking area. (*Photograph by Louis Checkman*)

TRAINS, AIRCRAFT, AND SHIPS

Kits and ready-made model train cars and locomotives are available in great numbers at 1:152, 1:120, 1:87, 1:76, and 1:48 scales. These are known as OOO or N gauge, TT, HO, OO, and O gauge, respectively. At smaller scales, simple abstract model trains may be carved out of balsa strips.

Small-scale aircraft can be quickly carved from balsa. If you want greater detail, however, purchase kits from your local hobby store.

Small-scale ships (1:500 and smaller) may be built out of balsa and cardboard. The former material is used to construct the hull and funnel. The board is used to make decks and bridge structures. Dowels may be used for round funnels, and wires for masts and derricks. Larger-scale boats can be purchased prefabricated or they can be carved from hardwood.

Showing Animation

Traffic animation is often used on certain types of models that are to be viewed by the general public. Motion greatly increases the crowd appeal of the exhibit. Figure 14-9 shows one possible construction of an animated road. For an additional effect, cars may also have working headlights. Electricity is carried through the conveyer loop to individual vehicles.

For very small-scale town-planning models, animation can be shown by representing each road lane by fabric or plastic tape strung over widely placed supports and then painting oblong-shaped vehicles on the tapes; air circulating above or below the tapes causes them to move up and down, creating the illusion that the cars are moving horizontally.

Night photographs are sometimes enhanced if the vehicles on the model have working lights. To install lights in 1/16" and larger scale models: drill out the non-working headlights of the vehicles; cement small lamps in the holes, using Elmer's glue; and run the wires of the lamps through the road bed, hiding each behind a wheel. Attach them to a transformer in a parallel hookup.

LAMPS, RAILINGS, AND SIGNS

Lights and signals are most easily constructed from wire, dowels, or copper tubing (if working lamps are intended). Lamps may be made from carved acrylic rod, variety store pearls, or miniature bulbs. Ready-made lights and signals are available in 1:152, and at 1/10", 1/8", and 1/4" = 1' scales (figure 14-10), but only at the 1/8" scale is there a wide selection of styles.

Large-scale wire and stripwood railings and fences

14-8.
Harbour Island
The Hillier Group, Architects
Modelmaker: Timothy Burton
Material: painted acrylic

The model consists of acrylic buildings, contours, and water on a wood frame base. Added scale elements include prefabricated metal cars and trees, and hand-carved wood boats with silk sails. (*Photograph by Leigh Photographs*)

are best made with the aid of a hardwood assembling jig; or pin them over an elevation drawing. Figure 7-5 shows a cutting guide that can be of great help in cutting equal-length stripwood stringers. The steel or hardwood bars should be drilled to take two screws each. The bars are individually clamped to the steel backplate and the holes extended into it. The holes are then threaded.

Small-scale ($\frac{1}{32}'' = 1'$ and larger) railings and fences can be made by scoring acetate sheet and coloring in the lines.

Storefront signs, traffic signs, display graphics, and other signs can be made in a number of ways. Make those that are needed in limited numbers from pressure-sensitive letters, transfer letters whose carrying sheet can be peeled away (provided the backing of the sign will not be adversely affected), decals that are transferred by the application of water, letters that are hand done with the aid of a lettering set stylus and guide, or letters cut from magazines and other similar sources.

Signs that must be duplicated a number of times can be made by rubber stamping, being commercially printed on paper or custom-made as pressure-sensitive transfers, or being photographically reproduced.

It is always advisable to form the sign on a sheet of Bristolboard or illustration board and then to apply it to the model rather than trying to work directly.

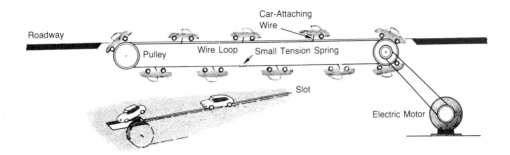

14-9.
Animated traffic

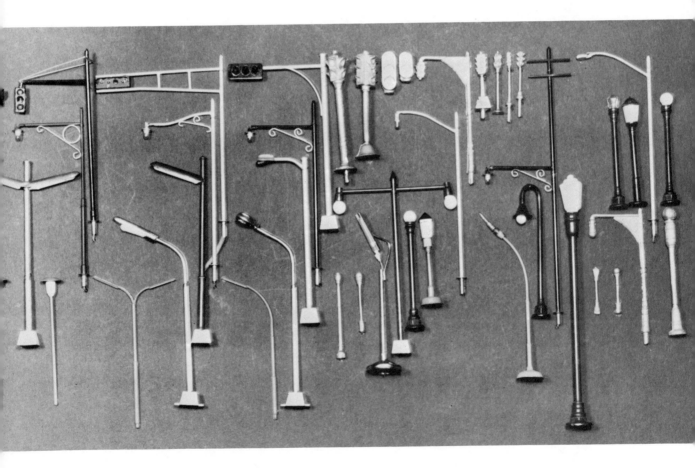

14-10.
Ready-made street lights and traffic signals. The ones shown here
are cast in metal or plastic and are available from various manufacturers. The scales range from 1″ = 152′ to ¼″ = 1′. Some
even have working lights.

Part Two

15:Massing Models

Models are arbitrarily divided into five overlapping categories:

1. Rough massing solid models used mostly for study
2. Solid models with selective details
3. Roughly detailed hollow models
4. Fully detailed hollow models
5. Engineering test models

The first two categories are reviewed in this chapter, with photographs arranged in approximate order of the complexity of models—from the simplest solid models to more detailed ones. Hollow models are discussed in Chapter 16, and engineering models in chapter 19.

SOLID MASSING MODELS

Massing models are most often used as a preliminary design aid. This need not, however, preclude their use for presentation. Those that are a study tool should be fabricated in a minimum of time with simple tools. Only when you have built and studied enough designs and reached a final concept should you build one of more durable materials for presentation use. Before final stage, however, it often becomes evident that a study model is, in fact, needed for some minor presentation use. Since the cost of a new model is not usually warranted, it becomes necessary to refurbish the rough design model. It is possible to plan ahead and, at the start, to build a more solid baseboard and a better-constructed model of an existing building, as well as to lay in a supply of model cars, trees, and so on. Later stages of the design model can also be built with a thought to permanency. Once the design has been completed, the model can be inspected and shabby looking or under-detailed parts rebuilt. This will result in an overall saving in time, and will allow you to present a detailed structure.

A solid massing model with detail, selectively chosen and ingeniously built, can look completely professional despite the speed at which it was constructed. Many such sensitive models are more impressive than professionally made, highly detailed, expensive models are. The important things to remember are: choose modeling materials with which the prototype can be best presented; try to select materials whose natural colors and textures require no finishing steps; show only the details that are important to the fundamental design concept.

The more adroitly constructed the model, the greater its use as a design aid. Consider modeling existing adjacent buildings or transporting the model to the site so that factors not taken into account in the drafting room become evident.

The site should be simply represented with laminated contours; or dry-mount a plot plan onto the baseboard (figure 15-1) and color it in effectively with pastels or pencils.

Rough Massing Models

Such models of buildings and town-planning projects may be made from any material that can be added to and cut easily. Thus, such pliable materials as clay and plasticine may be used, as may Styrofoam. Small, preformed, modular blocks of wood or miniature magnets (for very small studies) should be kept on hand for repeated use. With all these materials, you can eliminate a part or decrease a dimension with one chop of a knife or by taking away some of the blocks. Adding material is almost as simple, except that with Styrofoam the new material must be glued in place. Naturally, clay is the best material to use when modeling buildings with extensive curved shapes.

Incidentally, a lifetime supply of various sizes of pine or balsa block can be cut on a band or circular saw in an hour or two. Several hundred magnets with $\frac{1}{4}''$ to $1''$ dimensions may be purchased for a few dollars from a mail-order house.

Rough massing models may sometimes be constructed from paperboard that has been scored and bent into boxes (figure 15-2). To save time, each wall should have

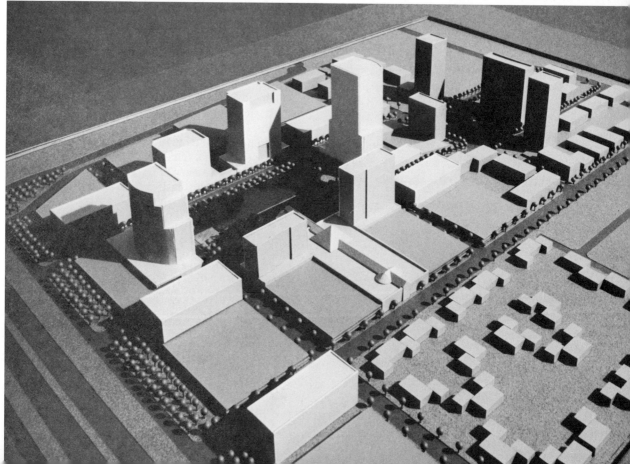

15-1.
Richard J. Hughes Justice Complex,
  Trenton, New Jersey
The Grad Partnership, Architects
Modelmakers: members of the
  architects' staff
Materials: matboard and color papers

The basic building forms and their relationship to the site are shown in this study model. The buildings were quickly made using matboard, with the circulation pattern of surrounding streets and the parking areas drawn directly on the base. (*Photograph by Louis Checkman*)

15-2.
Pin Oak Master Plan, Houston
Cesar Pelli & Associates, Architects
Modelmakers: Kevin Hart and Mark Schlenker of CP&A
Scale: 1″ = 100′
Material: painted chipboard

The relationship of the buildings in this planning project was studied with basic massing forms. These were simple chipboard constructions, the only details being the parapet walls and an atrium skylight on one of the low buildings. The smaller buildings were made out of wood. Cork was used on top of the chipboard base cover to define the block areas. (*Photograph by Kevin Hart*)

15-3.
Tour Fiat
Skidmore, Owings & Merrill, Architects
Modelmakers: SOM model studio
Scale: ¹⁄₁₆″ = 1′
Materials: wood and chipboard

This model was used to study the proposed building project in relation to existing buildings and street levels. The structure in the foreground is made out of chipboard. The other buildings are built out of solid wood blocks and cardboard. Chipboard was also used as the base cover material, with pantone paper applied to show the streets.

a tab for stapling to adjacent walls. Gussets or stripwood may be used to square up surfaces.

For presentation block models, use clay, plasticine, Styrofoam, cardboard, wood, or even acrylic blocks that come in the desired shape. To do a neat job, substitute a cutting jig or miter box and handsaws if power tools are not available. The varieties of wood that may be used are limitless, although balsa, naturally, is the easiest to cut. See chapter 8 for solid block and bread-and-butter construction techniques. Large clay or plasticine masses may be built on a cardboard or wood undershape to save material. Board may also be used to represent free-standing walls and other structures that would be

difficult to model with the plastic material.

If modeling a multifloor building on a small scale, construct it from laminations of illustration board, each floor represented by one layer. The plies of material in the board will very realistically represent the spandrels and glass areas of each floor. Every other layer may be indented to represent window strips, the unindented layers representing the spandrels.

If the building has extensive glass areas and the effect of glass is to be incorporated into the model, cut the buildings from acrylic. Opaque roofs and end walls can be created by sanding those surfaces, by painting them, or by covering them with Bristolboard.

If the project contains many buildings of the same general plan (such as a housing project), have a local carpentry shop mill a prototype shape in hardwood strips. Then cut the individual buildings from the strips. The walls of wood models may be stained or spray painted. Stipple paint on the roofs to create a contrasting effect. Roughly carved blocks may be covered with Bristolboard if other ways of finishing loom too large, or they may even be left rough.

SOLID MODELS WITH SELECTIVE DETAIL

When the design problems of basic massing have been solved, it may be wise to study the influence of windows, penthouses, setback floors, overhangs, and major textures on the design. Such forms as skylights, stair bulkheads, parapet walls, and recessed parts of a facade may also be introduced (figure 15-4). Care must be taken to keep all detail on a consistent level.

An acrylic or wood stamp will conveniently emboss clay with window shapes. Emboss or tool textures into the clay or, for detail, use embossed plastic building paper pressed against it.

15-5.
Cass Technical High School Addition, Detroit
Albert Kahn Associates, Inc., Architects
Modelmakers: AKA design staff
Scale: ⅛" = 1'
Materials: foam board and chipboard

This massing model features some elements of the buildings in detail. The existing buildings in the background are made of chipboard. Prints of the various elevations were laminated to their surfaces. The foreground buildings are paper-covered foam board with black tape used to represent glass. The steps and columns of the entrance are made of wood.

15-6.
Blade Runner
Warner Bros. (A Ladd Company Release)
Special photographic effects: Entertainment Effects Group
Materials: foam board and papers

Because these buildings were to be used in the background of the film's miniature set, they were made as simple forms: foam board boxes with various types of papers applied to show the spandrels and glass lines. (*Photograph by Mark Stetson*)

15-4.
Charlotte Downtown Development Plan
RTKL Associates, Inc., Architects
Modelmakers: RTKL model shop
    personnel
Scale: 1" = 50'
Materials: acrylic, polystyrene, and
    museum board

This more detailed massing study model was used throughout the design development of the project. Originally, only the gray buildings, which represented existing structures, were present on the base. The smaller of these were made from solid acrylic; the larger ones assembled, spackled, and painted from polystyrene sheets. As the design progressed, the featured buildings—made of white singleply museum board—were added. Atrium skylights are scored 1/32" plastic sheets. (*Photograph by David Whitcomb*)

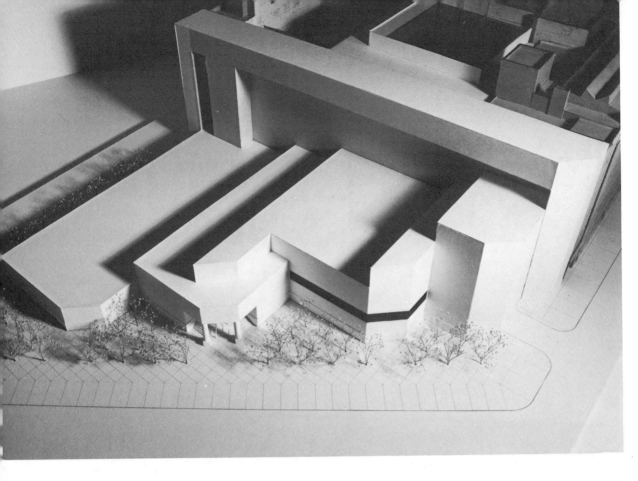

15-7.
Wrapped Reichstag, Project for Berlin
Christo
Modelmaker: Michael Sieler
Dimensions: 21½″ × 78¾″ × 65″
Materials: wood, fabric

This is a view of the model as it is being wrapped by the artist, Christo (on the left), with the help of an assistant. The understructure is built out of Finland birch of varying thicknesses, glued and nailed or screwed together. Detail elements were cut from solid birch and maple. The model was then sprayed with a light gray primer.
    The fabric is a sheer nylon dyed a light blue metallic gray. String was used to represent the marine-grade rope that would be used in the wrapping of the actual building. (*Photograph by Michael Sieler*)

15-8.
Although building details, such as the entrance pilasters and pediment, were simplified, their basic forms were evident through the fabric tied around the model. (*Collection of Rothschild Bank; photograph by eeva-inkeri*)

15-9.
The Gateway Mall
Hellmuth, Obata & Kassabaum, Architects
Modelmakers: HOK
Scale: ⅟₃₂″ = 1′
Materials: foam polyurethane and chipboard

The surrounding existing buildings in this model were cut from 5-pound blocks of foam polyurethane. The proposed buildings were made of chipboard, which was covered with colored papers and overlays to show the spandrels and glass lines. These easily rendered details enabled the featured buildings to be readily distinguished. The wood frame base was covered with matboard, and this was covered with cork to show the sidewalks and streets. The trees were made using cast metal armatures covered with steel wool; these were then painted and flocked.

To detail entire facades, apply black-on-white reproductions of the building elevations on cardboard or wood blocks (figure 15-5).

Individual windows may be stenciled onto the model. Cut the stencil from acetate, then spray paint or draw the openings. If you spray more paint on one or two corners of the windows, you will get a shadow effect. Indicate strip windows with tape (figure 15-6). These techniques allow windows to be represented at scales as small as 1″ = 100′.

To construct mullions and pilasters quickly, use stripwood or thread pasted onto the block. Make parapets by sheathing the walls of the block with thin Bristolboard and running it past the roof level. Balconies can also be made from Bristolboard. Use pressure-sensitive overlays or photostats of designs to represent plaza and paving textures.

Scribe spandrels and mullions into acrylic blocks, or represent them by first spray painting the protective paper and then cutting away the paper where the windows are to be.

To add further detail to a block model, cover the block substructure with one or more plies of paperboard cut out to represent doors, windows, and moldings (figure 15-9). Windows can be acetate with black paper behind them (to give the effect seen on a prototype building on a sunny day).

To give a quick indication of the scale of the model, make roughly constructed cars, people, and trees or use accoutrements that have been stripped from other models.

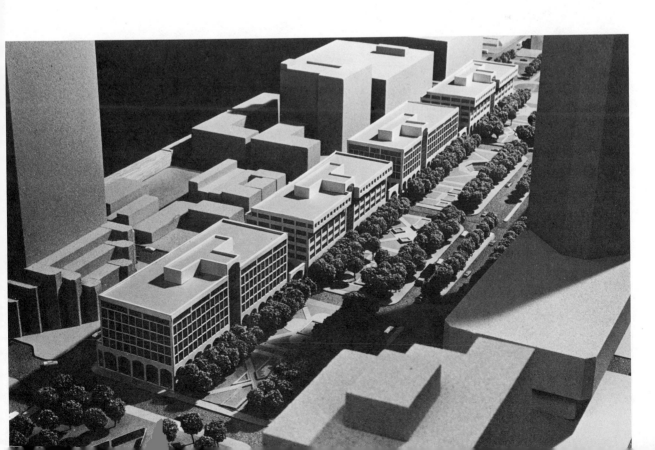

SOLID TOWN-PLANNING MODELS

Models are indispensible for the study and planning of urban areas, especially hilly sites where not only the plan layout but the relationship of buildings on different levels must be analyzed. Models are also used to present future planning schemes to the public. Some cities maintain up-to-date small-scale planning models that show all the buildings in the entire metropolis.

Use the usual construction techniques for the buildings included in town-planning models. These may also range from simple block forms to highly detailed constructions (figure 15-10). If there are basic building forms repeated many times, cast these (see chapter 8) or buy cast houses available from various companies.

15-10.
Dammam Towers, Dammam, Kingdom of Saudi Arabia
The Eggers Group, Architects and Planners
Materials: acrylic and wood

This model was used to present not only the relationship of the numerous high-rise buildings, but also their design. The buildings are made as solid block models, richly detailed with, among other things, balconies, windows, street level arcades. The large wood base was covered with chipboard, on which streets and walkways were painted. Trees were added as a finishing touch. (*Photograph by Gil Amiaga*)

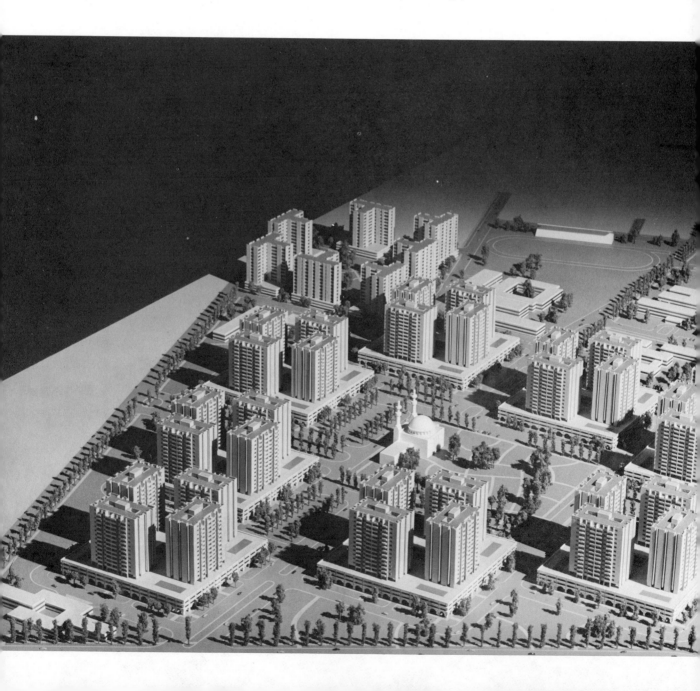

16:Hollow Models

Hollow models are usually more complicated to construct than solid block models because internal bracing is required and more detail, sometimes including interior building elements and furnishings, will be shown. A judicious evaluation of the degree of detail can result in huge savings of construction time without lessening the effectiveness of a hollow model. Often a roughly detailed model can prove as effective a study and presentation tool as a super-detailed, professionally made, acrylic one. Using easy-to-work-with materials that resemble the prototype and require little or no finishing is another way to save time and money.

INTERNAL BRACING

All hollow models require internal bracing to avoid warpage caused by room temperature changes, exposure of parts to artificial light or sunlight, applying other parts to the model, and painting. Models can be braced with an internal framework, or carcass, as it is sometimes called. This frame can be in an arbitrary form if the inside of the model will not be seen, or, on models where it will show, it can be disguised in the form of floors or interior partitions.

There are 50-year-old models built entirely from thin Bristolboard that, because of elaborate and well-placed internal buttressing, have resisted countless climatic changes and are as plumb as they were on the day they were built. A good rule to follow, then, is to put as much bracing as time permits into the model.

To brace the backs of walls or floors, run strip material parallel to the long dimensions of the surfaces or behind all four edges of the surface. Use plenty of cross braces with both systems. For plywood or cardboard with a discernible grain, run a good number of the strips at right angles to the grain of the outside plies. The grain of board can be determined by flexing it in both directions. The grain runs in the most easily bent direction. A better way to prevent flat surfaces from warping is to apply a backing sheet over the strips. This sheet should be made from the same material as the exterior or viewed face of the object.

Walls and floors can be simultaneously braced together and set into true 90° relationship by any of the methods shown in figure 16-2, or, in very large scale models, by metal angles screwed in place. Techniques A and B should be used on small and medium-size models to true up wall intersections. Techniques C and D can be used on larger models or where walls must be removable. If the model must be taken apart and the scale is small, the rods or dowels may be built into pilasters hidden inside the model.

If the back of the wall will be seen, it may still be attached to the floor at a true 90° angle by temporarily pinning or tack cementing the strips in place until the wall-floor joint has dried.

Professionally made acrylic models are braced with large pine blocks placed inside unseen parts of the building; with thinner pine strips where bulky blocks would be visible; and with plywood sheeting behind thin acrylic walling that might buckle without this additional stiffness.

WALL CONSTRUCTION

You can use any of the wall systems shown in figure 16-3. The first (A) is the easiest to construct, the strongest, and the one requiring the least number of precision cuts. It may be used on models as small as $\frac{1}{32}'' = 1'$. The other styles require individual cutting of each window or strip and extensive bracing of the wall material. Of all the styles, D, F, and I appear best when viewed from behind.

Figure 16-3J shows an alternative way of fastening the various plies that make up the wall. Pins can be used to fasten all but the outer ply; cement this layer to small pieces of paper speared by the pins. Simulated building material may be applied where needed.

16-1.
1299 Sansome Street Office Building, San Francisco
Hellmuth, Obata & Kassabaum, Inc., Architects
Modelmakers: A. Fakoor, A. Popal, Andy Laguana, and
  Adolpho Perez
Scale: massing studies and site model, $\frac{1}{16}'' = 1'$
       presentation model, $\frac{1}{8}'' = 1'$
Materials: Styrofoam, matboard, wood, and Plexiglas

The models in this series, showing the project development, range
from simplest solid massing studies to detailed hollow models. O:
the six models seen in the front row, the first three show the
building's general shape and floor levels. The next three show
different treatments of the exterior surface. One of these design
solutions is shown in its setting, in the background. The hilly site
contours are built up of laminated layers of foam board. On the
right is an $\frac{1}{8}''$ scale model of the building's stepped corner. The
$\frac{1}{4}''$ scale model on the left demonstrates the precast concrete
panel system. (*Photograph by Peter Henricks*)

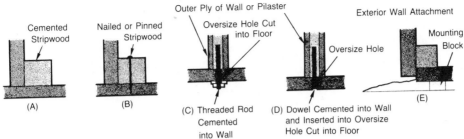

16-2.
Attaching walls to the floor or baseboard

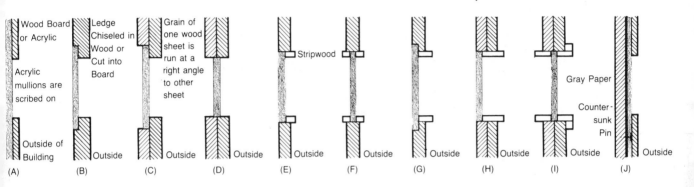

16-3.
Wall construction

Figure 16-4 shows many of the more sophisticated construction techniques used by a single professional modelbuilder in making acrylic, or acrylic and metal,

It is very helpful to be able to lay out wall materials directly from an elevation drawing of the building. Lay the drawing over materials and window corners. Transfer key points with a series of pinholes. This technique is better than using carbon paper because it does not deface the material as badly.

Attaching the Building to the Base

If the ground is constructed of laminations, cut out a depression to secure the building. Use mounting blocks to bring the building up to the proper level (figure 16-2E). If the model must be removable, do not cement the walls or the perimeter strip to the floor.

FLOOR AND ROOF CONSTRUCTION

Follow the instructions given on page 211 for bracing floors and roofs. Special care must be taken to construct an absolutely flat roof; otherwise, its corners will lift from the walls or, worse yet, warp the entire model.

To prevent this, mount roofs and floors to the walls by resting (not cementing) them on strips (wood or acrylic) cemented to the outside walls.

Try to cut out all floors simultaneously to ensure uniformity of shape. Roofs with complex shapes (mansards, folded plate, etc.) may, in some cases, have to be first mocked-up out of ⅛″ or ¼″ square balsa strip. Measurements for the final model may then be taken directly from the mock-up. Sloping roofs can be built on acrylic or stripwood framing that is a simplification of the prototype.

DOMES AND VAULTS

See the table in chapter 9 for ways to make domes and vaults. Professional modelmakers sometimes make large forms by draw-forming hot acrylic sheets over a plaster mold. Smaller ones may be vacuum-formed or hot-drawn from acetate or styrene and built up from several plies of Bristolboard or brown adhesive paper. In town-planning models, these structures may be molded in plasticine on carved wood molds. Ready-made acrylic or acetate hemispheres can often be purchased or cut from toy balls.

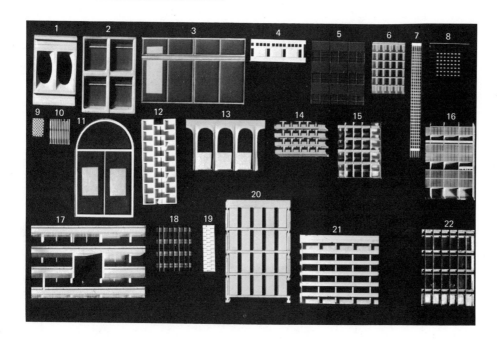

16-4.

Highly detailed wall and window assemblies. (*1*) Acrylic cut out then filed to shape. (*2*) Window frame made from extruded polystyrene. Extrusion was done by an outside shop, then cut into required thickness and other details carved into it. Window was constructed of acrylic into which rails were machined. (*3*) Metal inlaid into acrylic sheet. (*4*) Made from small pieces of acrylic butt- and dado-jointed together and cemented. (*5*) Acrylic with grooves cut into it. The spandrel panels were made from second plys of acrylic. (*6*) Acrylic. Verticals are represented by grooves cut into the backing sheet, horizontals by strips set into grooves in the backing. (*7*) Acrylic, with white paint rubbed into scored lines. (*8*) Acrylic strips joined in an egg-crate fashion. (*9*) Milled acrylic. Grooves were cut along a length of strip stock. The strip was then cut perpendicular to its long axis and the pieces joined together in a staggered fashion to form a checkerboard effect. (*10*) Milled acrylic. Equidistant grooves were cut into one side of sheet stock. The other side was then milled through in places to create the openings. (*11*) Acrylic with the frame painted on. (*12*) Individual pieces of acrylic strip butted together and cemented. (*13*) Cast metal. (*14*) Acrylic. Back sheet was channeled to receive strip acrylic balconies. (*15*) Acrylic. Back was made from square strips joined side to side. Some horizontal lines were painted; others were made from acrylic strips set into grooves in the back sheet as were the vertical lines. (*16*) Acrylic sheet for backing. A grid of strip material was mounted onto it and some of the voids were plugged with blocks. Fine horizontal lines were achieved by painting the entire surface of the block and then scratching away some of the paint to form lines. (*17*) Acrylic. Horizontals, columns and sunshades were set into grooves cut into the backing sheet. Some of the fine vertical lines were painted on spandrel strips (see description for No. 16). Other fine vertical lines (see second row of lines from top, left side of facade) were made by painting milled grooves. (*18*) Acrylic. Horizontals are painted; verticals are strips which were set into grooves cut into the backing sheet. (*19*) Milled acrylic sheet was then cut into the desired width. The resulting strips were cemented together in a staggered fashion. (*20*) Acrylic. Beams (running perpendicular to the facade) are milled strips which were set into grooves in the spandrel. Panels between the windows were set between the spandrels. (*21*) Acrylic. Horizontals and verticals were butt joined to the backing sheet. (*22*) Acrylic. Horizontal lines were milled into the backing sheet. Verticals are strips which were set into grooves.

NOTE: The white rectangles that appear under Nos. 3, 8, 11, 13, 15, 16 and 17 are strips of tape used to mount the assemblies to their display board.

the covering foil or
er material diagonally

Fold the material back
and cement it in place

ow Opening

Rear of Wall

Front Frame of Window

Rear of Wall

Rear of Wall

pplying Wall-Covering Material to Window Openings

ow construction

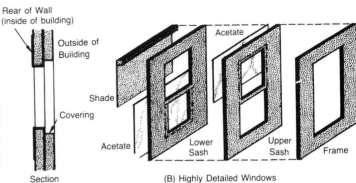

Rear of Wall
(inside of building)

Outside of
Building

Shade

Covering

Acetate

Section

Acetate

Lower
Sash

Upper
Sash

Frame

(B) Highly Detailed Windows

VINDOWS

Vindows can be represented by using acrylic sheets
or the wall construction. Paper or simulated building
materials can be applied to the surface except where
he windows are located (figure 16-5A), or the windows
an remain masked out until the walls have been painted
figure 16-6). Another way to construct windows is to
lace thin acetate between plies of materials (figure
6-5B).

Small-scale acrylic models usually have window mullion
etail scribed into the plastic walls. The lines are then
lled with paint. Any excess that spills over onto the
lass area may be removed with a swab stick dipped
a paint remover or thinner. Thicker mullions may be
epresented by thin tape.

Etched metal has also been used to represent window
valls. Large-scale models have mullions and window
ills built up from metal, acrylic, or wood strip material.
These strips are set into grooves milled into the side
f the building. A hypodermiclike applicator should be
sed to place cement in the grooves. Since both metal
nd wood have expansion rates different from that of
crylic, the mullions will buckle if the model is subjected
o wide temperature changes. Thus, this type of model
hould be protected from temperature changes.

The problem of having to show interior detail and to
onstruct the inside of the model neatly can be eliminated,
o a large degree, if you use windows glazed with dark
ransparent plastic or back up clear glazing with dark,
paque sheets. If the sheets are kept a fraction of an
nch behind the plastic, the effect will be more realistic.
f the windows are not too large and are handled cor-
ectly, the effect is much like that of an actual building
viewed on a very bright day.

WINDOW SCREENS AND BLINDS. Venetian blinds can
be simulated by a pressure-sensitive overlay with a
parallel line pattern. To make window screen (figure
16-9), carefully stretch nylon material and pin on the
work surface. Coat the window or window wall with
cement, place it on the nylon, and clamp it in place.
The excess material can be trimmed off when dry.

TINTED AND STAINED GLASS. To simulate tinted glass,
use colored acetate or acrylic, or spray the back of clear
acrylic with translucent lacquer. Stained glass may be
created by hand painting acrylic with translucent lacquer.
If the scene represented does not have to be completely
true to the prototype, choose from a fairly wide selection
of translucent acetate stained glass designs used for
quality Christmas cards. Custom-etched metal sheets
made to specification can also be used to represent
stained or etched glass.

ROUGHLY REPRESENTED WINDOWS. If a model is to
have many hundreds of windows, it may be practical
to have a rubber stamp or metal embossing die made.
Another method is to draft several windows which can
be cut out and mounted on the model. Windows can
also be drawn or painted directly on the walls of the
model (figure 16-7). Photographs of actual windows can
be printed to scale and added to the model.

READY-MADE WINDOWS. See figure 16-8 for examples
of the many ready-made windows that can be purchased.
To increase their usefulness, you can modify their shapes
according to your requirements. Ready-made windows
and windows built up from small parts should be attached
to walls before these are set into the model. The walls
should be clamped under books until the cement holding
the windows has dried.

16-6.
Mutual Benefit Life Headquarters Office Building
RTKL Associates, Inc., Architects
Modelmakers: Peter Doo, Associate Architect
Scale: ⅛" = 1'
Material: acrylic

This sophisticated model was built without elaborate equipme
A saber saw was the most expensive tool used. The ⅛" gree
tinted acrylic was cut with the saw, sanded, and joined with solve
The protective paper on the acrylic sheet was used as maski
during the painting. Narrow strips indicating curtain wall membe
were cut and pulled off. The surface was then spray painte
Remaining paper was pulled off, except at the spandrels, whe
it was simply left in place. (*Photograph by David Whitcomb*)

16-7.
Snake Building
Roger Brown
Dimensions: 91½″ × 23½″ × 12¾″
Materials: acrylic and wood

This is a creative method for showing interiors without having to actually build them. Windows and silhouettes of people are directly painted on the exterior of the acrylic and wood building. (*Photograph courtesy of Phyllis Kind Gallery*)

16-8.
Ready-made doors and windows. These are some examples of
ready-made windows and doors available from several manufacturers. Some are cast unpainted plastic or metal; others are printed
in black or white ink on acetate sheets or white on white paper.

16-9.
Maquette for Two Story House
Donna Dennis
Materials: paper boards and balsa wood

The walls of this model are made of pebble-board painted with
watercolor. Balsa wood strips were used for columns, porch pediment, and door and window frames. The screens were made of
nylon stocking mesh. Behind them are venetian blinds made of
paper strips. (*Photograph by eeva-inkeri, courtesy of Holly Solomon
Gallery*)

SKYLIGHTS

Saw-toothed factory and other skylights may be made by scoring and coloring thin acrylic sheet (figure 16-10). Represent mullions of large-scale versions with tape. Cut small-scale skylights from acrylic block; then score and paint mullion lines. Either blow or sheet-form bubble domes from clear acetate; if the scale allows, they can be cut from transparent pill casings (you can buy these empty and in several sizes from pharmacies).

DOORS

Most of the techniques used to make windows also apply to door construction. Revolving doors can be represented with acrylic tubing of the right diameter cut down to the height needed. For more detailed or larger-scale revolving doors, first cut the tube into two quarter-circle sections, then cut these to the correct height; doors, made from acrylic sheet, can be added inside the circular pieces.

READY-MADE DOORS. There are several commercially available lines of cast or printed windows and doors (figure 16-8). Because of the small number of scales in which they are made and their often outdated style, these are of limited value to the modelmaker. Modifications, however, can sometimes be made by filling or cutting off parts.

OPERATING DOORS. Functional doors may be made by inserting two pins, whose heads have been removed, into the top and bottom of the door. The pinpoints protruding from the door act as its pivot. Hinges may also be made from strips of linen or other thin fabric.

COLUMNS OR RIB VAULTS

Columns with capitals can be carved from wood or plastic, vacuum-formed from polystyrene, or cast. Vaulting can be formed from stripwood or plastic, or in any of the ways noted in chapter 9.

There are two ways of affixing columns to the model. In the first method, the columns can simply be attached to the adjacent floor slab, and then all the slab-column assemblies fixed one over the other. In the second method, all the floors can be clamped together, holes drilled to take the columns, the slabs blocked at appropriate distances apart, and dowels inserted that run continuously from the roof to the ground. Any columns

16-10.
JFK Library, Cambridge
I.M. Pei & Partners, Architects
Modelmakers: architects' model studio
Scale: $\frac{1}{16}'' = 1'$
Material: acrylic

This final presentation model of a proposed scheme was made out of acrylic plastic. The double glass facade consists of four facets joined along mitered edges. These edges had to be precisely cut because the joint lines would be visible through the clear acrylic. The internal supporting truss system was suggested on the surface with scored lines. The solid walls in the model were spray painted. (*Photograph by Nathaniel Lieberman*)

16-11.
St. Louis Centre
RTKL Associates, Inc., Architects
Modelmakers: members of the architect design team
Scale: $\frac{1}{16}'' = 1'$
Materials: acrylic sheet and tubing

Here, the skylights are Plexiglas tubes cut lengthwise and set on walls made of acrylic sheet. The supporting structure of these vaults and the mullions are indicated with chart tapes. The floor slabs are constructed of matboard and supported by wood dowel columns. (*Photograph by David Whitcomb*)

with complex shapes or with capitals can fit right over the dowels. If square columns are needed, use strip material in place of dowels. In many instances, spaces between square strips and round holes will not be seen on the finished model. If, however, these gaps prove to be objectionable, they can be plugged with a filler material. To prevent the filler from falling through the holes, construct a temporary jig that slips around the top of the columns. This will also provide a surface against which the filler can be compacted. A coat of release agent will keep the jig from sticking.

STAIRWAYS

Stairs require great accuracy in fabrication since the slightest imperfection can readily be seen against the regular pattern of steps. For the exact floor-to-floor dimensions of the stair run, measure the model, not the plan of the building.

Make small-scale stairs by cutting to the correct length stripwood or acrylic whose cross section equals the height and slightly more than the depth of the stair. Each strip will represent a step. Cement the strips one over another in a setback arrangement, each setback having the dimension of a step. When it is dry, turn the assembly over and sand the bottom smooth. Bristolboard or stripwood stringers can then be added, followed by wire or stripwood balusters and newels and then handrails.

Stairs may also be cut from an acrylic or hardwood block with a power jigsaw. Or cut them with a knife from a hard balsa block and face the treads and risers with Bristolboard.

Larger stairs and those with open risers may be constructed from cardboard, acrylic, or wood sheet. Pin the stair carriage to an elevation of the stair and add the treads and risers, using blocks of wood to support these at perfect 90° angles to the carriage while the cement is drying. If many similar stairs must be constructed, use a metal jig for notching the carriage and the outer stringers.

Ready-made stairs and ladders, made of cast metal or plastic, are available in various scales.

16-12.
Competition for the design of city government offices for Furth
Joseph Alfred Frank, Architect. Rolf Janke and Heinz Musil,
   Associate Architects
Scale: $\frac{1}{16}$″ = 1′

(A) shows the cores (which were each made from several bloc of acrylic) of the building being assembled to the acrylic floo The wood-positioning jig was used to hold the parts in place the cement set. In actual practice, the jig was placed in a vertic position to the work surface and parts of the building were stacke alongside it. The cores could also have been made of two piece of plastic inserted through holes cut into the floor slabs. This wou have necessitated the making of position blocks to keep each flo the proper distance from the next. (B) shows the columns of th building cemented in place. (C) shows the two-floor building place. Its columns were cemented against the floor and roof slab were set into grooves. Walls were made from acrylic sheet provide internal bracing. The entire model was painted the sam color as the interior. (D) shows the steps required to model th facades. The sheet second from left was scribed with all the require horizontal lines. Opaque areas were made with tape, spray paintin overlays of various types, or by leaving the protective paper the plastic in place and then painting it. The sheet second fro right has had the dark spandrel covers applied. These were mad from tape, spray paint, or strip material. The right-hand sheet shown with the roof grill in place. This was constructed with series of tapes. The facades were given beveled corners for neater joint. (E) shows vertical mullions being applied. These wer made from strip material which was cemented in place with th aid of the hypodermic solvent applier. Grooves had to be c through the overlay material to receive the mullions. (F) is of th completed model.

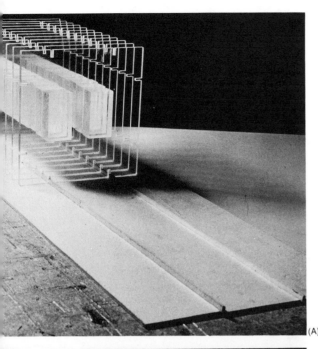

(A)

(B)

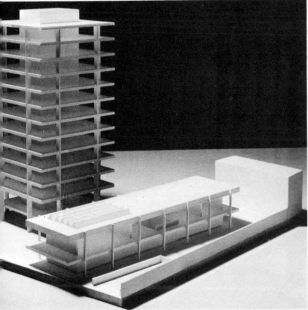

(C)

(D)

(E)

(F)

16-13.
Lever House
Skidmore, Owings & Merrill, Architects
Modelmaker: Theodore Conrad
Scale: 1/16″ = 1′
Materials: plastic, milled brass sections,
    and wood

The walls and floors of this precisely detailed
presentation model are made of acrylic plastic. Metal strips were used to represent the
mullions; columns are made out of wood.
The floor slabs, glued to the exterior walls,
serve as internal support for the model.

17:Interior Models

Models of interior spaces are of use not only to architects and interior designers but to office managers, house-holders, renting agents, and others engaged in the arrangement of movable elements within habitable space.

For a simple, nonpresentation, space-planning model, make two-dimensional cardboard cutouts and manipulate these on a floor plan. If the three-dimensional aspects of furnishing must be studied, construct simple models from wood blocks or from cardboard. Walls and floors may be made from cardboard taped or cemented together. More complex models showing all or most of the details of each furnishing element are quite time-consuming to construct and, in most instances, super-fluous since the appearance of various makes of furniture is well known.

Interior designers try to simplify construction by maintaining extensive collections of doll furniture, fabric samples, and small shapes. It is also expedient to save furniture from past models for reuse with or without modification. Constructing complicated pieces of furniture precisely, especially chairs, often costs as much as the purchase price of the full-size object. Therefore, highly detailed models of interiors are a rarity, especially if they are to be used solely for planning and client prep-aration. Detailed interior models are usually used as museum displays (and these are primarily period rooms) or in publications featuring highly original designs. To be economically feasible, the latter must either be sponsored by a manufacturer, an association, or the pub-lication, or be a labor of love by the designer.

Models are especially helpful in presenting the true volume of an interior area—especially, the relationship of ceiling height to other dimensions. The model should be constructed in a way that allows the viewer to see the interior from above, to study the plan layout, and (at eye level) to imagine the room as it would normally be experienced. It may be necessary to construct the model with one or more movable walls or in such a way that it can be pulled apart into sections. Larger-scale models sometimes have a hole cut into the baseboard into which viewers may insert their heads.

Interior models are also extremely useful in designing tight areas such as display booths, bathrooms, and kitchens.

The colors and textures of fabrics, paints, carpeting, and wood finishes used in an area may be studied on simplified models that contain template representations of furniture set on simply constructed cardboard floors. Sample swatches of the contemplated finishes can be mounted on the templates and walls to give a rough idea of how the color combinations will appear.

For efficient office-planning models, use ready-made cast furniture available from several companies. Exact clearances may be studied with this furniture and the layout tightened into a design that balances space-saving ideas with comfortable working conditions.

STAGE SET MODELS

Models are often used by stage set designers as pre-sentation devices and, despite certain problems, as design aids. Because it is impossible to represent lighting con-ditions and painted colors exactly (two extremely im-portant aspects of set design), models must usually be considered abstractions of the design. They may, how-ever, be used to study the profile of various parts and the general lighting and color. The model is usually a simplification of the design, and colors are made more intense. The overall mood derived from the model is more important than an accurate portrayal of the set. In the past, stage-set models were composed mainly of painted flats and had few three-dimensional model parts. The flats were often sent to the set constructor as a construction document. Theater-in-the-round re-quires more extensive model study to investigate the juxtaposition of design parts when viewed from all sides (figure 17-1).

17-1.
Space Theater for Mark-I Enterprises
Hugh Hardy, Architect
Modelmakers: members of the architect's staff
Scale: ¼″ = 1′
Materials: cardboard and wood

Walls, scenery, seats, and the seated people were made from cardboard. The bracing of the model and the roof truss were made of basswood strips. Standing people were bent from 3-ply Bristolboard. (*Photograph by Gil Amiaga*)

EXHIBITION AND DISPLAY MODELS

Models are extremely well received by the general public when they are used as parts of both commercial and noncommercial displays. They often become "show stoppers," especially when illuminated or animated. Fascination with models is such that not only window displays and corners of exhibition booths, but also entire world's-fair pavilions and tourist attractions have been successfully based on them. An example of the latter is Madurodam, a ½″ scale model of a city, port, and aerodrome which is a major attraction at The Hague, in the Netherlands.

Exhibition and store displays themselves are best represented by, and designed on, models. Actual graphics may be roughly drawn, photographically reproduced, and mounted in the model. Clearances and visual juxtaposition between parts of the design may be studied with greater accuracy with models than with sketches. Occasionally, a model is used in place of plans and elevations to describe a display design to the contractor.

FURNITURE

READY-MADE RESIDENTIAL FURNITURE. Dollhouse furniture, obtainable at variety and toy stores, is a marginal source of parts for the modelmaker. With luck, some dated or styleless samples can be cut apart, modified, and reassembled.

To avoid long, last-minute searches for out-of-production models, the designer should, despite the cost, maintain a good supply of such furniture. Over the years, new, interesting-looking specimens should be added.

FURNITURE LEGS AND PEDESTALS. Legs for small-scale models are best made from pins and wire. In

17-2.
Detailed Model Furniture
Modelmaker: Form and Function, Inc.
Scale: ¾″ = 1′

The frame of the room divider was made from square brass strips that were soft-soldered together and then nickelplated. Shelves were constructed of acrylic. The fiberglass chairs were simulated with vacuum-formed ¹⁄₂₀″-thick polystyrene, shaped on a plaster mold. Their bases were made of nails glued to the plastic and the crosspieces were filed from wire and soldered to the nails. The leather chairs are made of real leather and were frame fabricated from brass rods and strips. The three wood and wicker chairs have lathe-turned brass legs and brass frames, with seats made of thread woven over the frames. The small glass bottles, made from Pyrex rods, were heated and pulled into shape; the large bottle is ready-made. The bowl is vacuum-formed polystyrene and the silver canister and coffee pot are tin can metal bent into shape and soldered. (*Photograph by John Takeraas of Form and Function, Inc.*)

larger scales, they may be carved from stripwood or acrylic. Fancy, carved legs and pedestals can sometimes be improvised from stamped brass eyelets, collars, grommets, and bushings or from the ⅛″ to ⁷⁄₁₆″ highly decorative brass stanchions available from model boat supply houses.

CHAIRS. Bucket chairs, and other chairs with curved forms, may be cast (most often in several parts), vacuum-formed out of polystyrene (figure 17-2), or built from formed flat material. Bend thin Bristolboard over a balsa or hardwood mold that has been covered with wax paper. Then laminate the chair with several layers of board cemented together. Wire chair frames should be made with the aid of a hardwood bending jig.

For chairs and couches that do not have concave shapes, carve seats and backs from sheet balsa or cardboard.

Small-scale theater and church seats may be constructed, in simplified form, from Bristolboard bent to an *L* cross section. Each row of seats can be made as one unit, omitting rests. For added detail, notch the back of the row to represent individual seats. The entire unit can then be easily cemented to the floor in one piece. If the row must curve, notch another series of slits into the seat and carefully curve the row to the desired shape.

PILLOWS AND CUSHIONS. These are made from carved balsa on which fabric is cemented; or the balsa may be painted and, while the paint is still wet, flock applied to it. When cementing fabric to wood shapes, carry the material around to the sides of the cushion, where it will not be visible, and cement it there.

To create tufting or pleating, cover furniture with a very thin (about ⅛″-thick) sheet of foam rubber (the type used to protect delicate electrical and mechanical parts during shipping) and then cover the rubber with the upholstery cloth. Tufts are made by pushing small pins through the fabric and rubber. To form pleats, use pins with wire heads constructed in the form of a *T*. Insert these pins, their heads pointing in the direction

17-3.
Group of Small Chairs
Lucas Samaras

These chairs are made of various materials, most of which can be found around the house. Aluminum foil was pressed and shaped into the form of the high chair seen in the top row. The cloudlike chair next to it was made by wrapping a wood frame with cotton; tiny metal world globes were used for the chair's feet. On the right, the twisted wire chair has small stones tangled in its frame. The chair with a triangular seat is made with cotton swabs attached with airplane glue. The two smallest chairs, one of which rests on a wood pedestal, were modeled from clay. Wood and cardboard were used in making the pyramid-legged chair. The chair in front of this one only appears to be three dimensional—it is actually lying flat. The sturdy little chair to the left was carefully built out of matchsticks. Above it can be seen a chair made of thick string stiffened with glue. (*Photograph by Ferdinand Boesch, courtesy of Pace Gallery, New York*)

of the intended pleat, one head touching the next, through the fabric and rubber in rows.

CABINETS, TABLES, AND SHELVES. This type of furniture may be simply built from sheet wood, acrylic, or cardboard. Keep adjacent cabinet sides at 90° angles by cementing stripwood inside joints. Use polished, unpainted, clear acrylic to simulate aluminum and stainless steel frames. If you need a more exact facsimile of bright metal, construct the frame from soldered brass rod and send this out to be plated.

Cut cabinets and breakfronts from blocks of such woods as beech. Cover these with Bristolboard, colored paper, or Flexwood, on which such details as drawers have been scribed. Larger, more-detailed models may require individual parts to be vacuum-formed from polystyrene. Make marble tops from the materials suggested on page 144, and drawer pulls from pin or nail heads or from tiny glass beads.

RUGS AND CARPETING. Many materials with a fine tilelike texture are available for use as rugs and carpets. Among these is blotting paper, which is available in a wide range of colors. Use thick poster color applied with a dry brush to paint patterns on it. When cementing the paper in place, make sure the adhesive does not come through the paper. Felt, flocked paper, or velvet fabric may be used in larger-scale models. Glue these materials in place with rubber cement. Cover the backs of all fabric materials with adhesive tape so that they will not unravel when cut.

The office sample box may often provide fabric or wall coverings whose texture is reasonably close to the rug or carpeting desired. Patterns may be directly painted on most rug-representing materials or may, if the pattern is repetitive, be printed on with the aid of a lino or wood-block cut.

Use pieces of powder puff to represent fluffy bathroom mats. Make fur animal skin rugs from pieces of 100% wool blanket material. For Persian rugs, use color reproductions of actual rugs. Make sisal matting from pieces of raffia (a finely woven rush work) or, for small-scale models, colored buckram.

FABRIC

Modeling fabric presents two major problems: finding a material whose weave is not too oversized, and, when creating miniature drapes and other hanging fabrics, finding some way of approximating the folds and stiffness of the prototype.

Small swatches of certain fabrics will accurately represent the intended fabrics at model scale. Other materials that may be used are colored paper (including tissue paper) and box cover papers with woven texture patterns (obtainable from paper wholesalers). A trip to a large local retail fabric store, especially one with a large selection of remnants, can also provide much useful raw material. Fabric can also be painted with textile colors which do not bleed or stiffen the cloth. These are sold in large artist supply stores.

WEAVE. Good silk generally has a weave that is fine enough to represent rough upholstery fabric, but only at scales of over $\frac{1}{2}'' = 1'$. Shirt broadcloth (having about 80 threads per inch) can represent the same rough fabric in models of over $1'' = 1'$. It is almost impossible, however, to find fabrics that can be used to represent fine weaves at the scales over $\frac{1}{2}'' = 1'$.

FOLDS. In small-scale models, realistic folds can be made only with paper; use gift wrap or colored paper to represent the fabric. In large-scaled models, make folds by dipping fabric in a bath of one part Elmer's glue and one part water. After you remove the fabric from the bath, pull, fold and otherwise fashion it into shape as it dries. Test a scrap of the material to be sure the solution will not discolor it.

WALLPAPER AND PAINT

Colors and patterns may be spray painted or hand brushed directly on the model or on paper that can then be dry-mounted onto the walls. You can occasionally find a transparent pressure-sensitive overlay that will come close to simulating a wallpaper pattern. In some cases, box cover papers that have the appropriate, subtle textures can be used to represent fabric wall coverings. Flexwood is a good choice for wood finishes. All these finishes may be used only at $\frac{1}{4}'' = 1'$ and larger scales (especially the box cover paper). For smaller scales use finer paper.

ARTWORK

PAINTINGS AND MURALS. Often it is not very important that a painting or mural be modeled accurately. If such is the case, facsimiles of the correct size and approximate coloration will suffice. These can be chosen from miniature color reproductions of pictures (obtainable in postage stamp size from some art museums), postage stamps (United States and foreign), parts of colored postcards or prints that depict famous works of art, reproductions of paintings cut from art magazines, advertising copy taken from popular magazines, and so forth. If an exact replica of a painting or mural is needed, you may have to paint it yourself.

SCULPTURE. Small representational reliefs may be depicted with foreign coins and intricate patterns cast in plastic, metal, or plaster. If only a rough idea of the sculpture is required, make it out of charms, model people (filed or bent into artistic poses), pieces of costume jewelry, or whatever can be found in your scrap bins to represent various styles of art.

If an accurate reproduction is required, carve it from any dense wood or plastic with the aid of a small motor tool. Metal sculpture may be made from sculpt metal.

ACCESSORIES

Make books from cardboard of the proper thickness and covered with colored paper or parts of magazine advertisements that contain bits of small printing or pictures.

Mirrors may be made from smoothed tin foil, mirrored

17-4.
House
George Nelson and Company, Architects
Modelmakers: members of the architects' staff
Scale: 1″ = 1′

Columns of this presentation model were made from groupings of basswood *T* sections. The dome was vacuum-formed from polystyrene and the grill below the dome was made from expanded honeycomb material. Carpeting was cut from a towel. Books, bottles, and dishes are doll house accessories. The drawers, shelving, and desk were created from pinheads and the record player from wood and pins. The statues on the central tables came from charm bracelets and the wall clock and lighting fixture are made from wood and paper.

Plexiglas, or pieces of actual mirror. To represent antiqued glass, paint the foil or glass or cover it with a thin sheet of acetate.

Use hammered or pressed sheet metal for pots, pans, coffee services, and other similar objects. Vacuum-form dishware from plastic or form it with thin Bristolboard. The latter method requires plotting for the correct shape of paper required to form the vessel. Remove seams by filling with plastic balsa and sanding lightly. Small, 1″-diameter dishes and pots can sometimes be found in toy stores.

The easiest way to make bottles and glassware is to turn them from acrylic rods. To represent the contents of a bottle, carve the interior from the bottom and then fill the cavity with paint. Bottles 1″ to 1½″ high are sometimes available at toy stores or novelty supply houses (figure 17-4).

For pottery and planters, use the same techniques as for dishware or, if they have thick walls, turn them from wood or plastic. Use fine clay to carve or model nonsymmetrical shapes. If you need a large number of planters, the best procedure is to cast them in a low-melting-point metal.

LIGHTING FIXTURES. Improvise globes from empty gelatin pill casings, miniature light bulbs, or reshaped glass and plastic beads and buttons. Exact shapes may be carved from acrylic stock.

Covers for large recessed ceiling fixtures may be made from vacuum-formed acetate. Large varieties of ready-made clear plastic shapes can often be obtained from local plastic fabricators (sometimes they may be prevailed upon to provide a good selection gratis). These shapes are used in packaging to cover the small merchandise that is sold mounted on cards.

To roughly simulate crystal chandeliers, use short lengths of cemented-together acrylic rods. Sometimes spangles will give a feeling of realism to the modeled fixture.

Lampshades are best made from colored paper brackets, supports from wire, and bases from carved wood or acrylic.

To make working fixtures, see instructions on internal lighting of models in chapter 20.

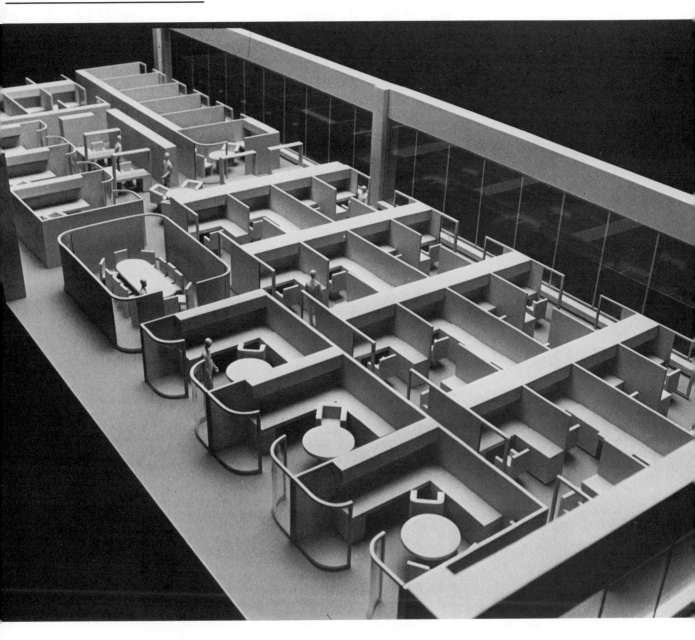

17-5.
Executive Offices for United Airlines
Metz, Train & Youngren, Inc., Architects
Modelmakers: members of architects' staff
Scale: ½″ = 1′

Because the interior model was used to study the space planning
of a typical office floor, the furniture was built in basic block forms.
The desks, chairs, and wall partitions were made out of wood,
the glass line and curved walls of acrylic. Figures are cast metal.
(*Photograph by Steve Grubman*)

17-6.
*Count Dracula's Beach House in East
    Hampton* (back view)
Ed Kerns
Dimensions: 24″ × 24″ × 24″

Here, the interior elements, including chairs,
tables, beds, and coffins, are basic forms
carved out of hardwood and embellished with
drawn details. The figures were also carved.
Paintings were cut out from art books. The
house and base were built out of plywood.
(*Photograph courtesy of Rosa Esman
Gallery*)

17-7.
Manufacturers Hanover Trust
Skidmore, Owings & Merrill, Architects
Modelmaker: Theodore Conrad
Scale: ½″ = 1′

This skillfully crafted presentation model
shows both the architectural design of the
building and the interior design of each floor.
The internal lighting of the model, placed
within each floor slab, not only reproduces
the lighting conditions of the actual building,
but also gives the model a showcase effect.

17-8.
Each model piece of furniture is an exact replica of the actual furniture proposed for the Manufacturers Hanover Trust building shown in figure 17-7. These include all the desks, chairs, tables, and couches. Intricate artwork, such as the mobile and the sculpted wall panel on the right, were made out of metal. Materials for the floor finishes and for the rugs and vertical blinds were carefully chosen to show properly scaled pattern, texture, and color. (*Photographs (figures 17-7 and 17-8) by Ezra Stoller*)

18:Special Models

Special models, of which there are various types, have a controlled viewpoint, which makes them of use mostly in the depiction of interiors, gardens, building entrances, and other parts of buildings. They are usually found in museum and fair displays and are made by the designer to present certain aspects of the project. Other special models are graphic representations of historical buildings.

PERSPECTIVE MODELS OR DIORAMAS

Dioramas are models that are meant to be viewed from one side. They are built in one- or two-point perspective.

The model parts closest to the viewing position are largest and those at the back are smallest. The backdrop scene is painted in perspective and the entire model is set into a box with one open side.

When planning a diorama, decide which is the least important side of the room or area that is to be depicted. This will become the viewing opening. Next decide on the vanishing points of the perspective. This can be done by making a series of sketches of the scene in the same manner in which a perspective would be planned.

Once you locate the vanishing points, transfer the drawing into the third dimension (figure 18-2). This is done with three or more sheets of cardboard.

18-1.
"The Founding of the New York City Stock Exchange Buttonwood Agreement, May 17, 1792"
Diorama on display at the Museum of the City of New York
Scale: 2″ = 1′ (at front of model)

This model was built 1′ wider on the left side, 6″ wider on the right, and 1′ higher than its glazed viewing opening. The background, rear quarter of the right wall, and all of the left wall were painted. The ground slopes up to and joins the backdrop and is painted on the left side in a 4″ curved, covelike sweep. This was done to soften the visual transformation between modeled ground and painted surface. The scene is lit from above. (*Photograph courtesy of Museum of the City of New York*)

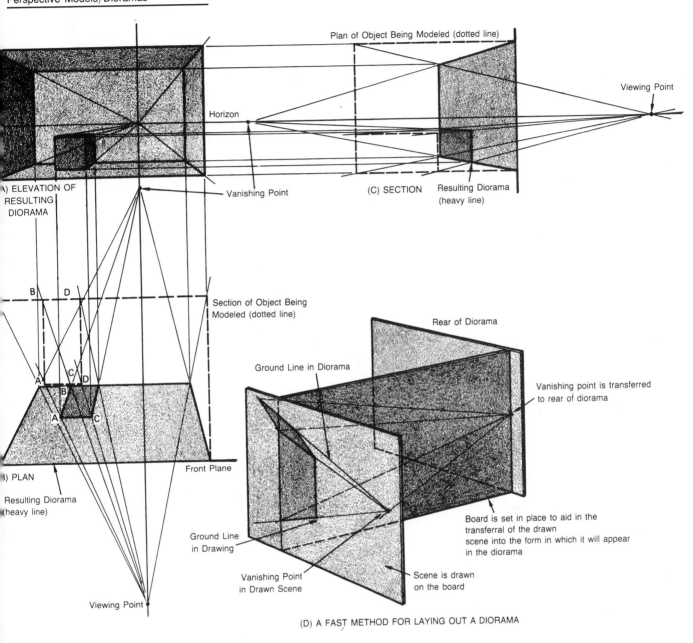

Plan of Object Being Modeled (dotted line)

Viewing Point

Horizon

(A) ELEVATION OF
RESULTING
DIORAMA

Vanishing Point

(C) SECTION

Resulting Diorama
(heavy line)

Section of Object Being
Modeled (dotted line)

Rear of Diorama

Ground Line in Diorama

Vanishing point is transferred
to rear of diorama

(B) PLAN

Resulting Diorama
(heavy line)

Front Plane

Ground Line
in Drawing

Board is set in place to aid in the
transferral of the drawn
scene into the form in which it will appear
in the diorama

Vanishing Point
in Drawn Scene

Scene is drawn
on the board

Viewing Point

(D) A FAST METHOD FOR LAYING OUT A DIORAMA

18-2.
Plotting a diorama

1. Attach the original sketch to one sheet and set another one behind it at a distance equal to the desired depth of the vanishing point of the diorama (figure 18-2D).

2. Transfer the vanishing point to the back sheet through a pinhole.

3. Use still other pieces of cardboard to represent the major walls or facades that will be in the diorama. Tape these to the first two pieces so that they intersect the rear board at the vanishing point.

4. Mark the height of walls as they appear on the front drawing and connect the top and bottom points

to the vanishing point. This will give the shape of the walls as they should appear in the diorama. A board representing the rear wall of the diorama may now be set into the mock-up.

From this rough setup, you can make working drawings for the diorama. It should be noted that not only do the side walls of the diorama converge but so do its floor and ceiling. Usually the depth of the diorama and vanishing point is located by trial and error. The rear wall is often located in such a position that objects appearing on it will be about half the size they would be if they were located at the front of the diorama.

Once you see the depth at which the backdrop is to be placed, you can determine which objects will be modeled in the round and which will be painted. The diorama in figure 18-1, for example, has painted flats for all of its left side and for the rear quarter of its right wall. Mock-ups of various objects may be quickly molded in clay to see whether their perspective is acceptable. If objects at various locations prove to look odd, it will probably be necessary to change the angle of the perspective. Sometimes there is almost no modeling in the round: the side walls and many freestanding objects as well as the rear wall are made as two-dimensional "flats" and only objects that can be seen into (past their front plane), such as chairs, tables, trees, and so on, are made in three dimensions.

Dioramas are usually lit from the top down, so the box into which they are built should have a section left off for top-mounted lights. The front glass may be sloped to prevent glare from the lights or reflections. Backdrops should be painted under the lighting conditions at which they will be displayed.

CYCLORAMAS. Cycloramas are the same as perspective models except that the sky background is painted on a curved wall, which starts at the front of the model box and curves behind the entirely freestanding model. Cycloramas are used to depict landscapes, freestanding buildings, and anything that requires a curved sky backdrop. The location of the lighting makes the sky appear luminous and detached from other parts of the model. As with perspective models, various objects in the cyclorama may be drawn on two-dimensional flats and placed in freestanding positions in front of the sky.

PEPPER'S GHOST

This intriguing name is given to a display device that automatically and instantaneously changes one modeled scene to another before the viewer's eyes. It can be used to show before and after, or stage 1 and stage 2 conditions, of a design project.

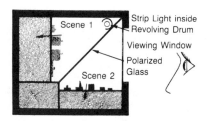

18-3.
Pepper's Ghost (section view)

Figure 18-3 shows a cross section of a Pepper's Ghost. The cycle runs as follows. Cyclorama 1 is illuminated by the bulb; the viewer is able to see this model through the polarized glass because of the high level of illumination behind the glass. A timer revolves the drum-shaped shutter around the bulb, redirecting its light away from cyclorama 1 and toward cyclorama 2; and, since the rear of the polarized glass is now in darkness and its front illuminated, the polarized glass becomes a mirror and projects the image of lighted cyclorama 2 to the viewer. The drum shutter revolves again, starting a new cycle. The less important scene should be in the second position, since it is not well illuminated and often appears less distinct.

TAKE-APART MODELS

Occasionally, an architectural project will require an overall model as well as models of certain interior spaces. This may be necessary in order to show the interrelationship of areas in a complex structure or to get a rough idea of interior decor. Combining both types of models into one take-apart one (figures 18-4 through 18-7) will result in considerable cost and time savings. For large buildings, a take-apart model will usually require at least a $1/8'' = 1'$ scale if interiors are to be shown in enough detail to be studied. A scale of around $1/16'' = 1'$ is required if a model merely illustrates the interrelationship of areas.

Parts of the model should be pegged or splined together. To simplify making a neat parting line, first construct the area immediately around the joint, put that area together, and then build the model. Removable roofs may also be constructed this way. The basic objective is to provide surfaces that are as massive and warp resistant as is practical.

Attach the buildings of small-scale multiunit developments and town plans to the baseboard with magnets or dowel them in place. These techniques may also be used to make a model demountable and thus easier to pack and ship.

18-4.
Shiraz Technical Institute, Iran
Hugh Stubbins and Associates, Inc., Architects
Modelmakers: F.W. Dixon Company
Scale: ⅛″ = 1′

This take-apart model was built entirely out of Strathmore board.
When all the levels are assembled, the building's overall design
can be viewed. The model rests on a cork-covered base, featuring
roads and landscaping. (*Photographs (figures 18-4 through 18-7)
by Steve Rosenthal*)

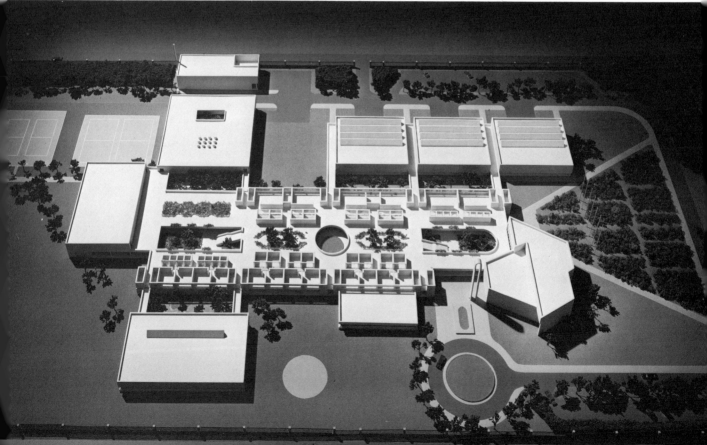

8-5.
Three levels of the building were made to be lifted off so that the interior space planning of each floor could be studied (see figure 8-4). The roof piece has been removed to reveal the third floor.

8-6.
In this view of the second floor, the way each floor level interrelates is more easily understood.

8-7.
With all the levels removed, the ground floor plan can be examined in relation to the site.

Take-apart models are especially useful for studying existing and historically significant buildings. In the 1930s, large dollhouse models were constructed in such a way that they could be opened and disassembled for blind children to explore the various rooms and house elements. Figure 6-16 shows a more recent student project, constructed for analyzing the interior and exterior design of a Le Corbusier building. The various levels can be lifted off to be examined individually and as they relate to a whole.

GRAPHIC ABSTRACTION MODELS

While take-apart models faithfully re-create most of the major building elements, another type of educational model is illustrated in figures 18-8 through 18-11. These were constructed to identify major perceptual or conceptual design components of various architectural examples. Materials and colors used in constructing these abstract models are chosen to represent the design concepts rather than to simulate the building materials.

18-8.
Graphic Abstractions of Historical Buildings
2nd Year History Course, taught by Professor Donald Wall,
  Catholic University, 1965

This first example is a three-dimensional diagram delineating the
structural framing of the Pazzi Chapel. Because only the columns,
beams, and arches are shown, the viewer's attention is focused
on these aspects of the building. The materials used were Strathmore
board and wood. (See also figures 18-9, 18-10, and 18-11.)

18-9.
In this study of St. Peter's Plaza, pins and small cardboard walls
were used to plot the columns of the colonnade. These were
connected to three separate viewing points with thread. All of these
elements establish a viewing system from within the plaza. For
example, by standing at the point where the lighter color threads
converge, the view of and through the colonnade is completely
unobstructed.

18-10.
The two aspects of the Hagia Sophia being compared in this model
are the building mass layout and the dome system. Size and
location of the building masses were suggested by clear Plexiglas.
The arches and the center dome ring were made of tinted acrylic
strips from which threads converge to a single point on the ground
plane.

COLOSSEUM

FLOW MODELS

When presenting or studying the designs of such build-ings as hospitals and factories, in which the inter-relationship of material, personnel, or utility flow is important, it can be extremely effective to present this flow on a rough model. A model of this type may be made by cementing prints of the various floor plans of the building to cardboard or wood sheet. Flow arrows may be drafted onto the plans and areas of similar use color coded. Vertical utility and transportation cores are made from stripwood, and holes to receive them are cut through the various floors. The model may then be assembled and studied, with the floors separated from one another by small blocks or pegs. If floor sheets are made to the correct thickness—that is, to represent the windowsill-to-windowhead dimension of the building, it may also be possible to use the flow model as a massing model once roof structures and other details have been added to it.

MIRRORING A PARTIAL MODEL

Models of symmetrical buildings, such as auditoriums, may be simplified by constructing only half the structure.

18-11.
Each of the five sections of this model presents a different aspect of the Colosseum's design. The bearing walls to the far left are made of wood. In the next section, arrows made of paper indicate the circulation system. In the center section are the descending tunnel vaults, made of paper held in shape with string. Lateral barrel vaults, to the right, are made of tubing.

Place a large mirror against the center line and, if viewed or photographed from the exterior, it will have the effect of an entire building. If the interior must be seen, cut a vision hole through the wall that is opposite the mirror.

Long interior spaces, such as corridors and halls, may also be abbreviated by building a typical section and placing mirrors at either end. The surfaces of both mirrors must be parallel to one another. Make a peep-hole in one of the mirrors by scraping off a small circle of its silvering, and then illuminate the model segment. When viewed through the hole, the area will appear to be of great length, and the only distraction, caused by the reflection of the viewing hole, will be a dark spot reflected from the opposite mirror.

19:Piping Design, Mechanical Engineering, and Structural Test Models

PIPING DESIGN MODELS

Piping design models (figure 19-1) are extensively used in the design of chemical- and petroleum-producing plants. Most major installations are designed on these models. The intricacies of pipe runs and intersections make it very difficult and inefficient, if not impossible, to rely exclusively on drawings for the countless references that have to be made to each part of the design before it can be completed. It has been found that models can produce savings by reducing overall drafting and designing costs, minimizing the number of field changes to be made, expediting the training of operating personnel, and saving time for clients and consultants.

The Fluor Corporation, one of the nation's largest refinery and chemical plant designers, uses three types of design models:

Plant layout models are simple preliminary models showing only the rough space requirements of the equipment and the general arrangement of the plant. When finalized, this model is photographed or drawn in plain view.

Piping layout models show the plans of all piping runs. These are represented by lengths of small-diameter wire. Clearances can be checked by placing a washer with an outside diameter equal to that of the intended pipe over the wire. Wires are coupled with sleeves. Plastic markers indicate the number of the line. This model is also photographed. Incidentally, center line piping models of this type are useful with photographic drawing because smaller pipes can be seen where normally they would be hidden behind other, larger lines.

Piping arrangement models are the same as the second type, except that the piping is represented by tubing of an exact scale diameter.

Often the model, along with dimensioned photographs, is sent in lieu of drawings to the construction site. The model is also used to aid in estimating; checking for errors made in the drawings; coordinating the design with the requirements of the safety, security, maintenance, and production departments of the company; and facilitating personnel training.

Models made from color-coded pipe should preferably be photographed in color or, if black-and-white film is used, it should be of an orthochromatic variety to help better differentiate the colors.

Component parts for making piping design models may be ordered from several companies. Architects and mechanical engineers can also use these parts in the planning of boiler rooms and other building areas containing extensive piping.

FACTORY-PLANNING MODELS

Study models that show the exact positioning of all production tools and equipment are of increasing importance in factory design (figure 19-3). As the costs of construction, land, and running an assembly line increase, so does the importance of designing the optimum utilization of space. Models are indispensable tools for the study of the complex interrelationships and clearances found among tools. They present the design easily to the many people who must check and work with it and who are unable to understand drawings fully. Not only will the designer and the client use the factory model, but so will the client's safety, security, maintenance, and production departments, who must analyze and solve various work problems. Even after the factory has been completed, the models can still help to solve material handling and storage problems that invariably crop up. Several modelbuilding companies specialize in factory and office layouts. Their service runs from building complete models of a prospective plant to supplying castings of furniture and tools for the designer's own use in the modelbuilding shop.

Models are usually built with an acrylic sheet floor

19-1.
Power Island Plant
Modelmaker: Industrial Models, Inc.
Scale: ¾" = 1'

The baseboard of this piping design model was made of plywood stiffened with white pine. Most pipes were standard plastic ones available ready-made from modelbuilders and manufacturers. Large pipes were made of acrylic tubes. Tanks, floors, and columns were also constructed of acrylic.

19-2.
Outland
Ladd Company Release
Dimensions: approximately 10' H × 30' L × 30' W

This special effects model was constructed out of acrylic plastic sheets, rods, and tubing. Various ready-made and specially cast plastic pipes, valves, and other piping design elements were adapted for use in this depiction of industrial architecture. (*Photograph courtesy of the Ladd Company*)

19-3.
Office and Factory Layout Model
Modelmaker: Model Planning Company, Inc.
Scale: ¼" = 1'

Columns, stairs, floor, and partitions of this design model were made in acrylic. Everything else was cast in metal by the modelmaker.

that is scribed with a 1' grid on its reverse side to aid in the placement of tools and to show clearances at a glance. Columns and partitions are also made from acrylic. Upper floors, stiffened by beams, are supported by channels or acrylic strips affixed to the walls of the model. Each floor may be cemented to columns and to one story of exterior walls and the assembly is stacked upon the next floor.

Partitions may be constructed out of acrylic. Place the plastic sheet over a full-size elevation, scribe in all details, and paint. Areas of frosted glass can be represented by sanded plastic.

Sometimes columns are made in two parts: a stubby socket and a full-length column fitting into the socket. This allows the long column to be removed and work to proceed without the danger of breakage. Roofs are often dispensed with, but they are sometimes constructed to serve as a dust cover and also as a device to keep unauthorized hands off the modeled equipment. Tools, equipment, and people are cast from metal and are held in place with double-faced pressure-sensitive tape.

Factory models are sometimes photographed from the top down. The negative is dimensioned and processed through a blueprint machine to create final layout plans.

MECHANICAL ENGINEERING MODELS

Test models similar to those used in architectural and interior design have found application in most of the mechanical engineering fields. Their use has been limited by the difficulty of finding the relationship between model and prototype characteristics and the cost of doing this. Since such test models require a great deal of capital, they are of greatest use to researchers in large engineering firms and universities. As basic formulas are developed, smaller testing laboratories may be able to apply them to their specific projects.

The following summary of some of the tests that may be performed on models is intended as a survey and not as an encouragement for architects or interior designers to undertake this type of testing on their own. The complexity of the measuring apparatus involved, ratios of similitude, and analysis make it too difficult for all but a relatively few specializing engineers to attempt model testing.

Heating Test Models

Studies in the temperature distribution of buildings have been performed on test models at the National Bureau of Standards. The complete validity of the use of models for this type of test has not been established. To be valid, a test must be conducted with a model whose walls and ceilings are of scale thickness and proportionate conductivity to the prototype. Heat input in the model must be proportionate to the square of the linear size reduction ratio. On some past tests, temperature was created by electric heating cables and was measured by copper thermocouples cemented to the walls of the model (to measure surface or air temperature) or attached to vertical posts. In the latter test, the thermocouple must be shielded from radiated heat by being housed in polished metal cylinders that are open at both ends.

Ventilation Test Models

Models have been used to predict the pattern of air flow through variously shaped rooms and fenestration. The models are made in something close to a $1'' = 1'$ scale, with all windows, doors, and other openings faithfully represented. One side of the room is constructed in clear plastic to allow visual observation of the test, which consists of mounting the model in a wind tunnel, blowing smoke into its windows, and then watching the smoke circulate through and out of the rooms.

Other ventilating tests employing smoke patterns have been made on models of landscaped areas to see how trees, other vegetation, and ground contours influence the flow of prevailing winds over a building.

Tests to determine only the direction of air flow can be performed on small-scale block models on which short strands of thin string are fastened at $1''$ or $2''$ intervals. The model is subjected to high winds in a wind tunnel; these are applied in the direction of prevailing winds on the prototype. By studying the directions assumed

by the strings, it is possible to locate areas of low or negative pressure and to design windows at these points to create a cooling air flow within the prototype.

The actual velocity of air moving through a building can be predicted by the wind tunnel testing of a model. Air pressure measuring gauges are mounted in the slip stream of the tunnel and at various locations in and around the accurately constructed, moderately large-scale, model. Air velocity is related to pressure by the following formula:

$$\text{velocity at any point in the actual structure} = \text{prevailing wind velocity at the site} \times \sqrt{\frac{\text{air pressure at the same point on the model}}{\text{free wind pressure in the wind tunnel}}}$$

The accuracy of results achieved with ventilation model testing is very high. It is often more practical to test models than full-size mock-ups because finding natural breezes that correspond to optimum test conditions is relatively difficult and testing a mock-up in a large enough wind tunnel would be very expensive.

Sun-Orientation Models

Models may be accurately used to test the shadows cast by parts of buildings and by landscaping. Block or final presentation models may be used with a spotlight representing the sun. The spot should have a parabolic reflector and a Fresnel lens so that it will produce light with parallel rays. Two interesting devices that simplify sun testing are the Heliodon (figure 19-4) and the Pleijel sundial.

The Heliodon consists of a small table that can be rotated about its horizontal and vertical axis. Adjustment about the horizontal axis is to compensate for the latitude at which the prototype building will be constructed. The vertical axis is adjusted to relate to the time of day. A light representing the sun is mounted on the post. By adjusting it up or down, the time of the year can be counterpoised.

The Pleijel sundial is placed on the model in correct north orientation. The light source is manipulated to make the shadow cast by the post of the sundial correspond to the desired day and time of day on the chart of the sundial. Light falling on the model will then correspond to this desired time.

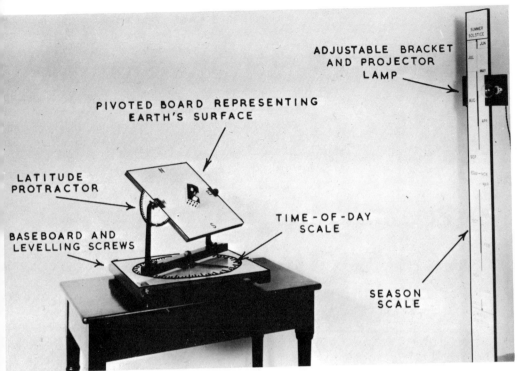

PIVOTED BOARD REPRESENTING
EARTH'S SURFACE

ADJUSTABLE BRACKET
AND PROJECTOR
LAMP

LATITUDE
PROTRACTOR

TIME-OF-DAY
SCALE

BASEBOARD AND
LEVELLING SCREWS

SEASON
SCALE

19-4.
The Heliodon. The model is placed on a pivoted board, which is adjusted to the correct latitude and time of day. The lamp on the vertical post is adjusted to the correct day of the year. The resulting shadows cast on the model are exactly what they should be for that particular point in time and space. (*Photograph reproduced by permission of Her Majesty's Stationery Office, Crown copyright reserved*)

TESTING INTERIORS. Special areas such as schoolrooms, laboratories, and art galleries are especially dependent on the correct engineering of their orientation and fenestration. Models are usually built at ¾" and larger scales.

QUANTITATIVE ANALYSIS OF INTERIORS. Detailed models may be used for precise photometric measuring to determine placement of windows and skylights that will avoid glare; color schemes; effect of light reflection from one colored surface to another; effect of light reflected from sky, grass, and other elements outside the building; and loss of color due to shadow. The high degree of accuracy that may be achieved allows the model to more than compete with expensive full-size mock-ups in the solving of pilot problems.

In general, since use of the real sky for model illumination is not considered consistently dependable, it is seldom used. Sun and sky may be presented in two ways:

1. *Hemispherical sky dome.* This method is often used in model testing (figure 19-5). Its interior is finished with a white reflecting material, such as texture paint, having an 85% coefficient of reflectivity. It is indirectly illuminated. The model is placed at the center of the dome, with its floor below the dome's horizon. This makes for a more naturally illuminated model ceiling, at the expense, however, of a less naturally illuminated rear wall. An artificial sky should only illuminate the ceiling of a model by bouncing its light from ground or floor, as does the real sky, which is why the model is placed low in the dome. To simulate an overcast sky, lighting of 100 lamberts is created at the horizon and 250 lamberts at the zenith of the dome.

To simulate a clear sky, intensities of 200 and 100 lamberts are used. In conditions of direct sunlight, the model is first tested in the dome and then removed from the dome and subjected, while in a darkened room, to the light from a spot. Readings obtained from these two types of tests are combined and the results tabulated. The reflection caused in the prototype by the ground is sometimes simulated on the model by back lighting a translucent baseboard. This allows the model to be mounted at the horizon line of the dome.

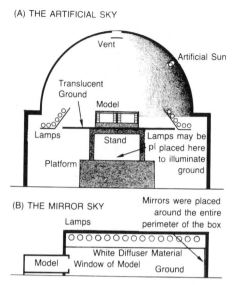

(A) THE ARTIFICIAL SKY

Vent

Artificial Sun

Translucent Ground

Model

Lamps

Stand

Lamps may be pl placed here to illuminate ground

Platform

(B) THE MIRROR SKY

Mirrors were placed around the entire perimeter of the box

Lamps

White Diffuser Material

Model

Window of Model

Ground

19-5.
Testing sun and sky conditions

2. *Mirror sky setup.* This is a more accurate way to represent a natural sky, especially when used to illuminate the model of a room that gets its light from a side window. The sky, in this case, is a mirror-lined box (figure 19-5B) from the top of which a ceiling of white translucent diffuser material, backed by rows of lights, is hung. This simulates a bright overcast sky (which is the minimum natural light condition to confront a building).

The modeled room to be tested in these sky models is divided into an imaginary grid, and light measurements are taken at each of the interesecting points. If the room is an office or school, the measurements are taken on horizontal surfaces. If it is an art gallery, they are taken on vertical surfaces. Models may be as small as ½" = 1' if limitations in the size of the artificial sky require this. More often, however, they are at a ¾" = 1' scale to allow more accurate light measurements. At this scale, error usually runs from 0 to 15% and averages under 5% if the reflectivity of the future landscape is known.

Interior surfaces should be exactly located, and they should all have the same reflective quality as the prototype. This is accomplished by painting them an appropriate value of gray. All detail need not be shown; only that which affects reflectance is necessary. Windows must be glazed with glass or similar transmission factor material. For accurate testing, the windows must have mullions or a factor to compensate for the lack of mullions must be used.

Terrain conditions also influence the amount of light

reflected into the model. Thus a representation of about 100' of ground should be constructed with the model. Grass is often assumed to have a 6% reflectance coefficient.

Photoelectric cells, some as small as 3" in diameter by ½" in thickness, record the quantitative light intensity. They can be permanently mounted at specific locations in the model or on a movable probe. The walls and ceiling of the model may be movable to facilitate the testing of alternate solutions.

QUALITATIVE ANALYSIS. To be adequate for qualitative analysis, a model must be built at between ¼ and ½0 of the size of the prototype. If it is too small, significant detail will be lost. If it is too large, it will seem to be a small room and not a model.

Occasionally, a highly individualistic design may be studied in model form for the effects that will be achieved with skylights or atypical windows.

The model is best viewed from a hole cut in its floor; this allows the tester to stick his or her head inside the model and to see the entire room by turning around. Viewing holes cut into walls or looking in through a window is less satisfactory. The interior of the model will appear more realistic if viewed with one eye closed through a weak (2-diopter) convex lens. Closing one eye will eliminate the normal stereopticon effect, created by both eyes, that contributes to the miniature look of a model. The lens aids the eye in adjusting to the short viewing distance.

Artificial lighting is almost never accurately studied in model form. Bulbs are hard to duplicate at small scales, since, to be really accurate, both globe and filament size must be scaled down. Lighting fixtures are also rarely studied in miniature form because of the problem of duplication and because it is often less expensive to build them in full-size mock-up than to attempt to construct them as models.

Acoustical Test Models

Rooms in which acoustics play an important role—auditoriums, theaters, and conference rooms, for example—may be tested in model form to determine their best overall shape, location, shape of necessary sound baffles, and wall, ceiling and floor surfaces. Models are made to the scale of about 1:10, which allows for accurate measurements of the degree of sound absorption and reflection and of the time it takes for sound to reverberate. Tests have also been performed on models of streets to determine the noise level that will be encountered in the surrounding buildings.

To provide acoustical similitude between model and prototype, not only the linear dimensions of the model must be reduced but the wave length and time scale of the sound as well. Thus, if the model is at a 1:25 scale and it is necessary to test the reaction caused by a 500 cycle per second sound, a 12,000 cycle per second sound must be broadcast into the model. Sound produced by a white noise generator is filtered, amplified and broadcast into the model at the desired point. Sound readings are taken from a sound level meter connected to a microphone placed at desired points in the model.

Fire Propagation Test Models

Several testing laboratories have tried to use models to aid them in formulating theories about the growth of flames, fires, and heat transfer in connection with

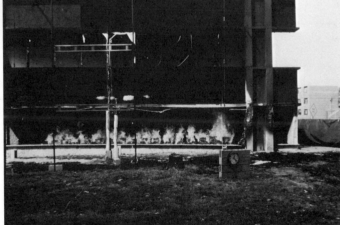

19-6.
Office Building
Skidmore, Owings & Merrill, Architects

Shown here is a 1:1 scale section of the structural system of a proposed office building. It was built to test the results of fire on the actual building materials.

19-7.
The effects of the fire on the structure shown in figure 19-6.

19-8.
Here, seven minutes have elapsed since the fire started.

such influencing factors as wind, window areas, shape and size of structure, and the amount of combustible material involved. Results have not been impressive because several, and often mutually contradictory, criteria of similarity must be achieved between model and prototype.

Tests on models of actual small assemblies—walls, floors, etc.—to study their fire resistance are more successful because of an absence of contradictory similitude criteria.

Detail Mock-Ups

Often it is worthwhile to build models of small portions of a design to aid in the visualization of important or complex detailing. The aircraft, automobile, and appliance industries make extensive use of full-size mock-ups made from easy-to-work nonprototype materials. These mock-ups allow full-size equipment to be put into place and clearances and details studied. Ships are often modeled at such large scales as 1:10 to allow for detailed investigation of all their parts.

Full-size mock-ups of window walls, windows, grilles, or custom-made wall textures are sometimes made by the modelbuilding shop from easy-to-fabricate materials. The appearance of these assemblies, including the shadows they cast, are studied and any needed modifications made. Figure 19-9 shows a typical window wall mock-up.

Structural engineers and, more infrequently, steel detailers also use detailed models, in full or partial size, to visualize complex intersections. These models are sometimes made of the actual building materials (figure 19-10), although this is extremely expensive. Models built out of cardboard or wood are quite frequently used to study intersections of geodesic structures and new fabricating systems. Models may also be used to test the practicality of welding reinforcing bar intersections in shell concrete structures. These tests can determine whether or not the bars will interfere with the structure as it develops its intended curved shape. Models are also useful for the complex design of mechanical equipment duct work and piping.

STRUCTURAL TEST MODELS

The use of models for structural testing is burgeoning. Engineers are being forced by the many new and highly complex structures to turn to models as a companion tool for the mathematical analysis of the strength and stiffness of their structures. Architectural students are being exposed more and more to laboratory work on model testing as many universities try to re-relate ar-

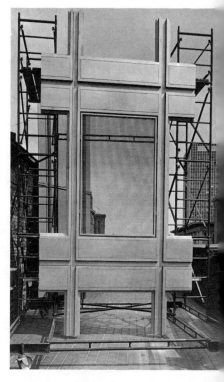

19-9.
Franklin Bank, Roosevelt Field Shopping Center
I.M. Pei and Associates, Architects
Modelmaker: the architects' model shop

This full-size mock-up of a portion of the window wall, served a an aid in the study of the shadows cast by various parts of the facade and helped to explain the design to contractors. The construction was made of wood and hung on a metal pipe scaffold (*Photograph by Acker Photo Service*)

chitectural design to structural engineering. The model serves this function well by presenting the visually oriented architectural student with a vivid picture that will help develop his or her intuitive judgment of structural action.

What Model Tests Can Show

Structural model testing can bridge gaps in knowledge about the assumed and actual forces acting on a structure. It is especially useful in the study of forces acting in three dimensions and in the study of the change in shape of a structure caused by loading.

Models may be used for qualitative analysis: the appraisal of basic deformations, rotations, and modes of failures. Some types of models may be used for quantitative analysis: the accurate measurement of these factors.

19-10.
Union Carbide
Skidmore, Owings & Merrill, Architects

This is a full-scale mock-up of a portion of a proposed office building. The construction duplicates the exterior elements and materials. It was also built approximately 10′ off the ground so that the design effect from below could be studied.

Testing can be used to determine force distribution, reaction to vibration, deflection, reaction to the application of prestressing, the existence of unusual boundary conditions, buckling, shrinkage and creep effects, compression, tension, shear, and, if micro materials are used, the ultimate strength and nature of failure.

Models may also be used as starting points for some structural designs. Antonio Gaudi designed ceiling vaults on 1:10 models. He built these models upside down, using cords to represent the struts of the vaults. The pull of gravity revealed the form that could best support the acting force vectors, which were represented by hung weights. After establishing the best design on the model, the structure was mathematically checked.

Models and Mathematical Analysis

In the design of some types of structures, models and mathematics share the design burden. With other structures, models must be used to obtain almost all the information. But even in these instances, the engineer usually makes occasional spot mathematical checks. Because models never provide more than a close approximation of the prototype, exact analogies cannot be made.

The use of models is necessitated, to a large extent, by four shortcomings of current mathematical analysis:

1. Formulas are often based on an oversimplification of what is happening in the structure; minor forces are often ignored.

2. To compensate for the differences between actual conditions and mathematical assumptions of what the conditions are, various large safety factors must be used to achieve conservative analysis. Thus, for example, "lightness," which many designers strive to achieve through the use of minimal materials, may well prove impossible.

3. Many complex structural problems cannot be solved with conventional, available formulas. Other structures require large amounts of time for the resolution of their parts into solvable units. While computers have helped to solve these problems to a great degree, models can be used as a check on the solutions.

Structures with inherently difficult problems include: umbrella structures, complex shells, space frames, domes, inflated structures, hyperboloid shells, geodesic and lamella structures, folded plates, and suspended roofs.

4. When solving a complete structure by resolving it into parts and analyzing these separately, the fact that other parts of the structure aid the part being tested is usually overlooked. Through the use of models, entire structures can be analyzed at once.

These four shortcomings of mathematical analysis can, in many cases, be overcome through the use of model testing in combination with mathematical computation.

Some engineers, however, are reluctant to accept the results of model testing, since tests often suggest the use of lighter structures than those to which they have become accustomed. Engineers also find that fees do not usually allow for model study, since it is more costly to use models than to rely on simplified calculations, with their inflated safety factors. The architect should attempt to have the cost of model testing included in his or her fee on all commissions that result in unusual structures. The cost of the model can often be made up by eventual savings in construction costs.

Structural Test Techniques

Similitude is the key factor in structural test models. The models must be similar to the prototype in geometry, load distribution, and response. If the model is being investigated within its elastic range, its Poisson ratio should be similar to that of the prototype. Each material, and its means of attachment to the model, must relate to the physics of the prototype. The engineer should design the model and its test with the same degree of intuition and judgment used for the structure itself.

If the model is being investigated beyond its elastic range and up to its ultimate strength, as can be done with models made from micro materials, the deformation and strength characteristics of these materials must be similar to those of the prototype. Both materials must have stress/strain curves that can be related to one another by formula.

If the deformation produced by any test is large enough to influence the behavior of the structure, the strain scale of the two materials' stress/strain curves must be exactly equal.

Large repetitive structures may sometimes be modeled and tested in part and the results applied to the overall structure. This requires preliminary investigation to determine whether or not the part selected is truly representative of the total assembly.

LOADING THE MODEL. Uniform loads may be conveniently represented on the model by concentrated loads produced by weights (figures 19-11 and 19-14), by vacuum pressure (figure 19-12), or by the pressure exerted through expanded air bags. Uniform loads caused by body forces may also be created by swinging the model in a centrifuge. Sometimes additional weights must be placed on a model to compensate for the lack of deadweight of the model material.

DIRECT TESTING. Direct measurement testing of strain is used to study conditions within elastic or inelastic ranges or to determine ultimate strength. Models used with the direct testing method must be constructed to exact shape, or they may be slightly simplified.

Strain gauges and measuring tools. Strain may be measured with electrical resistance strain gauges that consist of fine wires cemented to the models. As the model is subjected to loading and its resulting strain, the wires are also strained. This changes the area of their cross section and, in turn, changes their electrical resistance. The latter is read on an instrument that translates electrical readings into strain readings. Single strain gauges applied in the direction of the stress are used to measure bending or axial load on the surface of beams, columns, or truss members. Two gauges oriented in the direction of the stresses are used to measure the action of plate or shell structures when the direction of the principal stresses is known. Three gauges coupled together are used to measure the action in a plate or shell subject to bending or axial load in several directions.

In addition to gauges, linear differential transformers or precision levels may be used to measure deflection. Figure 19-12 shows one assembly of electrical resistance strain gauges and a dial gauge used to measure horizontal deflection.

Brittle lacquer coatings. Certain lacquers may be applied to modeled and full-size structural components made from deformable material. When the member is loaded, the lacquer will crack. These fissures give good indications of the direction and magnitude of stresses and aid the engineer in determining where to put strain gauges for quantitative analysis.

The magnitude of strain may also be measured directly from the amount of cracking. First, the number of cracks formed due to a given amount of deformation must be ascertained in a control test; then the cracks formed by succeeding tests can be counted. Comparing the number of cracks on the control test to the number in the latter tests can determine approximate stresses and their direction.

To test for tension, the model is painted with lacquer before it is loaded. To test for compression, the model is first loaded then, while the load is still in place, painted with lacquer. Once the paint has dried, the load is removed and cracks representing compression will appear.

INDIRECT TESTING. A second way of obtaining information is to keep loading a model until a desired deformation occurs in one place. The resulting deformations in other parts of the structure are then measured to obtain the internal forces and moments and the external redundant forces and moments. The indirect method can only be used to study the behavior of a structure within its elastic range. Models built for this technique

19-11.
A three-dimensional photoelastic model of a Gothic vault on which dead weight loading was applied. (*Photograph by Dr. Robert Mark*)

19-12.
The Kodak Pavilion at the 1964–65 New York World's Fair
Kahn and Jacobs and Will Burton, Inc., Architects
Lev Zetlin, Engineer
Modelmakers: Wiss, Janney Associates, Structural Engineers
Scale: 1:64

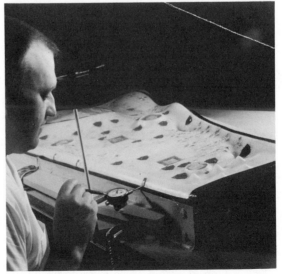

Structural tests performed with the aid of strain gauges were necessitated by the complexity of the shell concrete roof structure. The model was made from methyl mathacrilate. This material allows testing, performed within its elastic limits, to be accurately measured. Columns (not visible) were seated in plaster of Paris, and the entire assembly was mounted on a rigid base. The black line along the edge of the model was tape, which ensured an airtight seal. Loads were simulated by creating a vacuum below the model. Strain gauges and a dial gauge were used to measure horizontal deflection on the shell concrete roof structure.

are distorted because different scales are used in their lateral and longitudinal measurements.

Analysis of Plastic Models

The behavior of structures within their elastic limits may be quantitatively and qualitatively analyzed with the use of small-scale models made from nonprototype materials. Materials used, however, must be homogeneous and isotropic. The most popular of these materials are acrylic, polystyrene, vinyl, castable epoxy resin, and ethyl cellulose (aluminum, brass, and steel are used infrequently for this type of elastic analysis). The response of plastics to tests is sufficiently accurate and their machining and forming sufficiently simple to make them acceptable test subjects. Vacuum-forming, casting, and machining are used to form the model. Sometimes these small-scale plastic models are used to ascertain a preliminary basic deflection in a structure. Subsequently, more elaborate models are constructed of micro materials or nonprototype plastic materials and precisely tested.

Analysis of Micro Material Models

A greater number of stresses and conditions can be analyzed on models that are made from scaled-down prototype materials than on models made of plastic. These scale materials, referred to as *micro materials*, must have characteristics that are quite similar to those of the prototype.

Micro materials must have a stress/strain curve similar to that of the prototype material. If the curves are similar in shape, they can be nearly equalized by applying a factor to the two axes of the curve obtained by the model test. This will convert the model test results into those that would be encountered on the prototype structure.

Timber is extremely difficult to duplicate because of its cell and knot structure. However, balsa has been used for small-scale (1:30 to 1:20) models. The wood of the actual structure can be used on larger (1:5 scale or so) models. Scale pins are used to represent nails.

Perhaps the most similar material that can be found to test reinforced concrete is cement mortar with scaled down aggregates, but its slow drying time makes it inconvenient to use. Dental plaster, because of its very high tensile strength, may be used on ultimate load tests. Ultracal 30 gypsum plaster, with aggregates represented by crushed limestone and sand, is often used. Reinforcements may be made from wire mesh and threaded or deformed mild steel rods (figure 19-13).

Models have been constructed at a 1:5 to 1:15 scale with mock-ups of single beams and struts sometimes made at a larger scale.

A difficulty that hampers the selection of any micro material is that the yield point of any material increases as the size of its parts decreases. This affects shear, compression, tension, and other yield points. Sometimes the deflection that would result in a model is so slight that it is difficult to measure. This is one of the factors that encourages the use of models made of plastic. Plastics with their smaller moduli of elasticity (and greater deflection) are especially useful in the making of small-scale models.

Photoelastic Analysis of Plastic Models

Photoelastic analysis, unlike strain gauge analysis, allows one to view an optical pattern that is directly related to stress or strain acting along all parts of a structural member. It shows, however, only those stresses that occur on the surface of the model. A model of the structure to be tested should be constructed in a suitable transparent material such as gelatin, epoxy resin or acrylic.

The models are loaded (figure 19-14) and then heated to increase their deformation. Upon cooling, the stress is "frozen" in the model. The loads are removed and the model is viewed in a polariscope (figure 19-16). Polarized light passing through the specimen will reveal a pattern of light and dark areas called fringes (figure 19-15). This fringe pattern is caused by reorientation of the molecules of the model.

The results of photoelastic tests may vary slightly between the prototype and the model because of the differences between the Poisson ratio of the model and that of the prototype material.

The model can be tested again with different loads because reheating will erase the previous stress patterns. Three-dimensional models can be viewed in their entirety or sliced to reveal internal patterns. If the model is cut, however, it cannot be reused.

PHOTOELASTIC COATINGS. Certain aluminum coatings can be painted or cemented on modeled or full-scale structural parts, or the part can be polished. This creates a reflective surface that is then coated with a birefringent material. The structure is then loaded and studied through a reflecting polariscope (figure 19-19B). The stressed birefringent material will reflect a colored fringe pattern. By comparing each color, quantitative stress measurements can be made.

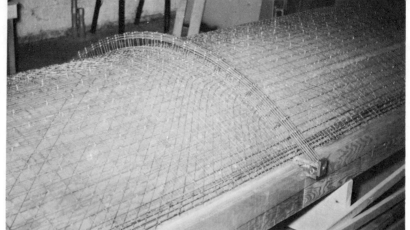

19-13.
Continuous, arch-reinforced roof shell model, showing the reinforcement before micro-concrete material was applied. (*Photograph by Dr. Robert Mark*)

19-14.
Partial dead-weight loading was applied to this model of the structural frame of the nave of Beauvais Cathedral.

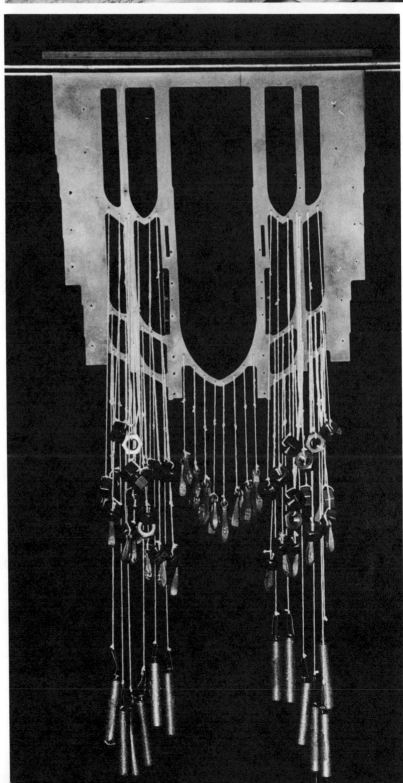

19-15.
The photoelastic pattern in the stress-frozen
model shown in figure 19-14.

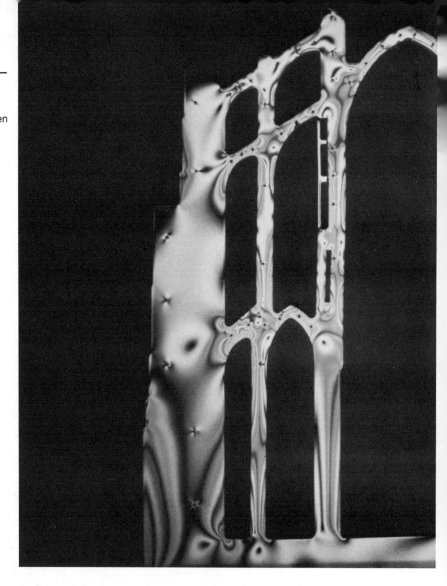

19-16.
The transmission polariscope of Princeton
University's Architectural Laboratory. The
components of the polariscope, designed by
Dr. Robert Mark, are (from left to right) a
view camera which can be removed to permit
direct observation, a Polaroid analyzer, a
model table, a polarizer, and a light source
box.

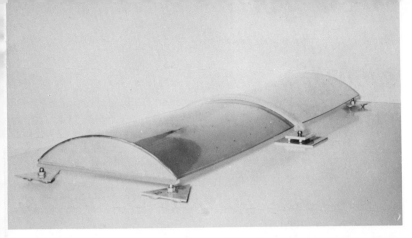

19-17.
Three-dimensional photoelastic model of the roof shell structure shown in figure 19-13.

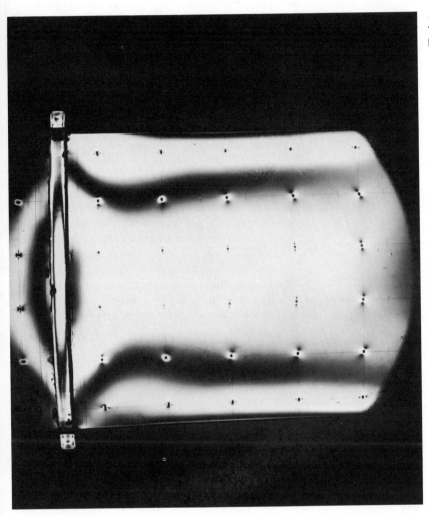

19-18.
The same model as it appeared in polarized light after stress freezing

Moiré Grid Analysis

If a simple grid pattern is viewed through a transparent sheet on which another grid pattern has been printed, a third pattern or fringe will be seen. This effect can be seen by using two sheets of overlay sheets: fringe results from the interrelationship of the two grids. If one of the grids were to be rotated, new fringes would form. Moiré grid testing makes use of this phenomenon. It may be used in the investigation of plates or sections of more complex structural components. One grid is photographically imprinted on the surface of the model; another grid is printed on a transparent sheet and held against that surface. The moiré fringe, caused by the deformation of the model, forms when the model is loaded. Strains involved can be found by analyzing the

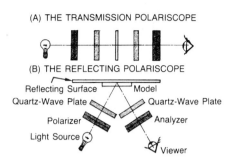

(A) THE TRANSMISSION POLARISCOPE

(B) THE REFLECTING POLARISCOPE

Reflecting Surface   Model
Quartz-Wave Plate   Quartz-Wave Plate
Polarizer   Analyzer
Light Source   Viewer

19-19.
Polariscopes

pattern. An alternate procedure is to use only the first grid and create a fringe by photographing the unloaded model, then loading the model and rephotographing it on the same film, with the camera in the same position.

By visually observing and counting the fringes as they form, it is possible to analyze qualitatively how the surface of the model became deformed as it was loaded.

Grid Analysis

A two- or three-dimensional grid is placed into a model made from a highly deforming material and the distortion of the grid is physically measured when the model is loaded. The grid is often used in a gelatin block model.

Wind Load Study

Sometimes a high building of unorthodox shape must be model tested to determine the wind loads or oscillations to which it will be subjected. For this test, the model is loaded with weights that represent live and dead loads. To simulate wind, strings are attached to its walls and pulled taut, or the model is placed in a wind tunnel. Wind pressure is calculated in pounds per square foot, which relates to wind velocity: wind pressure $= 0.0026 \times$ (wind velocity)^2.

Determining wind loads for the prototype requires that the model be subjected to wind speeds in excess of the winds that would be encountered by the prototype.

The air flow pattern around the model must be similar at all altitudes to that which is expected around the prototype. Wind gusts must also be accurately duplicated. Wind loading is applied from each angle that might affect the prototype. Deflection or strain is measured from the model.

Models may also be used to test qualitatively any flutter to which unconventional roof shapes may be subjected.

Another use of test models is in ascertaining the pressure that prevailing winds will cause on a high building. The building and all surrounding structures and landscaping must be accurately modeled and tested in a wind tunnel. Such tests will determine the pressure put on the windows of the building. This pressure must be taken into consideration when designing the window structure and its waterproofing.

MODELS OF RIVER SYSTEMS

Civil engineers often use models in the planning of dams and bridges and in other situations where hydraulic design is an important factor. Huge models employing loose bed materials and water are constructed of entire bay and harbor systems to study the causes of both currents and silting.

The shifting of land caused by flooding conditions is studied to see what effect it may have on bridge abutments. A model is made of a length of a river. Its horizontal scale, usually governed by cost considerations, may run between 1:100 to 1:300; its vertical scale is exaggerated (1:25 to 1:100) to allow for a more rapid flow of water. Underlying earth contours are built from concrete. The final earth levels are built up of crushed anthracite or sand to simulate the movable river bed. Water is run over the bed at a controlled rate of flow to simulate various flood conditions. Currents are made visible by surface floating confetti or by injecting fluorescent dye below the surface of the water. After each experiment, a contour map is drawn to show changes in the river bed. A similitude must be maintained between model and prototype conditions.

20:Displaying the Model

DISPLAY STANDS

The designer or modelmaker should give some thought to the various ways in which a model can be displayed. Occasionally, a project is of such importance that it is wise to design a special transparent cover and display stand for the model.

The viewing angle of the model should show it off to its best advantage. Models may be bracketed from walls so that they are viewed in elevation (figure 20-1), plan view, or with their ground plane at an angle to the wall. It is even possible to select a model-to-wall angle and a mounting height that permits the model to be viewed at pedestrian eye level or at almost plain view, depending on how close the spectator stands.

Display stands may be any available table or they may be custom-constructed from wood (figure 20-2). To improve tables cosmetically, encase them in painted plywood. All sorts of stand shapes may be custom-constructed from wood: boxes, pedestals, cruciforms, intersecting vertical walls, and so forth.

Large landscape or town-planning models should be mounted on very low stands or bracketed vertically from walls to allow them to be viewed from bird's-eye level. The importance of the display may justify placing the model with its ground elevation at eye level and building an elevated walkway around it to allow both pedestrian and bird's-eye level viewing.

Dioramas are most effective when their horizon line is at viewer eye level. Models of individual buildings and interiors are best viewed when mounted on a 4' or higher stand. This allows the spectator to look into the model at pedestrian level.

Mirrors may be necessary to show details that would otherwise be hidden from the viewer. They are especially useful when space considerations keep spectators on only one side of the model. This problem may also be solved by placing the model on a continually rotating turntable. Such mechanisms are sold by local store-fixture supply houses. Motors and their gear trains should be enclosed in a box that is lined with sound-deadening material.

THE MODEL COVER

The transparent model cover performs two necessary functions: it keeps dust and spectators' fingers from the model. One-piece hemispherical and square-base domes are commercially available. Domes must be set on or in the model base to allow for expansion; otherwise they may crack. Covers may be constructed from acrylic. These may be built in the form of a flattened arch, a low-hipped roof, a barrel vault, or just a plain box shape. Make provisions for periodically treating the cover with antistatic electricity spray; otherwise, the acrylic will be hard to dust. Display lights should not create reflections that will make viewing the model difficult. Sometimes this requires the construction of a cover whose shape will be compatible with the expected lighting conditions.

DEHUMIDIFIERS. Humidity sometimes affects even well waterproofed paper, cardboard, or wood models, so it may be necessary to install a dehumidifier inside the cover. Small slabs of camphor ice will suffice if the model is small. If it is large, an electric dehumidifier may be required.

SPECIAL DISPLAY EFFECTS

Internal Lighting

Lighting can greatly increase the realism and attractiveness of a model, thereby enhancing its value as a display and study tool (figure 20-3). Internal lighting can also be used to give a feeling of depth and, if located behind the model, can help kill reflections on transparent and translucent surfaces.

Miniature bulbs are sold in most model railroad and

20-1.
Everything I Have Is Yours
Ira Joel Haber
Dimensions: 118″ × 51½″ × 7″
Materials: mixed media

This is an interesting way to display models: the buildings are placed on separate shelves, which are bracketed to the wall at various angles. Because of their arrangement, the viewer is drawn to examine each piece in the grouping individually, or as an element of the whole. (*Photograph courtesy of Pam Adler Gallery*)

hobby stores. Slightly larger bulbs are available from hardware stores. Small and miniature bulbs usually require less than 110 volts and will accept either AC or DC current; they can be operated by either a transformer or a battery. Model train transformers, with a variable voltage throttle control, and low voltage step-down transformers (new or surplus) are inexpensive and convenient to use. Model train transformers allow the dimming of lights at will or the use of various voltages. Bulb life, which is pitifully low in some brands, may be extended by running the bulb at reduced voltage. This, however, will change the brightness of the light and alter the color of clear bulbs from white toward orange.

COMPUTING THE NUMBER OF BULBS. Bulbs should be of a voltage rating equal to that of the transformer. This allows the use of simple parallel circuitry (figure 20-4A). To estimate the maximum number of bulbs that can be used in a parallel hook-up with a transformer,

20-2.
Inner City 1977
Michael C. McMillen
Dimensions: 10′ × 12′ × 11′
Materials: mixed media wood construction

These large models were elevated on display stands so they could be more closely examined. The sound effects and low level of lighting in the room re-create a nighttime atmosphere. (*Photograph courtesy of Los Angeles County Museum of Art*)

first find the output wattage rating or current capacity of the latter. In addition, you must determine the wattage rating of the bulbs. The relationship can best be expressed as follows:

W_t (output wattage rating of the transformer) = E_t (voltage output employed) × I_t (rated current output in amperes);

W_b (wattage of each bulb) = E_b (rated bulb voltage) × I_b (the measured current drain (in amperes) of one bulb at the rated voltage).

Thus it follows that the maximum number of bulbs

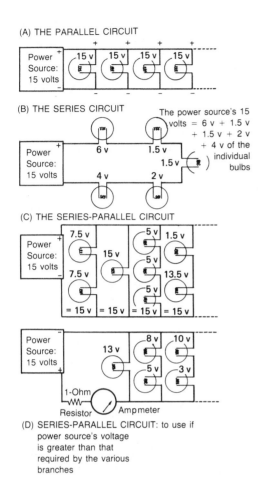

(A) THE PARALLEL CIRCUIT

Power Source: 15 volts

(B) THE SERIES CIRCUIT

The power source's 15 volts = 6 v + 1.5 v + 1.5 v + 2 v + 4 v of the individual bulbs

Power Source: 15 volts

(C) THE SERIES-PARALLEL CIRCUIT

Power Source: 15 volts

= 15 v = 15 v = 15 v = 15 v

Power Source: 15 volts

1-Ohm Resistor   Ampmeter

(D) SERIES-PARALLEL CIRCUIT: to use if power source's voltage is greater than that required by the various branches

20-4.
Circuits for internal lighting

20-3.
Ruckus Manhattan, detail of The World Trade Center
Red Grooms and The Ruckus Construction Company

Models are usually internally lit with miniature bulbs. Because of the large scale of this construction of the office towers, spotlights, suspended from the ceiling at the top, had to be used. Because portions of the translucent wall material are painted out, the effect of viewing the building at night is suggested. (*Photograph by Robert Mates and Gail Stern, courtesy of Marlborough Gallery, New York*)

(N) that can be powered by a transformer is:

$$N = \frac{W_t \text{ (output wattage of transformer)}}{W_b \text{ (wattage of each bulb)}}$$

Remember that if the wattage is not known, it can always be calculated by the rated or measured voltage and current if the formula $W = E \times I$ is used.

For example: The transformer has an output of 6 volts at 10.5 amperes, and the bulbs in use are rated at 6 volts. By connecting an ammeter in series with one bulb and the 6-volt source, the current consumption can be measured and is observed to be 1 ampere. Therefore:

$$N = \frac{W_t}{W_b}$$
$$N = \frac{6 \text{ volts} \times 10.5 \text{ amperes}}{6 \text{ volts} \times 1.0 \text{ amperes}}$$
$$N = \frac{10.5}{1}$$
$$N = 10.5$$

Thus the maximum number of bulbs that can be employed is 10. If 11 or more are used, the maximum wattage rating of the transformer is overdrawn, and it may burn out.

The parallel circuit is the type most commonly used. Each bulb is located independently of the others in a separate parallel branch. Thus, if one bulb burns out, the others will continue to burn. Since the voltage received by each branch will be the same, all the bulbs must be of the same voltage as the source.

An alternative hook-up method must be used when a higher-voltage transformer is used with lower-voltage bulbs. In this circuit, all of the bulbs are interconnected or hooked up in series (figure 20-4B). If one bulb burns out, the entire circuit will go dead. In a series circuit, the voltages of the individual bulbs are cumulative, so different-voltage bulbs can be used as long as their total voltage equals the output voltage of the transformer. The same transformer wattage considerations apply.

Combinations of parallel circuits, with branches made up of series circuits, can be used with a few bulbs of voltages other than those produced by the transformer (figure 20-4C). If one bulb in a series circuit of a parallel branch blows out, that entire branch, although not the whole parallel network, will be extinguished.

Another method is to use a dropping resistor to lower the transformer voltage to that of the bulbs (figure 20-4D), but this is not used as often as matching bulb voltage to transformer voltage (or vise versa). The resistor can be used in a series and parallel circuits or in branches of parallel combination circuits. An ammeter must be used with the voltage dropping resistor method. If all the bulbs are of the same voltage but have a rating of less than that of the transformer, a parallel circuit, with the appropriate dropping resistor placed after the transformer output lead, can be used.

The ammeter (which if working with an AC transformer must be designed for use with alternating current) is connected in series with the parallel branches after a resistor. Both the resistor and the ammeter are connected to either of the output leads of the transformer. The same procedure can be followed with a direct current hookup, but a DC meter must be used and polarity considerations adhered to. A temporary resistor (of about 5 ohms per desired volt drop) is used to simulate the current drain of the resistor that will be finally used. In figure 20-4D, a 2-volt drop is required. Let us assume that the ammeter reads 2 amperes. Using Ohm's law, we can compute the required resistance:

$$\text{resistance} = \frac{\text{voltage drop desired}}{\text{measured current}}$$
$$= \frac{2 \text{ volts}}{2 \text{ amperes}}$$
$$= 1 \text{ ohm}$$

Another criterion vital to the selection of the proper resistor is its heat dissipation power. Since a resistor converts electricity to heat, the more heat dissipation required, the greater the voltage drop needed and the greater the current drain. Heat dissipation can also be measured in watts and can be computed by the product of the voltage drop and the current drain of the resistor.

$$W \text{ (heat dissipation)} = E \text{ (voltage drop)} \times I \text{ (current drain)}$$

Be sure that the resistor selected has sufficient heat dissipation capacity; that is, be sure its wattage rating is high enough. Also be sure to locate the resistor in such a position that air can freely circulate around it in the model, or wrap it with aluminum foil to increase its radiating area.

To reduce the voltage to one bulb of a circuit, whether it be series or parallel, place the resistor into the circuit directly before that bulb and connect the ammeter at the same place to take the current measurement of just that bulb.

FLASHING BULBS AND WIRING. Independently flashing bulbs can be used in place of regular bulbs in parallel circuits. If flashing bulbs are used in series circuits, all the bulbs in the circuit will flash simultaneously; only one flashing bulb is necessary to achieve this effect.

Bulbs may be wired with 15-ampere-rated household wire, bell wire, or No. 22 or No. 24 wire, obtainable in model train and hobby shops. When selecting wire, be sure to specify the braided variety because this type will reduce breakage and wearing down. Keep wiring neat by stapling it in place in the model, taking care not to penetrate the insulation.

Painted circuitry may also be used to form electrical connections on any model surface. First varnish the surface on which the circuit is to be run. After the varnish has dried, paint the circuit lines with special silver conductive paint. Then insulate the lines with a second coat of varnish. All hook-ups should be provided with an on-off switch.

PLACING BULBS IN THE MODEL. Make some provision to cool all bulbs that are rated at over 10 watts. Besides creating a fire hazard, the heat from large bulbs may warp the model. It may be possible simply to cut ventilation holes in installation or it might be necessary to add a small electric fan of the variety used in electrical appliances. Holes should provide a constant draft in the model. Small air-intake holes should be placed low on the model and larger outlet holes at the top of the model.

Models constructed from acrylic and other transparent or translucent materials must have black painted interiors to stop the passage of internal light. If this does not block out all light leakage, place baffles around the bulbs or line the interior of the model with aluminum foil.

If the model is illuminated by a few high-wattage, unbaffled lamps, rice or white tracing paper may have to be cemented inside the windows of the model to eliminate glare.

There is no need to illuminate the model to the same intensity as the prototype. Both long photograph exposures and the eyes of the viewer will compensate for the lower intensity and the illumination will seem to be "in scale." Illuminated models are most effectively displayed in a dark room.

Professional modelmakers often use full-size fluorescent or cold neon tubes in large models. These cut down the number of bulbs and amount of current needed and also reduce the heat output of the lighting system. To prevent heat build-up, professional modelmakers sometimes wire a timer into the circuit; this periodically cuts off the lights for a few minutes of cooling. Despite these precautions, occasional fires have started inside models.

WORKING LIGHT FIXTURES. Light may be led from one place to another through a clear acrylic rod whose ends have been polished. One end of the rod is aimed at the light source; the other is used to represent a lamp. In this way multibulb marquees and other fixtures may be created with only one or two bulbs mounted in the center of the marquee as a light source.

Scale spotlights may be constructed from Bristolboard or sheet metal and lined with aluminum foil for greater reflectance.

Fluorescent tubes may be represented by polished acrylic rods. These are mounted behind slits in the ceiling of the model, with bulbs placed behind them. Parts of the rods that are visible through the slits can be lightly sanded.

ILLUMINATED SIGNS. Illuminated signs may be constructed in many ways. One method is to apply transfer letters to sheet acrylic. The sign is then painted and the transfer letters removed to leave transparent, illuminable letters on an opaque background. If opaque letters on a transparent background are desired, leave the transfers in place and do not paint the background. Another method is to use slide transparencies with lights shining behind them (figure 20-5).

Sound

Presentation models may warrant a recording that explains the project to the viewer. Use a tape recorder with a continuous tape to provide a running commentary, or a system in which picking up an earphone or pushing a button will start a record. Other, more theatrical effects have been achieved on occasion, including sounds associated with a particular project—organ music, waterfront sounds, or aircraft engines, for example.

Smoke and Fires

Some museum and exposition display models of factory complexes make use of smoke as an animation effect. Small amounts of smoke may be generated by the small units sold for use in model locomotives. These units generate smoke by electrically heating a pellet or liquid oil. Cartridges generate smoke for about one hour and they run on 3 to 6 volts. These devices have a rather limited smoke-making capacity—only enough for one smokestack. To produce a larger volume of smoke, it is necessary to construct a smoke machine from sheet metal. This can produce a sufficient quantity of smoke by electrically heating machine oil which is drawn to the electrical heating coil through a fiberglass wick. If the model is of a low building and does not have enough interior space for mounting such a smoke machine, place it under the model and conceal it with a wood skirt constructed around the baseboard.

If smoke is desired only for photographs, blow it through the chimney of the model by attaching a rubber hose and blowing cigarette smoke through it. Smoke may also be airbrushed on photographic prints.

It may occasionally be necessary to represent fires, especially for photographic purposes. To do this, use several small birthday cake candles burning among plaster of Paris logs. This is satisfactory in ¼" scale and larger models whose fireplaces have been constructed of nonflammable materials. A safer way to represent a fire is with a miniature bulb surrounded with tendrils of roughly cut red and yellow cellophane. Glowing coals can be represented by rear-lighted, roughened fragments of red or orange acrylic.

CLEANING THE MODEL

To begin with, all possible efforts should be made to keep dirt from collecting on the model. A display model should be fully enclosed by a cover. If the model does not warrant the expense of an acrylic cover, it should be draped with a sheet of plastic or paper when not being viewed.

If the model does eventually collect a coating of dust, remove this by carefully brushing it with a camel's hair or static electricity brush. Both can be obtained from photographic supply stores.

Flocked areas of foliage are best cleaned with a miniature vacuum cleaner. Modify an ordinary home-type cleaner by forming a wood plug to fit snugly into the end of the hose. Drill a hole into the plug and insert rubber or neoprene tubing. An entire set of cleaning tools may be made by cutting the openings of several lengths of tubing into various shapes. The insertion of ½" lengths of flattened or crimped metal tubing into the flexible material will form additional opening shapes. Make sure that the metal is inserted far enough inside the flexible tubing to prevent it from scratching the model's surface.

SHIPPING THE MODEL

The safest local deliveries are made in person. The modelbuilder or members of his or her staff can then set up the model and its display stand. (Very large or heavy models, however, should be sent by a trusted moving company specializing in art or museum display moving.) Deliveries of 100 or so miles can be made by the modelbuilder in a rented station wagon or truck. For longer distances, the model should be air freighted (either the modelbuilder or a moving company should supervise the delivery to the airport). Make sure the model is picked up at its destination by the architect or owner.

20-5.
60th and Third Avenue
Helmuth, Obata and Kassa-
    baum, Architects
Modelmakers: HOK
Scale: $\frac{1}{16}'' = 1'$
Materials: Plexiglas and
    cardboard

This model was designed to be backlit through the retail space. Slide transparencies were used to insert images of actual storefronts and people into the scene.

Shipping Crates

The modelbuilder should take the responsibility for constructing, or at least designing, any shipping crates that will be needed for the model. Small and medium-size crates should be framed with $1'' \times 1''$ to $1'' \times 2''$ pine and covered with plywood if the model is to be hand carried or shipped by air. If shipping is to be by truck, train, or boat, or if the crate is larger than about $3' \times 5' \times 2'$, cover it with wooden boards. When possible, consult a professional packing expert if the model is to be shipped long distances.

Models with one or more high buildings covering a small portion of the model's baseboard area should be constructed so that the high building can be detached from the base. This will diminish the total volume of the packing case. Construct blocks inside the case to hold the model in place. All large model shapes should be individually braced with these blocks. Use felt or sponge rubber to cover the places where the blocks contact the model. Screw or bolt the baseboard of the model into the case. You can also cast shock-absorbing pads made from casting rubber or foaming plastic to the contours of the model. Finally, affix instructions for unpacking, setting up, and cleaning the model, as well as suggestions for lighting, to the inside of the case.

Small carrying cases may be constructed in the same manner as packing crates are. They should have handles to simplify handling.

INSURANCE

Models may be insured to cover most of the unpleasant eventualities that might occur while they are in transit or on display. An underwriter will rate each model, its trip, and the exhibit in which it is to appear and will take into consideration the construction and packing of the model, how it is to be shipped, the fire rating of the building in which it is to be displayed, and the safeguards taken. Although all-risk (including breakage) insurance is available, even this extensive form will exclude payments for damage caused to the model "due to its inherent weakness."

21:Photographing the Model

The presentation model constitutes only half of a presentation technique. To be of complete use to the designer and client, a model must be skillfully photographed to make one or more balanced presentations of the project. As a general routine, it may also be useful to photograph the design and test model for permanent records. For this form of photographic record, the skills of the ordinary professional or skilled amateur photographer are sufficient. But the creation of a first-rate presentation photograph requires extremely specialized skills and equipment, so much so that there are several commercial photographers whose entire livelihood comes from photographing architectural models. There are also several lens systems designed specifically for photographing the architectural and interior design model, and no doubt more remain to be created.

MODEL PHOTOGRAPHY BASICS

Model photographers, both amateur and professional, must follow these basic rules in order to ensure quality presentations:

1. The picture should be taken from a viewpoint that makes the model look like an actual structure. The resulting vanishing points should also be similar to what could be expected with a full-size building.
2. The foreground, midground, and background of the picture must be reasonably in focus.
3. The model must have a compatible background. Also, as with all photography, such factors as lighting, correct film selection, and composition must be taken into account. Model photography is undeniably a complicated undertaking, but with the proper equipment and instruction, a fairly experienced amateur photographer should be able to produce professional results after practice that includes experimenting on several models. But the catch is that the proper equipment is expensive and the novice model photographer will have

to take several (perhaps a dozen) photographs for each good one. An assistant to help with the lights and reflectors can ease the strain. Many offices have one or more employees who can turn out decent model photographs, but few can produce results that would be mistaken for the work done by a specializing professional.

EQUIPMENT

The Camera

To qualify as a good camera for model photography, an instrument must have:

1. The ability to focus to within a few inches of the lens
2. Full negative size ground glass viewing (through the main lens to avoid parallax)
3. Negative size that allows for making good 8″ × 10″ enlargements
4. An interchangeable lens system for wide-angle lens use

Since color and black-and-white photos are often taken in the same photographing session, two cameras may be needed or, preferably, a camera with interchangeable film holders. The latter can be a press camera with cut film or, for black-and-white film, filmpack holders and, for cost conservation, an adapter to take roll color film.

THE PRESS OR VIEW CAMERA. As is shown in table 21-1, the press camera is the best-suited commercially made device for taking model photos.

The lens of a press camera is mounted at the end of an adjustable bellows and may be extended or retracted to focus on close or distant objects, respectively. On good press cameras, the lens may be swung and tilted in relation to the plane of the film. Tilting or revolving the lens forward or backward around its horizontal axis increases the depth of field of the camera. Swinging the lens or revolving it around its vertical axis can put

Table 21-1. Comparison of Cameras for Model Photography

Camera type	Sighted and focused through film-size ground glass	Focusable within inches of the lens without supplementary lenses, tube, or bellows?	Parallax problem on close-up shots?	Accepts interchangeable lenses?[1]	Distorts perspective by tilts and swings?	Film size sufficient for prints larger than 8″ × 10″?	Film of same proportion as 8″ × 10″ print?	Completely satisfactory, with modification (extension tube or bellows), for model photography?
35mm candid	No	No	Yes	Yes (except for cheap models)	No	Only if care is taken	No	No, because of lack of ground-glass focusing and small film size
35mm single-lens reflex or 2¼″ × 2¼″ single-lens reflex	Yes	No	No	Yes	No	With 35mm film size, only if care is taken; with 2¼″ × 2½″ size, yes	No	Yes, if small film size is no problem—get a magnifying lens (to aid in precise focusing) and a bellows
2¼″ × 2¼″ twin-lens reflex	Yes	No	Yes	Yes (except for cheap models)	No	Yes	No	Yes; get a magnifying lens and bellows
2¼″ × 3¼″, 4″ × 5″, 5″ × 7″, 8″ × 10″ or 11″ × 14″ press or studio camera	Yes	Yes (if bellows are of the double or triple extension variety)	No	Yes	Yes (with most makes)	Yes	Yes	Camera needs no modification; a 3¼″ × 4¼″ or 4″ × 5″ camera may prove the best all-around camera for model as well as full-size architectural and interior design photography

1. A parallax-correcting device is available for twin-lens cameras. It comes in three models: one is used when the lens is 10″–13″ from the subject; another when the distance is 13″–20″; the third for 20″–38″ distances.

a larger amount of vertical surface in focus. Most lenses may also be raised in relation to the film; this helps to eliminate convergence that is caused by aiming a camera up at high buildings. Lenses may also be slid from side to side in relation to the film to accentuate or eliminate the perspective of horizontal lines. A press camera would be an excellent choice for architectural and interior photography as well as for model photography.

Polaroid makes an adapter for their instantly developed film that fits press cameras. This adapter aids in checking exposure, shadows, and camera angle. It is conceivable that this might reduce the number of shots taken with regular film and thus effect an overall savings. If nothing else, it would allow a clearer anticipation of results before the end of the photographic session. A new 4″ × 5″ camera equipped with a wide-angle and a regular lens and all the film holders needed should cost no more than a good reflex camera.

When the lens of a press camera is extended far out of the camera, as in taking extreme close-ups, the f number indicated by the lens is no longer accurate. The true number may be found by the following formula: actual (effective) f number = lens-to-film distance × f stop indicated on the lens over the focal length of lens; or look up the actual f number on an effective lens aperture guide wheel. The more bulky the camera, the farther away from the model the centerline of its lens will be, no matter how close one tries to bring it. This is one of the few drawbacks of the press camera.

CUSTOM-MADE CAMERAS. An occasional model photographer will fabricate his or her own camera for close-up work. This type of camera might have the following features:

1. It is extremely small ($2'' \times 2'' \times \frac{3}{4}''$ plus lens) so that it can be set right into the model and has a lens center that can be placed on a scale 12 feet off the ground (when photographing $\frac{1}{8}'' = 1'$ scale models).
2. A pinhole (f 74) lens gives the camera a depth of field of from $3\frac{1}{2}''$ to $2'$.
3. A 25mm focal length lens from a 16mm motion picture camera is used to produce a wide-angle effect.
4. The camera uses 35mm film and is focused through a nonpinhole lens substituted for the pinhole shooting lens.

While cameras such as these work well, constructing them entails more trouble than most modelmakers are willing to accept.

Lens and Lens Extenders

The lens systems listed below may be used for model photography and will result in the described effects accompanying each.

1. The regular lens of a camera with an inexpensive portrait lens attachment permits focusing at closer objects but diminishes depth of field. (This type of lens attachment is not needed on a camera, such as a press camera, which has its lens mounted on a bellows system. Numbers 2 and 4 are also unnecessary for this type of camera.)
2. An extension tube inserted between the regular lens of the camera and the camera, as with the portrait lens, permits focusing at closer objects but diminishes depth of field. Tubes tend to flatten out the perspective of the subject.
3. A bellows inserted between the lens and the camera tends to flatten out the perspective of the subject.
4. Using a telephoto lens and moving the camera farther from the model increases depth of field but flattens the scene, making it look shallow.
5. Using a wide-angle lens improves depth of field of any given camera-to-subject distance and exaggerates depth of the scene, making it look deeper. The lens also makes the scene smaller and includes more in the picture. Most professionals use this type of lens for eye level close-up model shots. In fact, the wide-angle lens used on a press-type view camera is the combination of equipment most often used.
6. Using a disc with a small (pinhole) opening inserted at the focal point of the lens works like a large f opening, providing great depth of field. The scene is not fore-shortened or exaggerated in depth. A pinhole lens can give a picture that has a depth of field of from $6''$ to $3'$. The pinhole lens may be made of thin metal ($0.007''$ brass, for example) sheet. Drill a hole (a No. 71 drill often works well) in the center of the disc and chamfer the hole from both sides so that in cross section its sides look like Vs. Paint all but the chamfered hole a flat black. Blacken the chamfer by holding it over a lighted candle. Now rate the lens for its f number. In general, a pinhole lens with an opening smaller than f 120 is impractical on a 50mm lens. If the lens has a longer focal length, a smaller opening may be used. When a light meter is not calibrated to show the exposure required with an f opening as small as the one above, the exposure may be found with the following formula:

$$\frac{(\text{the square of the } f \text{ number}) \times (\text{the exposure recommended with any } f \text{ number shown on the meter})}{\text{the square of the above } f \text{ number (this is shown on the meter)}} = \text{the exposure to be used}$$

The disc must now be inserted in the lens at its exact focal point. It is advisable to have this operation done at a camera repair shop. Some photographs taken with a f 64 pinhole lens have had a depth of field from a few inches to $100'$.

21-1.
This photograph is of a midtown area where four new major buildings were to be constructed. It was taken with a fish-eye lens from the top floor of a nearby office tower. (*Photograph by Nathaniel Lieberman*)

21-2.
A photocomposite of the site and models of the new towers (see figure 21-1) shows how buildings collectively affect the skyline. The result is realistic for two reasons. The models, provided by individual architectural firms, are all highly detailed; and each model was photographed with a fish-eye lens to carefully match the same angle and lighting conditions of the midtown view. (*Photograph by Nathaniel Lieberman*)

7. The regular lens is used by most professional photographers for taking long, bird's-eye model shots.

8. Using a regular lens, moving the camera far from the model, enlarging the resulting print, and cropping off the unwanted border increases depth of field but also produces a flat-looking picture similar to that obtained with a telephoto lens.

LENS EXTENSION TUBES. These are used to allow the lens to focus on close objects. They are sold by the manufacturers of a large number of quality cameras to fit their own cameras. Tubes are inserted into the lens system of the camera, which, in turn, must be focused through ground glass (if the camera is equipped with it), since the distance scale on the lens will no longer be applicable. If the camera has no ground glass, depth of field and point of focus must be established in the following way:

1. Remove the back of the camera.

2. On the film rolls, insert a strip of tracing paper held in the position that would be normally occupied by unexposed film.

3. Use the paper as a substitute for ground glass. Open the lens aperture as wide as possible and experimentally move the camera forward and backward until the subject is in sharp focus on the paper.

4. Measure the distance from the lens to the part of the subject which is in sharpest focus and the distance from the lens to the closest and farthest parts of the subject which are in acceptably good focus. This establishes the new depth of field and the distance from the subject at which the camera must be held. Also note the width of the field that is captured by the lens.

5. Make a complete series of tests by placing the camera at various distances from the model. Another tube will naturally require a new set of tests.

Conversely, when constructing your own tube for general use or even for taking one specific shot, the length that will be needed may be calculated in the following way:

1. Locate the camera (with its back removed and tracing paper inserted into its rollers if the camera does not have ground glass focusing) at the distance from the subject at which the picture is to be taken.

2. Unscrew the lens of the camera and, holding it by hand, move it back and forth between the camera and the test subject until the image is in focus. Record the distance that the tube must span.

3. Construct the tube at that length.

The homemade tube may be made from a mailing tube painted dull black inside. It may be wedged on the lens. Before attempting to produce a homemade tube, however, ask the camera store or the manufacturer of the camera whether or not a tube may be inserted into the lens system and, if so, at what point.

PORTRAIT LENSES. These may be obtained in sets from the manufacturers of many quality cameras. The lens are numbered by strength, from 1^+ up to 10^+. They can be used one at a time or coupled to add up to a higher rating (this is done by simultaneously using a 3^+ and a 1^+ to equal 4^+, etc.). The stronger lens should be closer to the camera. Portrait lenses make depth of field rather unsubstantial. The following table explains what happens when a 35mm candid camera is used with a 50mm lens set at f 22, or what happens when a 2¼″ × 2¼″ reflex camera with a 75mm to 80mm lens is set at f 32:

Portrait lens(es) used	Camera focused at	Distance of lens to subject	Depth of field
1^+	4′	22″	4″ to 7½″ = 3½″
3^+ and 3^+	4′	5½″	⅜″ to ⅜″ = nil

The wider the lens is opened, the more the depth of field is diminished, and the center of clear focus moves in toward the lens. Naturally, the camera may be focused at over 4′, the camera pushed back, and a deeper depth of field achieved. Portrait lenses do not cut down the light that reaches the film, so their use does not require additional exposure factor.

BELLOWS. These may be obtained from the manufacturers of several quality candid and reflex cameras for use with their own camera products. They serve the same purpose as portrait lenses or extension tubes but have the additional feature of being able to be focused with greater versatility. Some even have tilts, swings, and other actions.

WIDE-ANGLE LENSES. The wider the angle of the lens (the shorter its focal length), the greater depth of field it can achieve. Objects in the foreground seem closer and those in the background appear farther away than with a regular lens, thus dramatizing the perspective of the photo. The lens also covers a wide arc, one which is closer to what is seen by the unaided eye.

PERSPECTIVE-CORRECTING LENSES. This type of lens is constructed so that its component optics can be shifted off axis. This performs the same basic correction as raising or shifting a press camera lens sideways. Thus a P.C. lens (as it is called) can be used to kill the convergence that will be photographed if you stand at he base of a tall building and take a picture of it with he camera pointing up.

MODELSCOPE. The Modelscope lens system, especially engineered for close-up and realistic, wide-angle photography of models, measures 12″ by about ⅟₁₅″ in diameter (at its front end). These dimensions allow the lens to be placed at scale eye level inside the models, between buildings, or into rooms so that prospective inhabitants can visualize how the finished edifice will look. In this way, the Modelscope allows an examination of the model in ways that were heretofore impossible. The instrument has an impressive depth of field (5mm to infinity when viewing by eye).

21-3.
Austin Condominiums
Greshman, Smith and Partners, Architects
Modelmakers: Rick Rosson and Jim Langford

This progression of photographs taken through a modelscope simulates a realistic eye level view of the building at four different points on the site.

Filters

Aside from color-compensating filters that allow the use of outdoor color film with artificial illumination and vice versa, filters are seldom used on model photography, but there are some exceptions. When taking black-and-white cloud shots for use as background, the various yellow filters may be used to accentuate the image of the cloud. The most dramatic cloud effects possible are obtained by using an infrared filter. It both increases the whiteness of the clouds (and in many instances records clouds on the film which are not visible to the naked eye) and darkens the sky.

Since a filter of a given color allows the passage of light of only that color, it is possible, when taking black-and-white photos, to accentuate areas of the model by using a filter. For instance, in a model that is green and blue, a green filter will allow all the light coming from the green parts of the model to get to the film. At the same time, much of the light coming from the blue part of the model will not be transmitted. The green parts of the model will, therefore, appear lighter, and more of their detail will be observable than without a filter. The blue parts will appear darker. A red filter will darken blues and greens almost to black, lighten reds and yellows almost to white, and only slightly darken browns. A yellow filter will darken blues, browns, and greens, and will lighten reds. These effects can be achieved with panchromatic film only. Orthochromatic film produces different results.

Filters cut the total amount of light that reaches the film; therefore, a longer exposure is needed.

Film

Most of the photographs in this book were taken with panchromatic film such as: Plus-X, Super XX, Tri-X, Royal Pan, or Super Panchro Press B. Choice of film seems to be one of personal preference, since most of these films work in the hands of those who know them, with roughly the same excellence.

Some films are better than others for specific applications. If the shots must be greatly enlarged, for example, use a fine-grain film (such as Ansco Super Hypan, or Kodak Panatomic-X or Plus-X) and fine-grain developer. Always use a film that gives good contrast between the dark and light areas of the photographs. Since a tripod must be used, film speed is of little importance.

If the model has both very dark and very light areas, it will be necessary to solve the problem of how to illuminate the dark areas so that their detail will be observable and yet not overilluminate and "burn" out the neighboring light parts. In these instances, it is best to use a film of moderate contrast and to overexpose the photo slightly. The negative can then be slightly underdeveloped in a soft working developer. This procedure darkens the white areas and lightens the dark ones.

Photographs that are to be made into color prints will be of better quality if they are taken on film that produces a negative, not on film that makes a slide. The negative may also be used to make color slides. If both color and black-and-white prints of a shot are desired, the picture should be shot on both types of film rather than trying to make a black-and-white print from a color negative. The latter procedure more often than not produces inferior results.

Light Meters

Light meters are an absolute necessity. Some people may develop an "eye" for judging light intensity and relating it to exposure time and lens aperture, but this is extremely hard to achieve and is always a gamble. Use a meter that measures reflected light, preferably a meter that only picks up light from a narrow angle. Take readings of various parts of the model, making mental note of how the readings change from part to part. This change reflects the degree of brightness (or darkness) of each part of the model. If the range is too great for the picture contemplated, consider changing the lighting. If the readings are satisfactory, decide which reading to "favor" when selecting exposure time and aperture. Keep in mind what this selection will do to the other parts of the picture: will it cause overly dark or bright areas or loss of detail due to under- or overexposure?

Correct exposure is more vital and critical in color photography than it is in black-and-white. An underexposed color photograph will result in a loss of color as well as in a dark print.

Some photographers take a test shot with a Polaroid camera. The immediately developed shot is studied to modify their lighting and exposure.

Tripods

Because it is always important to obtain the greatest possible depth of field, the lens will invariably have to be closed down as much as possible. This necessitates using long exposures. To make these extended exposures and to focus the camera and compose the picture requires a well-built tripod. To bring the camera close to the model, get a tripod whose head and central shaft can be placed on the tripod legs in an inverted position. This will allow the camera to be mounted upside down. Carefully place the legs of the tripod on the base of he model and lower the camera until its top almost ouches the model or its baseboard. This procedure will allow the camera to be brought in closer to the model han could be achieved by standing the tripod on the loor alongside the model and setting the camera upon t.

The tripod should allow the camera to be elevated to a height of at least 6'. Additional height may be obtained by mounting the tripod on a table. The tripod should have a head that can be swung 360°, precisely cranked up and down, and tilted up or down a full 180°. The tripod should be picked for its sturdiness, even if this means using a somewhat bulky and heavy model. Many finely constructed tripods have legs that telescope out to their full length. The sections are then made secure by turning a knurled sleeve. It is often hard to turn these sleeves to release them, so a monkey wrench may be a needed accessory in your equipment bag.

BACKGROUNDS

A model, unlike many other photographic subjects, does not usually have a ready-made background. This must be supplied by the photographer. One choice is to set up a board, painting, or photograph (figure 21-4) behind

21-4.
New York Convention Center
I.M. Pei & Partners, Architects

Because this model had to be photographed in a gallery setting, a large backdrop could not be set up. Instead, a large photograph, which was part of the model presentation display, was placed behind the model. (*Photograph by Nathaniel Lieberman*)

the model and photograph them together. Most professional photographers use either a large photograph of clouds or white clouds airbrushed on a blue paper background (the work of more than a few professional photographers can be identified by the cloud formations they invariably use). A photograph of the model can also be cut out and pasted onto a photo of a background; the resulting composition is then photographed and the new negative used to make all future prints. Or the model may be photographed against a prototype background (figure 21-5). Another solution is to use a wall, or sheets or rolls of plain white or colored paper or cardboard, as background.

For more complicated arrangements, use a large sheet of opaque glass for a screen on which color or black-and-white slides can be rear projected. A good substitute for the glass is tracing paper sandwiched between two sheets of plain glass or a sheet of tracing paper mounted in a wood frame. Make color slides for projection by using slide-producing color film. Black-and-white slides may be made directly if direct positive film is used, or favorite cloud shots may be sent to a processing lab and reproduced onto slides.

Interesting effects can be created with light. Use white or light gray material for black-and-white photos or blue material for color shots. Provide a halo or other model-framing effects with spotlights.

Photographing the Background

Because the background is flat, projected, or luminescent, and the model is three-dimensional, a different and sometimes conflicting lighting problem arises. Most photographers evenly floodlight their photographs or painted-on sky backgrounds (one 300-watt bulb or so per two or three running feet of background). They then spotlight and floodlight their model, being careful to achieve model lighting that is of an intensity consistent with that of the background and also being careful not to cast model shadows on the background. This approach is the simplest and should be used whenever possible.

Other photographers, on the other hand, sometimes light and photograph their background separately, having placed a black cloth over the foreground. They then cover the background with a black board or cloth, remove the cloth from the foreground, light it, and photograph it on the same negative. In this way they can achieve perfect exposure for both subjects. An alternative to this procedure is to illuminate and photograph the model, being careful that no light falls on the backdrop, and then illuminate and photograph only the backdrop. Both exposures are taken in the same frame.

Split Matting

In this method, the model and background are set up together but, with the use of masks, they are photographed (or printed) separately. The model and its background may be viewed through the ground glass of the press camera. Trace the silhouette of the model on a piece of tracing paper mounted on the glass. Cut two cardboard masks, one to obscure the foreground, the other to obscure the background. Put the background-obscuring mask in front of the film holder and photograph the foreground at the exposure needed. Then repeat this procedure with the foreground obscuring mask.

It is also possible to photograph the model in front of a black background; print this picture in the darkroom, with a cardboard mask covering the sky portion of the printing paper; and then cover the part of the print that has the image of the model with a mask, and print a sky negative on the print. This technique permits you to increase or decrease brightness and move cloud shots around in relation to the foreground.

Use stock photographs (see "Photographs-Stock" in the *Yellow Pages*) for the sky backgrounds or photograph your own (photograph the clouds through an infrared filter for a more dramatic shot). Another possibility is to use stylized backgrounds, representing a skyline or cityscape, cut from black board and mounted on the backdrop or on flats in front of a sky backdrop. An out-of-focus background sometimes works well.

LIGHTING

Lighting is used to create shadows that emphasize the form and texture of parts of the subject, to articulate curved surfaces, to illuminate deep recesses of the model, and to bring the overall illumination of the subject to a level that allows a reasonably short exposure time. All these uses should be kept in mind when arranging lights for each photograph. The arrangement may be creatively thought through for each photograph, a procedure that produces the best results. Or photographs may be mutually grouped into basic types and each of these types illuminated in an almost routine way. Surprisingly enough, this works well most of the time, and many successful photographers use a set order for placing their lamps. They use only slight modifications when they encounter an atypical model shape or texture that needs special treatment.

Basic light layouts are usually planned around: a main light that is used to represent the sun and that creates the major shadow; one or more secondary or "high"

lights to define important surfaces and textures and to create a separation between the model and its background; "fill-in" lights to bring out sufficient detail in areas that are put into shadow by the primary and secondary lights; and lights used to illuminate the background.

Lighting Equipment

The basic lighting equipment for a simple studio should consist of a main spotlight of as high as 750 watts (if the models are large), and several lamps with lower (200 to 300) wattage. The smaller lamps may have built-in reflectors that produce a flood or a spot effect, or they may be screwed into metal reflectors. The latter arrangement is cheapest in the long run. Sealed beam lights (650 watts) are useful for the illumination of large models. The life expectancy of the replaceable bulb of these lights is about ten hours, which is considerably better than that of most photographic bulbs.

Some of the lamps should be set into sockets that have clamp ends. Others can be set into sockets that screw into inexpensive tripods. A 10″ reflector, socket with clamp-on swivel end, and cord can be purchased from many camera stores.

Also available are miniature spotlights that, at the turn of a lever, will give the effect of either a spotlight or a diffused floodlight. Fresnel lenses placed over spots will soften their outline.

Metal or wood hoops that hold light-diffusing material are also available. These are mounted onto the reflectors by means of clips and serve to spread the light more evenly.

Have available a supply of extension cords, white cardboard that can be cut into light masks or used as reflectors, tape to hold the cardboard masks to the metal reflectors, a few square feet of tin or aluminum foil (this is pressed into a crinkled form and then cemented to cardboard) from which multifaceted reflectors can be made, and mirrors. In addition, color-compensating filters are essential when using outdoor color film with artificial lighting or when using a type of light that is not compatible with indoor color film.

THE MAIN LIGHT. Since the main light emulates the sun, it is usually a spotlight placed high above the model (figure 21-6). Try not to locate this light on the side of the model that represents north, since this can never happen in nature. If the primary light comes from over the camera, it will tend to flatten out the model. Illumination from the rear of the model silhouettes it and kills detail that is observable from the camera position. Side illumination usually gives the model an interesting shadowing of its mass but will reveal any crudity of

detail or sloppiness of construction. Front illumination produces the most satisfactory color rendition on color shots.

The overall illumination level of the photographic area may be raised by bouncing a large floodlight off the ceiling or walls of the room, or off sheets of white paper hung around the model or hung in front of the camera (with a hole cut out for the lens).

21-6.
Northwest Tower, Hyattsville, Maryland
VVKR Incorporated, Architects
Modelmaker: Architectural Presentations Associates
Scale: ⅛″ = 1′
Material: milled Plexiglas

A strong directional light source illuminates the front facades of these towers, drawing attention to the crisp detail of the models. (*Photograph by J. Alexander*)

SECONDARY LIGHTS. Floodlights are often used for secondary lights. These must be placed so that they do not cause secondary shadows, which are contrary to what can happen in nature.

The best position for secondary lights may be most easily established if you place the main light above the model and stand at various spots around the model, inspecting it for surfaces that need to be highlighted. When you see a surface that needs secondary lighting, place a lamp where you are standing and aim it at the surface to be illuminated; then go back to the camera and examine the lighting through its ground glass. Adjust the intensity of the secondary lights by moving them closer or farther from the model until a good balance is achieved.

Different types of surfaces require different types of lights. Matte surfaces generally require spotlights to bring out their detail. Shiny objects require diffused spotlights for detail and to prevent glare. To emphasize texture, have the light glance across the surface at a low angle. Incidentally, textures, because of the play of light and shadow they create, often contribute more to the tonal values in a black-and-white photograph than does the color of the material.

Spotlights create shadows that have a sharp edge and give little illumination of the area within the shadow. Floodlights produce an indistinct shadow line and illuminate the area within the shadow to a greater degree. Back lighting adds to the three-dimensionality of the subject. Test the effect of the lights by moving them around until the best composition is achieved. Try to imagine making a charcoal drawing of a group of forms, and use the lights to create the proper impression of mass on each form in the design.

If the model has both very dark and very light areas, both of which must be seen in detail, keep illumination off the white areas by masking the lights with cardboard cut in the proper shape.

Early morning and late afternoon sun and shadows can be simulated by lamps placed at low levels (figure 21-7). To produce shadows cast on the model by trees, hills, and buildings outside camera range (and those that have not been modeled), cut masks out of cardboard and hold them in front of a lamp.

FILL-IN LIGHTS. To prevent fill-in lights from casting shadows, place them at a low angle. If a mirror or white cardboard is used to bounce light from the main or from a secondary light, you may dispense with separate fill-in lights. Diffused flood lamps or a flood with a reflector may also be used as fill-in lights. Small mirrors may be placed inside or on top of the model to bounce light into small hard-to-reach areas. These mirrors may be obscured from the camera by parts of the model.

They may be held in place with tape and may be partially masked to provide any desired shape of reflecting surface. Small areas of the model may be illuminated if a mask is cut from cardboard and placed in front of a light.

If the illumination scheme does not throw enough light on the model to allow focusing through ground glass, use a hand-held, high-wattage lamp to pan around the model as it is checked through the glass.

Illuminating Shiny Surfaces

Some part or all of the model (figure 21-8) may have a shiny surface that causes unwanted reflections or light flares. To correct this, evenly light the shiny surface or spray it with matting spray. Very even illumination can be achieved by placing screens in front of the lamps or by constructing a "tent" around the model (the tent is made of white paper hung from rollers or from the ceiling of the studio). Position lamps inside the tent and aim them at its walls. The tent can also be constructed from an acetatelike material called matte Kodacel. Lights are placed outside this tent and are aimed toward the model at about the same position in which they would be arranged to illuminate a nonshiny model. The Kodacel evenly spreads out the light. For both these setups, the lamps should throw their penumbras above the view of the camera. Use floodlights, unless an area is to be highlighted, in which case use a spotlight.

Once you have taken care of the overall shine, you may bring out one or more controlled shiny highlights by introducing a spotlight directly on the model. Controlled reflections may also be created on the shiny parts with strips of gray paper pinned to the interior of the walls of the tent. If the reflection produced has too sharp an outline, subdue it by using an unevenly sprayed piece of paper.

Full tenting, naturally, will produce a more even, pristine lighting on the model—not the natural lighting caused by the main, secondary, fill-in light arrangement. But tenting allows a starting arrangement from which you can experiment introducing a main light to form a dramatic shadow.

Using matting spray is less complicated than using a tent. With the spray, any dramatic lighting scheme desired can be fully retained. Matting spray eliminates shine, replacing it with a luster. The spray broadens highlights and allows the camera to catch additional detail. Be sure that the spray used is compatible with all the plastic or painted surfaces to which it is applied. Photographers of still life often use a brush-on cosmetic liner such as screen and stage make-up, which is compatible with plastics, metals, etc.

21-7.
The New York State Pavilion at the 1964–
  65 New York World's Fair
Philip Johnson Associates, Architects
Modelmaker: Joseph Santeramo of the
  architects' model shop
Scale: ⅛″ = 1′
Materials: painted acrylic and brass

This photograph was taken with a 4″ × 5″
Sinar view camera, 90mm Angulon lens, and
Super Panchro Press "B" film. Two floodlights
illuminated the airbrushed background. One
750-watt spot placed low and to the right of
the model provided its major illumination.
Fill-in light was used to bring out some of
the detail lost in the shadow caused by the
spot. (*Photograph by Louis Checkman*)

21-8.
Gateway in Singapore
I.M. Pei & Partners, Architects
Modelmakers: architects' model studio
Scale: ⅛″ = 1′

Photographing models with large shiny surfaces, like this one, is not easy. This photo,
however, is an excellent example of how
reflections can be controlled to create realistic
effects. Lights were carefully positioned not
only to avoid glare, but also to draw out as
much detail as possible. (*Photograph by
Nathaniel Lieberman*)

Photographing the Model Out-of-Doors

While natural lighting produces a sharp shadow (if the sun is out) and eliminates the necessity of procuring and setting up artificial lights, its drawbacks make it of little use except for taking rush pictures when a lighting setup is not readily available. Besides the handicaps of wind, dust, and, possibly, an audience, outdoor setups will not provide the secondary and fill-in lights that are needed for truly polished photographs.

PLANNING THE PHOTOGRAPH

Photographic angles should be planned as carefully as the construction of the model is. You may have to make sketches to show the placement of lights and cameras. Important photographs must be especially well planned. Take many different poses of the model, even though these shots are not to be part of any foreseeable presentation. An hour or so spent taking a number of extra shots is not a waste of time. Many of these photos have a way of becoming "sleepers," and replace other photographs in the presentation. To decide on the angles to take, move the camera around the model, sighting it every 30° at three or more elevations.

Never assume that color shots can be copied in black and white. While occasionally the results will be satisfactory, most of the time the copy will have a rather odd-looking tonal quality. If a Kodachrome 35mm color slide is enlarged to an 8″ × 10″ black-and-white flat, it will lose sharpness. Only a quarter of the good color shots you may attempt to copy in black and white will turn out well. When taking color slides or photographs, also take a black-and-white shot from each viewpoint just for the records or for use in publications that cannot reproduce color.

Camera Viewpoint

Overall bird's-eye photographs present only moderate focusing or background problems (figure 21-9). It is with eye level and interior shots that serious complications arise. Select and plan these shots by determining the angles at which the actual building will be viewed and by determining which of these will make the best photographic presentations. Photographs should be composed like renderings or paintings, with foreground objects framing the model, with a carefully planned major center of interest, and, perhaps, with one or more minor centers of interest.

Convergence

To understand convergence, study photographs of actual buildings, interiors, and models. Note that photographs of buildings tend to have a more dramatic appearance. Their foreground elements seem closer to the viewer and their horizontal lines seem to converge more abruptly toward the horizon. Model photographs (especially those done by the unskilled photographer) often seem flat, with the foreground too close to the background. This is probably because they were photographed from a distance greater (when scale is taken into consideration) than that used to shoot a real building. To compensate for this, photograph the model from a close camera position, and use a wide-angle lens to make foreground elements appear to be closer to the viewer. This creates greater and more dramatic horizontal line convergence.

Focus

When photographing the front of an actual house, you would probably have to stand perhaps 100′ from the building to get its entire facade in the picture. To add interest and artistic balance, you might include a tree in the foreground of the picture, its trunk framing one side of the picture and its lower branches framing the top. Thus, you would focus the lens on the front facade of the house (100′ away), on the farthest parts of the house that would be seen in the picture (perhaps 140′ away), and on the tree (8′ away). To reproduce this scene with great clarity, the lens would have to have a depth of field (the distance between the closest and farthest objects that are in reasonably sharp focus) of from 8′ to 140′. This capacity is not at all uncommon among even low-priced cameras, as long as their focus

21-9.
Chase Manhattan Bank
Skidmore, Owings & Merrill, Architects
Modelmaker: Theodore Conrad
Scale: 1/16″ = 1′

The skillfully executed detail of the model is brought out by dramatic lighting and the camera angle used. Mullions and columns are made of metal extrusions precisely inlaid into the acrylic grooves cut in walls. Because these walls were clear, it was necessary to construct each floor slab. These floors and the interior columns contribute to the internal bracing of this hollow model. The exterior walls of all the surrounding buildings were made from wood, and tinted acrylic was used for the windows. The plaza was made from scribed wood. (*Photograph by Ezra Stoller*)

21-10.
One Logan Square
Kohn Pedersen Fox, Architects
Modelmaker: George Awad
Scale: ⅛″ = 1′

This photocomposite shows the proposed building in its intended site. The photograph of the site was taken from a helicopter at a time of day when the lighting brought out the sharpest detail and created no harsh shadows. The model, also shown in figure 21-11, was photographed at the corresponding angle and under duplicated lighting conditions. This second photograph was then superimposed on the helicopter shot. (*Photograph by Jack Horner*)

and lens openings are adjustable. A moderately priced candid camera, for instance, will produce a sharp image of objects from 10' to infinity when its lens is stopped down to f 8 and it is focused at 20'.

In photographing a ¼' = 1' scale model of the same house and tree, the following dimensions would be pertinent: lens-to-tree distance, 2"; lens to facade, 25"; and lens to farthest part of house, 35". Thus the lens must be capable of focusing sharply on objects that are from 2" to 35" from its lens. No unmodified candid or reflex camera can do this. A candid will produce a sharp image of objects 1'11" to 6'10" away if it is focused at 3' (its closest focus) and if the lens is closed down to f 32 (the smallest stop for the lens). To increase the depth of field, the lens must be closed down. This is accomplished by setting it at a high f number. Incidentally, the f number equals the focal length of the lens (the distance of the focal point of the lens to the film) over the opening of the diaphragm.

Taking this shot with a lens that cannot give a sharp picture of both the foreground and the house will result in a technically poor picture and, perhaps worse, one with an unrealistic, modellike feeling. Some photographers try to solve the focus problem by moving the camera back until the increasing depth of field covers the entire model. For example, on the ¼" scale model, the camera should be positioned about 2' from the tree. Thus it would be on a scale 100' from the tree and 200' from the house. This would result in a shot that is sharp from the tree to far behind the house (the ground between the tree and the camera would be blurred, but it could be cropped from the print); however, the tree would no longer frame the scene, and the location of the vanishing points of the house would change, altering the dramatic perspective that a photograph of an actual building has. All this makes the shot look like that of a model.

To make the close-up focusing capabilities of candid and reflex cameras more like those of press-type cameras, it is possible to use a portrait lens over the regular lens of the camera and to insert a lens extension tube or bellows between the camera and its normal lens in order to change its focal point. These two techniques will solve the problem of close-up focusing, but owners of candid and reflex cameras will still face the limitation of a shallow depth of field.

Press cameras with double and triple extension bellows have lenses that can be moved out many inches (or even feet) from the film plate, thus providing the possibility of focusing on objects that are fractions of an inch away from the lens. This allows the camera to focus on anything, but does not improve its depth of field. In fact, the closer a lens is focused, the shallower

its depth of field becomes. To gain the depth of field needed when taking close-up model shots with a press camera (or with other cameras that can be focused extremely close), use a pinhole lens that has a huge f rating, or a very expensive lens system with a large depth of field.

Foreground blurring is usually disturbing. However, background blurring often permits photographing a model in front of a crude backdrop. Also, a blurred background may, at times, minimize competition for the viewer's attention.

SPECIALIZED PHOTOGRAPHS

Photocomposites

Combining photographs of the model with other photographs can be used to add shots of existing buildings, backgrounds, and other surroundings to the presentation of the model (figures 21-10 and 21-11) (this may even eliminate model construction of existing buildings); to combine model photographs with rendered plans, elevations, or perspectives for an original presentation; to add photos of cars, people, furniture, and so on, to the model shot; or to combine all of the above in one presentation.

All shots to be included in the photocomposite must be planned so that the objects depicted are photographed from the same angle above the horizon and illuminated from the same side. When photocompositing shots of automobiles and the modeled facades along which they are parked or the street facades of existing buildings and the street facade of the model, be sure that the facades are all at the same angle to the camera. Work with prints that are double or more the size of the intended reproduction. When reproduced at half size, small miscuts and other blemishes will not be visible. Color backgrounds may also be combined with black-and-white model photos, and vice versa, for unusual effects. Correct-size photographs of people and cars may be pasted directly on prints of the photograph of the model. These may be either specially shot for the composite or come from a stockpile of pictures.

For more realistic photocomposites, shadows should be cast from the objects shown in one photograph onto another. Shadows may be made with overlay sheets.

Foreground objects, such as cars, trees, etc., may be photographs pasted on cardboard and set up in the model. The entire assembly (model and foreground entourage) is then shot. This helps to reduce the depth of field that is needed to make a sharp composition.

When attempting to superimpose a photograph of the

surroundings of the building onto the photograph of the model, use the following procedure:

1. Before photographing the model, visit the site and note the desirability of the background and the best angles and elevations for taking background shots. Determine whether or not a camera can be conveniently set up at these viewpoints. Make a sketch of the site, including the elevations of the roofs of surrounding buildings and other locations at which the camera will be set up. Bring the camera on this trip and, with its viewfinder, determine the borders of shots to be taken from desirable viewpoints.

21-11.
The One Logan Square model used in the photocomposite shown in figure 21-10.

2. When photographing the model, attempt to take some shots from each horizontal and vertical angle that was impressive at the site.

3. Use a lighting setup similar to natural conditions.

4. Select the best photographs for the composite, noting the direction of their illumination. You should revisit the site to match this lighting.

5. Take several pictures at the site from each of the selected angles, varying the exposures and filters. If a camera with a ground glass viewer is available, insert the negative of the model shot (protected by a cellophane envelope) into it and precisely match the angle of the background.

THE DUNNING PROCESS. This is a way to avoid the laborious cutting out of photographs to be used as overlays in a photocomposite. Photograph the intended background and make a slide of the shot. Tone the slide with transparent yellow dye and place it in front of unexposed film in the camera. Set up the model against a plain white board background, and then illuminate the model with yellow light and the background with purple light. In the photograph, the yellow light coming from the model will pass through the yellow slide and record the image of the model on the film. The purple light of the background will illuminate the slide and allow the detail on it to be transferred to the film. In the areas where no purple light comes from the setup, there will be no overlapping of background and model images since the background slide will not transfer to the film.

Photo Drawing

It is sometimes necessary to draw on a photo print. For interesting presentation pictures, combine techniques and render part of a project on the model photo. It may also be useful to add titles or dimensions to the photograph. In some cases, working drawings have been made by taking photos of the detailed design model and adding dimensions and notes to the prints. It has been found that in the design of complex piping, for example, this technique is more easily understood than conventional drawings are.

Various techniques may be used for lettering and simple drawing. White lines may be made on a print by applying a bleach solution with a ruling or drawing pen; or use white ink on matte prints. The solution is concocted from potassium iodide (2 ounces), iodine (90 grams), gum arabic (90 grains), and water (8 ounces). Use black India ink to make black lines on matte prints.

If an entire part of a print must be obliterated so the area can be rendered completely, mount paper on it and render this area with pencil, ink, or watercolor. The resulting modified print can then be photocopied and a supply of prints made from the resulting negative.

It is also possible to ink directly on the back of the negative, although this is not recommended because of the likelihood of failure. A safer procedure is to tape a sheet of acetate that is treated to take ink to the

negative and to do pen work on that. Both negative and sheet may then be printed together through the enlarger.

Follow these steps for extensive photo drawing:

1. Photograph the model.
2. Project this image through a magenta contact screen and contact print it on a high-contrast film. This results in a halftone or a screen positive, which is necessary if the model has been constructed of materials that have more than two colors, or if the model's shadows should show on the print. The screen brings about tone separation through its use of black dots on a white background or white dots on a black background.
3. Position the halftone over a positive showing the border lines and title block of the drawing. This sandwich is then printed on a sheet of autopositive matte film.

Other processes can also be used. The following one is simple and of use to the architect and designer:

1. Photograph the model (which should be painted with flat lacquers or paints to prevent undesirable highlights). Use Royal Pan film and illuminate the model from all sides by diffused light. Avoid overhead lights since they cause deep shadows.
2. Develop the negative and make a Kodalith film at the desired scale.
3. Draw on the film with pencil or ink. Parts of the photo image may be removed with standard drafting room eradicators.
4. Make diazo, blue-line, or black-line prints of the results. The size of Kodalith film limits the drawing to a 24″ × 36″ maximum.

Black-and-White Photographs of Color Models

When photographing a color model in black and white, make sure its colors end up in a reasonably pleasant and contrasting assortment of gray tones. If a model is painted in several harmonious colors and appears in a black-and-white print to have too many similar tones of gray to provide contrast, correct this problem with lighting that raises or lowers the tones of various surfaces or with color filters that distort the brightness of certain colors. Make a test exposure of color charts of the paints, boards, and other materials with each type of black-and-white film used. Study these tests and determine which colors must be specially illuminated or filtered in any photograph.

"Night," "Sunset," and "Fog" Photographs

Night photographs make interesting secondary shots of any model that is internally lit. The lights of the model must provide even lighting, or at least lighting that is as constant as is desired. Some bulbs may have to be shielded to prevent them from shining into the camera. Small reflectors whose outside surfaces are painted black can be mounted in front of objectionable model lights to prevent glare from reaching the lens. Additional lights can be made by mounting miniature bulbs on dowels, 2' to 3' long, held to illuminate those parts of the model that do not have enough light. The lights of the model may also be augmented by placing small flashlights inside the model or behind it.

While it is usually best not to allow an unshielded miniature light to be photographed, sometimes doing just that can add the realistic touch of halation to the picture. Halation is the spreading out of light coming from an unshielded bulb to form a sunburstlike radiance pattern. It makes the picture look as if it were taken in the rain. Halation may be created by taking the picture through a piece of insect screening. This forms four-pointed stars; to create eight-pointed stars, take it through two pieces of screening held so that their threads cross one another diagonally.

For dramatic *sunset* (or sunrise) photographs, low-light the model from its side or rear. The internal lights of the model may burn too strongly into the film if exposure is based on the internal plus the low level external illumination of the model. To rectify this, expose the photograph with the model illuminated only by the external lights. Then, without moving the camera and on the same film, take a shot that is exposed only by the internal lights of the model. This procedure may also be used when photographing interior shots that are illuminated by miniature lights as well as by auxiliary photo lamps.

Fog can be simulated in photographs by smearing Vaseline on a sheet of clear glass and holding it about a foot in front of the camera lens, or by placing a diffusion disc over the lens.

Photographing Tight Places

A modelscope can be used to photograph viewpoints inaccessible to the camera. Another method is to shoot them off a mirror aimed at the desired view. The camera must be focused for the distance from lens to mirror plus the distance from the mirror to the image.

DARKROOM TRICKS

Once a negative is out of the camera, there are several creative innovations that can be used to process it. It is generally a good practice to select a processing laboratory that is geared to and noted for high-quality work. The premium price—and it may run an additional 100%—is very little considering that it has to be applied only against developing negatives and making contact sheets, master prints, and 8″ × 10″ negatives. The rest of the photos may then be made by a regular printer as contact prints from the 8″ × 10″ negatives.

Among the things that may be achieved in the darkroom are:

1. Manipulation of the enlarging processes to compensate for negatives or parts of negatives that are too dark or too light.
2. Burning an interesting horizon halo into the enlargement. This is done by cutting a cardboard template in the shape of the horizon and allowing the light of the enlarger to burn in the halo while the rest of the print is kept dark by the template.
3. Enlarging through a "homemade" or commercially obtainable screen (a texture printed on clear acetate), usually placed in contact with the printing paper.
4. Achieving a soft diffused focus by enlarging the negative through a diffusing filter.
5. By tipping the easel of the enlarger, printing pictures of models of high buildings with convergence similar to the distortion found in photographs of actual buildings.
6. Achieving photocomposites in the darkroom by printing parts of several negatives on one piece of enlarging paper.

For this last darkroom technique, the negatives must be masked and individually projected through the enlarger. Masks are made by tracing parts of the negative on a sheet of tracing paper and then transferring this to a sheet of cardboard (mask 1), or by projecting the image of the negative through the enlarger on a sheet of cardboard, and then tracing and cutting out the intended lines of demarcation (mask 2). Mask 1 must be used while sandwiched with the negative. Mask 2 is placed on top of the enlarging paper. These techniques of achieving photocomposites have their drawbacks inasmuch as it can be fairly difficult to cut masks accurately.

The emphasis of certain parts of the finished photo can also be altered. A background may be partially eliminated by putting a black or white acetate overlay sheet over it. These sheets are covered by a film that

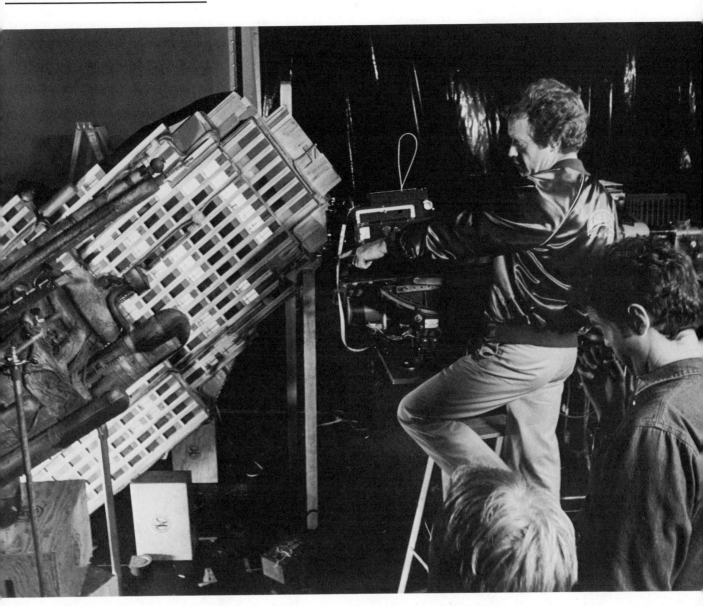

21-12.
Blade Runner
Warner Bros. (A Ladd Company Release)

The camera angle in this movie shot is from the point of view of a character in a flying vehicle. Because the vehicle must appear to be spiralling down from above, one model has been tipped to afford views of the roof. Otherwise the camera would have had to be suspended from above, which would have made filming the sequence more difficult.

comes in various shades of gray. The shade may be removed to the desired outline by scraping with a stylus or by using a liquid remover. The acetate sheet is pre-pared, then mounted on top of the photo, and the assembly is sent to be photocopied.

THE PRESENTATION

Making contact prints of all the photos taken provides much information about the composition, contrast, and technical accuracy of each photo. Examine the prints under a magnifying glass that has the capacity of enlarging sections to the size they will be on an 8″ × 10″ print. In this way, it is possible to study the sharpness

21-13.
Querelle, full-scale movie set reconstruction
Triumph Films

This is a full-scale movie set reconstruction of a house (seen elevated on a platform in the background) and a highly stylized bridge. The sequence in this setting was filmed with a camera that could be moved along a track.

and grain that will appear on future enlargements. Also, note what pictures are needed for the various presentations of the project. These presentations may include some or all of the following: photos for the client; for the office portfolio; for the basic press kit of the project; for an extended press kit for special publications; for the mortgagee, government agencies, etc.

Certain shots must obviously include overall bird's-eye views and three-quarter or full front shots of the major facade. Beyond these staples, a combination of the importance of the view and the quality of the photo must be considered. Sometimes one or two great shots of the project will satisfy basic presentation requirements. But there are many instances when none of dozens of photos are acceptable. In this case, choose a handful of the best and analyze what steps to take, when reshooting, to improve them. Whether there are good results or bad, it is desirable to summarize what went wrong, concluding with a list of the major errors (underexposure, uneven lighting, etc.) to increase your awareness of these problems in the future.

Have the photos that will be the backbone of the mass-produced presentations photocopied on 8″ × 10″ negatives if more than three prints are needed. All the pictures subsequently ordered may then be contact prints rather than more expensive enlargements.

Coloring Enlargements

Enlargements may be colored with transparent oils or watercolors obtainable at photo supply stores. Since it is hard to apply color to glossy prints, and colored matte prints are often dull looking, use paints with enlargements made on semimatte, rough paper. Prints should not have too much contrast. They should have detail and not impenetrable black in shadow areas.

PUBLICATION

Send as many prints as possible to each relevant publication. It is impossible to foresee which secondary shots will catch the eye of an editor. Each photo should have the name of the firm stamped on the back and the name of the project written in soft pencil (so you do not make an impression through the print). Prints should be glossy (they reproduce best when rephotographed) and double-weight (less likely to crease with handling). Send all submissions packed between at least two sheets of corrugated cardboard. Do not rely on the legend "Photographs—Do Not Bend" to save the package from rough handling.

Appendix 1: Suppliers

The following is a list of manufacturers and suppliers of materials and tools that have been mentioned in the book. The addresses of these suppliers are also given. Most of them have catalogs that list the products they carry as well as current prices.

TOOLS AND MATERIALS

Workbenches/Storage Units/Spray Booths
Abbeon Cal, Inc.
Arrow Star, Inc.
Babco, Inc.
Sears, Roebuck and Company

Hand Tools
Abbeon Cal, Inc.
Albert Constantine & Son, Inc.
Craftsman Wood Service
Garrett Wade Company, Inc.
John Harra Wood and Supply Company
Hyde Manufacturing Company
Jensen Tools, Inc.
Mohawk Finishing Products, Inc.
Moody Tools, Inc.
Warren Tool Corporation
X-Acto

Power Tools
Rudolf Bass, Inc.
Bethlehem Model & Pattern
Dewalt
Edmund Scientific
Garrett Wade Company, Inc.
John Harra Wood and Supply Company
Jensen Tools, Inc.
Porter-Cable Corporation
Rockwell International
Sears, Roebuck and Company
Sig Manufacturing Company
U.S. General Supply Corporation

Adhesives
Ambroid
Borden Chemica
Loctite Corporation
Pratt & Lambert
Mohawk Finishing Products, Inc.
Testor Corporation

Paints
Binney & Smith, Inc.
Floquil-Poly S Color Corporation
Mohawk Finishing Products, Inc.
Pratt & Lambert
Testor Corporation

Airbrushes
Badger Air-Brush Company
Binks Manufacturing Company
Paasche Airbrush Company
X-Acto

Ready-Made Products
A.D.S. Company (office furniture)
A.H.M., Inc. (trains, scale building kits)
Alexander Scale Models (detail building elements)
Architectural Model Supply Company (vehicles, trees)
Egon (trees)
Engineering Model Associates, Inc. (figures, structural/piping/electrical scale elements)
Holgate & Reynolds (plastic simulated building materials)
Life-Like Products, Inc. (trains, building kits, landscaping)
Microform Models, Inc. (figures, furniture, pipes/structural shapes)
Midwest Products Company (wood strips and shapes)
Northeastern Scale Models, Inc. (wood sheets, structural shapes, siding materials)
Revell, Inc. (vehicles)
Woodland Scenics (landscaping)

Art Supplies/Drafting Materials
Abbeon Cal, Inc.
Art Brown & Bro., Inc.
Charrette Corporation
Karl Art Supply
Utrecht Art & Drafting Supply Centers

Paper
Amoco Foam Products Company
International Paper
Monsanto Plastics & Resins Company

Clay/Plaster
Activa Products, Inc.
American Art Clay Company, Inc.

Metal/Soldering Equipment
Bernzomatic Corporation
Harrington & King Perforating Company, Inc.
Jensen Tools, Inc.
Microflame, Inc.
Multicore Solders
Mundt Perforations, Inc.

Plastics
AIN Plastics, Inc.
Caloric Color
Coating Products, Inc.
Commercial Plastics & Supply Corporation
Midwest Products Company, Inc.
Smooth-On, Inc.

ADDRESSES

Abbeon Cal, Inc.
123 Gray Avenue
Santa Barbara, CA 93101

Activa Products, Inc.
P.O. Box 1296
Marshall, TX 75670

A.D.S. Company
Indianola, PA 15051

A.H.M., Inc.
401 East Tioga Street
Philadelphia, PA 19134

AIN Plastics, Inc.
300 Park Avenue South
New York, NY 10010

Alexander Scale Models
P.O. Box 7121
Grand Rapids, MI 49510

Ambroid
600 West Water Street
Taunton, MA 02780

American Art Clay Company, Inc.
4717 West Sixteenth Street
Indianapolis, IN 46222

Amoco Foam Products Company
Shadowood Office Park
2111 Powers Ferry Road N.W.
Atlanta, GA 30339

Architectural Model Supply Company
115B Bellam Boulevard
P.O. Box 3497
San Rafael, CA 94902

Art Brown & Bro., Inc.
2 West 46th Street
New York, NY 10036

Arrow Star, Inc.
637 William Street
Lynbrook, NY 11563

Artype, Inc.
3530 Work Drive
P.O. Box 7151
Fort Myers, FL 33901

Babco, Inc.
60-10 Maurince Avenue
Maspeth, NY 11378

Badger Air-Brush Company
9128 West Belmont Avenue
Franklin Park, IL 60131

Rudolf Bass, Inc.
45 Halladay Street
Jersey City, NJ 07304

Bernzomatic Corporation
Olney Street
Medina, NY 14103

Bethlehem Model & Pattern
343 Ranch Street
Bethlehem, PA

Binks Manufacturing Company
9201 West Belmont Avenue
Franklin Park, IL 60131

Binney & Smith, Inc.
1100 Church Lane
P.O. Box 431
Easton, PA 18042

Borden Chemical
180 East Broad Street
Columbus, OH 43215

Bourges Color Corporation
20 Waterside Plaza
New York, NY 10010

Caloric Color
176A Saddle River Avenue
Garfield, NJ 07026

The Castolite Company
Woodstock, IL 60098

Cello-Tak Manufacturing, Inc.
35 Alabama Avenue
Leland Park, NY 11558

Charrette Corporation
1 Winthrop Square
Boston, MA 02110

Coating Products, Inc.
Division of Tyco Laboratories, Inc.
580 Sylvan Avenue
Englewood Cliffs, NJ 07632

Commercial Plastics & Supply
    Corporation
630 Broadway
New York, NY 10012

Albert Constantine & Son, Inc.
2050 Eastchester Road
Bronx, NY 10461

Craftsman Wood Service Company
1735 West Cortland Court
Addison, IL 60101

DeWalt
Division of Black & Decker, Inc.
715 Fountain Avenue
Lancaster, PA 17601

Dimensional Products, Ltd.
P.O. Box 484
North Conway, NH 03860

Dremel
Division of Emerson Electric Company
P.O. Box 1468
Racine, WI 53401

Edmund Scientific
101 East Gloucester Pike
Barrington, NJ 08007

Egon
3829 Villanova
Houston, TX 77005

Engineering Model Associates, Inc.
1020 South Wallace Place
City of Industry, CA 91748

Floquil-Poly S Color Corporation
Route 30 North
Amsterdam, NY 12010

Fome-Craft Corporation
830 Broad Street
Portsmouth, VA 23707

Garrett Wade Company, Inc.
161 Avenue of the Americas
New York, NY 10013

John Harra Wood & Supply Company
511 West 25th Street
New York, NY 10001

The Harrington & King Perforating
    Company, Inc.
5655 West Fillmore Street
Chicago, IL 60644

Holgate & Reynolds
1000 Central Avenue
Wilmette, IL 60091

Hyde Manufacturing Company
Southbridge, MA 01550

International Paper
P.O. Box 5380
Statesville, NC 28677

Jensen Tools, Inc.
1230 South Priest Drive
Tempe, AZ 85281

Karl Art Supply
230 East 54th Street
New York, NY 10022

Keuffel & Esser Company
40 East 43rd Street
New York, NY 10017

Life-Like Products, Inc.
1600 Union Avenue
Baltimore, MD 21211

Loctite Corporation
4450 Cranwood Court
Cleveland, OH 44128

Microflame, Inc.
3724 Oregon Avenue South
Minneapolis, MN 55426

Microform Models, Inc.
Webb Drive
Merrimack, NH 03054

Midwest Products Company, Inc.
400 South Indiana Street
Hobart, IN 46342

Mohawk Finishing Products, Inc.
Route 30 N. Perth Road
Amsterdam, NY 12010

Monsanto Plastics & Resins Company
800 North Lindbergh Boulevard
St. Louis, MO 63166

Moody Tools, Inc.
42-60 Crompton Avenue
East Greenwich, RI 02818

Multicore Solders
Westbury, NY 11590

Mundt Perforations, Inc.
South Plainfield, NJ 07080

Northeastern Scale Models, Inc.
P.O. Box 425
Methuen, MA 01844

Paasche Airbrush Company
1909 Diversey Parkway
Chicago, IL 60614

Polk's Model Craft Hobbies
314 Fifth Avenue
New York, NY 10001

Porter-Cable Corporation
P.O. Box 2468
Jackson, TN 38301

Pratt & Lambert
625 Washington Avenue
Carlstadt, NJ 07072

Revell, Inc.
4223 Glencoe Avenue
Venice, CA 90291

Rockwell International
Power Tools Division
400 North Lexington Avenue
Pittsburgh, PA 15203

Scale Models Unlimited
111 Independence Drive
Menlo Park, CA 94925

Sears, Roebuck and Company
Chicago, IL 60684

Sig Manufacturing Company, Inc.
Montezuma, IA 50171

Skil Corporation
4801 West Peterson Avenue
Chicago, IL 60646

Smooth-On, Inc.
1000 Valley Road
Gillette, NJ 07933

Special Shapes Company
P.O. Box 487 R
1356 Naperville Drive
Romeoville, IL 60441

The Testor Corporation
620 Buckbee Street
Rockford, IL 61101

U.S. General Supply Corporation
100 Commercial Street
Plainview, NY 11803

United States Products Company
518 Melwood Avenue
Pittsburgh, PA 15213

Utrecht Art & Drafting Supply Centers
Spruce Street
Philadelphia, PA 19102

Warren Tool Corporation
P.O. Box 68
Hiram, OH 44234

Woodland Scenics
P.O. Box 266
Shawnee Mission, KS 66201

X-Acto
45-35 Van Dam Street
Long Island City, NY 11101

Zauderer Associates, Inc.
P.O. Box 342
Mt. Vernon, NY 10551

Appendix 2: Metric Conversion

ENGLISH TO METRIC

Length
1 in.	= 25.4 mm
1 ft	= 0.3048 m
	= 304.8 mm
1 yd	= 0.9144 m
1 mi	= 1.609 344 km

Area
1 sq. in.	= 645.16 mm^2
1 sq. ft	= 0.092 903 m^2
1 sq. yd	= 0.836 127 m^2
1 acre	= 0.404 686 ha
	= 4046.86 m^2
1 sq. mi	= 2.589 99 km^2

Volume
1 fl. oz	= 29.573 53 mL
1 pint	= 0.473 176 L
1 gal.	= 3.785 412 L
1 cu. in.	= 16 387.1 mm^3 (or mL)
1 cu. ft	= 0.028 317 m^3
	= 28.3168 L
1 cu. yd	= 0.764 555 m^3

Temperature
°F	= $\frac{9}{5}$ (°C + 32)

METRIC TO ENGLISH

Length
1 mm	= 0.039 370 in.
1 m	= 1.093 61 yd
	= 3.280 84 ft
1 km	= 0.621 371 mi

Area
1 mm^2	= 0.001 55 sq. in.
1 m^2	= 1.195 99 sq. yd
	= 10.7639 sq. ft
1 ha	= 2.471 05 acre
1 km^2	= 0.386 102 sq. mi

Volume
1 mL	= 0.061 024 cu. in.
	= 0.033 814 fl. oz
1 L	= 0.035 315 cu. ft
	= 0.264 172 gal.
	= 2.113 378 pint
1 mm^3	= 61.0237 × 10^{-6} cu. in.
1 m^3	= 1.307 95 cu. yd
	= 35.3147 cu. ft

Temperature
°C	= $\frac{5}{9}$ × (°F − 32)

Index

666 657